P9-AOS-371

aei studies on

CONTEMPORARY ECONOMIC PROBLEMS

william fellner, editor

1976

aei studies on
**CONTEMPORARY
ECONOMIC
PROBLEMS**

aei studies on
CONTEMPORARY
ECONOMIC
PROBLEMS
william fellner, editor

American Enterprise Institute for Public Policy Research
Washington, D. C.

ISBN 0-8447-1319-8

Library of Congress Catalog Card No. 76-21977

Printed in the United States of America

CONTRIBUTORS

William Fellner—*Editor*

Sterling professor of economics emeritus at Yale University, former member of the Council of Economic Advisers, and past president of the American Economic Association. Resident scholar with the American Enterprise Institute.

Phillip Cagan

Professor of economics at Columbia University, research staff of the National Bureau of Economic Research, and former senior staff economist for the Council of Economic Advisers. Adjunct scholar with the American Enterprise Institute.

Harold O. Carter

Chairperson of the Department of Agricultural Economics at the University of California, Davis, and former senior staff economist for the Council of Economic Advisers.

Richard Erb

Former assistant director of the Council on International Economic Policy, and staff assistant to the President. Resident economist with the American Enterprise Institute.

George M. von Furstenberg

Former senior staff economist with the Council of Economic Advisers. Resident economist with the American Enterprise Institute.

Gottfried Haberler

Galen L. Stone professor of international trade emeritus at Harvard University, and past president of the American Economic Association and International Economic Association. Member of the Academic Advisory Board and resident scholar with the American Enterprise Institute.

Marvin Kosters

Former associate director for economic policy at the Cost of Living Council. Director of research of the Center for the Study of Government Regulation and resident scholar with the American Enterprise Institute.

Geoffrey H. Moore

Director of business cycle research for the National Bureau of Economic Research, senior research fellow at the Hoover Institution, Stanford University, and former U.S. commissioner of labor statistics. Adjunct scholar with the American Enterprise Institute.

Herbert Stein

A. Willis Robertson professor of economics at the University of Virginia, former chairman of the Council of Economic Advisers, and former vice president and chief economist of the Committee for Economic Development. Adjunct scholar with the American Enterprise Institute.

Murray L. Weidenbaum

Edward Mallinckrodt distinguished university professor at Washington University, St. Louis, and former assistant secretary of the Treasury for economic affairs. Member of the Advisory Council of the Center for the Study of Government Regulation and adjunct scholar with the American Enterprise Institute.

Marina v. N. Whitman

Distinguished public service professor of economics at the University of Pittsburgh, and former member of the Council of Economic Advisers and National Price Commission. Adjunct scholar with the American Enterprise Institute.

CONTENTS

GUIDE TO THE VOLUME

William Fellner

Purpose of the Study: The Common Core

This volume—the first product of what is planned as a continuing effort—was motivated by the conviction that the future of our economic and political system depends largely on whether we shall be able to overcome a difficulty with which the American economy has been faced in the decade since 1965. The decade was one of accelerating inflation and one in which, aside from a short initial span, we were clearly unable to "buy" low unemployment rates in exchange for the inflation. On the contrary, the decade ended with steep inflation, low capacity utilization and high unemployment rates. The common core of the studies included in the volume is described by a concern with these events and an appraisal of the prospects for coping with the difficulties they have created.

When it is described in general terms, our problem shapes up as one in macroeconomics—the branch of economic research relating to broad aggregates, such as the level of output, of employment and of unemployment, and relating to averages, such as trends in the general price level. But we cannot properly appraise problems of macroeconomics without making an effort to tie our analysis in with processes developing in specific areas of the economy—that is, with structural problems usually considered the subject matter of microeconomics. It is necessary to accept the fact that at the present time we do not possess a usefully integrated theory that would include "macro" and "micro" analysis in the same formal apparatus. This, however, provides no valid excuse for paying little attention to the interplay of microeconomic (structural) forces with forces typically explored in macroeconomic (aggregative) research. The neatness of

1

any analysis linking aggregative to structural problems suffers from the unavailability of a unified formal framework but formal elegance is not the supreme objective of empirical investigations. It is necessary to take a good look at the micro-implications of results reached through macro-analysis as well as the other way around. The present volume attempts to do this, and in this regard too our work will be further developed as our project progresses.

The common core of these studies may be described in a slightly more expanded form than was done in the introductory paragraph. What can be said about our effort is that the aggregative studies on the outlook for overcoming our difficulties—the studies focusing on demand management including, of course, monetary and fiscal policy—were written in awareness of their structural implications; and that the studies concerned with specific problems were written in awareness of their bearing on the "macro" problem of returning to a sustainable path in our overall performance.

A General Appraisal of Essentials

The problems I shall discuss in the present section clearly belong among the "essentials" with which the participants in the project have concerned themselves, but the reader should keep in mind that we made no attempt to agree on joint answers to the specific questions encountered in our inquiries. I should therefore take individual responsibility for this section of these introductory observations. As I go along, I shall call attention to the fact that not all contributors have the identical first preferences in answering two of the questions to be discussed in this introduction. One of these differences relates to the characteristics of the price trend at whose stabilization we should direct our efforts, leaving room for an intervening period of transition; the other relates to the desirable behavior of the monetary authority in exceptional cases of steeply rising specific costs.

Past and Present Difficulties and the Outlook for Overcoming Them. In the United States and elsewhere policies have been strongly influenced by the hypothesis of a trade-off between inflation and unemployment. The skeptics were proved right in their suggestion that such a trade-off exists merely temporarily, as a purely short-run phenomenon, and that policies trying to build on this trade-off for achieving high employment by inflationary methods will fail.

It has by now become inevitable to accept the burden of an adjustment process on the way back from accelerating inflation to the neighborhood of what may be regarded as the normal growth path for the U.S. economy. Along that path monetary and fiscal policies—"demand management" policies—will have to aim for the aggregate demand that neither exceeds nor falls short of the requirements of normal growth with a reasonably predictable behavior of the price level to which market decisions can adjust. Meanwhile, during a transition period, "gradualism" requires our accommodating the cyclical recovery of real output from the recession of 1973–1975 and accommodating inflation at a decelerating rate, in addition to normal growth. If during the recovery we should not observe the speed limit these requirements impose on the real rate of expansion, we shall soon be back in the same unacceptable situation from which we have now begun to depart.

We must remain committed to helping that part of our population reasonably regarded as suffering substantial hardship, but it is not possible for us to live up to this commitment by temporarily raising the employment level through an inflationary stimulus—that is, essentially by fooling the public about the real incomes that will turn out to correspond to their money incomes. That method would backfire in the future as it has in the past—indeed it would probably backfire with even less delay than it has in the past.

A realistic appraisal of the outlook suggests that the shortening of the delay with which a policy of promoting inflationary disequilibria would be likely to backfire could turn out to be a saving grace. Not only has it become more difficult for policy makers to talk themselves into the belief that there might after all exist a long-run trade-off between inflation and unemployment but, given the by now widespread doubts about that hypothesis, it has also become more difficult for them to visualize themselves as benefiting in the next election from the political advantages of short-run inflationary stimuli and to visualize their successors as being in charge at a later date when such a policy boomerangs. With the public at large obviously worried about the price trend, we seem to have arrived to a point at which there has developed a receptiveness for the views of those of us who strongly urge a rejection of the hypotheses that were supposed to justify the inflationary policies of a past period.

There remains, however, quite a bit of resistance to breaking away from past demand policy practices, and that resistance needs to be overcome. So far as I can see the resistance has two roots, to be discussed in the next two subsections, though the arguments on which the resistance is based have so far been less well integrated than had been the initial hypothesis of the long-run inflation-unemployment

3

trade-off. The hypothesis of the long-run trade-off had indeed gradually become sufficiently well articulated to make one feel confident as to *what* has proved unrealistic about it—this being essentially the conjecture of its proponents that it is possible to raise the level of activity by generating a steady rate of inflation, a nonaccelerating and sustainable rate. Belief in the realism of that contention has greatly weakened, and the remaining resistance to turning away from past policy practices and to adopting a program of gradual return to a noninflationary course now has roots of a somewhat different kind.

The Belief that the Recent Inflation Resulted Mainly from the Weather and the Greed of the Oil Producers, Not from Inflationary Policies. It is often argued that the really bad part of the recent inflationary experience was not policy-made but was an inevitable consequence of the coincidence of various accidental factors. Among these the 1973 shortfall of farm-product supplies as compared to the demand for these products at given prices, the subsequent cartel-induced significant rise of energy-material prices, and the correction of the earlier overvaluation of the dollar (hence the rise in foreign-currency rates) are those most frequently referred to in the argument.

These factors, it is sometimes suggested, got us into the truly uncomfortable phase of the past inflation. It has even been maintained that when the specific cost increases of recent years occurred the authorities should have adopted a more expansionary policy line. In order to "accommodate" the sale of any given aggregate output at the higher prices reflecting the cost increases, it is claimed, they should have promoted the creation of greater nominal demand relative to the available supply of goods and services. The lesson from the past experience would then not be that we have carried expansionary policies too far, but if anything the contrary. Along these lines it is argued that an appreciable rise of the general price level was inevitable and all that policy restraint could accomplish was to reduce the level of economic activity with little effect on prices. This is supposed to be true at least concerning the worst phase of the recent inflation—the phase that started in 1973.

Now, it is quite true that if demand management policies are conducted on the assumption that the real output potential would remain "normal" and the output potential is in fact reduced by shortages, a temporary increase of the price level is apt to occur. All that can be said about this is that errors in forecasting are inevitable and that they presumably tend to cancel out in the longer run. Yet it is *also* true that even if the shortages *are* foreseen and demand management policies are shaped with the objective of keeping aggregate nominal demand in line with a more limited aggregate real supply, the economy may nevertheless experience a temporary rise of the *general* price level, and not merely a rise in specific prices. This is so because the reduced amount of aggregate demand *may* for a while be used up for the purchase of a further contracting quantity of output—a recession output—at generally rising prices.

What, however, must not be overlooked is that if a "cyclical" setback of output is needed for making the public accept an inevitable real burden—say an oil-price or farm-price burden—then realization of this fact can be delayed but not avoided by raising aggregate demand and by thus "accommodating" a pass-through of specific cost increases into the general price level. A delayed recession, when the inflationary process touched off by the accommodation needs to be stemmed, is likely to be more pronounced because the difficulties of adjustment are magnified by the intervening process, in the course of which the inevitable real burden is passed back and forth among the various sectors. Changes in the relative cost and price structure must indeed be taken for granted and some of these will at times express themselves in rising raw material costs, but to conclude from this that such changes must be made to take place about an inflationary general price trend would mean creating a hopelessly inflationary environment in the future. Policy makers would be falling into a trap if they followed the advice to raise aggregate nominal demand relative to the real output potential of the economy in order to accommodate a price pass-through whenever specific shortages raise specific costs. In my contribution to this volume, I will further elaborate on the deficiencies of the principle of "accommodated" pass-throughs of specific cost increases into the consumer price index and into the general GNP deflator. Mine is not the only contribution to the volume in which this problem will be discussed, and it should be noted here that Phillip Cagan leaves the question open whether in exceptional cases of large specific cost increases—in "unusual" cases—the accommodation of pass-throughs by additional demand creation might not nevertheless have a desirable cushioning effect that outweighs the risks. However, he is keenly aware of the dangers of going too far in that direction by making the accommodation of specific cost increases the rule.

It must, of course, be recognized that even if a pass-through were not "accommodated" by demand management policies—that is, even if aggregate demand were not raised relative to the economy's real output—specific cost increases could nevertheless lead to a one-time increase of the general price level. This possibility exists especially if the specific cost increases are large, since in that case an adverse cyclical development *may* prove necessary for achieving the acceptance of the burden by the relatively disadvantaged sectors. Meanwhile producers may be charging generally higher prices for a recession output. In any event, there is this much truth in the contention that even under a policy of restraint the specific cost increases of 1973 and of 1974 might well have translated themselves into a rise of the *general* price level. But in those circumstances the money GNP would not have risen (as it did) by more than 10 percent at an annual rate in all quarters of 1973 except the first, nor would the year-over-year increase in money GNP from 1972 to 1973 have come out at 11.5 percent. It should be obvious that such increases in aggregate nominal demand could not help including a very significant inflation component in an economy that by 1973 was operating at a high level of resource utilization. This is the basic fact with which the explanation of the recent inflationary phase in terms of special and accidental factors does not come to grips.

Needless to say, the specific cost increases in various areas of material shortage did add considerably to our difficulties but in an analysis of our accelerating inflation it is exceedingly unconvincing to try to take the main emphasis off the large discrepancy between the very rapid growth of money GNP (hence of aggregate demand) on the one hand, and the very limited further "real" growth potential of the economy on the other. I recommend engaging in the following imaginary experiment: tell any professionally educated person, who is (we shall assume) *uninformed* about the specific commodity problems of 1973, that in the final quarter of 1972 the American economy had a measured unemployment rate of slightly more than 5 percent and had capacity utilization rates falling in the high ranges by past standards, and tell him also that from that quarter to the final quarter of 1973 the money GNP rose by 10.9 percent. You may be certain he will conclude that you are describing a highly inflationary economy. The specific commodity problems of the year 1972–1973, and the resulting specific cost increases, would have caused a temporary increase in the general price level in any event, but it is clear that overly expansionary policies would have produced *steep* inflation quite aside from these complicating factors.

I do not believe that the rapid growth of aggregate nominal demand would have resulted from any desire of the authorities to accommodate the specific cost increases—a desire founded on the assumption that a durable gain could be made if these specific increases were allowed to lead to an enlarged nominal demand relative to the available aggregate real supply of goods and services. In 1973 the authorities moved towards a policy of restraint, not towards a policy of greater accommodation, and for this they deserve high praise. But the period of demand policy laxity that started about 1965 did not come to an end before 1973, though there occurred brief interludes during those years in which insufficient attempts were made to dampen the inflationary process. Even now it is a matter of guesswork whether the determination expressing itself in the anti-inflationary conduct of demand management policy since about 1973 will last. What needs to be remembered here is that monetary and fiscal policy affect aggregate demand with lags, and the rapid increase in aggregate nominal demand experienced in 1973 was mostly a consequence of policies adopted in 1972. It was not a consequence of any desire to accommodate specific cost increases but rather a consequence of the fact that the post-1965 period of overly expansionary demand management was brought to an end belatedly.

The Belief that Demand Policy Restraint Must Lead to Long-lasting Stagflation. During periods in which the authorities are willing to resort to inflationary practices in an attempt to play safe against cyclical setbacks, the money-wage- and price-setting practices in the economy will be strongly influenced by the ability of the public to "figure out" this willingness of the policy makers. If most major participants in market processes are convinced that, when inflationary wage- and price-setting behavior emerges, lax demand policies will validate that behavior, and if each member of the public senses that most others have also figured out the authorities in this same fashion, then inflationary wage and price tendencies are in fact apt to develop. Consequently, if an investigator bases his conclusions on data observed for a long past period of lax policies, he is almost certain to conclude that even a consistent and fully credible anti-inflationary policy would have a hard time overcoming the obstinacy of inflationary wage- and price-setting practices. Such a conclusion can easily be derived from the experience of a past period in which demand management was not guided by credible anti-inflationary objectives but was known to build on a short-term (temporary) inflation-unemployment trade-off. In fact this conclusion—essentially, the conclusion that, given the inflationary antecedents of the present situation, it would take a very long time and possibly a major depression to overcome a "sabotaging" behavior of the markets—has been repeatedly suggested by investigators estimating behavior patterns (structural relations) from the data available for a past period.

7

But it is wrong to jump to the conclusion that the public would act in the same way if it were convinced that the authorities would persist in generating no more aggregate demand than is compatible with declared price-level objectives. If the same investigators who are telling us now that demand policy restraint would not really work had used their present techniques of price level forecasting in past eras, they would have had to warn every government that its stabilization effort after a major inflationary span would result not in price level stabilization but in continued inflation with rapidly shrinking output. What in fact made these stabilization efforts successful was that the participants in the market processes knew that as a result of a credible change in policy it was they and the other participants who had to adjust to "obstinate" authorities rather than wait for the authorities to adjust to "obstinate" wage- and price-setting practices.

Given significantly inflationary antecedents, a *sudden* change to a strictly noninflationary policy—to one aiming for a horizontal trend of the general price level—has, of course, always caused a shock, and the dislocations caused by our post-1965 inflationary processes have so far not become grave enough to justify this kind of shock treatment. A policy aiming for a gradual return to normalcy can achieve its objectives, provided the policy acquires credibility and is followed through consistently. Under such circumstances past cost commitments, entered into in the years of steep inflation, would indeed continue to express themselves for a while in the price trends, but the money supply and the budget would have to be managed in such a way as to leave room merely for a significantly diminishing inflation rate as the economy recovered from the recession. We may conceivably have already started moving along such a course—a course along which a sufficiently determined policy could *continue* to move—though it took the greater part of the recession to arrive to the point at which inflation ceased to accelerate and started decelerating. On this occasion the lag with which a reduction of the inflation rate became observable was unusually long; deceleration occurred when the contraction phase of the cycle had almost been completed.

The explanation of this lag does call for recognition of the role of significant specific cost increases in the recession year 1974, particularly of the role of energy price developments. But the duration of the lag was undoubtedly influenced also by the length of the preceding inflationary span, and by the steepening of inflationary expectations during a period of accelerating inflation. In all probability it was influenced also by uncertainties about the persistence of the authorities who had, to be sure, turned around to a policy of restraint but on earlier occasions had not been able to resist the temptation of giving up prematurely and trying again for the advantages of a short-term trade-off between inflation and unemployment. Completing the adjustment successfully means not pretending to have achieved the objective before the economy has returned to the neighborhood of its normal growth path with a steady behavior of the price level to which price expectations in the markets can remain geared.

To this generally valid proposition I will add a personal judgment which differs from that expressed in Herbert Stein's contribution and possibly from the views held by some other contributors to the volume. I find it very difficult to imagine that a steady price trend could be established by any method that would fail to move consistently towards approximate horizontality of the trend, and would fail to restore that condition at the end of the adjustment process. I will suggest that if for the sake of short-run advantages the authorities should "settle" for trying to stabilize an inflation rate of, say, 6 percent or 4 percent, then wage- and price-setting practices would be based on the assumption that the same short-run considerations will lead the authorities to correct these figures upward whenever more inflation needs to be generated to accommodate the behavior developing in the markets.

The Measured Unemployment Rate. In an economy with an unemployment compensation system—and more generally with transfer-payment entitlements characteristic of the Western industrialized world—it is impossible to make firm predictions about the measured unemployment rate that will establish itself along the normal growth path. This is particularly true of countries in which the composition of the labor force is subject to appreciable changes, as has been the case in the United States. It is very likely that changes in labor-force composition and in transfer entitlements have raised the measured unemployment on the normal growth path beyond the 4 percent estimated for the mid-1950s. On the other hand, it is equally likely that the present measured rate of 7.5 percent contains a substantial component reflecting the temporary difficulties of an adjustment period following the era of inflationary overheating. But such a statement leaves open a fairly wide range, and the main point here is that in these circumstances no "normal rate" can be quantified as a target. The target can only be the employment level corresponding to the highest sustainable output path—a path that does not involve the temporary "stimulus" (fooling effect) produced by inflation.

If one's time horizon for appraising policy results is of reasonable duration, one must obviously not try to make the public believe that practically all persons who in some sense are looking for a job can obtain a job on whatever terms the persons in question regard as acceptable. That particular objective could be achieved at best for a short period by expressing the acceptable terms as acceptable *money* incomes and by using inflationary methods for making the *real* incomes come out smaller than was expected at the time when workers and employers entered into commitments involving the money incomes in question. In no other sense can a job be secured for everyone who wants a job, without regard to the terms of employment and the capabilities of the employee. We must develop adequate programs for helping the needy and also for training those who are capable of acquiring skills they do not possess, but it must be clearly recognized that inflationary techniques for temporarily reducing the unemployment rate represent no substitutes for workable programs of income maintenance.

"Incomes Policy" and Other Euphemisms for Political and Economic Control of the Wage and Price Structure. In comprehensively controlled political and economic systems the wage and price structure is determined mostly by decisions of a political character, rather than by market forces and collective bargaining. By their own standards those systems are "workable," but the standards in question involve a high degree of dependence of all individuals on the political authority, they place very small weight on the objective of adjusting the product mix to the desires of the public, and they involve lack of concern with the creation of appropriate incentives for risky innovations. This is not accidental: reliance on market forces is needed for achieving these objectives which have all along been held high in successful modern economies. Comprehensively controlled countries can, of course, force high proportions of their populations onto payrolls, and "eliminate" unemployment in that particular sense.

The standards so described being unpalatable, the practice has been spreading lately of using vague terminology for suggesting that we can eat our cake and yet have it—provided we are willing to rely on measures of administrative wage and price control that are described by less offensive words. It is usually suggested that the applicability or the de facto enforcement of the planned wage-price interferences would be less comprehensive than are those of police states. With reliance on measures describing a half-way house between the world of comprehensive wage-price controls and that of market forces, we could allegedly make the general wage and price level as well as the wage and price structure behave in a desirable fashion. This we could allegedly achieve even if expansionary monetary and fiscal policies were pressed to a point at which major inflationary disturbances would otherwise develop.

Yet there is no reason to believe that the economic inefficiences that are introduced into a system by politically motivated interferences with the wage-price structure could be avoided by spottiness of the interferences or by going easy on enforcement. At the same time there are good reasons to believe that results that are inevitably shaped by the political influence of power groups will be considered inequitable and after a while unacceptable in societies in which dissent is not suppressed. Periodic experimentation with such controls, leading to "off and on" regulations, would result in an increase of the uncertainties surrounding the economic decision-making processes and to a significant lowering of the economy's performance. This would further complicate the basic problems that must be faced in the coming years—the problems to which this volume is addressed.

In the end a country may opt for the kind of permissive society that develops under modern democratic institutions and where the wage-setting and corresponding price-setting practices can be *influenced* by demand management policies as well as by requiring adherence to various general rules—but cannot be *controlled* in any detail. Or, alternatively, a country may opt for a strictly controlled society. In the former case the country in question is likely to adopt arrangements involving quasi-guaranteed subsistence, and there is no way in which such a country could force its entire labor force onto payrolls without intervening periods of unemployment. Market inducements for achieving such a result would have to be inflationary ones leading to unrealistic real-income expectations—and would therefore backfire without much delay. Rigorously controlled societies *can* achieve practical absence of measured unemployment all the time, but they can achieve it only at a sacrifice of political and economic objectives to which we have all along attributed great significance.

Relating the Individual Studies to the Main Theme

The reader will find in the studies relevant information and analysis beyond what needs to be stressed in an attempt to indicate their bearing on the central theme of the volume. Here I will merely comment on some of the ways in which the studies relate to the common theme.

Turning to the individual contributions, we note that Phillip Cagan's analysis of monetary policy and Herbert Stein's analysis of fiscal policy include discussions of problems touched upon in the preceding section, and my study on the criteria for shaping demand management policies is also concerned with these and with closely related problems. Cagan attributes a good deal of importance to the complications that specific cost increases have caused, and to the dilemma they may pose for those in charge of demand management by means of monetary policy. That problem is discussed in some detail. The author calls attention also to the recent poor performance of money-demand regressions and discusses possible causes of the high negative residuals observed for recent quarters. Stein examines various hypotheses concerning the reasons why, in our postwar experience, a noninflationary period has been followed by a steeply inflationary one. In his discussion he takes account of the fact that the sharp price increases of 1950–1951 did not touch off a continuing inflationary process and that the post-1965 span has different characteristics in this regard. Among the hypotheses relating to the more recent period, the effect of overly expansionary policies on expectations and thus on wage and price behavior receives considerable emphasis, though other contributing factors are also given attention. In his discussion of the relation of monetary to fiscal policy, Stein reminds us that not in all cases has easy money been a mere response of the Federal Reserve to the credit market tightening effect of expansionary fiscal policy. The bearing of the Cagan and Stein analyses, and that of my paper, on the volume's main theme should be self-explanatory.

It is equally obvious that the main theme of the volume requires an exploration of developments in the labor market, and the study of these developments by Marvin Kosters is presented immediately after the three demand management studies. One of the interesting propositions that Kosters develops relates to the degree of wage resistance to anti-inflationary policies. The author stresses the role of specific factors of timing, attributing considerable importance to the question whether the wage *structure* moves towards an acceptable shape or away from it, when at the onset of an anti-inflationary policy effort those wage rates react first which are free to react at that time. Attention is thus directed to the question where an economy finds itself in its bargaining calendar at various critical stages of policy making, and also to the recently increased role of escalator clauses which render automatic some degree of wage response to the slope of the price trend.

In the next paper Geoffrey Moore suggests that in some analytical contexts, including that of the present volume, greater emphasis should be placed on the "employment ratio" than on the unemployment rate as we measure it. He argues that in efforts to link labor-market tightness or labor-market ease to money-wage and price developments, better results are obtained by interpreting tightness as expressing itself not in a low measured unemployment rate but in a high employment ratio—that is, in a high proportion of employed persons in the noninstitutional population aged sixteen and over. This is another way of saying that, when exploring changes in the variables affecting the rate of wage and price increase, we should place the emphasis on the proportion of the population that is employed (or is not) without regard to what proportion of those not employed shows up as "unemployed" by the criteria used in evaluating the census surveys. Moore finds higher employment ratios for the highly inflationary cycle that reached its peak late in 1973 and its trough early in 1975 than for earlier cycles, though the unemployment rates were higher during the recent cycle.

With a different purpose in mind my study also explores employment ratios as well as unemployment rates, and I observed a very similar difference between their behavior in the recent cycle on the one hand and in earlier cycles on the other—though not strictly the same difference as Moore observed, because I have not followed his procedure of including the members of the armed forces in the population while excluding them from the employed. The difference between the trend in the employment ratio and the trend in the unemployment rate reflects an upward trend in the proportion of the "nonworkers" classified as unemployed by the census surveys. Hence, to unchanging or rising employment ratios there corresponded rising unemployment rates. It is shown in my study that the proportion of nonworkers classified as unemployed has increased significantly for adult women and for teenagers, as it has for the population when this is viewed as a whole, but that the same proportion has *decreased* significantly for adult males (whose weight in the total labor force has, however, decreased appreciably). This, in turn, may help us to understand why the observed increase in the unemployed proportion of *all* nonworkers—the proportion that is "looking for a job" and hence is regarded as unemployed—has not had the tightness-reducing (wage-moderating) effect in the labor market that might otherwise have been expected. That is to say, we have here a trend limited to adult females and to teenagers, with the trend moving in the opposite direction for adult males.

In her analysis of international interdependence, Marina Whitman covers a substantial range of problems that tie in closely with the central theme of the volume, since it has become impossible to appraise domestic prospects without regard to interactions between the United States and the rest of the world. On realistic assumptions the nature and the extent of these interactions depend on the exchange-rate regime as well as on substitutability relations among sectors within the various economies. The author regards the shift from the Bretton Woods system to exchange-rate flexibility as an important step in the effort to avoid the transmission of unwanted processes from one country to another, but she also considers in some detail the limitations on the insulating effect of flexible rates. In her discussion of the potency and the limitations of the insulating effect of rate flexibility she distinguishes among types of change abroad that may raise the question of insulation. These are types of change that may influence domestic variables through international transactions, and inflationary trends originating in foreign countries represent only one of the changes raising this question.

As for the harm done by inflation, George von Furstenberg's investigations have led him to the conclusion that, when it comes to an appraisal of the harmful effect of high but steady inflation rates on domestic investment in the long run, the tax-raising effect of inflation under an unindexed tax system deserves much less attention than it sometimes receives. On the other hand, another harmful effect of inflation, stemming from real losses suffered in monetary assets and from the increasing dependence on external financing, deserves much more attention. Indeed, on the assumptions of the model he develops, the burden resulting for corporations from the taxation of merely nominal (inflationary) revaluations is outweighed by the tax deductibility of the merely nominal component of interest payments (that is, of the component representing merely an inflation premium). Yet on the author's assumptions applying to high and steady inflation rates, book profits and dividend payments vanish in the long run, along with corporate income tax payments, equity financing may cease to be available for raising funds, and creditors find it increasingly risky to supply the funds needed for investment in the absence of equity financing.

Without detracting attention from the role of demand management in generating inflationary expansion, both Gottfried Haberler and Murray Weidenbaum stress in their essays the role of institutional rigidities in raising costs and prices. Noting that the recent inflationary trend has significantly outlasted the expansion phase of the cycle, Haberler points out that in a fully competitive economy the inflationary expectations generated by the post-1965 experience could not have led to the coexistence of a steep upward trend in money wage rates with undercapacity output—indeed, with shrinking output and with significantly rising unemployment during the recent recession. The author's argument overlaps an argument developed in my paper, inasmuch as I take the position that it is inconsistent to accept a number of competition-limiting factors—even to consider some of them desirable—and at the same time to set employment policy goals that could at best be achieved in the absence of those factors. Some rigidifying factors seem acceptable to most of us even at a cost—income-maintenance programs being one illustration—but the fact remains that the true nature and the consequences of many rigidifying elements of our institutional structure are widely misjudged by the public. These elements of the structure are costly without serving the purpose they are supposed to serve, or at least without serving it well enough to provide reasonable justification for the cost. Weidenbaum raises and discusses this problem in connection with a number of specific government regulations.

Several of the studies so far considered concern themselves with structural problems rooted in various sectors of the economy but their concern is not with individual sectors in the particular sense of specific industries or specific groups of industries. Turning to sectoral problems in the latter sense, we may say that, aside from oil, agriculture has rightly attracted the most attention during the past few years, and this is the area surveyed in Harold Carter's study. Our generation is not the first in whose mind doubts have arisen whether the Malthusian-Ricardian fears of basic resource scarcities will not shortly prove to be justified, after an era during which technological and organizational progress was winning the race over diminishing returns from land by a comfortable margin. Carter discusses trends in food production and consumption in general with particular emphasis on grains, and he distinguishes between trends in acreage planted and trends in output per unit of land in various parts of the world. He concludes that we are unlikely to have entered into an era of chronic shortages—on the contrary, he considers it likely that the "real" price of grains will start to decline again after not changing much over the near term. But he makes allowances for the possibility that the future variability of grain prices will be greater than was their variability in the past, and he therefore suggests that the question how best to organize stockpiling programs does indeed deserve a new look.

Richard Erb's study surveys and analyzes two major special areas—oil and the metals. Future oil and energy prices are, of course, a matter of substantial importance for the appraisal of our economic prospects, and in this regard the author concludes that the key question is likely to lie in the behavior of Saudi Arabia. So far the Organization of Petroleum Exporting Countries has not developed an allocative system characteristic of well-functioning cartels that can systematically achieve their pricing objectives, but Saudi Arabia has the required capability of effective quantity adjustments within wide limits. Insofar as the Saudi decisions will be governed by economic considerations rather than by considerations relating to the Arab-Israeli conflict, they will essentially be investment decisions based on a comparison of the yield (gradual appreciation) of "oil in the ground" with the yield of the assets that can be acquired for the sales value of exported oil. The author calls attention to the policy problems these considerations pose to the West. Concerning the specific metals markets that he analyzes, Erb concludes that while recent price developments in these markets were widely believed to be dramatic and unusual, this view loses much of its validity if allowances are made for the rapid increase of the general price level. The "real" metals prices discussed by the author typically started from a base level that was low by previous standards, then tended to overshoot during the phase of rapidly rising world demand, but soon came down, mostly to the pre-boom level or below it.

It is now time to let the authors speak for themselves.

MONETARY PROBLEMS AND POLICY CHOICES IN REDUCING INFLATION AND UNEMPLOYMENT

Phillip Cagan

Summary

In 1973 efforts to curb inflation were set back as (1) the domestic business expansion gained speed and intensified market pressures to raise prices and (2) international prices of basic commodities (primarily oil, food grains, and metals) rose sharply in response to expanding world demands and restricted supplies. The inflationary outburst led most countries to adopt policies of mild but increasing restraint on monetary growth. There followed a contraction in aggregate demand, in the United States, moderately at first (beginning in the fourth quarter of 1973) and then precipitously (in the fourth quarter of 1974). The contraction in economic activity turned around in the first quarter of 1975 and a moderate recovery ensued. The high inflation rates of 1973–1974 receded by 1975 to reveal an underlying inflation rate of 6 to 7 percent, which should decline gradually if excess capacity continues in most sectors.

The business contraction was more severe than the moderate decline in growth of the money stock can account for. A special contribution to the business contraction was made by the exogenous fall in the real value of money balances. The world price increases raised costs to U.S. manufacturers and pushed up the domestic price level by about 10 percent in 1973–1974. This produced a 10 percent decline in real money balances, which the public sought to restore by lending and spending less, thus contracting aggregate expenditures. While econometric equations of the demand for money balances indicate that actual real balances outstanding fell below the quantity demanded, the equations went way off track in predicting subsequent behavior. The breakdown of the equations has added to the difficulties of interpreting monetary policy in the business recovery. The recovery, though stronger in 1975 than the equations predicted on the basis of the accompanying moderate rate of monetary growth, did not satisfy many policy critics who proposed more stimulative measures to achieve a rapid reduction of unemployment. The Federal Reserve followed what was overall a conservative policy of reducing unemployment gradually to maintain strong market pressures to curb inflation.

Previous efforts to curb inflation (in 1966–1967 and 1969–1970) had sought a period of mild restraint in which the increase in unemployment was to be small and short-lived. Those policy choices were based on the assumption that the faster any given reduction in the inflation rate was achieved the greater would be the total amount of unemployment endured. The optimal path on this view was one that spaced the unemployment evenly over the period in which the inflation rate was reduced. This policy prescription assumed that the trade-off between inflation and unemployment is nonlinear. Yet the evidence for nonlinearity in the U.S. trade-off is far from firm. If the trade-off relation approximates linearity in the relevant range, a rapid reduction of inflation does not have the disadvantage of greater total unemployment, while it does have the advantage of reducing the risk of encountering another round of inflationary pressures before the previous one is under control.

The economic recession of 1973–1975 began a process of reducing inflation. Business cost cutting is expected to slow the rate of increase in unit labor costs and thence in prices, even though the advance of wages may not let up until after the inflation rate subsides substantially. By mid-1976 it was clear that this process was at work, but whether the speed of the process would be sufficient to justify the sizable excess capacity in the economy remained to be seen.

The controversy over monetary policy during the 1973–1975 recession and ensuing recovery raised the issue of how to deal with inflationary disturbances from abroad. The foreign influences on basic commodity prices in 1973–1974 increased manufacturing costs and were passed through to selling prices before policy restraints on aggregate demand could prevent the increases in the price level. A policy of not accommodating the imported price increases would require a period of slack demand in which the price level, though it initially rose above its trend path, was eventually brought back through a period of lower inflation rates than would otherwise have occurred. To avoid the period of slack demand, policy could expand monetary growth sufficiently to support the price level on a higher trend path. Such a policy of accommodating foreign disturbances on prices is consistent with a full employment goal, but accommodation is bound to increase the long-run average rate of inflation if inflationary pressures from outside the country occur with any regularity.

The response of policy to the 1973 outburst of inflation was not expressly accommodative—indeed monetary growth has declined and the inflation has slowed. But there is little indication that the 1973–1974 rise in the price level will ever be reversed. Indeed, policy makers had difficulty merely bringing the runaway rate of inflation under control. This experience raises doubts about our chances of avoiding the long-run inflationary consequences of such disturbances should they prove not to be a rare occurrence.

The New Environment

The fury of the inflationary storm that burst upon the Western economies in 1973 has compounded the difficulties in carrying out anti-inflation policies and has shaken what remained of confidence in their effectiveness. Not only is there apprehension over our apparent vulnerability to such outbursts of inflation, but also there is confusion and difference of opinion over how best to deal with them. Before 1973, inflation had with few exceptions reflected an overexpansion of aggregate demand from too rapid monetary growth, for which the policy prescription is first to persevere in mild restraint until inflation simmers down and thereafter to avoid overexpansion. In that case inflation is the vehicle by which excessive money balances are reduced to the desired level in real terms. But part of the inflation in 1973 appeared to be different. Special conditions conspired to raise the prices of many basic commodities well beyond a level attributable to prior monetary growth. When these increases passed through to prices of finished goods and services, real money balances were reduced *below* the desired level. Faced with deficient balances, the public attempted to restore them to the desired level by selling other assets and reducing expenditures. Monetary policy was then faced with a range of choices from (1) accommodating the increases in the price level by expanding the money supply faster until real balances reached the desired level to (2) holding back and enduring a period of economic retrenchment during which desired real balances would be reduced to the lower actual level. In view of the severity of the 1973–1975 recession and despite the continuing rise of prices, monetary policy can be described as pursuing a course closer to the second than to the first of these two extremes.

In recent years there had formed in the United States a consensus of sorts for a middle-of-the-road policy of maintaining mild slack in the economy until inflation was "subdued." The question of how much slack should be maintained after the inflation fell below 4 or 5 percent per year was not settled. But, until that issue had to be faced, policy had been guided by a consensus that we should reduce the rate of inflation—slowly to be sure—and keep it low as economic activity expanded. That at least was the announced intention, even though it was not always achieved. In 1973 and 1974, policies to subdue inflation not only suffered another temporary setback because of the resurgence of domestic inflation but also appeared to have entered a hostile new environment subject to inflationary disturbances from outside the country. In addition to braking the momentum of the ongoing inflation, policy somehow had to combat the effects of new outside disturbances as well.

Preventing outbursts of inflation and bringing the long-run average rate down below 5 percent and holding it there now appears more difficult and costly than had been imagined even after the sobering experience of the 1970 recession (which temporarily slowed but did not arrest the inflation). In the new environment it has become harder to maintain the view that inflation will succumb to a careful policy of containment. No one can be sure which policies are still feasible and will actually be carried through. The 1973–1975 recession began again a process of slowing inflation. The high rates of 1973–1974 have receded, but an underlying rate of 6 to 7 percent per year still persists. The test for policy will be its ability to continue reducing inflation even as the economy approaches full production in 1977 and later years.

This essay reviews recent and prospective price behavior, the short-run policy issues raised by foreign influences on U.S. prices, and the problems of consistency between long-run objectives and responses to short-run developments.

Recent Foreign Influences on U.S. Prices. The outburst of inflation in 1973 reflected a variety of international developments that raised prices throughout the world. World prices of basic commodities rose sharply, beginning late in 1972 with food grains reduced in supply by crop failures, spreading to nonfood materials under the demand pressure of cyclical upswings in most of the industrialized countries, and capped by the quadrupling of the price of petroleum by the OPEC cartel in late 1973. There was in addition to these worldwide developments the devaluation and floating of the dollar exchange rate beginning in 1971, which raised the prices of U.S. imports.

None of these foreign influences was the result of a concurrent rise in U.S. aggregate demand. The devaluation reflected past U.S. inflation, and in the floating of the exchange rate, dollar prices of imports previously held in place by a fixed exchange rate were set free to adjust upward. The explosion in world commodity prices was fueled by expanded monetary growth in the major industrial countries in 1971–1972, which was in turn supported in no small measure by a growth in world monetary reserves from an outflow of U.S. dollars.[1] Although not independent of prior U.S. developments, the price increases of basic commodities nevertheless came mostly in response to world demand and supply conditions and were much greater (as shown below) than demand conditions within the U.S. economy alone can explain. Once under way, the price increases generated their own effects on U.S. incomes. The main effects occurred through the balance of foreign payments and the terms of trade. The sharp rise in the price of petroleum reduced U.S. incomes in real and nominal terms in early 1974, though from the third quarter of 1973 to the first quarter of 1974 U.S. incomes rose because increased grain exports at increased prices expanded farm receipts from abroad. But the resulting effects on net aggregate U.S. expenditures, relatively minor from an overall view, were temporary. Given that monetary growth did not rise to sustain them, and other things the same, the rising prices of the scarce commodities reduced the demand for all other goods and services, and aggregate demand did not change, except perhaps temporarily.

Yet, while aggregate demand is the main determinant of the general price level in the long run, recent price increases of imports were passed through the economy as cost increases and thereby raised the general price level before offsetting demand pressures on other prices took effect. Demand pressures work very slowly; their impact is initially on output and only much later on prices.[2] Consequently, the run-up in the price level resulting from the cost increases is reversed, given unchanged monetary growth, only after a long period of reduced output. In the meantime, wages advance in response to the higher cost of living, making the period of reversal very long indeed.

Much remains to be learned about the reasons manufacturing prices respond to cost increases so quickly and to demand pressures

---

[1] See David I. Fand, "World Reserves and World Inflation," *Banca Nazionale del Lavoro Quarterly Review*, no. 115 (December 1975).

[2] This pattern of price behavior is discussed in Phillip Cagan, *The Hydra-Headed Monster: The Problem of Inflation in the United States* (Washington, D.C.: American Enterprise Institute, 1974).

so slowly. The reason given by current theories in the literature [3] is that sellers in most industries have implicit understandings with workers and customers (and sometimes explicit contracts) to keep wages and prices close to a long-run equilibrium level in order to avoid uncertainty and search costs. These understandings do not preclude price adjustments, but the adjustments generally occur in response to changes in costs only and not to current demand conditions. Hence prices reflect unit costs of production, while changes in inventories and production absorb changes in the quantity demanded. Reduced demand does eventually affect prices, but mainly as the derived demand for input materials lowers prices in basic commodity markets, from which lower materials prices work through the economy as lower or less rapidly rising costs. This sequence of events describes the behavior of prices in recent decades.

The importance of foreign influences in 1973 and 1974 is indicated by the rise in U.S. import and export prices relative to general prices. From the fourth quarter of 1972 to the second quarter of 1974, while the consumer price index rose 15 percent, the unit value of total imports rose 68 percent, and even with fuels excluded it rose 39 percent—which was also the rise in the unit value of total exports (see Table 1). The effective dollar exchange rate depreciated 7 percent. Even with fuels excluded, therefore, import and export prices rose about six times more than the depreciation in the exchange rate and two and a half times more than the consumer price index.

To what extent did these increases raise costs and push up other prices? The direct effect of a rise in input prices on output prices in the various sectors of the economy can be estimated with the use of input-output weights for U.S. industries. To be complete, the estimates must make some allowance for the effects on substitutes, because a rise in import prices will pull up the prices of substitute domestic inputs. A study for the Joint Economic Committee, which made such estimates,[4] found a moderate effect on general prices from the third quarter of 1971, when the dollar was first devalued, to the second quarter of 1974. In that period the price deflator for personal consumption expenditures rose 18.6 percent. The study attributed a rise of less than 1 percent to the depreciation of the dollar and a rise

---

[3] See Arthur M. Okun, "Inflation: Its Mechanics and Welfare Costs," *Brookings Papers on Economic Activity*, 1975(2), pp. 351-90.

[4] Same source as for Table 1. The estimates are biased upward by the assumption that the input weights for each industry are constant and that the rise in prices of domestic substitutes is the same as that of the corresponding imports. The estimates may be biased downward by a failure to allow for increases in all substitutes.

Table 1

INDICES OF U.S. DOMESTIC AND WORLD PRICES, 1972-IV TO 1974-II

Year and Quarter	U.S. Dollar Price of Weighted Foreign Currencies	Import Prices (unit values)		Export Prices (unit values)	Consumer Prices
		Total	Nonfuel		
1972 IV	100.0	100.0	100.0	100.0	100.0
1973 I	104.1	103.8	103.6	103.9	101.5
II	106.9	112.5	112.6	108.7	103.7
III	108.8	116.8	116.1	116.1	106.0
IV	106.9	127.0	123.3	124.2	108.5
1974 I	104.0	147.8	126.6	134.3	111.5
II	107.2	168.3	138.9	139.2	114.8

Source: R. Berner, P. Clark, J. Enzler, and B. Lowrey, "International Sources of Domestic Inflation," Joint Economic Committee, *Studies in Price Stability and Economic Growth*, No. 3, 94th Congress, 1st session, August 5, 1975, p. 5.

of 4.5 percent to the effect over and above exchange depreciation of higher import prices including sympathetic rises in domestic substitutes. The combined effect of depreciation and additional increases in import prices accounted for three-tenths of the total inflation over the period. We must also add the pressure of foreign demands on U.S. commodities traded in world markets, which raised the input costs of these commodities to the U.S. economy. Even with this addition, it still appears that a substantial part of the 1973 inflationary outburst in the United States reflected excessive domestic demand.[5]

[5] In the Joint Economic Committee study cited in Table 1, the Federal Reserve Board's econometric model was simulated to measure demand as well as cost effects. In the simulation the estimated effect of the depreciation of the exchange rate on the consumption deflator was 2.8 percentage points, compared with less than one point with the input-output analysis noted in the text. The estimated effect of the extraordinary increases in import and export prices was 4.5 percentage points, the same as the estimate from input-output analysis noted in the text for import prices alone, apparently because deflationary demand effects exactly offset the added inflationary effects.

An estimate of the rise in the private nonfarm deflator resulting from price increases of fossil fuels alone from the second quarter of 1973 to the first quarter of 1975 is 1.5 percent. This figure, based on producer sales data, is consistent with the input-output estimates above. See Charles L. Schultze, "Falling Profits, Rising Profit Margins, and the Full-Employment Rate," *Brookings Papers on Economic Activity*, 1975(2), p. 450n.

Figure 1

INDUSTRIAL WHOLESALE PRICES, QUARTERLY, 1971–1976

(1972 IV = 100)

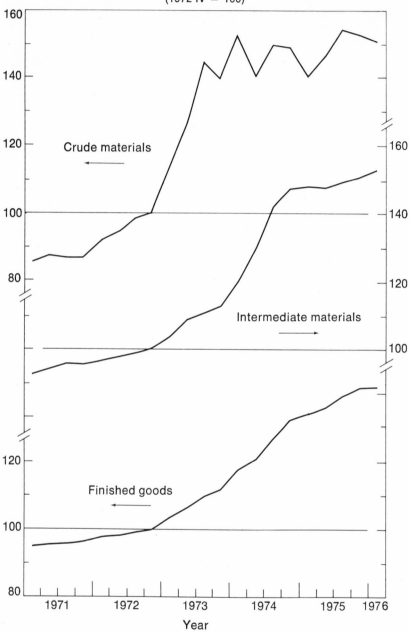

Year

Source: Bureau of Labor Statistics.

It took about two years for all the foreign-induced cost increases to pass completely through the price structure. This can be seen in Figure 1 from the timing of quarterly price movements in crude, intermediate, and finished goods. The inflation rate for wholesale crude materials jumped from 15 percent in 1972 to 39.5 percent in 1973. The index of these prices then stopped rising and fell in the first half of 1974. According to the monthly data, the index fell at a 16.5 percent annual rate over the first half of 1974, but the decline erased only a fraction of the 1973 increase. Although the index fell 14 percent from its peak in August 1973 to a trough in June 1974, by the end of 1974 it had recovered and was below the earlier peak by only 5 percent. For all of 1974 the index actually rose 7 percent (in quarterly averages), bringing the total increase for 1973 and 1974 to 49 percent. The contribution of this increase in materials prices to manufacturing costs took a year to pass through the entire economy: wholesale prices of intermediate materials and finished goods did not begin a comparable rise until 1974. Prices of intermediate materials rose 30.5 percent in 1974, up from 12.5 percent in 1973, and prices of finished goods 18.5 percent, up from 11.5 percent. These high inflation rates came down sharply during the first half of 1975 (in the case of intermediate materials to a level below the 1972 rates), and then partly recovered in the ensuing business recovery during the second half of 1975. Finished goods prices continued rising more rapidly than the other two indices in 1975. (The lag in the price index of finished goods would have been even longer if it were not for the inclusion of consumer foods.) The passing of price increases from crude to intermediate and then to finished goods with a year's lag meant that the total index of wholesale prices rose substantially in both 1973 and 1974.

The pattern of recent price movements therefore shows a large blip from materials and food costs superimposed on a moderately accelerating inflationary trend: the blip was a sharp rise in the level of prices which temporarily raised the rate of increase, and the accelerating trend reflected the accumulation of past pressures and the emergence of new pressures as the business expansion gained speed during 1972. The price deflator for the private nonfarm sector, which in the first quarter of 1973 had an annual rate of increase of only 4.2 percent, then had a 9.3 percent rate in the fourth quarter (see Figure 2). Not all of that acceleration yet reflected the 1973 blip in materials costs which subsequently passed through successive stages of production and by the end of 1974 raised the inflation rate for the private

Figure 2

RATE OF CHANGE OF PRICES, PRIVATE
NONFARM SECTOR, QUARTERLY, 1970–1976

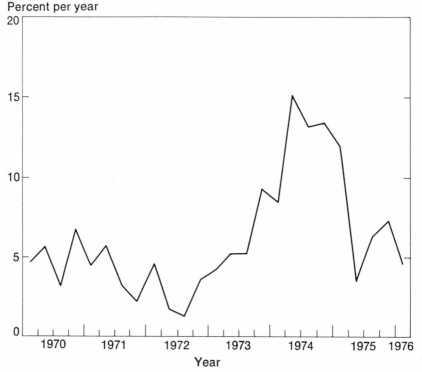

Source: Bureau of Economic Analysis.

nonfarm sector to 13.4 percent. The rate for this sector receded in early 1975 at the trough of the recession, but the blip left a trail of cost increases that continued coming through the production pipeline for a time thereafter, not to mention an accumulation of cost-of-living increases in the wage "catch-up" of negotiated labor contracts later on. While the inflation rate for the private nonfarm sector had declined by the fourth quarter of 1975 to 7.3 percent, it remained well above the 2.8 percent of 1972.

On the assumption that the 21 percent rise in the private nonfarm deflator from mid-1973 to mid-1975 would, if there had been no price blip, have instead roughly equalled the 5.1 percent annual rate reached in the middle two quarters of 1973, we may conclude that the blip added 10.5 percent to that index—which doubled the increase in the index—over the two-year period.[6]

Overexpansion from the 1970 Recession. The foreign influences would very likely have had much less effect on prices than they did if the domestic business expansion had not accelerated price increases at the end of 1972 by pushing the economy into the zone of demand-pull inflationary pressures. Monetary policy had been too expansive during 1972. Recovery from the 1970 recession had begun slowly but progressively picked up speed. In 1971, after a first-quarter jump reflecting settlement of the General Motors' strike, dollar GNP rose in the next three quarters at an annual rate of 7.5 percent. In 1972 and 1973 the annual rate rose to 11 percent. By 1973 capacity utilization in manufacturing had returned to the neighborhood of the peak rates reached in the booming second and third quarters of 1969.[7] Supply bottlenecks developed in various industries. Unemployment fell below 5 percent, a level which because of changes in the composition of the labor force was no longer consistent with reasonable price stability.

Nominal wages were not a source of increasing pressure on prices. As is usual for the late stages of a cyclical expansion, they trailed price increases. Average hourly earnings for the private nonfarm sector rose by 6.5 to 7 percent during 1972 and 1973, about the same rate of increase as in 1971. But unit labor costs rose considerably

---

[6] A times-series regression estimate (Franco Modigliani and Lucas Papademos, "Monetary Policy for the Coming Quarters: The Conflicting Views," *New England Economic Review*, Federal Reserve Bank of Boston, March-April 1976) finds the underlying inflation rate in 1974 to be from 4 to 5 percent and thus attributes slightly more than half the total rate to foreign influences.

The domestic inflation rate of 5.1 percent may partly reflect a measurement catch-up from the removal of price controls (see Michael Darby, "The U.S. Economic Stabilization Program of 1971-74," in *The Illusion of Wage and Price Controls* [Vancouver, B.C.: Fraser Institute, 1976]) and so may misrepresent the lower "true" rate. In that event the remainder attributable to the foreign influences would represent more than half of the total "true" inflation rate.

In the light of these studies, the mid-1973 inflation rate, and the fact that the Joint Economic Committee estimate is probably low, the half-and-half assumption in the text for the division between foreign and domestic influences seems to represent a reasonable order of magnitude.

[7] The Federal Reserve capacity utilization index was 83 percent in 1973, a bit below its level of 87 percent in the first three quarters of 1969. The Wharton index was 96 percent in the three final quarters of 1973, about equal to the percentage in the first three quarters of 1969.

Other evidence suggests that these indices understate the actual level of capacity utilization in the economy in 1973 (see Geoffrey H. Moore, *How Full Is Full Employment?* [Washington, D.C.: American Enterprise Institute, 1973], pp. 24-27).

faster in 1973 and 1974 than in 1972, as output per man-hour fell sharply. It does not seem implausible to attribute the serious deterioration in productivity growth to the spreading inefficiencies and distortions of an inflationary environment. In any event, profit margins generally fell, so that the decline in productivity growth, together with the rise in materials costs, accounted for the increasing pressure on prices.

Instead of slowing monetary growth during 1972 as activity approached full capacity, policy allowed the growth to increase.[8] From 6.5 percent in 1971, M_1 growth spurted to 9.2 percent in 1972. Although growth rates of more broadly defined monetary aggregates did not rise in 1972 over 1971, they remained high in comparison with the years before 1971. Net borrowed reserves of member banks rose over the second half of 1972, suggesting that the Federal Reserve was willing to see banks under pressure to curtail expansion, but such pressure had limited effect that year and the next. The expansion of monetary growth in 1972 was not pursued to ease tightening financial markets (as is sometimes the case), because interest rates in fact fluctuated within a low band during 1971 and 1972 and only began to rise above it in 1973. The expansive policy appears to have been simply a mistake related to the price controls: the Phase II controls in effect during 1972 apparently held back some of the early signs of rising inflationary pressures and lulled policy makers into the belief that unemployment could be pushed to around 5 percent without inflationary consequences. The rate was above 5.5 percent during most of 1972, but, as the expansion gained speed, it dropped rapidly during the closing months and fell below 5 percent at the beginning of 1972. Complacency about renewed inflationary dangers turned out to be a disadvantage of the controls more serious than their allocative distortions.

Such complacency was widely shared, to be sure, as late as the first quarter of 1973. The sixty-odd professional forecasters in the ASA-NBER survey[9] of December 1972 expected on average that the GNP deflator in 1973 would rise 3.5 percent, up only slightly over 1972. In the February 1973 survey they expected a small bulge in the inflation rate for the first quarter of 1973 then under way, but no lasting escalation, and the expected rate for the year remained at

[8] This is discussed in my "Controls and Monetary Policy, 1969-1973," in *A New Look at Inflation* (Washington, D.C.: American Enterprise Institute, 1973).

[9] Quarterly survey conducted by the American Statistical Association in the fourth quarter of 1972 and compiled by the National Bureau of Economic Research (mimeographed).

3.5 percent. The actual rate for 1973 was 7.6 percent, and it was still climbing as the year ended. When the Phase II price and wage controls were replaced in January 1973 by the milder set of Phase III controls, the change appeared to be justified by a continuing low rate of inflation—but with hindsight one wonders whether the Nixon administration might have detected the coming inflationary storm and wisely acted early, recognizing that later, when the public would think that the tight regulations of Phase II were most needed, they would be impossible to enforce and politically difficult to abandon. (And, indeed, the administration was forced to tighten controls again later in 1973.) No doubt the removal of Phase II in early 1973 permitted some previously suppressed inflationary pressures to surface during that year, but this accounts for only about two percentage points [10] of the price explosion that then occurred.

The Recession of 1973–1975. As a result of the price explosion, real money balances (M_1 deflated by the price index for the private nonfarm sector) fell 9.75 percent from mid-1973 to mid-1975 (see Figure 3), which happens to correspond in timing and magnitude to the price blip of 10.5 percent noted above.[11] Without the blip, in other words, monetary growth would have kept real balances constant: such a policy would have been too tight for the economic slowdown which developed but still better than the policy of allowing them to decline. Insofar as the price blip originated from crop failures and demand conditions outside the U.S. economy (as it did for the most part) and monetary growth was not at the same time expanded commensurately, the blip reduced real money balances *below* their desired level. Such a reduction had consequences altogether different from those of a reduction following monetary overexpansion, in which the resulting spurt of prices reduces real money balances *toward* their desired level. The economic effect of reducing real balances below their desired level is contractionary, just as though nominal monetary growth had been curtailed, and the immediate effect was a rise in short-term interest rates. Prime commercial paper rates rose above 10 percent in the second quarter of 1973, receded somewhat during the next two quarters, and then rose steeply to almost 12 percent by mid-1974. Part of this rise in interest rates may have resulted, to be sure, from the increase in inflation rates, as compensation to lenders for the depreciation in the purchasing power of dollar securi-

---

[10] Based on estimates for the period from the first quarter of 1973 to the third quarter of 1974 in Darby, "The U.S. Economic Stabilization Program."

[11] A price rise of 10.5 percent reduces real money balances to $1/1.105 = .905$ or by 9.5 percent.

Figure 3
REAL MONEY BALANCES, QUARTERLY, 1969–1976
(1973 IV = 100)

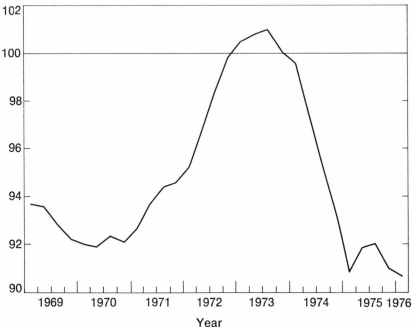

Source: Ratio of M_1 to private nonfarm deflator. *Federal Reserve Bulletin*, various issues, and Bureau of Economic Analysis.

ties. To that extent the rise in nominal interest rates reduced the demand for money balances and offset the tightening effect of the actual reduction in real balances on the economy. But it seems unlikely that a full adjustment of interest rates to the change in the inflation rate occurred so quickly. If we put all the evidence together—the sharp reduction in real money balances, the estimates of the desired level of the balances discussed later, and the fall in aggregate de-mand—it points to a decline in real balances *below* their desired level. This decline then contributed to the tightening of financial markets, to the rise in interest rates, and thus to the deepening contraction in economic activity in the fourth quarter of 1974 and the first quarter of 1975.

What could policy makers do about the decline in real money balances? Monetary growth cannot affect real balances in the long run, since economic behavior adjusts them to the desired level as determined by public preferences, GNP, interest rates, and other variables. But when actual real balances deviate from the desired level in the short run, monetary growth can have an effect on real balances by bringing them closer to the desired level or by influencing the desired level itself through effects on GNP and interest rates. In 1973–1974 a speed-up in nominal monetary growth would have counteracted the effect of the rise in prices in reducing real balances. That would have kept the balances at the desired level and have prevented the subsequent contractionary adjustments in aggregate demand.

To have expanded monetary growth, however, would have precluded any resistance to the outburst of inflation. The Federal Reserve authorities favored the standard response of monetary restraint. M_1 growth remained around 6 percent per year through most of 1973 and early 1974, down from around 7 percent for most of the second half of 1972 (see Figure 4). It is likely that the authorities desired even slower monetary growth in early 1974 but compromised in an effort to hold back a sharp rise in interest rates. The authorities revealed their preferences by reducing monetary growth after midyear when interest rates finally fell. In the second half of 1974 M_1 growth dropped to 4 percent per year, resulting in a further reduction in real balances. The mild business recession which began at the end of 1973 became severe in the fourth quarter of 1974 with a precipitous decline of industrial production—12 percent in six months. The relatively mild decline in growth of the money stock does not itself appear sufficient to have precipitated such a severe downturn in activity, and the large reduction in the real value of money balances was apparently crucial.

In 1974 one problem for policy makers was the unusually confusing business picture in the first three quarters. At first the mild decline in output seemed to result from production cutbacks necessitated by the oil embargo from October 1973 to March 1974. It is still not entirely clear whether a business recession of the traditional kind—that is, with deficient aggregate demand—began then or in the fourth quarter of 1974. Despite declining real final sales for the national economy after a peak in the third quarter of 1973, inventory accumulation was extremely large. The rapid increases in crude materials prices engendered fears of shortages, and users of crude materials sought large inventories as insurance against supply shortages and as a speculation on further price increases. In the three quarters from the fourth quarter of 1973 to the second quarter of 1974, inventory investment was two-thirds larger in real terms than

Figure 4
MONETARY GROWTH RATES, MONTHLY AND
SEVEN-MONTH CENTERED AVERAGES, 1972–1976

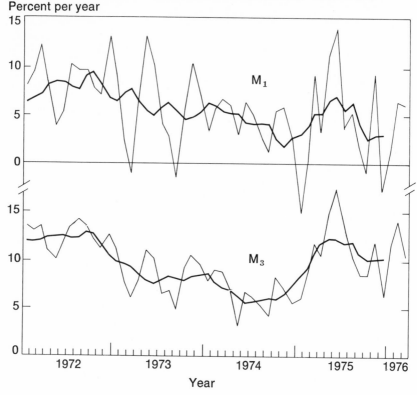

Note: M_1 is currency outside banks plus demand deposits at commercial banks. M_3 is M_1 plus time deposits at commercial banks other than large negotiable CDs plus deposits at thrift institutions and credit unions.
Source: *Federal Reserve Bulletin*, various issues.

in the preceding three quarters when sales were still expanding. The inventory accumulation could not have been primarily an unintended result of a shortfall in sales. Although sales failed to rise as anticipated, the accumulation was much larger than could conceivably be attributed to estimates of higher sales. It turned out to be excessive, and suddenly in the fourth quarter of 1974 the inventory overhang seemed to be recognized as unnecessary, unprofitable, and oppressive, so that purchases for stock, new orders, and production all plummeted. As these events were unfolding, President Ford held his conference of experts and public opinion leaders to discuss policies to curb inflation.

For ill-timing this matches President Truman's strictures against inflation in the closing months of 1948 as the economy was entering recession. A big difference, however, was that, though wholesale prices kept rising rapidly in the recession of 1973–1975, they declined sharply in the 1948–1949 recession.

As the depth of the decline in business activity became clear by the end of 1974, some commentators [12] called for a large increase in monetary growth to make up the reduction in real money balances. But the Federal Reserve was afraid that open market purchases beyond the normal scale of such operations would disrupt financial markets [13] and (by heightening expectations of inflation) worsen the trade-off between inflation and output. In retrospect the Federal Reserve could have cushioned the decline in real balances and moderated the fall in economic activity, which turned out to be more severe than was desirable. Yet it is also clear that raging inflation distorts and clouds economic developments and makes it difficult to determine a policy that will subdue inflation with the lowest feasible unemployment path. Whether an error in setting policy once recognized can be quickly rectified is not known, but certainly massive shifts in policy are not part of the traditional art of central banking.

The steep decline in economic activity hit bottom in the first quarter of 1975. With the aid of expanded monetary growth and a tax reduction and rebates, most of the inventory paring ended and the economy turned around. The rebound was vigorous. Real GNP rose at an annual rate of 8.5 percent in the second half of the year. Excess capacity, however, remained large (about 30 percent), and unemployment was still above 8 percent at year-end, finally falling below that level in January 1976 (to 7.8 percent).

Problems in Selecting a Policy for the Early Part of Recovery

How Much Monetary Growth Was Desirable? With the recovery well under way in the second half of 1975, attention turned to the appro-

---

[12] See Franco Modigliani and Lucas Papademos, "Target for Monetary Policy in the Coming Year," *Brookings Papers on Economic Activity*, 1975(1), pp. 141-63, esp. p. 159; Edmund S. Phelps, "Creating Money for Tax Rebates," *New York Times*, January 26, 1975; and James Tobin, "Monetary Policy and the Control of Credit," in A. T. Sommers, ed., *Answers to Inflation and Recession: Economic Policies for a Modern Society* (New York: The Conference Board, 1975).

[13] The tax rebates offered an opportunity to increase the money stock quickly through Treasury operations (see Phelps, "Creating Money"). The rebates did shift Treasury holdings into public hands, a fact that accounts for the rise in monetary growth in early 1975. But the Federal Reserve did not favor this result, and subsequent growth was low in order to offset the rebate increase.

priate policies for a strong expansion that would reduce the large unemployment without at the same time interfering with a further decline in inflation. In the prevailing view, the unemployment and inflation goals were not considered in conflict, because the business trough had been so low that two years of strong expansion would not remove all the excess capacity in the economy. So long as a return to excess demand was avoided, inflation would decline as cost increases from past excess demand worked their way through the price system and eventually petered out. Strong fiscal and monetary stimulants were widely proposed, since without them most forecasters saw a sluggish recovery. Despite the strong rebound in the third and fourth quarters of 1975, forecasts at the end of that year predicted a relatively slow recovery of 6 percent growth in real GNP for 1976 and less in subsequent years, a forecast with which the administration concurred. For such a path, unemployment would remain above 7.5 percent through 1976 and 1977.[14]

The arguments for expanding monetary growth given in early 1975 and cited above could be applied equally to the 1976 recovery. If the momentum of rising prices at 6 to 7 percent per year had been built into the economy for the year ahead, as was generally believed, outstanding money balances would depreciate at that rate without having much immediate effect on the rate of inflation. On this line of reasoning, the best policy was for the money stock to grow at a rate sufficient to provide for short-run growth in real balances and output. Then, as the inflation rate gradually moderated, growth in the money stock could be reduced commensurately. Without growth in real balances in the short run, however, the drag on aggregate demand would for some time depress output rather than the inflation rate. Alarm was sounded in the press that without adequate stimulus the recovery could be aborted.

Proponents of this view were ready to admit that, in past cyclical recoveries, output expanded faster than real balances (as indicated by a rise in the velocity of money, the ratio of GNP to M_1). The typical increase in velocity had been 6 percent in the first year of recoveries since 1954, though less in the second year. The forecast of 6 percent growth in real GNP implicitly assumed such a rise in velocity in 1976. But critics found this outcome unsatisfactory and wanted faster growth in output to remove the excess unemployment within two years. Some called for 10 percent or more output growth in the first

[14] *The Budget of the U.S. Government* (Washington, D.C.: Government Printing Office, 1976), p. 41.

year.[15] With built-in inflation of 6 to 7 percent, that meant 16 to 17 percent growth in dollar GNP. This implied monetary growth of 10 percent if velocity rose the typical 6 percent, and it was thought that velocity might rise much less (its first-year recovery from the 1970 recession having been 2.5 percent).[16] Velocity did rise at a surprising 10 percent annual rate in the second half of 1975. But the rapid rise reflected an initial spurt from a deep recession and was thought unlikely to continue. Moreover, some argued that a rapid rise in velocity was not all to the good, because such a rise usually came about through a rise in interest rates. With the large projected Treasury deficit, a sharp rise in interest rates would crowd out private investment and partially offset the fiscal stimulus—and many thought the administration budget provided insufficient stimulus to begin with. To avoid this crowding-out, some proposed that stable interest rates be made the target and high monetary growth (10 percent or more) be made the means to achieve vigorous business recovery.[17]

The Federal Reserve was sympathetic to those who wanted stable interest rates but was not prepared to pursue such high monetary growth. In May 1975 and subsequently during the year, it announced a target growth path for M_1 between 5 and 7.5 percent for the year ahead,[18] in line with monetary growth in 1973 and the first half of 1974. This target allowed for virtually no rise in real money balances until inflation slowed considerably.

Economic events have a way of giving an ironic twist to the best-laid proposals of economists. During the second half of 1975, financial markets were unexpectedly easy despite the spurt in output and the large Treasury deficit, and interest rates generally declined. The Federal Reserve refrained from pursuing monetary expansion aggressively, and monetary growth actually fell below the announced target. M_1 growth slowed in the second half and rose only 4.5 percent for the year.

---

[15] Modigliani and Papademos, "Monetary Policy for the Coming Quarters," and Benjamin M. Friedman, "Monetary Policy for the 1976 Recovery," *New England Economic Review*, Federal Reserve Bank of Boston, January-February 1976, pp. 3-16.

[16] Friedman, "Monetary Policy."

[17] Modigliani and Papademos, "Monetary Policy for the Coming Quarters."

[18] The corresponding target for M_2 was 8.5 to 10.5 percent and for M_3 was 10 to 12 percent. See statement of Arthur F. Burns before the Committee on Banking, Housing and Urban Affairs, U.S. Senate, May 1, 1975 (*Federal Reserve Bulletin*, May 1975, p. 286), U.S. House of Representatives, July 24, 1975 (*Federal Reserve Bulletin*, August 1975, p. 495), U.S. Senate, November 4, 1975 (*Federal Reserve Bulletin*, November 1975, p. 747). The successive extensions of the target did not, however, allow for corrections of previous divergences.

35

Usually interest rates rise in a business recovery, and proponents of a stable interest-rate target then call for faster monetary growth to hold down the rising rates. On the other hand, those who believe that monetary growth should be kept stable argue for the contrary policy—not to accommodate the expanding demand for credit but to allow interest rates to be pulled up by market forces. Events in the second half of 1975 upset both views. Proponents of stable interest rates, who wanted a vigorous recovery, could not by the logic of their position criticize the low monetary growth so long as interest rates did not rise. Proponents of stable monetary growth, who were leery of overstimulating the economy through overfast monetary growth, had in consistency to urge that interest rates be reduced further in keeping M_1 growth from falling below the target. The Federal Reserve could relish the confusion visited upon its critics on both flanks.

The appropriate policy depended in theory upon the reasons interest rates were sagging. If a shift in the demand for money balances had reduced the desired quantity of balances at the given level of interest rates, the public would adjust by increasing its demand for other financial assets and thus by bidding interest rates down. In that event the money supply target could appropriately be lowered.[19] Under the circumstances in 1975, however, it seemed more likely that the decline in rates reflected a weak demand for inventory and capital financing, more than offsetting the effects of the large Treasury borrowing. (Treasury securities may also have gained new takers who had become wary of municipal offerings as a result of New York City's well-publicized difficulties.) To counter a decline in business borrowing, the appropriate policy was to reduce interest rates even further by maintaining or even raising the original monetary growth path. In that event stable monetary growth was closer to a stimulative policy than was the actual growth or the growth which a stabilization of interest rates would have produced. (Eventually, as business recovered further and borrowing increased, financial markets would tighten, and the policy debate would be back on its usual track—arguing whether to hold down interest rates or monetary growth, since one or the other would have to rise.)

---

[19] In the literature this case is analyzed as a leftward shift in the LM schedule, for which a policy of offsetting changes in the money supply in order to stabilize interest rates is shown to stabilize aggregate demand as well. The companion case noted next in the text is a leftward shift in the IS schedule, which requires the opposite policy of lower interest rates and higher money supply. See, for example, William Poole, "Rules-of-Thumb for Guiding Monetary Policy," in *Open Market Policies and Operating Procedures—Staff Studies* (Washington, D.C.: Board of Governors of the Federal Reserve System, 1971), pp. 135-89.

The 4.5 percent growth of M_1 in 1975 was not viewed by the Federal Reserve as a departure from its announced policy. Although M_1 growth was low, the growth rates of the other monetary aggregates stayed on target. M_3, for example, grew 12 percent to meet its targeted range of 10 to 12 percent (see Figure 4). The divergence of M_1 from target was attributed to a shift in public preference from checking accounts to savings deposits, to which the slowing of M_1 growth was an appropriate accommodation. This was a special case of a shift in the demand for money balances noted above. Partial support for this interpretation came from a November 1975 change in Federal Reserve regulations—a change that allowed businesses to acquire and hold savings deposits with commercial banks. A survey estimated that $2 billion in savings deposits had been subsequently acquired. In line with this interpretation, the Federal Reserve widened its M_1 target in February 1976 for the year ahead to 4.5 to 7.5 percent and kept its targets for the other aggregates unchanged.[20]

But it could be questioned whether this interpretation of the divergence was correct. Although it is tempting to interpret a divergence between the growth rates of M_1 and M_3 as a shift between M_1 and M_3 by holders, such a divergence often reflects instead a shift between M_3 and nonmonetary financial assets which does not affect the demand for M_1. In the recession a desired increase in M_3 was encouraged by the decline in market interest rates while deposit rates offered by thrift institutions were unchanged. Such an increase in the intermediation of lending alters the channel of credit flows but does not change the total flows. There may also be an expansion of commercial bank time and savings deposits, drawing reserves away from the backing of demand deposits. As a result, M_1 growth falls (as happened in 1975) unless the Federal Reserve drops its target range for the federal funds rate fast enough to prevent such a development—as apparently it did not. The growth of time and savings deposits often occurs at the expense of nonmonetary financial assets and may not, as noted, reflect a corresponding reduction in desired holdings of demand deposits. In that event, the authorities should push interest rates down further to counteract the reduced business investment responsible for the sagging interest rates, and M_1 growth should not be allowed to decline.

---

[20] Statement of Arthur F. Burns before the Committee on Banking, Currency, and Housing, U.S. House of Representatives, February 3, 1976 (*Federal Reserve Bulletin*, February 1976, pp. 119-25). The target was changed again in May to 4.5 to 7 percent for M_1 and to 7.5 to 10 percent for M_2 and left unchanged (since November 1975) at 10 to 12 percent for M_3.

A divergence in the growth paths of the various monetary aggregates is hard enough to interpret under ordinary circumstances—though the interpretation is often crucial in choosing the proper policy—but in this period interpretation is further confounded by a failure of the standard econometric equations for money demand to explain events consistently with past experience.

What Went Wrong with the Money-Demand Equations? These equations relate the demand for money balances primarily to real GNP and interest rates. At first, events were consistent with the equations. The rise in interest rates in the first half of 1974 was accompanied by a fall in the real value of money balances. Thereafter real GNP fell sharply, a fall that was accompanied by a further decline in real balances. But the subsequent fall in short-term interest rates after mid-1974 should have then increased real balances, whereas the actual quantity of real balances continued to fall sharply.[21] The

[21] A typical money-demand equation for M_1 is the following from a recent study by Anna J. Schwartz and Phillip Cagan (*Journal of Money, Credit and Banking*, vol. 7, no. 2 [May 1975], Table 7, line 4):

> quarterly change in log of real money balances = .11(log of desired real balances *minus* log of real balances in previous quarter)

where

> log of desired real balances = .86(log of real GNP) − .19(log of commercial paper rate) − .19(log of average interest rate paid on savings deposits).

The coefficients were estimated by a regression fit to quarterly U.S. data from the first quarter of 1951 to the fourth quarter of 1971 with an R^2 of .99. No claim of superiority is made for this equation; its statistical properties are somewhat inferior to those of others. But it is similar in form to most others in the literature—see, for example, Stephen Goldfeld, "The Demand for Money Revisited," *Brookings Papers on Economic Activity*, 1973(3)—and serves for illustration. All equations with similar variables exhibit a growing discrepancy in 1975 between the desired and actual balances though the exact numbers may differ, on which see James Pierce, "Interest Rates and Their Prospect in the Recovery," *Brookings Papers on Economic Activity*, 1975(1).

When the above equation is applied to 1973–1975, the implied discrepancy of desired real balances over the concurrent actual balances in percent is:

Quarter	1973	1974	1975
1	—	+2.9	+8.9
2	+4.5	−1.4	+10.3
3	−2.4	−1.7	+10.1
4	+1.6	+3.3	+14.0

Although the differences before 1975 are not out of line with the usual standard errors of extrapolation for such an equation (which run lower than the percentages above because of allowance for delayed adjustments), the large and growing differences beginning in the fourth quarter of 1974 are unusual and puzzling. To be sure, when the equations are re-estimated including 1975 data, they will give estimated coefficients that fit the data better and show smaller equations had gone haywire. In his testimony to Congress in January 1976, Federal Reserve Chairman Burns cited the continuing discrepancy between such equations and actual events in support of his contention that the pursuit of specified monetary growth targets was virtually impossible and—even if possible—undesirable.[22]

The equations do allow for the emergence of *temporary* discrepancies between the quantity of real balances the public desires to hold and what they actually hold at any moment. If the foreign influences on prices were, as seemed likely, independent of past U.S. developments, the decline in real money balances could not have been desired by the public and therefore would lead everyone with deficient real balances to make adjustments—mainly a selling of other assets (which raises interest rates) and a reduction of expenditures on goods and services (which contracts output). The adjustments do not increase actual real balances—given an unchanged rate of inflation— but work instead to reduce the quantity demanded. The equations thus allow for gradual adjustments which remove discrepancies over a period of time. After mid-1974, however, the estimated shortfall in the actual balances held from the quantity demanded grew larger, and such an outcome is consistent with the equations only if the actual balances are increasing toward the larger desired quantity. Instead of increasing, however, real money balances declined in all but the second and third quarters of 1975 (Figure 3). A string of discrepancies of such large size was indeed unusual, and the equations will have to be taken in for repairs.

It was not clear what had gone wrong. One possibility was incomplete or inaccurate data. This had been a concern for some years because of the rapid growth of Eurodollars, thought to be an inflationary source of world monetary growth not counted in any national money supplies (in part because adequate data are lacking). Some Eurodollars might be serving as substitutes for domestic dollar holdings, in which case they would belong in the U.S. money supply, though they are omitted. Interpretation of the data is subject to some dispute, but the amounts in question appear to be small. Eurodollars held by U.S. non-bank residents were about $10 billion at the end of

---

error terms. But unless the equations are respecified in some way to make 1975 consistent with previous years, they will still show an unexplained shift. On the basis of past relationships, it may be said that the sharp decline and low level of actual real balances were not consistent with falling interest rates after mid-1974 and the recovery in real GNP in the second half of 1975.

[22] According to Burns, the Federal Reserve's equation for M_1 demanded was off by 6 percent, which is less than that given by the equation in the preceding footnote but still sizable (*Federal Reserve Bulletin*, February 1976, p. 123).

1974 ($40 billion for nonresidents).[23] These are all held as time accounts and are a tiny fraction of the comparable M_2 of $600 billion.

Another development raising questions of data completeness was the new transfer service on some savings deposits, which thereby acquire characteristics similar to checking accounts. NOW savings accounts (negotiable orders of withdrawal) originated in Massachusetts in 1972 when a court decision confirmed a savings bank's contention that the law did not preclude customers from withdrawing savings deposits by a written order to pay (essentially a check). The Massachusetts legislature did not act to close the loophole, and NOW accounts spread through the state. Similar accounts were then offered in other states. In addition, savings and loan associations and market investment funds are offering overnight or "same day" transfers into a customer's commercial bank checking account by phone orders, so that depositors can receive interest on balances up to the very day of a check transfer. The competition this provided to commercial banks has led the Federal Reserve to allow the commercial banks to offer phone transfers of savings accounts to their depositors. These developments are creating interest-bearing deposits that are transferable by check. They are spreading rapidly, and there is now virtually no chance of stopping their growth. It is only a question of a few years before they will have to be treated in the law and the data as regular checking deposits—and interest payments allowed, perhaps, on all such deposits. Nevertheless, the magnitude of these substitutes for M_1 are not yet consequential. NOW accounts at all institutions in Massachusetts and New Hampshire were $500 million in May 1975.[24] Similar developments in other states were still far behind. These small amounts cannot explain the recent failure of the money-demand equations.

Another possible explanation of the failure of the equations is that a crucial variable has been omitted that previously happened not to play an important role. Wealth at first seems to be such a variable. The real value of financial wealth declines under rapid inflation as well as with a rise in interest rates and fall in the stock market. The erosion of real wealth held by individuals has proceeded apace since the mid-1960s, however, and was not as severe in 1973–1975 as in some previous years. It could provide a partial but hardly a full explanation. One development unique to recent

---

[23] These figures exclude Eurodollars in foreign banks located outside the eight countries that report to the Bank for International Settlements. The figures in the text are based on reports of the Bank for International Settlements, U.S. Treasury, and Federal Reserve Board.

[24] Unpublished Federal Reserve survey.

years was the foreign-induced price blip (discussed above) that reduced real money balances. If the adjustment to this disturbance were slower than to others resulting from variations in monetary growth, it could throw the equations off track. A slower adjustment in this case seems possible. When large price increases that do not reflect prior monetary growth reduce real balances, real transaction balances can be maintained by drawing on balances held in store for contingency or financial purposes. Such nontransaction balances might then be drawn down well below desired levels, possibly for some time.[25] This might help explain the discrepancy.

The explanation must wait, however, for a careful analysis of the data in the light of subsequent developments. Econometric models can miss actual developments by a wide margin at various times, and money-demand equations are particularly unreliable in the short run. The latest fiasco is another reminder to view the results of these equations with extreme caution. While the failure of these equations does not show that any particular explanation of recent events was wrong and any other explanation correct, it does make the interpretation of monetary developments more difficult than usual. In particular it makes uncertain the size of the shortfall of actual from desired real balances and therefore the size of the contractionary pressures that have resulted and will result from adjustments to the shortfall. The early 1976 recovery in GNP suggests that the contractionary adjustments have already largely occurred, contrary to what would appear from the equations.

It was unclear, therefore, whether contractionary adjustments in real money balances were incomplete and more were still to come. Yet, even if the adjustments had been completed by 1976, the business recovery would require an expansion of real balances from their present reduced level to support an expansion in economic activity. Even without precise estimates, the interrelation between monetary growth, the inflation rate, and the level of economic activity meant that, if monetary growth only barely matched the underlying inflation rate, something had to give. If real money balances did not rise, interest rates would begin to rise to retard the recovery. The resulting slack in the economy would then hasten the decline of inflation, to be sure, and help to raise real balances for a given rate of monetary growth. Given the expected slow decline in the inflation rate, however, the recovery would be slow and the slack would persist for a

---

[25] Steps to restore these depleted balances, when undertaken, would act as a drag on aggregate demand.

long time. Those were the alternatives facing policy makers even though the magnitudes were uncertain.

Why a Conservative Growth Target? Although the M_1 growth target of 4.5 to 7.5 percent was high by historical standards, therefore, it was low given the ongoing inflation rate of 6 to 7 percent. Federal Reserve policy could only be described as conservative. By past experience the target growth rates appeared capable of supporting a 6 percent expansion of output at best, and probably much less, unless inflation declined faster than it was expected to. A more rapid recovery for 1976, followed by slower growth in 1977 and beyond, seemed consistent with a continuing reduction of inflation and reduced unemployment. The forecasts of the economy made inside and outside the government did not differ substantially. The decision not to adopt a more ambitious path of economic recovery was intentionally conservative.

On one level, a conservative policy reflected a desire to avoid further stimulus that might not be reversible later. The timing and magnitude of increases in the budget, once undertaken, might not be controllable for political reasons, and an expansive monetary growth might be difficult to slow down. Inflation was running out of control, and the two previous failures of monetary restraint to stop inflation—in 1967 and 1970—made the consequences of another failure appear serious indeed. It was a case of going slow because of the risk that the brakes would be unable to take hold when needed. Against this conservative attitude, the liberal counterview reflected a willingness to risk overshooting, consistent with the traditional liberal judgment that unemployment was not to be endured merely on the grounds that there was a "fear of inflation."

Even though the two views did not reflect widely different forecasts for the economy, there were unstated but important differences in the risks and costs attached to alternative policies. These centered around the feasible recovery paths in the trade-off between inflation and unemployment and the effect of inflationary expectations on prices.

The first difference concerned the optimum speed of reducing inflation. The usual "Phillips curve" relationship between the inflation rate and unemployment is used to answer the question, "What level of unemployment produces a particular rate of inflation?" The standard Phillips curve shows a diminishing effect in the reduction of inflation from higher and higher levels of unemployment. The implication is that, in the short run, the trade-off favors less unemployment with higher inflation. But an important question for 1976 was, "Given the fact that policy is committed to a first-stage reduction in inflation to below 5 percent per year, what path for the economy will achieve that reduction and minimize the total man-hours of unemployment?" Should we have high unemployment for a short period or low unemployment for a long period?

The question arises because the effect of unemployment on inflation is influenced by the expected rate of inflation, and the expected rate depends in part upon the past history of inflation. Suppose prices are currently rising at a rate that agrees with expectations. In such a situation employment will be at or near the full employment level, because the long-run trade-off is very small or zero. If policy actions are introduced to slow aggregate demand, they will raise unemployment and begin to reduce the inflation rate. In time the expected rate of inflation will also decline. Then a further decline in the actual inflation rate can occur, as the expected rate declines, without any further increase in unemployment. The faster the expected rate of inflation declines, the more the actual rate can be reduced by any given amount of unemployment.

Is there an optimum policy for reducing inflation? Clearly, the least unemployment is achieved by staying as close as possible to full employment, allowing just enough unemployment to produce a slow reduction of inflation. Carried to its extreme, however, this policy would take forever to achieve the desired reduction in inflation. That is clearly unacceptable, and some time limit has to be set for attaining the desired reduction. We may suppose that some time limit is provisionally chosen, say four or five years, to achieve a certain reduction in the inflation rate, and the resulting amounts of unemployment whenever they occur, no matter how much later, are estimated for all feasible paths. What is the optimum path to make the total unemployment as low as possible? In general it is best to keep the level of unemployment the same in each quarter over the period in which the inflation rate is to be reduced. Any higher level in one quarter does not produce a sufficiently greater reduction in inflation to justify the lower level of unemployment then possible in another quarter. (That is a consequence of assuming nonlinearity in the short-run Phillips curve.) After the target reduction in the inflation rate is achieved, the expected rate of inflation (and, therefore, unemployment) will remain high for a while, but will gradually come down: the expected rate of inflation will fall to the actual inflation rate and unemployment will fall to the full employment level. Although, during this terminal phase, unemployment will fall below its levels during the previous period of declining inflation, there is no way to depart from equal unemployment levels during that period in order to reduce the total amount endured still further.[26]

The optimum policy therefore is one of reducing inflation, in the time period selected, along a steady path that produces equal levels of unemployment and excess capacity during the period of reduction. This requires that the gap between the actual and expected inflation rates be kept constant over the selected period of reduction. In this policy the inflation rate would initially drop and then decline further as the expected rate declined. If, for example, the target reduction in inflation were four percentage points in four years, and the expected rate adjusted by the full amount of the gap in one year, the optimal policy would reduce the inflation rate by equal one-point steps per year. If the expected rate adjusted in one year by less than the gap, the optimal inflation rate would be reduced by more at the beginning and less over the period. In all cases unemployment would be kept at a constant level over the period until the target inflation rate was achieved, after which unemployment would gradually decline.

It is clear that the level of unemployment in 1974–1975 and as projected for the ensuing years departs appreciably from such an optimum path.[27] Instead of being kept constant, it rose sharply in 1974 and then has been falling, while inflation is still above what can be considered a desired rate. The critics of this path, as noted above, have called for a faster recovery to achieve a lower level of unemployment as soon as possible.

One reason for a more conservative policy would be to achieve the desired reduction in inflation sooner—say, within two or three years rather than five or six. The choice here depends on the relative costs to the economy and the public of inflation and unemployment. Despite all the discussion of these costs and the strong views held by those who decry unemployment and those who decry inflation, economic research has barely scratched the surface in measuring the costs of inflation and therefore has little to offer for a compara-

---

[26] Lucas Papademos analyzes the optimal path in a paper to be published.

[27] Edward Gramlich, "The Optimal Timing of Unemployment in a Recession," *Brookings Papers on Economic Activity*, 1975(1), pp. 167-80, suggests that unemployment was too low at the beginning—that is, that a more rapid reduction in inflation would produce less total unemployment for the targeted decline in inflation to 4 percent by 1980. Gramlich's study, however, is concerned with minimizing inflation for a given average level of unemployment, whereas the text discussion asks the significantly different question how to minimize total unemployment given that the inflation rate is to be reduced by a certain amount in a specified period of time.

tive evaluation of the widely cited cost of lost output from unemployment. Policy makers nevertheless have to make a judgment how much to try to reduce inflation within a given period of time. Since the economic costs of rampant inflation are very serious indeed, the desire for a speedy reduction is understandable, though the 1975–1976 level of unemployment has remained higher than probably anyone believes is needed.

But why does policy not pursue a constant level of unemployment, in whatever amount is found desirable, to be consistent with the optimal path described above? One answer is that the cyclical nature of economic changes makes it practically impossible to prevent some continuing recovery from a deep recession. The depth of the 1973–1975 recession clearly caught policy makers by surprise, and the cyclical recovery was bound to bring a continuing reduction of unemployment. To reduce unemployment to the desired level and then hold it there until inflation fell to the target rate would require a degree of control over the economy beyond our present competence. Given our lack of control over the direction of cyclical movements, a continuing recovery with a substantial average level of unemployment (as we are having) is consistent with an intention to achieve a substantial reduction of inflation over a selected period. It is a second-best policy to an optimal one of constant unemployment at the same average level.

But is constant unemployment optimal? That depends, as noted, upon nonlinearity in the short-run Phillips curve. Despite the widespread assumption of nonlinearity, the evidence for the United States is unclear and does not show whether the relationship is (1) close to being linear or (2) strongly nonlinear. If it is linear, there is in general no optimal path for reducing inflation. It can be done sooner or later within the period selected, and the total unemployment produced will be the same. This ambiguity of the evidence on linearity can lead policy makers to emphasize the advantages of reducing inflation sooner rather than later.

It is doubtful, of course, that optimal paths have been estimated by policy makers, since not enough is known of the possibilities to be precise. The discussion of optimal paths nevertheless helps to make explicit some relevant considerations in policy decisions that are seldom spelled out.

Miscalculation and the awareness of its possibility play a major role in policy decisions, especially in the present struggle to subdue inflation. It is one thing to have a theory of an optimal path; it is quite another to apply such a theory to the economy in a particular period. One worry already mentioned is that the cyclical recovery, if pushed too rapidly, might not be easily stopped and could mistakenly go so far that it would set off new inflationary pressures. Another worry is that we might set a target that takes us too far— that is, a policy of slowly subduing inflation assumes we know what level of unemployment is noninflationary and that we know where to stop a cyclical recovery. The evidence of inflation and unemployment since World War II (adjusted for changes in the composition of the labor force affecting overall unemployment rates) placed noninflationary "full employment" in 1975 at 5.6 percent.[28] So long as unemployment was kept above that level, inflation would presumably continue to decline until it practically disappeared. But one could worry, as the authorities did, whether the past evidence still applied. Had escalating inflation since 1965 made wages and prices more sensitive to impending inflationary pressures? Price and wage responses to economic conditions had clearly changed since World War II in a way that seemed to be related to the public's expectations about inflation.[29] If the public were to base its expectations of inflation on all available information, and not simply on an extrapolation of past inflation rates, policy excesses (such as rapid monetary growth or any rapid expansion of aggregate demand that carried the danger of overshooting) would affect anticipations of inflation.[30] Anticipations strengthen the momentum of an ongoing inflation by affecting the rate of increase carried along in wage and price contracts, in administered pricing, and in commodity futures prices. As a result, the inflation rate responds weakly to downward pressures and strongly to any upward pull. To counter these effects on price behavior, the authorities want a policy which is capable of restraining inflation in appearance as well as in fact.

In the final analysis, the justification for a conservative policy rests on its success in reducing inflation fairly rapidly and on its

---

[28] Modigliani and Papademos, "Monetary Policy for the Coming Quarters."

[29] See Benjamin B. Klein, "Our New Monetary Standard: The Measurement and Effects of Price Uncertainty, 1880-1973," *Economic Inquiry*, vol. 13, no. 4 (December 1975), pp. 461-84.

[30] This is the argument of a new literature on "rational expectations" that claims partial empirical support. See Robert E. Lucas, "Some International Evidence on Output-Inflation Tradeoffs," *American Economic Review*, vol. 63, no. 3 (June 1973), pp. 326-34, and Thomas Sargent, "A Classical Macroeconometric Model for the United States," *Journal of Political Economy*, vol. 84, no. 2 (April 1976), pp. 207-37.

One need not accept all the implications of fully "rational expectations" to recognize the importance of the point that economic behavior can be influenced by expectations about government policy.

ability to absorb future foreign disturbances on prices and still keep inflation under control. The critics contend that additional restraint would be unproductive and that virtually the same reduction in inflation could be achieved in the same time with less unemployment. Since no one can yet be sure of the answer, the evidence on this issue that present policy is producing will affect future policy debates and decisions—as well as the inflation rate—for some time to come.

Policy and Inflation in 1976

For a conservative policy to have general appeal, therefore, it must make substantial inroads against inflation. As of early 1976 the process of moderating inflation could be said to be on schedule but not clearly ahead of schedule. The inflationary blip of 1973–1974 subsided by the second half of 1975, but there remained an underlying and strongly entrenched 6 to 7 percent rate of inflation. None of the forecasts of future inflation at the beginning of 1976, including the administration's, saw a decline in this underlying rate by much more than one percentage point a year. This implied a period of three years of excess capacity to reduce the annual rate to 3 to 4 percent. No one could be confident that such a period could be traveled without renewed inflationary pressures.

The pessimism of these forecasts was derived from past experience. While past recessions initially reduced some prices, particularly those of crude materials, price increases continued coming through the pipeline of production costs. Most wage rates showed little effect from higher unemployment and continued rising with the cost of living. Consequently, a recession narrowed profit margins but had only a small effect on the rate at which the overall price level rose. Following the 1958 recession, when the inflation rate was much lower than it is today, inflation did not expire until mid-1960, two years later, and another business contraction in 1960–1961 prevented any immediate overexpansion of business activity. Moreover, the small effect of recessions on prices appears to be diminishing.[31] Although inflation had also moderated within two years following the 1970 recession, the short-run improvement was clouded by the imposition of price controls in August 1971.

Over the long run the inflation rate has eventually reflected changes in the rate of monetary growth. The monetary growth rate

---

[31] Cagan, *The Hydra-Headed Monster*, Chapter 1, and "Changes in the Recession Behavior of Wholesale Prices in the 1920s and Post-World War II," *Explorations in Economic Research*, vol. 2, no. 1 (1975), pp. 54-104.

has been coming down since 1972, and if that trend is not reversed, it is bound to be reflected in the inflation rate. The question, of course, is whether reversal of that monetary growth trend can be resisted during the transition to lower inflation, given the various pressures for monetary expansion generated by unemployment, an upswing in economic activity, and foreign influences. Despite the pitfalls awaiting anti-inflation policies, those responsible for policy (having benefitted from the lessons of past experience) are better prepared today than they were in the past to persevere with a policy in which the benefits appear slowly and to avoid the impatience which led to controls in 1971 and overexpansion in 1972.

Although the basic inflation rate no longer moderates perceptibly during the period of cyclical contraction in business activity (and the absence of immediate results generates widespread disappointment and confusion), a recession does break into the inflationary process and work to slow it down. The drop in capacity utilization stimulates cost cutting, and productivity improves. Although the improvement is not evident at the recession levels of production, it shows up when output recovers. Output per man-hour rises, and the increase in unit labor costs moderates, despite an undiminished advance of wages. Early in the recovery, depressed crude materials prices and profit margins recover, but if markets remain slack the slower rise in unit labor costs moderates the upward pressure on manufacturing prices. In time, the slower rise in the cost of living works to reduce wage increases, labor costs put less pressure on prices (which reduces the feedback on wages), and so on through the process of winding down inflation. There may be many exceptions to the pattern and timing of these developments in any particular episode, but this has been the typical sequence when it was not interrupted by new inflationary pressures.

The key to winding down inflation seems to be a reduction in the rate of increase in unit labor costs resulting from an improvement in productivity growth. It does not matter that this improvement initially bolsters profit margins, for profit margins do not rise indefinitely, and eventually the upward pressure on prices moderates, assuming the recovery in materials prices tapers off.

In the terms of this pattern, the 1975–1976 recovery presents a mixed but not discouraging picture. Although prices receded from the high inflation rates of 1973–1974, the private nonfarm deflator (the best overall measure of inflation) still rose at an annual rate of 6.7 percent in the second half of 1975. But the essential process of deceleration was at work beneath the surface and began to appear

Figure 5

UNIT LABOR COSTS AND PRICE DEFLATOR,
PRIVATE NONFARM SECTOR, QUARTERLY, 1970–1976

(1975 II = 100)

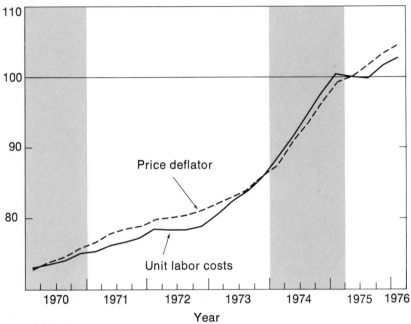

Note: Shaded areas are business recessions.
Source: Bureau of Economic Analysis.

in prices in early 1976. Output per man-hour for the private nonfarm sector began to grow again in the second quarter of 1975, after two years of decline. The growth faltered in the fourth quarter of 1975 but resumed in the first quarter of 1976. These statements are based on preliminary figures and are subject to subsequent revision. As the figures stand at present, they point to a deceleration of unit labor costs (see Figure 5), which eventually induces slower price increases.

The effect on prices showed up in the first quarter of 1976 when the annual rate of increase of the private nonfarm deflator fell to 4.6 percent from the 6 to 7 percent range of the second half of 1975 (Figure 2). Prices of wholesale finished goods were virtually constant in the first quarter of 1976 (Figure 1). The inflation rate will probably not remain so low over the next several quarters, since profit margins were still below normal and the pattern of wage contracts appeared to require a higher rate of inflation. Although average hourly earnings for the private nonfarm sector rose at an annual rate of only 6 percent in the first quarter of 1976 (compared with 8 percent for 1975 and 9.5 percent for 1974), earnings will probably rise faster than 6 percent for the remainder of the year in view of the heavy schedule of collective bargaining in 1976. But earnings show clear signs of deceleration, and, if productivity growth continues around 3 percent per year, considerable room for reduction of inflation exists. There is a basis for optimism, therefore, that the underlying inflation rate in 1976 will fall below the 6 percent rate projected at the beginning of the year. Success would confirm the efficacy of a conservative monetary policy and encourage its continuance. Failure would put the direction that future policies will take under a cloud of uncertainty.

The Problem of Price Blips

Blips in the rate of inflation such as the one produced by foreign influences in 1973–1974 present a perplexing problem. Should monetary policy ignore or accommodate them? The problem is similar for any exogenous source of inflation—a category which in some views includes union wage demands, administered pricing in concentrated industries, and purchases of scarce commodities in wartime. Only wage pressures have been a serious recurring problem, and then only in a period of excess demand and subsequently when wages catch up with past inflation. The events of 1973–1974 have introduced foreign influences as a potential source of sudden large price increases which policy has little chance of preventing and which can only be reversed through prolonged restraint on aggregate demand. Foreign trade previously played a small role in the U.S. economy, and such disturbances had not seemed important. World agricultural prices have risen sharply in past episodes (such as 1920–1921 and 1950–1951), but the repercussions on the aggregate price level were short-lived and reversible. Although it is not clear when the situation changed, the United States is not an isolated economic island today. Many countries have long experienced the vicissitudes of foreign trade effects, but now, with expanded international trade and with inflation rampant throughout the world, outside influences have become stronger than ever for all countries.

Our present floating exchange rates, instituted in 1971, in theory insulate the domestic economy from some foreign influences, but they do not solve this problem. The exchange rate will accommodate changes in the general price level between countries, but changes in prices of selected traded materials affect relative prices and cannot be offset by movements in exchange rates. If a rise in world prices of crude materials were to increase the value of imports and exports equally, the exchange rate would not change. If imports rose more, the exchange rate, if not held constant by the intervention of governments, would depreciate, reinforcing the effect of world price increases on domestic costs. Only if our exports increased more than our imports would the exchange rate appreciate and offset part of the rise in world prices.

Changes in world prices of crude materials and foods will therefore occasionally initiate cost increases in the economic pipeline and thereby begin to raise domestic prices. If aggregate demand is not raised to allow for a higher price level, the economy will adjust through a long period of slack demand in which other prices rise less rapidly than they otherwise would have until the price level as a whole falls in line with the unchanged path of aggregate demand. If the trend of prices is otherwise upward, the level need never actually decline, but its rate of increase would have to slow for a while after the initial spurt.

To avoid the effects of such an adjustment on output and employment, monetary policy could accommodate the growth path of aggregate demand to price blips. An accommodative policy raises aggregate demand to absorb the price blip, allowing a higher rate of price increase temporarily to support a higher level of prices, after which the special influence ends and the inflation rate is again determined by domestic conditions. In 1973 and 1974 this would have meant an extra 10.5 percent growth in the money stock, since the foreign influences raised prices by approximately that amount. The argument for such an accommodation is that policy is confronted with a *fait accompli*. The fundamental problem is that cost increases pass through the price system rapidly while the offsetting effect of deficient demand works slowly. Policy cannot stop the cost increases from passing through to prices and can subsequently reverse the effect on prices, therefore, only by a prolonged period of restraint.

While avoiding the loss of output from slack demand, a policy of accommodation subjects prices to higher and higher levels with every upward blip, unless downward blips occur with the same frequency and can be accommodated with equal ease. Most materials prices fluctuate up and down with considerable volatility but are partly offsetting and do not ordinarily affect the general level of prices. But 1973 showed that coordinated movements can occur on a scale that provides strong upward pressure on the general price level. Perhaps if prices and wages were more flexible these increases would not become embedded in the price structure and would be easily reversed. But we do not expect them to be reversed or to be offset by downward blips, in part because policy steps in to prevent deflationary episodes and in part because market participants do not expect deflation and behave in such a way as to reduce its likelihood. In this way the price system has become increasingly prone to inflation.

We cannot simply adopt the rule of accommodating every blip that comes along, however. Some price increases, though interpreted as an exogenous development, could result in part from prior monetary growth and, if accommodated, would lead to a self-reinforcing inflationary process. Since the origin of price increases is not always an easy matter to determine, such an outcome is a distinct possibility. There is also the matter of implementation. Which price increases are to be accommodated? Some would soon reverse themselves if not accommodated, since not all commodity prices are equally passed through to manufacturing prices. Policy cannot wait to see the effects on the price level, for to do so would entail the decline in output which an accommodative policy is intended to avert. The main problem of accommodating blips, however, is that such a policy would almost certainly result in a higher rate of inflation in the long run. It would mean that every rise in the relative price of certain commodities would require a rise in the entire price level. The rise in the price level would perhaps even induce a further rise in the initiating commodity price (as by an oil cartel) in order for that price to maintain its higher level relative to all other prices, subjecting the initial rise to a multiplier effect. The resulting higher trend of prices over the long run could not fail to affect expectations of the average inflation rate and so make basic commodity prices influenced by speculation quicker to rise when any disturbance occurred.

Yet a hard line according to which disturbances are not allowed to raise the long-run price trend will prove equally difficult to follow. The foreign price increases in 1973–1974 reduced real money balances and contributed to the severity of the recession. Because of the difficulty of reducing the underlying inflation rate, it does not seem likely that policy can be sufficiently restrictive to reverse the foreign influences, inasmuch as reversal would require that the price level end up no higher than it would have been had these influences never occurred. Monetary policy in 1975–1976 has been conservative in the sense of seeking a speedy reduction of the inflation rate, yet there is no intention and little likelihood of *reversing* the effects of the 1973–1974 foreign price increases on the domestic price level.

Indeed, these and future such increases will no doubt in fact be largely accommodated.

To avoid the long-run inflationary consequences of accommodation, a middle course would be to accommodate unusual price blips, but no more frequently than the occurrence of past wartime inflations, and force the economy to adjust to all others through changes in relative prices and not in the general level. This would require that outbursts of world inflation as in 1973 be rare occurrences. Given the U.S. contribution to world monetary developments, control of domestic demand pressures could help dampen the future development of world inflationary pressures. But if the pressures continue, it is doubtful that any country can cut itself off from their domestic influence. A middle course of not accommodating most inflationary disturbances will not, therefore, be easy to pursue. As a result, our new susceptibility to foreign disturbances adds to the uncertainty whether policy will be able to contain inflation and reverse the upward trend in inflation rates of recent decades.

FISCAL POLICY: REFLECTIONS ON THE PAST DECADE

Herbert Stein

Summary

The outstanding fact about the decade from 1964 to 1974, in economic terms, was the great inflation during it and the high rate of inflation that was running at its end. There are still many things about this period that we do not know. We do not know how much less the inflation would have been if aggregate demand had risen less rapidly, and how much the cost would have been in the form of lower output and employment. We do not know how much the rapid growth of aggregate demand was due to fiscal policy, how much to monetary policy, and how much possibly to other factors.

Still, it seems a reasonable deduction from our experience and from economic analysis that if aggregate demand had risen less rapidly we would now face a less painful choice between price stability and high employment. The rapid demand expansion generated inflationary expectations and momentum that subsequently made economic stability more difficult to achieve, even though there was some transitional benefit in higher employment. More restraint on aggregate demand would have been a wiser policy.

Although the relative roles of fiscal policy and monetary policy in affecting aggregate demand remain a subject of debate among economists, it is probably prudent in analysis as well as in policy to assume that both have significant influence. The question with which this essay deals, therefore, is why fiscal policy contributed to an excessively rapid rise of aggregate demand in the period from 1964 to 1974.

The history of the previous two decades provides part of the explanation. During the postwar period, up to 1961, there was a *common view that inflation was the dominant economic problem. The policy predicated on this view helped to hold down the rate of inflation. However, success on this side was accompanied by three recessions in the period from 1954 to 1960. National concern in public policy then shifted to the problem of unemployment. Unemployment was seen not only as a problem of avoiding recessions and promoting rapid recoveries, but also as one of holding the economy continuously close to "potential"—defined as the output that would be produced when unemployment was 4 percent. It was thought that there would be no serious problem of inflation as long as output was below its potential, and that such inflation as did arise could best be handled by incomes policy.*

The economic problems of the Vietnam War were approached in accord with this line of thinking. The President was reluctant to ask for a tax increase in 1966, because he feared that the congressional response would be harmful to his spending programs for the war and the "Great Society." But beyond that, during the period through 1968, the anti-inflationary policy was weak and hesitant because the size and durability of the problem of inflation was underestimated inasmuch as there was great fear of falling below the arbitrarily defined "potential," and an excessive confidence in the possibility of fine-tuning the economy.

By 1969 public and governmental attention to the problem of inflation had increased and it was recognized that slowing down the inflation would involve more pain and time than had been thought previously. Nevertheless, the administration continued to underestimate how long it would take, and how much unemployment would be involved. As this underestimate became apparent, the policy of "gradualism" in checking inflation became impossible to sustain, especially in the presence of the widespread belief that there was a painless way to do it, namely incomes policy or price and wage controls.

After price and wage controls were imposed, in August 1971, fiscal and monetary policy became excessively expansive, especially in the early part of 1972. The controls misled policy makers into thinking that there had been a more lasting reduction of inflationary forces and inflationary expectations than was actually the case. Moreover, the economy still appeared to be significantly below its potential, an appearance that later turned out not to be true.

After the beginning of 1973 fiscal and monetary policy became increasingly restrictive. The continued strength of inflationary forces was clear as was the impossibility of relying on controls as a durable solution to the problem. This fiscal and monetary restraint contributed to the sharp recession of 1974–1975, though it was not the only cause of that recession. It also contributed to some slowdown of the inflation rate. This episode is not yet over, and it remains to be seen whether an appropriate degree of restraint can be maintained to prevent the acceleration of inflationary pressures and permit high employment to be regained without raising the inflation rate once more.

Several conclusions may be drawn from this experience:

(1) It is essential to avoid random fiscal shocks to the economy— shocks such as the big increase in the deficit after 1965 resulting from unwillingness to face the financial requirements of the Vietnam War. The new congressional budgetary procedures reduce the prospect that major fiscal decisions will be made without adequate attention to their stabilization consequences, but they do not entirely solve the problem.

(2) Many of the errors of the past decade were due to the fact that economists do not know enough. We need, and can get, improvements in economic statistics. We also need significant advances in economic analysis, which will not be produced by more and better statistics alone, but which may be facilitated by more intensive application of economic reasoning to the problems revealed in the past decade.

(3) We should avoid commitment to any unemployment rate as a guide to fiscal and monetary policy. Political pressures will almost certainly force the unemployment goal down to a point that is unattainable, or unattainable without unsustainably escalating inflation. The unemployment goal of fiscal and monetary policy should be a steady moderate growth of aggregate demand so that the effort of workers to find jobs by moderating their wage demands is not frustrated by a parallel decline in the growth of nominal GNP.

(4) Demand policy should firmly resist an increase of the inflation rate above what now seems to be the underlying rate—about 6 percent. Our experience shows the difficulty of getting the underlying rate down once it has been allowed to increase. However, a commitment to get the inflation rate down to zero, or to any other very low number, in the near future seems unbelievable and (partly for that reason) too costly.

(5) There seems to be little possibility of specifying a rule of fiscal policy, on the model of the full-employment budget rule, that would be appropriate in the light of present uncertainties about the optimum path of the economy, and that would find enough support to serve as restraint against ad hoc pressures on the budget.

(6) We must disabuse ourselves of the notion that price-wage controls can relieve us of the difficult choices that fiscal and monetary policy otherwise must face. Belief in controls as a way of permitting us to have full employment and no inflation, simultaneously with budget deficits and easy money, has been a major impediment to realistic thinking about economic policy.

Introduction

This essay is an effort to throw light on some current issues of stabilization policy, and especially of fiscal policy, by reviewing the experience of the decade from 1964 to 1974. The decade is interesting, of course, because there was much inflation during it, and a high rate of inflation at the end of it—even if the inflation rate in 1974 is heavily discounted for the numerous transitory elements that played their part. And even with the end of that decade, we still confront the inflation problem—both the problem of reducing a rate that is high and the problem of avoiding acceleration to an even higher rate. Fiscal decisions are debated, and to some extent made, according to their possible effects on the inflation rate. What we would like to know is how and why fiscal policy contributed to the inflation of the past decade, and how and at what cost that contribution might have been avoided.

Even now, there is no well-established body of knowledge of what the relations were among such variables as the unemployment rate, the inflation rate, fiscal actions, monetary actions, and so on, so that we cannot be sure why anything happened, or what the results would have been if policy had been different. In that state of ignorance, to derive lessons from the decade is to make bricks without straw, but that is the usual condition in which policy is discussed and made.

I do not pretend to remedy that basic state of ignorance: I only offer a touristic account of the period by one who was there, and some speculations about it.

Inter-decade Comparisons

Provocative questions about the decade from 1964 to 1974 are raised by comparison with the decade from 1949 to 1959. There are striking similarities between the two. Each opened with a medium-sized war, accompanied by considerable inflation. The average unemployment rates of the two decades were about the same. But the earlier one was much less inflationary on the whole and at its end than tne later. What accounted for the difference, and what was the role of fiscal policy, or of demand management in general? There are three main interpretations of the difference between the inflation-unemployment experience of the two decades.

(1) One common explanation is that there has been an exogenous structural change, unrelated to the growth of demand, that has raised the inflation rate for any given rate of utilization of our productive capacity. This structural change might be connected with an increase in the power of businesses and labor organizations, or in their methods of operation, or in our systems of income maintenance for the unemployed, or in something else. In view of this change, the explanation runs, the authorities had to choose between a rapid expansion of demand, which would support a low unemployment rate with a high inflation rate, and a slower expansion of demand, which would have yielded more unemployment but less inflation, although possibly not much less. They chose the more inflationary course.

(2) A second explanation is that even though the unemployment rates in the two periods were about the same, the economy was operating closer to potential in the second decade than in the first. This is suggested, along the lines of Moore's argument in this volume, by the fact that employment rates were higher in the second decade than in the first.[1] It is also suggested by the lower rates of unemployment in some key sectors of the labor force, such as adult males, in the second decade. In other words, demand policy was pushing the economy to a higher level, in comparison to its potential, even though the aggregate unemployment rates were about the same, and this resulted in the greater inflation, at least in part.

(3) The third explanation is that demand policy itself created the unfavorable trade-off between inflation and unemployment with which we have been living and contending for most of this decade. The argument runs that rapid expansion of demand, while it may temporarily reduce unemployment, will increase the inflation rate. That leads to the expectation of more inflation, especially if the policy of rapid demand expansion is believed to be the permanent policy. This expectation leads to continuing inflation, even when demand is not rising rapidly. As a consequence, continuing rapid expansion of demand yields only more inflation, and not less unemployment, than

---

[1] Geoffrey H. Moore, "Employment, Unemployment and the Inflation-Recession Dilemma."

would have been experienced if the expectation of inflation had not been unleashed in the first place.

In this view, the rapid expansion of demand in 1965–1968 not only generated a rising rate of inflation during those years but also created the expectation of continuing inflation. This expectation made it difficult to slow down the inflation rate in 1970–1971 without a prolonged and deep recession. This "solution" was not accepted; instead only a shallow slowdown in the economy was brought about and even that was shortly terminated by strongly expansive measures. As a result, the inflationary expectations generated in 1965–1968 were not eradicated but intensified and solidified. This in turn at least helped to set the stage for the post-1974 situation in which a deeper and longer recession was needed (or would have been needed) to check the inflation.

These three explanations are not mutually exclusive. All of these factors could have been operating at once, and indeed, they would reinforce each other. In particular, if there were structural changes operating to make it more difficult to slow down inflation without unemployment, this would have strengthened the conviction that the government would not take the measures needed to check the inflation, and so would have strengthened inflationary expectations that would further worsen the trade-off.

The quantitative significance of the three explanations is difficult to appraise. The second explanation does relate to factors that can be seen and measured. That is, we can see changes in the age-sex composition of the labor force, in participation rates and in rates of productivity growth that would increase the likelihood of inflation resulting from an effort to keep unemployment at the rates of 1950–1960. But we do not know whether those changes are sufficient to explain our inflationary experience. For one thing, it is hard to distinguish the direct effects of these factors from the effects of the expectations set up by the effort to hold the unemployment rate down in spite of them.

The structural changes cannot be discerned as easily as changes in labor force composition. Probably the most common claim is that we suffer from the increasing power of big businesses and big labor unions. However, there is little evidence of that increasing power, unless one accepts the result itself—more rapidly rising wages and prices—as evidence. There was a time, in 1969 and 1970, when we thought we were going through a phase of increased aggressiveness and ambition on the part of unions seeking more nearly total exploitation of their economic power. Various explanations were offered for this—a new generation of labor leaders and members, the general anti-establishmentarianism of the times, the tide of rising expectations that was sweeping the country and the world and finding expression in both political and economic demands, and other such psychological or sociological factors. However, in retrospect all of that analysis seems unnecessary and the behavior of unions seems explicable in more conventional economic terms. That is, the large wage demands of unions can be fully explained by the fact that wages and prices have been rising rapidly and are expected to continue to do so.

There seems to be more substance to the argument that increased availability and size of benefits under unemployment compensation and income maintenance programs, including the food stamp program, together with the increased private financial resources of American workers, have increased the ability of unemployed workers to hold out for their desired and expected wages. But again, the degree to which this explains the pattern of 1964–1974 is uncertain.

The idea that inflation and inflationary policy would generate expectations of inflation that increase the difficulty of achieving high employment without inflation is plausible in general and seems realistic as a description of our experience. But even here there are mysteries. There was a time when some thought that the way to end inflation was to have it—that is, that a rise of prices would not only reduce the real money supply but would also create a belief that prices could not go on rising. Now we are convinced that the opposite expectations are generated. But even in our own recent experience that seems not always to have been the case. After the great surge of prices of 1950–1951 the rate of inflation fell very sharply, long before the 1954 recession, and probably not significantly as a result of the Korean War price-wage controls. After the smaller but longer inflation of 1955–1957, in circumstances that might have been thought more typical of our experience than the Korean War inflation, the inflation rate came down rather promptly. In those cases a rise of the inflation rate did not become solidified in expectations.

Why then did the rise of the inflation rate from 1965 to 1968 apparently have so durable an effect on expectations? The rise was not especially great—from about 1.5 percent to about 5 percent. The period of the inflationary expansion was not especially long. The inflation was triggered by (or at least associated with) an event that would almost certainly come to an end—the heavy U.S. involvement in Vietnam. To derive the history of the next decade from the original sin of failing to raise taxes in 1966, as is sometimes done, puts a heavy burden on the expectation theory.

One difference between the 1950s and the period after 1965 is that in the earlier period price increases were believed to be once-for-all, and expectations were generally geared to a continuation of present price levels, while in the later, price increases were believed to produce new price increases, and expectations were generally geared to a continuation of present rates of increase. In the earlier period it was noted that when prices went up they never came down, and in the later that when prices went up they continued to go up. The expectation that the future would be like the past came to be an expectation about the continued rate of inflation rather than about the continued level of prices.

It may be that the difference in expectations between the two periods was not entirely attributable to the difference in the actual behavior of the inflation rate but was also attributable (to a significant degree) to differences in public perception of what policy was or would be. Perhaps there was something in the way that President Eisenhower spoke and acted, aside from the things he did to control inflation and aside from the actual inflation rate of his time, which led the public to believe that inflation would be controlled—whereas they would not believe the same thing given the same objective facts from Presidents Johnson and Nixon. But while this may be an important observation, it is extremely difficult to verify.

These different explanations for the high inflation rate of the decade from 1964 to 1974, when the unemployment rate was about the same as in the earlier periods of lower inflation, have somewhat different implications for evaluating the appropriateness of the decade's demand management policy. If there were some force at work inevitably giving us a high inflation rate, to slow down the growth of aggregate demand would have been futile, since that would have only reduced output and employment without reducing inflation. Even in the less extreme condition where independent forces had only made the restraint of inflation much more costly, without making it impossible, wise policy might have been to accept the inflation rather than pay the cost.

The expectation theory seems to imply that policy was too expansive, since a more restrained policy would have kept the expectation of inflation low and would have permitted the achievement of high employment without inflation. This implication about policy is not necessarily correct. The expectation theory suggests that the cost of checking inflation does not go on forever; it does not deny that there may be some transitional cost in employment foregone or unemployment suffered during a period in which the expectation of price stability is defended, or restored if it has been lost. When the matter is viewed in retrospect, it always seems that the cost would have been worthwhile. Thus, in 1970–1971 it seemed clear that policy should have been less expansive in 1965–1968 to spare us the necessity of going through 6 percent unemployment in order to get the inflation rate down. And in 1975–1976 it seems clear the policy should have been less expansive in 1971–1972, tolerating more unemployment for a longer period, in order to spare us the necessity today of running an unemployment rate of 7 to 8 percent in the process of slowing down inflation. But this apparent clarity with which we see the wisdom of more restraint in the past may only be a case of retrospective myopia, which makes all past costs look smaller than any present ones. Hardly anyone thinks we should have had a deeper recession in 1975 or a slower recovery in 1976 in order to make price stability more easily attainable in 1980. But that may seem clear in 1980.

Nevertheless, I believe that the rate of demand expansion was too great from 1964 to 1974. In 1975 and 1976 the American people are paying a price, and are willing to pay a price, to slow down the rate of inflation. The price would, in my opinion, have been smaller if it had been paid earlier. The terms of choice deteriorate as inflation proceeds, and especially as it accelerates. The inertial factors that prolong inflation grow stronger the longer they continue unchecked. Surely it would cost more to get the inflation rate down to zero today than it would have in 1964. And probably the cost of merely stabilizing the rate of inflation, as distinguished from getting it down to zero, is greater today than it would have been in 1964, because we have experienced not only high but also accelerating inflation.

This is, however, a difficult decision, because it is difficult to balance objectively the problems one is living through today against the problems of a time which, although only a few years back, is fading from our memories.

It is nevertheless possible to say in a more objective sense that the demand management policy of the decade was too expansive. If the authorities of the Johnson and Nixon administrations followed policies that led us to the coexistence of 7.5 percent unemployment and 6 percent inflation in 1976, it was not because they foresaw and chose that outcome. The outcome was the result, at least in part, of accidents and errors even given the intentions and preferences of the earlier times. Specifically, there were three kinds of accidents and errors:

(1) Demand management policy often turned out to be different from what any authority responsible for economic stabilization wanted.

(2) Even when the preferred policy was implemented, the desired and expected behavior of aggregate demand did not always follow.

(3) Even when the desired and expected behavior of aggregate demand was achieved, the expected behavior of prices and output often did not follow.

These will be illustrated in the more detailed account of the decade presented below mainly in terms of fiscal policy. I do not, however, intend to write a fiscal history of the decade in the sense of writing a history in which the primary moving force is fiscal policy. The relative roles of fiscal policy and monetary policy (and of other things) in determining the behavior of aggregate demand is one of the important unresolved issues of economics, and it certainly will not be resolved here. It seems to me useful to assume for the purposes of this essay—as I think it is prudent to assume for the purpose of making policy—that fiscal policy does influence the rate of change of aggregate demand. Even if this is some day proved not to be the case, and if it is proved that only money matters, this essay may not on that account turn out to be irrelevant. The making of monetary policy in the period under review was influenced by much the same perceptions and objectives as the making of fiscal policy. By looking at the history of fiscal policy, where the record is more open than it is in the case of monetary policy, we may learn something as well about the determinants of monetary policy.

The tendency (common in political discussion) to blame all, or almost all, of the inflation in the past decade on fiscal misbehavior is an oversimplification. Thus, President Ford said in his 1976 State of the Union Address that the American people have learned that the way to hold down the cost of living is to hold down the cost of government.[2] If they have learned that, they have learned something economists do not know.

Federal spending (in the national income accounts) increased by over 150 percent from 1964 to 1974. This is an enormous figure, over twice as much as in the less inflationary decade from 1949 to 1959. But the fact that the later decade was more inflationary goes far to explain the greater rise of nominal expenditures. Everything rose much more in nominal terms in 1964–1974 than in 1949–1959, and it is hard to tell what is pushing and what is being pushed by the

---

2 "State of the Union Address," *Weekly Compilation of Presidential Documents*, vol. 12, no. 4 (January 26, 1976), p. 45.

inflation. Real spending by the federal government rose by a smaller percentage in the later decade than in the earlier. Spending rose relative to GNP in both periods, but not by much in either and by about the same amount in each. Federal expenditures rose from 16.0 percent of GNP in 1949 to 18.7 percent in 1959 and from 18.6 percent in 1964 to 21.3 percent in 1974.

The behavior of the deficit is more relevant to the increase of nominal GNP than the behavior of the spending side of the budget alone. In the earlier decade (calendar years 1950–1959 inclusive) the budget was almost exactly in balance. In the later decade the total deficit was $82 billion. That was about seven-tenths of 1 percent of the actual GNP in the decade, or 1 percent of what the actual GNP would have been at 1964 prices (to take out of the calculation the rise of inflation of nominal GNP that the deficit might have caused). These are fairly large figures when compared with the difference in the annual rates of growth of nominal GNP in the two decades, which is the difference between 5.7 percent in the earlier decade and 8.3 percent in the later one.

However, aside from the effect of the accumulating federal debt, there is no reason why a high average deficit, if stable, should cause nominal GNP to rise at a rapid rate. An economy can settle down to a constant nominal GNP, or a slowly rising nominal GNP, with a large stable budget deficit and a large stable excess of private saving over private investment. It is easier to see that a rapidly rising deficit would cause a rapid increase in nominal GNP. But in fact, for the period as a whole the deficit was not rapidly rising. Relative to the size of the GNP, or to changes in it, the change in the deficit between the beginning and the end of the decade, or between the first half of the decade and the second, was small. There were surges of increase in the deficit, as from 1965 to 1967 and from 1969 to 1971, but they were followed by declines in the deficit. These surges may have caused increases in prices, or in the inflation rate, which were irreversible, but there is no reason why the sequence of rising and falling deficits should have produced a rapid increase of nominal GNP if there were no substantial trend toward larger deficits.

The growth of the debt may be a more convincing representation of the effect of fiscal policy on the rapid rise of nominal GNP during the decade than are budget deficits. The federal debt held by the public increased by about 37 percent from the end of 1964 to the end of 1974. The debt actually fell as a proportion of the GNP, from 41.5 percent to 25.6 percent. Much of the GNP rise was due to inflation, but the debt in nominal terms rose a little less even than

CONTEMPORARY ECONOMIC PROBLEMS 1976

the GNP in real terms. In the earlier decade the debt rose little and also fell in relation to the nominal GNP. In fact the decline in the ratio of debt to nominal GNP was almost exactly the same in the two decades. But since the rate of inflation was much greater in the second decade, the decline of debt relative to real GNP was much larger in the first. If there is some tendency for the ratio of federal debt to the national income to decline, and to decline at a roughly constant rate, the rise of the debt could explain the inflationary growth of nominal GNP later in the period. However, the existence of such a tendency has not been established and seems to have little a priori rationale.

The connection between fiscal policy and inflationary expansion of demand is sometimes found, or at least sought, through monetary policy. The federal deficit is believed to necessitate monetary expansion, which creates or intensifies the effect of the deficit. But it has not been shown either that there is a logical necessity for such a linkage or that it has commonly existed in fact during the past decade. The linkage is usually said to exist because the Federal Reserve follows a policy of stabilizing interest rates, so that when budget deficits produce a tendency for interest rates to rise the Federal Reserve will increase the rate of monetary expansion in order to prevent that. Merely to use interest rates as a guide to monetary policy, or even as the target of policy, does not necessarily produce this linkage between deficits and monetary expansion if the interest rate target is variable. If the interest rate target is high in circumstances in which budget deficits would tend to cause high interest rates, then the deficit will not call forth monetary expansion. What is necessary for the linkage between deficits and monetary expansion is that the interest rate target should be stabilization of interest rates at a level which (given the deficits) cannot be maintained without excessive monetary expansion.

There is no good reason for the Federal Reserve to tailor its operations to the needs of fiscal policy in this way. The long debate over the policy of supporting the prices of government bonds in the years before 1951, which ended with the abandonment of that policy, concluded that there was no national benefit from holding interest rates down in this way that was worth the inflationary consequences.[3] If budget deficits that would otherwise be noninflationary are made inflationary by the monetary response, the correction should be sought in monetary policy.

---

[3] Herbert Stein, *The Fiscal Revolution in America* (Chicago: University of Chicago Press, 1969), chapter 10.

However, there is little evidence that the Federal Reserve acted consistently to do this during the past decade. The connection between the rate of monetary expansion and the size of the federal deficit was loose and variable. There was rapid monetary expansion in 1971 and 1972 when there were also large deficits, but interest rates were not rising and the depressed state of the economy made a case for both deficits and rapid monetary expansion to promote recovery. There was rapid monetary expansion in 1973, despite a rather small deficit. There was slow monetary expansion in 1966, when the deficit was small, and in 1975 (at least in M_1 terms) when the deficit was large.

On the whole, there was too much monetary expansion from 1964 to 1974, but it would be wrong to blame this mainly on fiscal policy. Insofar as there was both too much monetary expansion and too big budget deficits it was not primarily because the deficits were causing the monetary expansion but because both fiscal and monetary policy were making the same errors.

It is not my intention in these remarks to absolve fiscal policy of a share of the responsibility for the inflation. It is my intention to suggest some uncertainty about the size of the share and about the nature of the connection. The most probable assumption is that economic policy was too expansive from 1965 to 1968, too weak in slowing down the expansion from 1969 to 1971, and too expansive again in 1972. Fiscal policy shared in these errors. What follows is an attempt to explain why that happened.

The Pre-1964 Experience

A brief reprise of earlier experience is helpful to an understanding of the past decade.[4] Having gone through World War II with the expectation that our postwar problem would be a tendency to depression, we discovered in the first years after the war that the situation was actually quite different. From about 1948 to 1960 inflation was generally considered to be the dominant problem. Concern with inflation was a major issue in the 1948 election campaign and helped to explain the moderate governmental response to the 1949 recession. When the Korean War broke out in the summer of 1950, both the public and the private reaction was to expect a repetition of World War II inflationary conditions. Consumers rushed to buy and businesses rushed

---

[4] This experience is documented in Stein, *The Fiscal Revolution*, pp. 197-453.

to raise prices. The government raised taxes and imposed an excess profits tax. Soon thereafter, early in 1951, price and wage controls were imposed.

This turned out to be over-reaction. Prices rose sharply in the year from mid-1950 to mid-1951, but thereafter the rate of inflation settled back to about 1.5 percent per annum. This seems not to have been the result of the price-wage controls, as there were few if any shortages and many prices were below their ceilings. The initial price increases had outrun the underlying demand conditions.

Despite what now looks like the good inflation record after mid-1951, President Eisenhower assumed office in January 1953 thinking that inflation was his main economic problem, and he continued to think that throughout his eight-year administration. When he came into office, prices were still high—that is, they had not come down from the Korean War surge, but had continued to rise, even though slowly. It was not perfectly clear that the controls, intended to be temporary, were not restraining some price increases. Moreover, there was a budget deficit, considered to be inflationary. The view that inflation was the main problem was not, of course, confined to the President but was widespread.

Partly because of this concern about inflation, the government was reserved in taking steps against the 1954 recession. There was a tax cut, but the tax cut was in the cards anyway, regardless of the recession, and the administration resisted suggestions to do much more than that.

Despite the moderate character of fiscal policy, the 1954 recession was followed by a strong boom in 1955 and 1956. During those two years prices rose by about 6 percent, for the two years combined. This confirmed many people in their worries about inflation, especially as it was our first peacetime experience with inflation in many decades. In a policy statement dated May 1958, *Defense Against Inflation*, the Research and Policy Committee of the Committee for Economic Development said: "While we have behind us a long experience of inflation, only in the last few years has the possibility of inflation as a permanent way of life in America been generally recognized as real." [5] Work on this statement had been largely completed in 1957. The fact that the committee decided to issue it in May 1958, despite the economy's then being at the bottom of the worst postwar recession to date, was indicative. It was not widely thought that the

---

[5] Research and Policy Committee of the Committee for Economic Development, *Defense Against Inflation: Policies for Price Stability in a Growing Economy* (New York: Committee for Economic Development, May 1958), p. 12.

recession had removed the underlying inflation problem. The committee was struck by the fact that despite the recession the price level did not retreat, even though the rate of rise slowed.

It was mainly on the ground of the continuing inflationary danger that President Eisenhower and the Democratic leadership withstood the call for a tax cut to revive the economy during the 1958 recession, a call that came from a wide variety of sources. And this same concern with inflation turned the government quickly in the direction of restrictive fiscal and monetary policy soon after the recovery began. The administration brought the budget into balance in 1960, despite the unemployment rate of 5.5 percent in that year. There was a large full-employment surplus on the conventional definition of full employment as 4 percent unemployment. Partly for this reason the economy fell into another recession.

The 1960 recession was a turning point in popular and official attitudes toward the economic problem. It was the third recession in six years. The unemployment rate in each recovery was higher than in the preceding one—less than 3 percent before the 1954 recession, around 4 percent in 1956, around 5 percent in 1959. This seemed an ominous trend. Meanwhile, the inflation rate had been rather steady around 1.5 percent from 1952 to 1960, except for 1955–1957, which was far enough behind to be minimized. As a result, unemployment rose above inflation in the common view of what was the basic economic problem. The concentration of economic policy on the struggle against inflation was thought to have overstayed its appropriate time. Balancing the budget in 1960, which meant a large full-employment surplus, came to be regarded by later students as the worst error of fiscal policy in the postwar period.

These views were not confined to President Eisenhower's Democratic opponents. They influenced Richard Nixon, who regarded the overly restrictive fiscal and monetary policy of 1960 as one of the main causes of his defeat in the presidential election of that year. However, the new view of the economic problem was most thoroughly and precisely articulated by the economists of the Kennedy administration. Three aspects of their formulation of the problem were of special importance when the economy ran into the Vietnam War five years later.

(1) The goal of policy is not simply or mainly stabilization—the avoidance of recessions and quick recovery from them if they occur. The goal is to keep continuously up to the potential of the economy. This was the reaction to the mistake of 1959–1960, when recovery was accepted even though it fell short of the economy's potential.

(2) The potential output of the economy is the output it would produce if 96 percent of the labor force were employed and 4 percent unemployed. This potential rises along a fairly smooth trend, as the population and productivity grow.

(3) There will be no serious inflation so long as the economy is operating below its potential as thus defined, and such inflation as occurs in that condition of the economy should not be met by restraint of demand. Instead, it should be met by "incomes policy," meaning direct government restraint on private wage and price decisions, rather than indirect restraint through influence on the market conditions in which these decisions are made.

The recovery from the economy's low in 1961 proceeded irregularly. It was fast at first, then seemed to lag in 1962, and then gathered momentum again. By mid-1965 the unemployment rate was down to 4.5 percent. During this rise of output and employment the inflation rate had remained fairly stable around 1.5 percent, although by early 1965 there were some signs of a rise of industrial wholesale prices. The stability of the inflation rate at a low level was attributed by the administration in part to its guidelines for prices and wages. The vigor of the rise of the economy toward potential in 1964 and early 1965 was considered to result from the tax cut that had been proposed by President Kennedy at the end of 1962 and that was finally enacted under President Johnson in early 1964. Confidence was high that the economy could be kept near potential without inflation by an active and flexible fiscal policy combined with a voluntary incomes policy.

The Vietnam War Inflation

In mid-1965 the major increase of spending for the Vietnam War intruded upon this scene of economic success and confidence. Within three-and-a-half years the rate of inflation, which had stayed for some time around 1.5 percent, had risen to 5 percent. This happened as the unemployment rate fell to 3.3 percent at the end of 1968, significantly below the target 4 percent. In the inflation from mid-1965 through 1968 there is less reason than in any of the later episodes to say that the inflationary expansion was needed to get the unemployment rate down to an acceptable level. But why, it may be asked, did the flexible policy that had been so successful earlier work so poorly in this period?

An important part of the answer is the subordination of stabilization considerations to other considerations in the early part of the period. The economic advisers to President Johnson have reported that they urged the President to ask Congress to raise taxes at the beginning of 1966, to slow down the expansion they saw resulting from the Vietnam War expenditures. He rejected this advice, and apparently not because he rejected the economic argument underlying it. He did not want to raise the issue of a tax increase with Congress for fear that Congress would respond by cutting expenditures for the war or for the Great Society programs. He preferred to take the risks of inflation rather than the risks of cuts in these programs.

This is a leading example of a situation that has often occurred. The President and the Congress may be able to agree on some overall aspect of the budget, such as the size of the deficit or of total expenditures, but they frequently cannot agree on the specific way in which the overall budget is to be allocated. The President is opposed to giving up Program A; the Congress is opposed to giving up Program B. Each would rather sacrifice the overall goal of limiting the budget—which may mean accepting an inflationary policy—rather than sacrifice the particular program it prefers. Of course this may not be a bad result: economic stabilization is not everything. There may be expenditure programs so important that they are worth having even if the cost is inflation. This would seem more credible in the case under consideration if the Vietnam War had been more successful. However, that is irrelevant to the general principle.

The problem is that the choice between sacrificing programs and sacrificing price stability may not be an unbiased one. Public perception of the responsibility of identifiable public officials for inflationary fiscal policy may be less clear than public perception of the responsibility for particular government programs. For that reason the official would have a greater preference for the inflationary course than the public does, because he will not be blamed for it.

However, President Johnson's inability or reluctance to deal with the Congress on the tax issue in 1966 is not the whole story of the Vietnam War inflation. By the fall of 1966 he was willing to suspend the investment tax credit as an anti-inflationary measure. By the beginning of 1967 he was prepared to ask for a tax increase. But the suspended investment tax credit was soon restored. When the President asked for a tax increase in 1967 he did not ask for its immediate enactment. When Congress got down to considering the tax increase it took months to reach a conclusion. And when the increase was finally enacted, the administration and the Federal Reserve decided that its restrictive effect needed to be diluted by more rapid monetary expansion.

The policy of this period cannot be explained by presidential-congressional "politics" without reference to the economic goals and perceptions of the time. Indeed, it is possible that if the President had seen the inflationary danger in a sufficiently vivid way, he might have been willing to risk asking Congress for a tax increase at the beginning of 1966. There were, in my opinion, a number of economic factors that tended to make the moves toward anti-inflationary fiscal policy hesitant and weak:

(1) As the economy drew near to the promised land of potential output and full employment that the administration officials had been seeking for five years, they were reluctant to suppress the demand expansion that was getting them there. At the beginning of 1966, as we were crossing over the threshold into excess demand, the Council of Economic Advisers wrote: "Under the influence of favorable fiscal and monetary policies, the economy has achieved the best balance of over-all demand and productive capacity in nearly a decade." [6] (The reference to nearly a decade was presumably a reference to the inflationary boom of 1955–1957.)

A year later, at the beginning of 1967, after about three months of interruption in the boom, the Council was again worried about falling short of potential. It said: "As 1967 opens, inflationary forces set in motion during the period of overly rapid expansion are still alive, although their strength is waning. But now there is also a renewed challenge to sustain expansion; any further slowdown would be undesirable." [7] Again what might now seem an explosive situation in 1966 is described as an achievement: "A major economic accomplishment of 1966 is that the United States made essentially full use of its productive potential." [8]

(2) The dimensions of the inflation in prospect were repeatedly underestimated. The council forecast a rise of 1.8 percent in the GNP deflator for 1966; it turned out to be 3 percent. The 1967 increase was also 3 percent against a forecast of 2.5 percent, and the 1968 increase was 4.0 percent as against a forecast of 3.0 percent. [9] The main reason for these underestimates had to do with the notion that inflation would not speed up so long as there was a gap—that is, so long as output was below its potential. Of course, (1) there

[6] *Annual Report of the Council of Economic Advisers 1966* (Washington, D.C.: U.S. Government Printing Office, 1966), p. 39.
[7] Ibid., *1967*, p. 38.
[8] Ibid., *1967*, p. 42.
[9] Ibid., *1966*, p. 54; *1967*, p. 63; *1968*, p. 55.

was no basis for thinking that potential output necessarily implies 4 percent unemployment, (2) the estimation of potential even given the unemployment rate was difficult and the estimates were probably too high at that time, and (3) in any case the idea of the potential did not necessarily imply that prices would be stable when there was an excess of potential over actual output. (A second and probably less important reason was confidence in the ability of the government's incomes policy to restrain price and wage increases. This confidence, of course, was related to the belief that the inflation in sight was largely caused by something other than excess demand.)

(3) In retrospect, the most striking aspect of the economic policy thinking of that period is the degree of faith in what was then called "fine tuning." Both policy and the economy were assumed to be capable of turning around in a few months. It was thought that the inflation problem could be dealt with by short spells of restrictive medicine, after which the economy would proceed in stability. Thus, the council thought that by March 1966 the combination of fiscal and monetary policy was already providing adequate restraint to the upsurge that had begun in mid-1965. It said: "The question of whether a different timing or different magnitude of fiscal actions might have produced a more favorable balance in 1966 will long interest and challenge analysts of economic policy. But the main lesson is clear from the record: economic policy was used effectively to restrain the economy during 1966, much as it had been used during the preceding 5 years to stimulate demand." [10] At the beginning of 1967 it was thought that stimulative policy would be needed for the first half of the year, after which restraint would be needed. Thus a tax increase was proposed to take effect in the second half of the year. Again, in its report for 1969 the council thought that a brief slowdown in the early part of the year would check the inflation, after which expansion should be resumed. [11]

These attitudes all represented the continuation into 1965–1968 of the thinking that had dominated 1960–1965. Inflation, or at least excess-demand inflation, was not thought to be a real and durable problem or even possibility. Therefore, demand management policy turned to fight it only fitfully. The Johnson administration continued to fight the battle of the gap too long, just as, in my view, the Eisenhower administration continued to fight the battle of inflation too long.

[10] Ibid., *1967*, p. 50.
[11] Ibid., *1969*, pp. 55ff.

Gradualism—1969–1971

By the time of Mr. Nixon's inauguration in 1969 the balance of national attention and concern had shifted. When he said that inflation was the nation's number one economic problem, no one disagreed. Also, there was more recognition than formerly that the process of stopping the inflation would be difficult. As the new Council of Economic Advisers said in its first public statement, "We have run out of easy ways to do things." [12]

The administration, and much thinking outside it, placed a great deal of emphasis on the momentum of inflation built up from 1965–1968. It was believed this momentum would prolong the inflation through wage contracts adopted during the inflationary period, through the drive of other workers to catch up with the bigger contracts, and through the general expectations of higher prices and wages. This momentum would have to be checked by a period of restraint on the growth of demand. During this period of restraint prices and wages would at first continue to rise rapidly, and output and employment would fall. But after a while the price and wage increases would slow down, the expectations of inflation would subside, and it would be possible to regain high employment with less inflation. Whether there was some problem beyond that, some remaining rate of inflation after the consequences of excess demand had been eliminated, was uncertain. In any case that problem would be encountered later, if at all.

The question was how severe and long the restraint should be or would have to be. There were some, not in the administration, who advocated a sharp crackdown, squeezing the inflation rate down to zero, without regard to output and employment consequences, showing that the government meant business, and setting the stage for subsequent stability. But the administration could not adopt this recommendation, which seemed peculiarly inappropriate for the second Republican President since Herbert Hoover. No one could be sure that once so sharp a decline had been precipitated it could be stopped and reversed when it had served its purpose. There was a strong possibility that once such a course was under way there would be a popular revulsion requiring a forced recovery to an inflationary condition worse than the initial one.

The administration economists did not believe that so risky a course was needed. They believed that much more moderate restraint,

---

[12] Testimony of Council of Economic Advisers to Joint Economic Committee, February 1969.

continued for a long enough period, would gradually check the inflation. This theory, known as "gradualism," was the one on which the administration operated. It called for a slowdown in the rate of rise of aggregate demand, nominal GNP, to be achieved by reduction of budget deficits and of monetary expansion. That part of the program was carried out. But the inflation rate did not subside as fast as was expected, or as fast as was considered satisfactory, before the program was radically changed in August 1971 with the freeze of prices and wages. There were two main interrelated reasons for the failure of gradualism:

(1) The administration constantly overestimated the speed with which inflation would subside. Its view of the determinants of the inflation rate was similar in character to the view of its predecessors, although different in degree. The inflation rate would decline when the unemployment rate was above 4 percent. But the speed at which the inflation rate declined would be limited by the lagged effects of past inflation rates. Taking account of these lags was thought to correct the errors that had previously been made in estimating inflation. The Council of Economic Advisers repeatedly called attention to the presence of these lags. Nevertheless, the inflation did not decline as fast as was forecast in 1970 and 1971. The estimates assumed the inflation rate was more sensitive to the unemployment rate in the neighborhood of 4 percent than it turned out to be. Also, the lags were apparently much longer than the estimating system contemplated.

Since nominal GNP rose at about the expected and intended rate, when inflation continued at a rate higher than forecast, output and employment fell more than forecast. At the beginning of 1970 the CEA was forecasting that the rate of inflation at the end of the year would be about 3.5 percent.[13] Actually it was about 5.5 percent. The unemployment rate was about 6 percent, compared to the 4.5 percent forecast. That the economy was not running along the forecast path became clear by the middle of 1970. One option then considered within the administration was to adopt a more expansive policy, to get the unemployment rate down closer to the predicted path. The policy of gradualism required a sustained period of slack in the economy; the willingness of the public to accept such a policy for a long period might be greater if the unemployment were not so high. The more expansive policy was considered by its advocates not to endanger the struggle against inflation because it would still leave the economy operating below its potential for a long time. In fact, it was argued that a more rapid expansion would help to slow the

---

13 Unpublished Council of Economic Advisers memorandum, January 1970.

inflation by raising productivity. However, in the more conventional view, this option did involve a risk on the inflation side. The other option was to stick it out with the demand-restraint and the 6 percent unemployment rate until the desired slowdown of the inflation was achieved.

(2) Neither of these options was attractive. However, if there had been no other, one of them would have been adopted and might have worked. But in fact there was another that seemed to avoid the difficulties of the first two. That was "incomes policy," or price and wage controls. This quickly became the preferred option outside the administration. In fact, outside the administration it was almost the only option by the spring of 1971. Soon thereafter it became the administration's option also. As a result, we will never know whether the policy of gradualism would have worked. It was adopted by the administration and accepted by the public on the basis of an over-optimistic estimate of the results it could achieve. When this became clear the credibility of the policy was compromised and the policy could not be reestablished on a more realistic basis because there was a widespread belief that price and wage controls were a less painful option.

Expansion with Controls

In arguing against controls before August 15, 1971, the administration commonly referred to the experience of other countries in which the existence of price and wage controls diverted attention from the need for fiscal and monetary retraint, and indeed created a temptation to overly expansionist policies. For this reason, it was argued, the controls would prevent a durable solution to the inflation problem. Thus when the controls were adopted the administration believed this at least was one mistake it would not make, since it was aware of the unfortunate experience of others. However, the administration did indeed fall into that trap.

The New Economic Policy of August 15, 1971, which introduced the controls, also called for a moderate dose of fiscal expansionism in the form of tax reduction. In the circumstances, with 6 percent unemployment, the administration believed such a move was safe— that is, not inflationary—aside from the expectations and fears it might set up. With the controls being established, the creation of inflationary expectations did not seem a serious danger. As a further concession to fears of inflation and to conventional thinking about the budget, the expansionary fiscal move was put in a package that contained equal amounts of tax reduction and expenditure reduction. The main effect of this was to generate attacks from economists who claimed that such a balanced package could not be expansionary. This argument went on at a level of simple-mindedness that none of the participants would have accepted from a freshman student, and it need not be reviewed here.

The New Economic Policy was successful in holding down price increases in the last months of 1971. However, the unemployment rate was still 6 percent in December. It was against that background that fiscal decisions were made for the remainder of fiscal year 1972 and for fiscal year 1973.

The decision made was to escalate spending sharply in the first six months of calendar 1972 and to slow it down thereafter. This would yield a deficit in the full-employment budget for fiscal 1972, but full-employment balance would be regained in fiscal 1973. The rationale was similar to that of the smaller move made on August 15, 1971. There did not seem to be excess demand in the economy; the absence of shortages despite the strict price controls was evidence of that. The inflation that had been going on during the recession had resulted from expectations and momentum generated earlier and the controls were checking them and helping to eradicate them. Even with the proposed fiscal stimulus, the unemployment rate was expected to remain at 5 percent at the end of 1972—an expectation that turned out to be correct. The fiscal stimulus seemed safe if it were not continued too long, this being the reason for concentrating it in the first half of the year. In the event, the plan was partially frustrated by congressional enactment of a large increase in social security benefits to take effect in the fourth quarter of calendar 1972. As a result, the swing back to a full employment surplus only appeared in 1973, at which time, however, it was quite strong.

A similar line of thinking motivated monetary policy. Fairly rapid monetary expansion seemed appropriate in the early part of the year, with more restraint later. However, the move to restraint turned out to be small, and this may have been a case when interest rate considerations were a serious impediment to correct policy, though interest rates did remain well below their 1969 and 1970 levels. In any case, 1972 turned out to be a year of large monetary expansion.

Whether the fiscal policy of 1972 was too expansive is even now not entirely clear. The common criticism at the time was that the administration was stepping on the brakes too soon. By the end of the year the inflation rate was down to about 2.5 percent and there were no significant shortages. But in retrospect it is probably true that the policy was too expansive and set the stage for the shortages and excess demand pressures that emerged in 1973.

The controls contributed to this error. They misled the government about the extent to which the earlier inflationary expectations and inflationary spiral had been permanently eliminated and therefore about the inflationary danger that would remain when high employment was regained without controls. A second source of error was the one that had misled policy for the previous seven years—wrong calculation of what full employment and capacity utilization were and of the distance the expansion of demand could go before it became excessive. There seemed to be more room than there later turned out to be.

Back to the Old Time Religion

During 1973 and 1974 fiscal policy became increasingly restrictive, as may be seen by the rise of the full-employment surplus to an annual rate of $32 billion in the third quarter of 1974. This policy resulted directly from renewed emphasis on the demand-restraint attack on inflation, and the reasons were obvious: the inflation rate was skyrocketing, while the controls could no longer be relied upon to stop it. Unemployment was falling and was no longer the dominant problem. There was, moreover, increasing recognition that pursuit of low unemployment targets was likely to be self-defeating, because it only stimulated inflation which in turn prevented the reduction of unemployment.

On some occasions during 1973 and the first half of 1974 the administration considered moving to a still more restrictive fiscal policy. But it concluded that to ask for a tax increase would be futile, since Congress would not grant it. Neither did it seem possible to cut total spending because of the serious difference between the administration and the Congress over priorities. It was thought that Congress would not cut non-defense spending without a cut of defense spending on a scale that the administration considered unsafe. In the end the swing to large full-employment surpluses came about through an interaction of the inflation (which reduced the real value of the expenditures while increasing the real taxes) with the effort at expenditure restraint.

The story of this episode of fiscal history is not yet complete. The fiscal restraints of 1973 and 1974 contributed to the 1974–1975 recession, which in turn contributed to the slowdown of the inflation rate in 1975 and 1976. We do not yet know whether this will turn out to have been only another interlude like others, in which there is no durable reduction in the underlying inflation rate although some more transitory influences, like the oil price increase, are left behind. But there is a possibility that the wave of accelerating inflation may be brought to an end by persistence in restrictive policy. If that is what happens, there will surely be some who will say this was another case of continuing the struggle against inflation unnecessarily long and paying too high a price for it. But not many who participated in the struggle will take that view.

Concluding Observations

The experience briefly recounted here suggests a number of lessons. Some of them are obvious, and perhaps for that reason are commonly overlooked. Others are not only not obvious but are also not certainly true, though they seem to me the most prudent deductions from what happened.

(1) Avoidance of random economic shocks from the fiscal side is important. By "random" I refer to fiscal action that was not determined by stabilization considerations or even heavily influenced by such considerations. It is, of course, true that fiscal policy that is governed by stabilization considerations can be mistaken and destabilizing. But it does not therefore follow that results will be improved by disregarding the effects of fiscal actions on inflation, output, and employment. In the period reviewed here, the leading case of strong fiscal actions that did not sufficiently weigh overall economic consequences was the failure to raise taxes or cut other expenditures when the Vietnam War spending was speeding up in 1965 and 1966. The administration's view of the fiscal requirements of stability at the time may not have been entirely adequate, but still the outcome would have been better for the whole decade if the President had followed that view more closely. Another example, with less durable consequences, was the decision to raise social security benefits substantially in the second half of 1972.

The recent major revision in the congressional budgetary procedures will help to avoid error of this kind in the future. The new procedures require the Congress to act upon the budget as a whole, and not merely upon its numerous pieces separately, and create a staff whose research will highlight the macroeconomic consequences of overall budget policy. One may raise questions about the new procedure. Will the staff be sufficiently liberated from the patterns of analysis and judgment which led to (or rationalized) inflationary behavior in the past decade? Will the analysis become the handmaiden of decisions made by the congressional leadership on other grounds, once the leadership discovers that the analysis has important effects on the behavior of the Congress and the reaction of the public? Will the whole congressional procedure serve as a source of independent study and judgment if the President and the Congress should be of the same party? For the reasons underlying these questions and for others it would be going too far to say that the new procedures assure adequate attention to the macroeconomic effects of fiscal decisions. But they certainly are substantial progress in this direction.

(2) If part of the problem in the past ten years has been that policy did not listen enough to economics, the other part of the problem has been that economics did not know enough. The two parts of the problem are connected: economists would have been listened to even more than they were—they were listened to a great deal—if they had known more. The thing that economists were farthest from knowing in the past decade was how the rate of inflation would respond to changes in aggregate demand, and possibly to changes in other variables, such as the determination of the authorities to check inflation. But of course there were many other things we did not know. Moreover, ignorance is going to remain for a long time, and policy will have to be made in spite of it. Given the degree of ignorance, some policies will be better than others. But none will be perfect, or even as good as we would like.

The most readily remediable aspect of our ignorance is the inadequacy of our statistics. After a decade in which inflation has been our main economic problem we do not even measure the price level particularly well. The wholesale price index is still confused by the difference between list prices and realized prices. The consumers' price index is based on consumers' budgets that are more than ten years out of date. But many other statistics relating to the inflation-unemployment problem are also lacking or unreliable. We do not know what kind of jobs the unemployed are looking for, or at what wage rates. We have no index of wage rates or of labor compensation with constant weights. Measures of capacity utilization are highly uncertain, as are measures of inventories. The nature and location of economic "potential," on which so much economic thinking rested in the past decade, are quite unclear.[14]

[14] Pioneer work on this subject was done by Edward F. Denison in *Accounting for United States Economic Growth: 1929-1969* (Washington, D.C.: Brookings Institution, 1974).

The improvement of statistics will not by itself cure our igno-rance. Even with much better statistics we would still suffer from lack of reliable theories. The behavior of the price level is an example: We have what is probably a good theory about the rate of inflation at infinity, relating it to the rate of monetary expansion. We have what is probably a pretty good theory about the rate of inflation next month, which is a lagged consequence of this month's inflation of prices and costs at earlier stages of processing. But in between next month and infinity we are largely in the dark. And, of course, there are many other economic questions critical for the policies under discussion here in which uncertainty is great and controversy in-tense; how to remedy this kind of ignorance is a great problem. Perhaps we can do nothing but wait for the genius to emerge who will show us how to look at things in a new and clarifying light. But that is probably too defeatist a counsel. Economists should be able to organize themselves to focus more constructively on the real problems of our time than they have hitherto.

(3) We should avoid becoming committed, by law or consensus, to the achievement of any specified unemployment rate by fiscal and monetary policy. We do not know what unemployment rate is the lowest attainable, or the lowest attainable without unsustainably accelerating inflation. But we can be quite confident that if an un-employment target is set in the political process, competition among politicians will force the number down too far. The special signifi-cance attached to the unemployment rate of 4 percent during the 1960s and early 1970s was a serious impediment to reasonable policy. The current effort to enshrine a 3 percent unemployment rate for adults in the national consciousness, through the Humphrey-Hawkins bill, would, if it succeeded, make things even worse than they are now.

This does not mean that we should return to the pre-Keynesian condition of indifference to the unemployment rate—if there ever was such a condition. It should remain the responsibility of fiscal and monetary policy to maintain a condition of aggregate demand such that the efforts of workers to find employment by accepting wage rates consistent with their productivity are not frustrated by con-traction of demand. The objective should be reasonably steady growth of nominal GNP, so that a decline in the rate of wage increase will reduce the unemployment rate if workers are dissatisfied with the unemployment rate. But the objective cannot be to manage fiscal and monetary policy so as to achieve some predetermined unemployment rate regardless of the behavior of wages.

In formulating the objectives of fiscal and monetary policy it is necessary to have some idea whether unemployment is too high in the sense that it would decline if adequate demand were forthcoming to absorb more workers at the desired price level. For example, let us suppose we were prepared to accept an inflation rate of 5 percent, and it were known that our long-run trend of real output was 4 percent per annum. We might then set as a goal for aggregate demand a 9 percent increase. But if we were to start from a position in which the unemployment rate is "high," say 8 percent, we might expect that output would rise by something more than 4 percent, without exceeding the 5 percent inflation target. In that case it would be desirable to aim for something more than a 9 percent rise of nominal GNP.

This kind of thinking can lead to errors and has done so. If the expansion of demand is too great there may be an excessive inflation rate, with little or no reduction in the employment rate. And this raises the question whether to accept and validate the higher inflation rate and to later repeat the whole process in a further effort to get the unemployment rate down. There is no way to avoid this choice. If the unemployment rate is disregarded and the growth of nominal GNP is held to its trend rate (9 percent in this example), we may sacrifice a reduction of unemployment that would not be inconsistent with the goal for inflation. But the experience of the past decade warns us that this choice must be made with judgment, moderation, and flexibility. We have constantly overestimated the speed with which the inflation rate and unemployment would decline. Unless we learn something more than we have learned so far—and something different from what we have learned—we should be wary of aiming for an increase of nominal GNP much above its trend rate. We should not push insistently for a particular rate of reduction of unemployment. And we should not cling stubbornly to some predetermined unemployment goal if the actual rate does not reach it despite a period of reasonably steady growth of nominal GNP.

(4) We should firmly resist any rate of expansion of demand that would support a rate of inflation faster than the 6 percent or so which now seems to be our underlying rate. Our long experience is that an increase in the inflation rate is difficult and painful to undo and yields no lasting benefit. A more difficult question is how much restriction of demand should be imposed in an effort to get the inflation rate down—perhaps to zero. It can be argued that unless the effort is made to get the rate down, the private sector will in the future expect every surge of the inflation rate to be followed by

upward revision of the government's goal, with the result that holding to the present rate would be impossible. Moreover, if the credibility of a policy of getting the rate down to zero were accepted, businesses and workers might act in a way consistent with that outcome, and the pain of reducing the rate might turn out not to be serious.

Still, after the experience of the past decade, it will probably not be possible for us to establish the expectation of something like zero inflation without our going through a period in which that actually is the rate. Nothing the government says will be believed without such a demonstration, and the demonstration is likely to be extremely painful. Moreover, aside from the question of believability, there is no reason now to prefer a zero rate, or even a 3 percent rate, to a 6 percent rate. The rate has been around 6 percent for over seven years, and interest rates, wage contracts, annuities, and many other arrangements have been adjusted to it. On balance, what seems crucial is to try to assure that the rate does not rise above 6 percent, or gets back promptly if it does. Beyond that, if opportunities arise to get the rate lower they should be taken, but no great sacrifice should be made in order to achieve that.

(5) As the previous discussion has suggested, a fixed rule for fiscal policy, such as a requirement for balancing the budget at high employment, does not seem feasible or appropriate at the present time. Such rules have merit as ways of keeping the economy on its optimum path when the economy is on that path. It was recognized from the beginning that they did not prescribe the fiscal behavior that would be ideal if there were perfect foresight and control, but they seemed likely to lead to better policy than we would otherwise get in our real state of ignorance and political pressures. They were considered to be practical ways to harness the popular attachment to budget-balancing to the stabilization objective.

It is probably true that if the government had adhered to the rule of balancing the budget at full employment from 1965 on the economic history of the decade would have been more satisfactory than it was. But since the government did not, a number of serious difficulties have emerged. Most important, "full employment" no longer objectively defines the optimum path of the economy. Both the desirable rate of inflation and the desirable rate of unemployment have become uncertain. For example, at the end of 1969 the optimum rate of unemployment seemed to be something above the "full-employment" rate (whatever that is), the optimum rate of inflation was above zero, and it was quite unclear what budget surplus or deficit would be appropriate on the optimum path of the economy, inasmuch as we were running a surplus. Even though keeping a balanced budget on the optimum path of the economy might have been stabilizing, the move to a balanced budget from a surplus might have been destabilizing. In other words, the rules implied that the budget was in its prescribed position and the economy was in its prescribed position, and in that case keeping the budget position stable would help to hold the economy where it should be. But the typical condition of the past ten years was that neither the budget nor the economy was in its prescribed position, and the optimum position of the economy was difficult to discover objectively. In these circumstances, the rule said little about what to do.

Moreover, the theory of the rule was that a considerable body of moral support could be mustered behind it, mainly carried over from the moral imperative of the old-fashioned balanced budget. In fact that turned out not to be true. Mr. Nixon tried in 1971 to establish it as national policy that there should not be an excess of expenditures over revenues at full employment. This effort evoked no favorable response in the country, and it was particularly derided by "fiscal conservatives" who apparently did not regard it as offering any protection against large and politically motivated deficits. The possibility of devising a reasonable satisfactory rule, or getting adherence to it against any temptations, seems small. There is no present escape from trying to make better discretionary decisions in the circumstances we encounter from time to time. This may not, however, be a permanent situation. We may yet learn a more satisfactory rule and generate strong support for it.

(6) The possibility that we might resort to price and wage controls, and the fact that later we did have such controls in force, was a serious obstacle to clear thinking and firm decision making on fiscal policy. It first misled the public, and then misled the administration, into thinking erroneously that there was a painless way out of the situation that had developed by 1969, if not earlier. Nothing could do more to bring the country to realism about fiscal policy than recognition that controls are not a magic wand and that the hard facts of life must be faced.

CRITERIA FOR DEMAND MANAGEMENT POLICY IN VIEW OF PAST FAILURES

William Fellner

Summary

(1) Monetary and fiscal policies must be managed once again with the objective of generating no more demand for goods and services—no more money GNP—than is required for achieving the best real output results compatible with a sustainable behavior of the price level. The price level behavior must be one to which market expectations can become conditioned. To acquire the needed credibility, a policy engaging in this conditioning effort should consistently aim for a gradual return to an approximately horizontal price trend.

This is the only price-level target that can be made credible—that is, will not be interpreted as subject to periodic upward revisions by the authorities—and the money-wage- and price-setting practices of the markets will adjust only to a credible target. Over a reasonable time horizon the employment level cannot be raised by accommodating inflationary market behavior.

(2) In the United States the present policy line is expected to lead to an approximately 12 percent increase in money GNP for 1976 over 1975, with the year-over-year inflation rate less than 6 percent after a rate close to 10 percent for 1974 over 1973, and close to 9 percent for 1975 over 1974 (as measured by the deflator). We would then obtain a "real" rate of growth of more than 6 percent for 1976 over 1975—a rate which, of course, contains a substantial cyclical recovery component in addition to the normal long-term growth rate. Assuming the required persistence, the authorities could make such a near-term development fit into a sequence gradually leading to noninflationary normal growth. But at the end of that sequence, in a state of noninflationary normal growth, we should have no more than a 5 to 6 percent increase in money GNP (the annual compound rate having been

CONTEMPORARY ECONOMIC PROBLEMS 1976

5.2 percent from 1951 to 1965) and the course therefore requires an appreciable reduction from the now expected 12 percent. Implied in the course described is a gradual (but cumulatively significant) moderation of money-wage increases, in response to the actual and prospective behavior of the price trend.

(3) Persistent significant budget deficits over longer periods have become a characteristic of our post-1965 inflationary span. A strong case can be made for avoiding deficits along our future normal growth path in order to avoid their adverse effect on capital formation, and avoidance of actual deficits would presumably imply "full-employment surpluses" along that path since the path is apt to imply a measured unemployment rate higher than that serving as a basis for computing the "full-employment budget." To move effectively towards a balanced actual budget we should reduce our large current deficit by significant amounts year after year. The trend in fiscal expenditures will have to be made consistent with this objective.

(4) Money growth rates are a matter of substantial importance for demand management, and the Federal Reserve should continue to discuss its policies with the legislative and executive branches of the government. However, it would be inadvisable to go beyond the principle that the various methods of demand management policy must be reconciled by contacts maintained among reasonable individuals in charge of these policies. In recent years the Federal Reserve has made a significant contribution to reversing a trend toward rapidly accelerating inflation, and it is very unlikely that this result could have been achieved if the monetary authority had been exposed to the same political pressures as the legislative or the executive branch of the government. Even in periods in which the Federal Reserve was far too expansionary, "integration" of the monetary authority with the government in the narrower sense would not have improved monetary policy.

One institutional change overdue if future monetary policy is to have the required freedom of action is a change in the methods intended to ensure the viability of thrift institutions. The present interest-rate ceilings on deposits—the contemporary counterparts of usury laws—serve even this narrow purpose poorly, and occasions are apt to recur in which the monetary authority is strongly tempted to adopt unduly expansionary policies in an effort to keep nominal interest rates from rising. Overexpansion can achieve such an objective temporarily at best, inasmuch as it generates inflationary processes and these raise the interest rates on which lenders insist and which borrowers are willing to pay.

(5) Any suggestion for formulating a policy goal in terms of a numerically specified unemployment rate implies wholly unrealistic claims for what economic analysis can perform. Measured unemployment rates simply do not mean what they appear to mean, and it would be a major mistake to commit ourselves to a number whose relationship to desirable economic and social objectives is exceedingly loose. What can be firmly said is that generating inflationary trends in order to reduce measured unemployment rates is a policy that can at best be only temporarily successful and that must be expected to boomerang badly after a short while: it is not a feasible way of providing support for the needy—which, of course, remains a significant objective in all Western economies. The best sustainable output and employment results, for which our demand management policies must consistently aim, will inevitably be influenced by the properties of our market structures, including the structure of our labor markets, and by the availability of transfer payments. We must not first consider various rigidifying factors in our economy desirable or at least acceptable and then pretend that the consequences of these factors for the employment level are unacceptable.

(6) There is nothing in our past experience to suggest that the employment policy goals that could be achieved with reliance on administrative wage and price controls can be more ambitous than those achieved without; and there is much to suggest that renewed experimentation with controls would once more get us into substantial difficulties. The criteria for regulating the wage structure by administrative decisions are exceedingly vague, and the same is notoriously true of the criteria for deciding what the appropriate profits should be on risky innovative ventures on which large losses can be suffered by the unsuccessful. It is practically inevitable that in systems using direct wage-price controls these matters should be decided under the influence of vote-getting considerations, though most of the problems in question are of a highly technical character that makes them unsuitable issues for popularity votes. Also in a country of our size that we hope will shy away from becoming a police state, the enforcement of such regulations would inevitably be spotty and haphazard. This would be bad enough per se and it would further increase the temptation for any government to be guided by political considerations in deciding on what and on whom to concentrate its enforcement effort. Vague euphemisms, such as jawboning, social contract, and incomes policy, belong in a vocabulary ideally suited for evading the basic issues.

Dispensing with the Hazy Distinction between Voluntary and Involuntary Unemployment

Introduction. Demand management by means of monetary and fiscal policies can make a significant contribution to economic welfare, but the possibilities open to these policies are nevertheless much more limited than has been assumed in the recent past. Some of the failures of the more distant past—particularly of the 1930s—resulted from underestimating the promise of demand management techniques; recent failures have resulted from underestimating their limitations.

In particular, the possibilities of reducing our measured unemployment to small size by demand management depend to a considerable extent on which of the competition-reducing "rigidities" in the economy are regarded as reflecting deliberate political value judgments (or are considered irremovable) and thus are taken for granted, and which are regarded as reflecting correctable misjudgments about the true consequences of measures previously taken. Rigidifying factors cause unemployment, and it will be seen that the unemployment they cause is a mixed bag of what one would like by common sense to call "voluntary" unemployment on the one hand and "involuntary" unemployment on the other. These consequences of competition-reducing factors—only in part "knowingly" accepted ones—explain why measured unemployment in general is a mixed bag of voluntariness and involuntariness. The contents of that bag are incapable of being separated. A reasonable demand-management policy should not set its goals in terms of numerically specified measured unemployment rates. Attempts to do so can only lead to destabilizing the economy by generating inflationary processes or to ill-advised experiments with direct controls or to a combination of the two.

The Weakness of the Link between Measured Unemployment and Reasonable Policy Objectives. In the United States a person aged sixteen years or over is regarded as having been unemployed during a survey week if—according to the information obtained in the monthly Bureau of the Census survey from someone living in the same household—the person had no work during the week but was available for work *and* if the person either was looking for work some time during the past four weeks or would be reporting to a job within thirty days. Assume now for illustration that in a given year 40 of 100 persons of the American civilian population aged sixteen or over are neither employed nor self-employed—that is, that they are, for the time being nonworkers. Assume also that according to the monthly surveys during that year 4 persons of these 40 nonworkers are to be regarded as unemployed by the criteria explained above. Since the civilian labor force in relation to which the unemployment rate is defined includes the employed (or self-employed) 60 persons *and* the four persons falling in the unemployed category, the "measured unemployment rate" of the year is obtained by dividing 64 into 4. This would yield an unemployment rate of 6.3 percent for the year.

Presenting the figures in this fashion gives the impression that in that year 10 percent of the nonworkers—4 persons out of 40— were involuntarily unemployed while 90 percent of the nonworkers —36 out of 40—were voluntarily unemployed. Public opinion and policy makers have often implied that this is a justified impression, but they have implied this for no good reason. A somewhat more detailed discussion will follow later, and at this point it is enough to say that we do not know on what terms an unemployed person would have accepted work, nor do we have this information for those non- workers who are not included among the unemployed.

This statement concerning the essential lack of information about conditions of employment that would be acceptable to nonworkers is not invalidated by three additions that should be made for the sake of completeness and that could conceivably be viewed as very minor qualifications. The *insured* unemployed are supposed to be available for a job in their geographical neighborhood, provided that the job is comparable to the one they had held (a provision that is believed to be interpreted leniently in most places); on the other hand, we have indications that the unemployed identified as job-leavers have given up their former jobs because they are looking for jobs on terms more suitable to them; finally, for a small proportion of the nonworkers, who are often described as "discouraged" and who are not counted as unemployed, the surveys do provide the information that they would be looking for a job if they considered the outlook for getting one more favorable.

The distinction between involuntary and voluntary unemploy- ment cannot be drawn satisfactorily according to the criteria under- lying the Census surveys nor according to any other reasonable criteria. But this does not matter much for our developing a reason- able policy, because policy appraisals can do without the distinction.

A reasonable policy should aim for the highest sustainable output path along which all who desire employment on terms commensurate with their productivity would in fact obtain employment. *This is the legitimate objective of employment policy.* Achieving this objective cannot eliminate hardship problems for the entire population. The alleviation of the remaining hardship cases calls for measures in the nature of subsistence aid, and while such aid can to some extent be coupled with work and training opportunities in the public or private sector, the alleviation of the hardship cases remaining when the feasible objectives of employment policy proper are achieved is essentially a separate problem of subsidizing the needy. It is unreasonable to try to commit the policy makers to some specific "measured unemployment rate" that would be observable under the best feasible employment policy. Nor would it be reasonable to try to decompose that unemployment—or for that matter the unemployment of a recession period—into voluntary and involuntary components.

Elaboration on the Weakness of the Link. In 1973—the peak year of a business cycle—42.2 percent of the civilian noninstitutional population aged sixteen and over (for short, 42.2 percent of the "population") was not working in the United States. Only 7.0 percent of this 42.2 percent—that is, 3.0 percent of the population—was regarded as unemployed, and this was 4.9 percent of the civilian labor force. Hence the 1973 unemployment rate was 4.9 percent, as Table 1 shows.

In 1975—the trough year that followed the 1973 peak—44.0 percent of the population was not working, and 11.8 percent of the 44.0 percent was identified as unemployed. Thus, the unemployed accounted for 5.2 percent of the population, and the unemployment rate, expressed in relation to the civilian labor force, came to 8.5 percent.

Compare now the recent business cycle with that which turned down in 1957 (though the lowest yearly unemployment rate of that cycle had been reached in 1956).[1] That downturn was followed by a trough in 1958. We find that then also between 42 and 43 percent of the population was not working at the high activity levels of 1956 or 1957, and that this percentage increased then also to roughly 44 percent for the trough year 1958. Yet during that cycle a smaller percentage of the nonworkers showed up as unemployed in the household surveys: in 1956 5.8 percent and in 1957 5.9 percent of the nonworkers (as compared to 7.0 percent in 1973), and in 1958 about 9.0 percent of the nonworkers (as compared to 11.8 percent in 1975).

---

[1] In 1967 a few changes were made in the questions asked during the Census surveys, but the "lack of comparability" introduced by these changes is clearly not sufficient to throw doubt on the validity of the propositions developed in the text.

Table 1
UNEMPLOYMENT AS A PERCENTAGE OF NONWORKERS
AND OF THE LABOR FORCE AT CRITICAL STAGES
OF TWO BUSINESS CYCLES

Year (1)	Percentage of Civilian Noninstitutional Population[a] That is Not Employed or Self-Employed (2)	Percentage of Column 2 Regarded as Unemployed[b] (3)	Unemployment Rate (defined in relation to the civilian labor force) (4)
Entire Civilian Noninstitutional Population			
1956	42.5	5.8	4.1
1957	42.9	5.9	4.3
1958	44.6	9.1	6.8
1973	42.2	7.0	4.9
1975	44.0	11.8	8.5
Adult Men (20 and over)[c]			
1956	15.4	19.3	3.4
1957	16.2	19.3	3.6
1958	18.8	28.7	6.2
1973	21.3	12.3	3.2
1975	25.2	21.5	6.7
Adult Women (20 and over)[c]			
1956	65.1	2.4	4.2
1957	65.0	2.3	4.1
1958	65.4	3.5	6.1
1973	57.8	3.7	4.8
1975	57.7	6.4	8.0
Teenagers of Both Sexes[c]			
1956	54.7	10.4	11.1
1957	56.1	10.3	11.6
1958	60.1	12.5	15.9
1973	54.0	14.4	14.5
1975	56.6	19.0	19.9

[a] Here and in what follows: sixteen years and over.

[b] For instance, the first entry means 5.8 percent of 42.5 percent, that is, 2.5 percent of the entire civilian noninstitutional population.

[c] Here Column 2 also relates only to those falling in this category of the population.

Source: *Annual Report of the Council of Economic Advisers and Manpower Report of the President,* various years.

As can be seen from these data, the difference between these two cycles—separated from one another by a span of fifteen to twenty years—is *not* shown in any difference between the working and nonworking proportions of the population in the various phases of the cycle. Rather, it is shown in a difference between the proportion of the nonworkers regarded as unemployed. Recently a larger proportion of the nonworkers was looking for a job (at least at some time during the four weeks preceding the surveys) than was the case in the 1950s.

The figures show, however, a very different trend for adult men (twenty years and over) on the one hand, and for adult women on the other. The trend for the population results from offsetting trends observed for its various components. There has been a significant *increase* in the proportion of the adult male population that is not working and a significant *decrease* in the proportion of the adult female population. On the other hand, the proportion of the adult male nonworkers counted as unemployed declined significantly, while the "unemployed" proportion of the adult female nonworkers increased appreciably, with the result that the "measured unemployment rate" for adult men was roughly the same in the recent cycle as it was eighteen years earlier, while for adult women that rate increased. Teenagers have had a declining ratio of nonworkers to their population and yet a rising unemployment rate.

Before disaggregating by sexes we found that measuring the unemployment rate has recently involved identifying somewhere between 7 and 12 percent of the nonworking population as unemployed, depending on the "cyclical" characteristics of the year. When we disaggregate by sexes we find that, for the recent cycle, this comes down to identifying something between 12 and 22 percent of the adult male and only something between 3.5 and about 6.5 percent of the adult female nonworkers as unemployed according to the Census definition.

It is necessary to distinguish between two conclusions that could be and often are drawn from figures of this sort. One of these conclusions is clearly reasonable and the other is not. The number of those capable of obtaining jobs on terms commensurate with their productivity is influenced by policies, and it is clearly reasonable to try to shape these policies in such a way that this number be as large as it can be under policies placing the economy on the highest sustainable output path. On the other hand, it would be quite unreasonable to conclude that our definition of unemployment captures those members of the population who make an effort promptly to obtain jobs on terms on which such an effort would be most likely to succeed quickly. Nor would it in all cases be desirable that job seekers should do so, instead of finding the jobs for which they are best suited. The statement made here cuts both ways (as was already said) for two reasons: not only do we have no information on the terms on which a large number of those defined as unemployed would be willing to accept jobs, but we know little about the circumstances under which those nonworkers who are at present not "looking for work" would be tempted to enter into the labor force.

The weakening of the labor market from 1973 to 1975 expressed itself more convincingly in the fact that the nonworking proportion of the population (including the armed forces in the population as working) rose from 41.5 to 43.3 percent—or the nonworking proportion of the *civilian* population rose from 42.2 to 44.0 percent—than in the fact that the measured unemployment rate jumped from 4.9 to 8.5 percent.[2] Expressing the jump in the latter way attributes too much significance to the distinction between "looking for a job" on terms that are unspecified, and "not looking for a job" in some ill-defined sense.

If it were true that in 1973 4.9 percent and in 1975 8.5 percent of the civilian labor force were *involuntarily* unemployed while the remaining very large proportion of the nonworkers were *voluntarily* unemployed, then the measured unemployment rate would, of course, acquire much more meaning. But in almost all cases of joblessness these two elements are mixed in such a way that an attempt to separate them would involve intellectual acrobatics. We shall now consider some of the difficulties that such intellectual exercises would have to overcome, and it should be clear enough that in reality these difficulties *cannot* be overcome.

Specific Reasons for the Nonoperational Character of the Distinction between "Voluntary" and "Involuntary." (1) To begin with an element of *involuntariness:* even in an economy with no labor unions and no minimum wage legislation, unemployed individuals or groups of unemployed persons could in most cases not go to a major employer and offer their services successfully at the lowest wage acceptable to

---

[2] When expressing the nonworkers as a percentage of the population including the armed forces, we include here the armed forces both in the population and in "employment" (which is not the procedure followed by Geoffrey Moore in his study). When expressing the same percentage for merely the civilian population, we exclude the armed forces from the population and thus also from those regarded as working or nonworking. Measured unemployment, on the other hand, is always expressed as a percentage of the civilian labor force, defined as consisting of the civilian "employed" (including the self-employed) and of those identified as unemployed in the monthly surveys.

these workers. A major plant cannot be run with a work force that is under a constant threat of being fired and replaced by the next persons offering their work at a lower wage. This is another way of saying that even in countries with practically no union power in the formal sense workers in major establishments have in fact behaved and would always behave in many ways like members of an organization, and not like a work force consisting of atomistic units. Thus, even aside from other institutional factors, the fact that an unemployed person has the will to underbid the employed would not always be enough to secure him a job.

(2) If unions represent a sizable fraction of the labor force (which should be taken for granted for advanced industrial countries) and if employment opportunities of various sorts are subject to minimum-wage legislation (the true consequences of which are widely misunderstood) or to other competition-reducing regulations, then the number of those who would be willing to underbid the employed but cannot do so increases, and so does the element of *involuntariness* in unemployment. At the same time, an element of *voluntariness* may enter here to the extent that the temporarily unemployed members of the labor force effectively support the arrangements that tie their hands because they believe these arrangements to be in their own *long-run* interest.

(3) Quite aside from union rules and other regulations affecting wages, even the desire of the unemployed to underbid the employed would be limited by their inclination to hold out for wage demands they consider appropriate if the cost is likely to be unemployment of only limited duration. This introduces an element of *voluntariness* into the problem in any event, and this element becomes significantly enlarged if unemployment compensation is available. On the other hand, to the extent that in a weakened labor market the unemployed turn out to have overestimated the probability of obtaining employment on the desired terms within the span they had in mind, an element of *involuntariness* (or at least of miscalculation that is hard to distinguish from involuntariness) gets mixed in with voluntariness. This is true not only of the unemployment of job losers and of new entrants and re-entrants into the labor force but even of the unemployment of job leavers. The latter accounted for more than 16 percent of the measured unemployment at the cyclical peak level of activity late in 1973 and for more than 10 percent even at the cyclical trough level in mid-1975.

(4) Were it not for these somewhat involved considerations, the characteristics of the present unemployment problem in the United

States would lead one to conclude that the unemployment we are facing is in fact *voluntary*. At first sight it would appear that linking our measured unemployment to the concept of involuntariness is unequivocally wrong—"100 percent wrong." This appearance arises because in a first round of reasoning one would arrive at the conclusion that there cannot be a real problem of involuntary unemployment if real-wage rates are rising (as they are at present)—that is, if a rising real-wage trend is *not* effectively underbid by the unemployed who are supposed to account for 7.5 percent of the labor force. Indeed, the results of such a first round of reasoning have sufficient validity to remind us strongly of elements of voluntariness involved in the problem. Yet what was said on the first three points above also has sufficient validity to lead us to a more balanced final appraisal.

A balanced appraisal suggests that trying to distinguish voluntary from involuntary unemployment in economies of the Western type is a hopeless effort. That effort should be replaced by an effort to ascertain the presumptive effects of alternative policies on the sustainable level of economic activity. An environment needs to be created in which the number of those who want employment on terms commensurate with their productivity can obtain the employment they are looking for, and can do so on the highest output path sustainable in the economy.

Vague Speculations about Future Measured Unemployment Rates. If one nevertheless cannot resist the temptation to engage in vague speculations, the following may be added. Taking account merely of changes in the composition of the labor force, a measured unemployment rate of roughly 5 percent may have been the "equivalent" in the early 1970s of the roughly 4 percent that used to be regarded as expressing practical full employment in the circumstances of the mid-1950s. Along these same lines, the 5 percent would have to be raised somewhat because of continued recent shifts in labor force composition, and the resulting higher figure would then have to be raised again as a result of the significant extension of unemployment compensation. If this were the whole story, our speculations might land us in the neighborhood of 6 percent unemployment for practical full employment, and it would not be particularly astonishing if they landed us somewhat *above* that round number. But this is *not* the whole story, partly because the teen-aged proportion of our labor force will decline in the future and partly because the population cannot be fully described by its age-sex characteristics and its reactions to the availability of transfer payments.

Educational opportunities have in general been increasing, and it is to be hoped that specific means will be developed for coupling some amount of employment in various sectors of the economy with job training. Also, while the availability of "subsistence"—by means of transfer payments going to those qualifying as needy—should be taken for granted in the Western world, there is hope for offsetting the negative employment effect of such arrangements by increasing the attractiveness of the environment in which work is performed. All this remains conjectural, however, and it belongs to an area other than that of demand management policy whose objectives cannot be usefully quantified in terms of measured unemployment rates.

Review of the Record and Discussion of the Policy Line Suitable for Its Improvement

General Discussion of the Record. The mismanagement of our demand policies and of those of other countries has resulted largely from a lack of clarification of the problems briefly considered in the preceding section. In the United States this mismanagement started about 1965, and a more than temporary and better than very hesitant effort to correct the consequences dates back no further than to 1973.

The monetary and fiscal policies of the period from 1965 to 1973 were strongly influenced by the fear that a determined effort to prevent inflation would be incompatible with reasonable employment-policy objectives. This has proved a misconception, except insofar as it was possible to derive short-run employment-policy advantages from generating inflation of unexpected steepness—accelerating inflation—and thereby to induce workers and also employers to accept commitments on the assumption that they will be earning higher real incomes than could in fact be earned. The resulting real-wage disappointment of workers was not, however, associated with benefits to the employers in general.

Real-profit trends were very weak even for a post-1965 period defined as ending with the cyclical peak year 1973. From 1965 to 1973 the *pre-tax, pre-depreciation* gross book profits of the nonfinancial corporations rose no more than by about 15 percent when these "gross profits" are deflated for price changes, while the nonresidential fixed business investment of the country is estimated to have risen by about 45 percent in constant dollars. Even if net interest on borrowed capital is added to the pre-tax "gross profits" (not deducting depreciation charges) we obtain only a 25 percent increase of that sum of gross returns, after correcting for the price change. This has to do with the fact that productivity trends weakened significantly during this period, and the nonfarm sector's terms of trade deteriorated domestically as well as internationally, leaving the question open to what extent these changes reflected specific circumstances in those years and to what extent they should be regarded as predictable consequences of inflation in general. Yet it is difficult to imagine an accelerating inflationary process that would not lead to a significant weakening of the productivity performance, with substantial adverse effects on profits, if no earlier than by the time when it becomes inevitable to shift to policy restraint in order to stem the process. The post-1965 period did, of course, have some "accidental" properties of major importance—particularly during 1973 and 1974 in the crude materials area—but the fact that as a result of accelerating inflation the real-profit as well as the real-wage experience became disappointing is not a phenomenon belonging in the world of accidentals.

In the eight-year period from 1965 to 1973 occasional attempts were made to dampen the process, but these attempts were short-lived and their success was at best temporary. That period was preceded by a period of practical price stability. From 1951 to 1965 the consumer price index (CPI) had risen only at an annual compound rate of 1.4 percent, and the "all commodities" component of the CPI—the component remaining after exclusion of the "services"—had risen at no more than 0.8 percent (the GNP deflator at 1.9 percent). Thereafter, from 1965 to 1973, the rate of increase of the CPI was 4.3 percent, that of its "all commodities" component 3.8 percent (and that of the deflator 4.4 percent). By the early part of 1973 these inflation rates reached and shortly thereafter exceeded 7 percent, and while from then on a consistent effort has been made to use demand management policies for gradual reduction of the inflation rate, inflation in fact moved into the double-digit range before it was reduced.

From 1951 to 1965—during the period of approximate stability of the general price level—the money GNP had risen at an annual compound rate of 5.2 percent; from 1965 to 1973 the rate of increase of money GNP was 8.0 percent, with an 11.5 percent increase from 1972 to 1973; and thereafter the compound rate diminished to 7.4 percent for 1974 over 1973 and to 6.3 percent for 1975 over 1974. In bringing about both the accelerating and the decelerating phases of this development demand management policies—monetary and fiscal policies—played an essential role.

From 1951 through 1965 the average yearly deviation from federal budgetary balance on the national income accounts basis had been a deficit of $1.4 billion, while for 1965 through 1973 the yearly average was a deficit of $7.8 billion—a far greater proportionate increase than that shown by the money GNP. From 1951 to 1965 the rate of increase of the money aggregate defined as M_2 had been 4.5 percent, while for 1965 to 1973 this average rate was 8.0 percent. From the first half of 1972 to that of 1973 the increase of M_2 exceeded 10 percent.

Indeed, the rate of increase of M_2 jumped to 8 percent for the first time in the postwar period just before the inflationary span that followed 1965: it jumped to that level for 1965 over 1964 and this preceded the time when the significant stepping-up of both defense and of nondefense government expenditures led to the emergence of large budget deficits. Yet by the earlier standards 1965 would surely not have been a year calling for additional stimulation. From 1964 to 1965, money GNP rose by about 8 percent, real GNP by between 5.5 and 6 percent, and the unemployment rate declined to 4.5 percent for the year on the average. At that time demand management policy nevertheless became much more ambitious than it had been before. It remained more ambitious for many years, aside from brief interludes during which the damage was not undone.

By 1973, however, it was imperative to bring about a deceleration of inflation, since continued acceleration would have caused even greater difficulties than the overdue shift to restraint; and a *stable* rate of inflation of appreciable height would be unattainable. A promise to aim henceforth for the stabilization of a prevailing inflation rate despite emphatic past assertions that a rise of inflation to that level would be considered intolerable would have lacked all credibility. The 1951–1965 record, surveyed above, may be viewed as one of practical stability of the price level, and the limits of tolerance in this regard are small. Authorities purporting to aim for stabilizing an appreciable inflation rate would rightly be suspect of a strong inclination to correct the target upward whenever it became tempting to administer a short-term inflationary stimulus. Credibility is essential for the success of demand management policy because policy makers can be successful only if the money GNP generated *in view of their price level objectives as well as of their real-growth objectives* is used up in the markets in accordance with these policy objectives rather than for price increases combined with contraction of output. A demand management policy lacking credibility will lead the markets to sabotage the policy effort by using up the money GNP in this fashion, with a high probability that the authorities will give up before inflation is under control. By 1973 it had become clear that policies would have to be oriented to anti-inflationary objectives, and at that time monetary policy did in fact shift to restraint.

Even though subsequently monetary policy was directed at promoting recovery from the recession of 1973–1975, the money growth rates have so far remained compatible with a significant reduction of inflation during the recovery. Fiscal deficits declined appreciably during the late part of the expansion (1973). They rose to a very high level during the recession, and it will take the appropriate measures of fiscal restraint to eliminate them gradually in the course of the recovery.

"Passing Through" Cost Increases. Recently some critics of demand policy restraint have maintained that the restraint was greatly over-done inasmuch as when raw material prices (and thus raw material costs) rise as a result of natural or man-made scarcities, a pass-through of these increases into other prices (hence into the CPI and the overall deflator) must be taken for granted. The critics argued that such price pass-throughs need to be accommodated by keeping aggregate demand correspondingly higher relative to the real output of the economy. But this argument is unconvincing. Once the real burden arising from the specific cost increases—in the present case resulting from the rising prices of farm products, of various metals, and later particularly of energy products—has become inevitable, the rest of the community must necessarily accept a corresponding diminution of its *real* income. A policy "accommodating" pass-throughs in prices and thus in nominal values (dollar amounts) can merely cover up the real-income diminution temporarily by generating an inflationary process in the course of which the burden is passed back and forth among sectors, with the result that the economy is destabilized. At the end the users of the materials whose relative prices have risen must "get stuck" with the burden in real terms, and they must come to realize that under inflationary circumstances they are charging the cor-responding costs to one another, back and forth, noticing only gradu-ally that they are facing rising prices not only as sellers but also as buyers. The results of a policy given to accommodating pass-throughs in this fashion can only be short-term delusion of the public and increased difficulties of adjustment. The reasonable policy posture in such a situation is to face the public with the true nature of the problem by *not* raising nominal demand relative to the economy's output potential and thus making it clear to buyers of the high-price materials that if they pass the cost through into the general price level they will suffer a reduction of their sales volume. If they nevertheless insist on such pricing policies for a while, it is preferable to face them and the economy with the adverse consequences promptly instead of first destabilizing the system by creating an inflationary smokescreen. At the outset our policy makers may not have had a very clear view of the deficiencies of the theory of the accommodated pass-through, but at the end they did take determined anti-inflationary action in the United States and in some other countries, and for this they deserve credit. How persistent they will be is as yet a matter of guesswork.

Inflation and Unemployment. When we compare the post-1965 inflationary period with the noninflationary period from 1951 to 1965, we find that only for a short while was the poor price record of the inflationary period associated with low measured unemployment rates. The accelerating price increase of the years from 1966 through the cyclical peak year 1969 was accompanied by a decline of the unemployment rate to 3.5 percent, with the average for those four years at 3.7 percent. This is 1.2 percentage points lower than the 1951–1965 average. However, the forces generated during that period temporarily moved the inflation rate up to about 6 percent (as expressed at a yearly rate). For 1970 through 1973—from a recession year through the next peak year—the average unemployment rate was 5.3 percent, which is 0.4 percentage points higher than the 1951–1965 average, though by the late part of 1973 the unemployment rate had declined slightly below that average. Thereafter demand policy restraint was applied much more consistently than it had been before, in an effort to put an end to the renewed significant acceleration of inflation, and the unemployment rate rose to 8.5 percent for the cyclical trough year 1975. Such was the unemployment-rate record of a ten-year span in which inflation rose from the 1 to 2 percent range of the 1951–1965 period (essentially from a "negligible" rate) to about 12 percent expressed at an annual rate for what was the worst *quarter* in terms of the recent inflation. The worst quarter was the last quarter of 1974, just before inflation began to moderate near the end of the recession. The specific cost increases of 1973 and 1974 did play a role in these developments, but mainly by contributing to the prolongation of the lag between the belatedly applied demand-policy restraint and the moderation of inflation (see the introductory Guide).

In terms of averages for longer spans, the period from 1951 to 1965, with its inflation rate of less than 2 percent, thus had an unemployment rate of 4.9 percent; the following ten-year period, with its inflation rate of 5.3 percent, had an unemployment rate of 5.0 percent. Near and at the tail end of the 1973–1975 recession we went through one quarter with a 12 percent annualized inflation rate and through one quarter with an 8.7 percent unemployment rate. For any reasonably chosen time horizon the hypothesis of a trade-off between inflation and unemployment has proved an illusion. That illusion has caused significant damage.

Conclusion. The conclusion I suggest is that demand management policy must aim for the level of aggregate nominal demand (money GNP) that is consistent with reasonably foreseeable price-level objectives of the policy makers and with a real-output trend that can establish itself when the market expectations have become conditioned to the price level objectives. The "payoff" from unexpected inflation is the temporary stimulus produced by the overestimation by the public of the available real incomes, and a high price needs to be paid subsequently for that stimulus. Given the need to condition market expectations to a foreseeable behavior of the price level, a gradual return to an approximately horizontal price trend is the only safe target.

There is nothing in the facts that would suggest normalcy could not gradually be restored. We have seen that what first changed about 1965 (at the end of a fourteen-year period of approximate price stability) was the behavior of the authorities. The public's behavior changed in response to a change in the line of policy. The accelerating inflationary trend of the post-1965 period originated in a more ambitious demand-management policy which, neglecting brief interludes with no lasting effect, did not turn around before 1973.

However, this implicit praise of the 1951–1965 record requires some elaboration involving qualifying observations, and there is need for further discussion on the feasibility of a return to a noninflationary policy after the recent events.

Allowances Needed When Using the
Period 1951–1965 as a Frame of Reference

Appraisal of the Significance of Labor Force Composition. In retrospect, the 1951–1965 record looks better than that of 1965–1975, but it is essential to pay attention to those weaknesses of the earlier record which a price-level-oriented demand-management policy could presumably avoid in the future. It is important to do so because a price

Table 2
COMPOSITION OF THE CIVILIAN LABOR FORCE
BY FOUR AGE-SEX GROUPS
(in percentages)

Year (1)	Adult Men (20 years and over) (2)	Men (25-64 years) (3)	Adult Women (20 years and over) (4)	Teenagers of Both Sexes (5)
1951	65.6	55.2	27.8	6.6
1965	60.2	50.7	31.8	7.9
1969	57.4	48.2	34.0	8.6
1975	54.9	45.3 a	35.6	9.5

a 1974 figure.
Source: See Table 1.

level-oriented policy, as it is here conceived, should aim for the best output results compatible with the objective of conditioning market expectations to a sustainable behavior of the price level.

During the fourteen years of price level stability preceding 1965 the measured unemployment rate was slightly less than 5 percent on the average but it showed a rising tendency. For the subperiod 1951–1955 the average yearly rate was 3.8 percent, for 1956–1960 it was 5.2 percent, and for 1961–1965 it was 5.5 percent—though by 1965, before what may be regarded as the beginning of the inflationary span, the rate had again been reduced to 4.5 percent. One of the important factors influencing this trend was the change in the composition of the labor force which has continued beyond 1965, but had progressed far already during the period 1951–1965. This can be seen from Table 2.

Adult women have a higher measured unemployment rate than adult men because there are more entrants and reentrants into the labor force among women than among men. Judging by data for recent years, this seems to be the only reason for the difference between the unemployment rate of adult women and of adult men (twenty and over), since the difference disappears if new entrants and reentrants are excluded for men and women alike. Teenagers and those from twenty to twenty-four have a higher unemployment rate than prime-age males also for the additional reason that their attachment to a specific job is less durable than that of those in the older age classes even while they do remain in the labor force. In the interpretation of trends in the measured unemployment rate it is important to take account of these large shifts in labor force composition. It is necessary for the most recent period to take account also of the significant extension of unemployment compensation in duration as well as coverage.

The Importance of Other Factors: The Improving Quality of Foresight Illustrated with Troika's Performance. Yet the matter cannot be appraised simply by placing the emphasis on the changes in the age-sex composition of the labor force and on extended unemployment compensation. At least *some* of the other changes might have been expected to work in the other direction—that is, to lower the unemployment rate. The change in the white-collar/blue-collar mix belongs among these, and so does the rising level of education. Furthermore, a point that needs to be stressed in this context is that the outlook for avoiding "unnecessary" cyclical movements has improved: in spite of all the limitations of foresight, the predictive ability of the economics profession at large and of the various groups on which policy makers rely for professional advice was more limited in the period 1951–1965 than it is now. The business cycle history of that period included the recessions of 1953–1954, 1957–1958, and 1960–1961—a record that could in all probability be improved under a future policy aiming for a return to approximate general price stability. This is all the more true because the demand policy restraints that presumably contributed to the last of the three recessions listed above (1960–1961) were motivated in large part not by the objective of price stability but by what were then considered the binding requirements of a system of fixed exchange rates, with the dollar convertible into gold in circumstances in which suspicions about the viability of that system started to spread in the markets.

As for the foresight of policy makers, there exists to my knowledge no dependable numerical evidence on which an appraisal could be based for the period preceding 1962.[3] However, each year from 1962 on the *Annual Report* of the Council of Economic Advisers (CEA) has included a forecast made in the month of January for that same calendar year. Because these forecasts originate in the team

---

[3] For the earlier forecasting record of private forecasters, see Arthur M. Okun, "A Review of Some Economic Forecasts for 1955-57," *Journal of Business*, July 1959; and Geoffrey H. Moore, "Forecasting Short-Term Economic Change," *Journal of the American Statistical Association*, March 1969 (where the appraisals of other authors are also cited).

work of the CEA, the Treasury Department, and the Office of Management and Budget (OMB), they have been nicknamed "Troika" forecasts. For our present purpose the forecasting record for *money GNP* (rather than for its "real" equivalent) is of particular interest, because the policy recommended here is that of a gradual return to promoting the creation of that aggregate *current-dollar* demand (nominal demand) which leaves room for normal real growth at an approximately stable price level. Even during a transitional period on the way back to such normalcy it would be the creation of *nominal* demand that mattered. Even with room left for inflation at a decelerating rate and for the supernormal real growth rates of a recovery period, this room or leeway would need to be determined in current-dollar amounts (money GNP).

In other words, what must be avoided is the setting of goals in terms of real GNP on the assumption that money-wage and price-setting practices can be estimated from past relations observed during a period in which demand management policy was known to be lax and during which that policy was trying to exploit an alleged inflation-unemployment trade-off. Once the need to shift to a new policy has been recognized, what primarily matters is the foresight of the authorities in estimating the money GNP that will be generated, since the new policy must create an environment in which markets adjust their practices to the available demand expressed in current-dollar terms. This is how successful stabilization policies have always worked in the past.

A definite improvement of foresight can be seen when the five-year period from 1962 through 1966 is compared with the nine-year period from 1967 through 1975. Whereas the average deviation of the predicted *level* of the money GNP from the actual *level* is 1.5 percent of the actual level for the period 1962 through 1966, it is only 0.7 percent for the period 1967 through 1975. The average deviation is, of course, much larger if the deviation of the predicted *rate of change* of money GNP is expressed as a percentage of its actual *rate of change:* this kind of "average deviation" was close to 10 percent even for 1967–1975, and it had been close to 21 percent for the preceding five years.[4] The record in forecasting real GNP—which, as

[4] The following method was used for computing the numerical values of the deviations. The January forecast for the money GNP of year *t* was compared with the *then available* preliminary figure for the money GNP of year *t*-1, where the latter figure can be read from the statistical appendix of the Council of Economic Advisers report of year *t*. Assume for illustration that this comparison implied the belief on the part of the Council of Economic Advisers (and of Troika) that year over year the money GNP would rise by 7.5 percent. Assume also that,

was explained, matters much less for the present purpose than the record in forecasting money GNP—is distinctly worse, not so much because we observe higher percentage deviations of the predicted from the actual *levels* of real GNP but because even the same deviations in *levels* correspond to much higher percentage deviations of the predicted from the actual *rates of change*. Furthermore, wrong predictions were repeatedly made even of the *direction* of the impending "real" change. But the claim remains convincing that trying to direct demand management policies to the creation of effective current-dollar demand in the range deemed to be appropriate has become a reasonably promising endeavor, and that the relevant forecasting performance has improved considerably.

These claims are convincing despite the fact that it would be impossible fully to articulate the procedures followed by "Troika" or by any other reasonably successful forecasting group. While the econometric models of most forecasters would indeed represent detailed and complex "dynamic theories," the successful forecasters have all along been undertaking ad hoc judgmental adjustments of the model results, in view of new information currently coming in. As for the Troika, its forecasts are made after consulting the econometric models of various investigators, but the Troika forecasts are heavily judgmental, all the more because agreement must be reached among the various agencies participating in the effort.[5]

disregarding the January 1976 benchmark revisions of the GNP, the most recent information on the increase of the money GNP from t-1 to t disclosed an actual increase of 7 percent. Then the level of the money GNP of year t was said to have been overestimated in the proportion 1.075 to 1.07. The rate of increase was said to have been overestimated in the proportion 75 to 70. This calculation deliberately implies that for the present purpose the 1976 benchmark revisions of the GNP should not influence our "correct hindsight" which is compared with the foresight to be appraised. Yet the results would not have been affected significantly by proceeding differently in this regard, and for 1975 over 1974 it was necessary to use figures including the new benchmark revisions because no pre-1976 data were available for the year 1975 as a whole.

[5] A grossly simplified ("naive") quantity-theoretical method, postulating a one-to-one relationship between the proportionate increase of M_2 from one half year to the next and the proportionate increase of money GNP from the second of these two half years to that which follows, would have yielded almost twice Troika's average deviation for 1967 through 1975, but that method would have yielded a significantly lower average deviation than that of Troika for 1962 through 1966 (indeed, into 1968). Yet the two methods are not strictly comparable, because some of the data needed for using this "naive" quantity-theoretical method for predicting the money GNP of any calendar year are not yet available in the month of January, and it would have been necessary to rely on guesswork when using the "naive" quantity-theoretical alternative to the methods employed by Troika for its January forecasts.

Basic Requirements of Success

Why Market Behavior Has Been Adjusted to Firm Demand Policies in the Past. The post-1965 mistakes in demand management have been caused primarily not by the limitations of foresight concerning money GNP, but by the deficient hypothesis of the inflation-unemployment trade-off. In the effort to identify the prospective "real" equivalent of a change in money GNP it has generally been assumed that, given the past price trends, price expectations and wage- and price-setting practices are uninfluenced at any given level of employment by the public's expectations concerning future demand-management policy. If the conviction that the authorities have changed from a lax to a firm policy made no difference, then for a long period ahead we would have to continue to accommodate the practices developed in an inflationary era, in order to create an acceptable level of output and employment. Yet in such circumstances all past stabilization policies after inflationary interludes would in fact have failed. They would have resulted in continued steep price increases coupled with protracted large-scale unemployment. The experience of a few recent quarters again points to a strong influence of a changed policy posture on the expectations and behavior of the public, even though doubts about the future consistency of the change in posture have not disappeared.

In past periods in which the monetary and fiscal authorities were credible in their determination to leave room merely for reasonable real-growth objectives at an approximately stable price level, the money-wage-setting and pricing practices fell in line with policy objectives. It is unconvincing to argue that the decision makers in markets individually have no incentive to adjust to a firm demand policy. While decision makers in the markets cannot collude with a large number of others in this adjustment, they do know they will suffer a significant competitive disadvantage if the others adjust their wage- and price-setting practices and they individually do not. Moreover, given a truly credible demand policy, they know *also* that if the others do not adjust, then demand policy restraints will cause a recession—in which case they individually will be less badly off by having abstained from an inflationary wage-price behavior and by thus having at least partly avoided the fate of the others.

The Passing of the Era of the Gold Standard. It needs to be recognized that in some past periods of sustainable price-level behavior it was not so much a *direct* policy commitment to price level targets that acquired credibility as a commitment to an international monetary system that at the time of its dominance proved incompatible with major inflationary deviations. The international gold standard was such a system, but it involved arrangements that in the present circumstances would not be viable. The significance of the gold standard for the problems discussed in this paper derived from its rightly expected incompatibility with major inflationary disequilibria, but to tie the hands of the authorities by gold reserve (or similar) requirements has subsequently not proved to be a necessary condition of a credible commitment to an approximately horizontal price trend. The Bretton Woods gold exchange standard, which prevailed in the period of stable prices from 1951 to 1965, but which also ceased to be viable in this world of widely differing inflation rates, did not tie the hands of the authorities in the same way that the gold standard tied them. Dollar creation is not subject to the limitations to which gold mining was subject, and under the Bretton Woods arrangements the willingness of the monetary authorities outside the United States to keep their reserves in the form of dollars proved very large indeed.

At the end of the 1950s there did, to be sure, occur an interlude in which a gold outflow from the United States caused our authorities to adopt temporary demand-policy restraints, mainly by bringing about a large swing from deficit to surplus in the federal budget. But the interlude was brief, though our gold stock continued to show a declining trend thereafter. Any explanation of the recession of 1960–1961 *should* take account of the demand restraints in question. Yet comparison of the price developments before that recession with those thereafter (through 1965) make it appear exceedingly unlikely that the recession in question would in any sense have been required for ensuring the favorable price performance of 1951–1965. The essential characteristic of that period as a whole was the credibility of a policy commitment to general price stability, and this commitment reflected itself in monetary as well as fiscal policy. Both monetary and fiscal policy subsequently became much more expansionary than they had been, with monetary policy changing in this regard before inflationary behavior patterns began to emerge in the markets. The extra dose of fiscal restraint that had been temporarily induced by balance-of-payments considerations at the end of the 1950s was not needed for achieving the price level objectives of the pre-1965 period.

The Requirement of Consistency and Credibility. There is no reason to take a defeatist attitude on the possibility of once more gearing market expectations to the objectives of a noninflationary policy. Nor does past experience suggest that achieving the objective requires reliance on wage and price controls. On the contrary, the experience with wage and price controls strongly supports negative conclusions about their effectiveness. Experience also suggests that consistency and credibility of a policy aiming at noninflationary growth is of crucial significance. Any skepticism the public may develop about the consistency of such a policy will be self-justifying, because it will lead to continued inflationary cost-price behavior. This, in turn, is apt to result in an inclination on the part of the authorities to deviate from their policy line to an increasing extent, for fear of long-lasting "stagflation."

The conclusions of this analysis are incorporated in the Summary that begins this paper. The Summary also contains some supporting arguments that are not repeated subsequently.

WAGES, INFLATION, AND THE LABOR MARKET

Marvin Kosters

Summary

Inflationary conditions give rise to market adaptation that reflects the concomitant shrinkage in the monetary unit as a measure of value. Current price and wage adjustments in part reflect changes in related costs and prices that have occurred during the interval since earlier adjustments were made. Future adjustments are influenced by the terms of contractual arrangements—such as interest rates or scheduled wage increases—established to compensate for inflation. Forces that foster continuation of an established inflation trend assert themselves with particular pervasiveness in the labor market. In that market prominent features include: (1) relationships between workers and employers that are frequently long term in nature or covered by contractual arrangements, (2) equity considerations that are influenced by relationships among wages and between prices and wages, and (3) decisions on wage adjustments that are made only periodically.

To the extent that the sensitivity of rates of wage increase to changes in aggregate demand is limited by inertial forces in the labor market, changes in aggregate demand are initially largely translated into variation in employment and output rather than into changes in wage and price inflation. When a reduction in aggregate demand growth (made to curb inflation) results in a cyclical rise in unemployment, the economic dislocations of the adjustment process become particularly evident. Moreover, if unemployment is viewed as the relevant measure of labor market conditions and as the main channel of influence on rates of wage increase, continued inflation combined with high unemployment may be viewed as a symptom of a failure of

In preparing this paper, I have benefited from assistance by Andrea Haines.

wage changes to respond to demand conditions. But it may be more appropriate to view these circumstances as the reflection of limitations on the speed with which a complex series of labor market adjustments can take place—these being adjustments toward a' new equilibrium in the average rate of wage increase and in the pattern of relative wages. It is possible to identify several features of the labor market that significantly influence the speed with which the transition to a new labor market equilibrium consistent with a reduced rate of inflation can take place:

(1) Wage adjustments resulting from new wage decisions can be expected to be more responsive to current labor market conditions than wage adjustments resulting from decisions reached earlier. While most short-term wage adjustments result from new wage decisions, many current wage adjustments affecting a significant proportion of the work force are based on multi-year contracts or survey methods that primarily reflect labor market conditions prevailing earlier.

(2) Differences in productive contributions among workers with different work experience, occupations, and skill levels imply a structure of wage differentials that reflects these differences. For full equilibrium in the labor market, essential conditions include both an average rate of wage increase consistent with the rate of price increase (with appropriate allowances for normal productivity growth and temporary cyclical or sectoral disturbances) and balance in the structure of relative wages.

(3) One of the significant channels through which labor market conditions influence wage decisions is the pressure that asserts itself for maintenance or restoration of equilibrium in the structure of relative wages. The acceptability of particular wage positions is conditioned by forces of custom and tradition—forces that also place limitations on the speed of adjustment toward new relative wage patterns.

(4) The effect of earlier labor market conditions on current wage adjustments works not only through the direct impact of wage increases scheduled under multi-year contracts (or based on survey information), but also through the structure of relative wages that itself reflects the cumulative influence of wage decisions made in the past.

(5) The size of average wage adjustments and changes in the structure of relative wages are influenced by the terms of contractual and other wage-setting arrangements and by the timing of major wage negotiations. The outcomes of new wage decisions reflect the entire spectrum of current labor market conditions, including departures

from equilibrium relative wage patterns that may have built up. Unemployment measures represent only one broad channel of influence on wages, and influences through other channels are in part rooted in conditions prevailing in the past. The coexistence of high unemployment and large average wage increases during a transition to lower inflation reflects the influence of forces asserting themselves through channels other than current unemployment that must be accommodated in order to achieve restoration of labor market equilibrium.

(6) The widespread introduction of cost-of-living escalator provisions into multi-year wage contracts during the first half of the 1970s represented in part an adaptation to the experience of high and variable inflation during the preceding decade. During the surge of inflation in 1973–1974, cost-of-living escalators reduced the tendency for lagging relative wages of workers under long-term contracts as compared to the period 1965–1970.

(7) Major long-term wage agreements and contracts with strong cost-of-living escalators are disproportionately concentrated in sectors with average wages in the top half of the overall distribution of wages in the economy. Wage behavior for a large proportion of workers in the top part of the distribution is accordingly closely linked to price behavior. Average wage increases significantly slower than those produced by strong escalators in multi-year contracts could therefore not be achieved without a widening of wage differentials.

(8) The close connection between price and wage behavior in the current labor market environment has contributed to translating the decline in inflation in 1975 and early 1976 into a reduction in average wage increases. The close linkage between price and wage behavior, together with the relationship between this linkage and the structure of relative wages, constrains the potential role of an incomes policy in facilitating a transition to reduced inflation. Current conditions give emphasis to the importance—and the promise—of cautious demand-management policies to regain durable price level stability.

Introduction

Wages and their behavior are of central importance in a discussion of the overall performance of the economy no matter whether production and employment conditions or inflation problems are the issues of primary concern. The economic significance of wage behavior arises in part from the sheer magnitude of employee compensation as a component of the national income. Price-level increases are closely related to average wage increases because wages represent costs of production. In addition, prices define the purchasing power of wages, and thus translate money wages into workers' real income. Wage levels and wage trends influence overall production and employment rates through consumption and savings decisions by the recipients of the wage income, through hiring decisions by employers, and through job search and acceptance by members of the work force.

Relationships between wages also play an important economic role by influencing labor allocation geographically and among industries, occupations, and skill categories. However, issues of a social and political character also arise in connection with wage trends, the wage share, and comparisons among wages. Questions of social and individual equity are frequently discussed in terms of wage share and relationships between wages. These extra-economic issues shape the institutional characteristics of the labor market and complicate analysis of wage movements. The social and institutional aspects of wage behavior that influence adjustment processes in the labor market interact with economic aspects of labor market behavior to determine price, cost, and employment performance in the economy.

The labor market is an obvious starting point for an analysis of employment and unemployment. But since it is the market for only one factor of production, it would be inappropriate to consider only the labor market in an analysis of inflation. Inflation reflects conditions of supply and demand in all factor and product markets, and the labor market represents only a single factor market, albeit a disproportionately large one. In analyses of inflation, however, attention is often focused on the labor market for reasons that go beyond its size. The rate of wage increase has usually responded to changes in aggregate demand only after considerable delay. Rates of price change have responded with less delay, and they have shown more variability than rates of wage change. This insensitivity of wages has influenced both cost and employment conditions. Persistent cost trends follow from sluggish adjustment in wage trends, and this condition has introduced corresponding inertial tendencies into rates of price increase. Cyclical unemployment has also been in part a reflection of sluggish wage adjustment. When aggregate demand growth has been reduced below rates sufficient to support a continuation of prevailing rates of wage and price increase, the usual experience has been job rationing and unemployment in a labor market that fails to clear at the wage levels produced by these trends instead of a rapid decline from established trends toward market-clearing wage levels in response to the change in the market environment. Consequently, in addition to the unemployment normally accounted for by entry into the work force, job changes, and production and employment shifts, there have been periods with high and persistent cyclical unemployment.

The tendency for average wages to continue rising during and immediately after recessions at rates near those at which they had risen during preceding boom periods was particularly noticeable in the recessions of 1970 and 1973 (see Figure 1). While rates of price change showed the larger and more timely response, labor costs that continued to rise at nearly stable rates placed limits on the extent to which price increases decelerated. Since a systematic relationship between the unemployment rate and rates of wage and price inflation had come to be expected on the basis of historical experience (as interpreted by the prevailing orthodoxy), and since such "Phillips curve" relationships had come to be viewed as reasonably reliable, it was somewhat unexpected that in the recessions of the 1970s, inflation was persistent despite high unemployment and low resource utilization rates.

These conditions raised questions about the efficacy of aggregate demand-management policy as a stabilization tool. The apparent lack of a stable relationship between unemployment and inflation—this stable relationship being the simple form of the conventional analytical framework—gave rise to serious doubts whether inflation, employment, and production performance could be adequately explained by conventional theory and models in which a predominant role was assigned to price and wage adjustments in the marketplace in response to demand and supply conditions. The apparent gap between experience and conventional theory stimulated interest and inquiry in two general directions—toward possible sources of the problem and toward possible remedies for the difficulties it raised.

Renewed attention was focused on possible sources of rigidity and inflationary bias that might be impeding or delaying market adjustment processes. Possible sources identified included business pricing practices, government regulatory practices establishing rates and standards, and the role of labor market institutions such as collective bargaining agreements and contract provisions. Remedial policies that made use of some form of direct intervention into market adjustment processes (by restraining large movements in prices or wages, or by supplementing forces for adjustment or speeding up their effects) also were the subject of considerable discussion and some experimentation. If disturbances that might be expected to be

Figure 1

QUARTERLY MEASURES OF PRICES, WAGES, AND UNEMPLOYMENT, 1950–1975

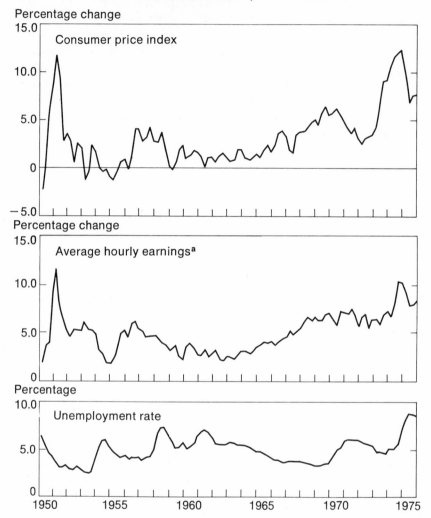

Note: Rates of increase in consumer prices and average hourly earnings are annual rates computed from quarterly data at two-quarter intervals. The unemployment rate is the quarterly average for all civilian workers.

a Percentages are based on quarterly averages of the manufacturing average hourly earnings index, seasonally adjusted, for the period from 1950 to 1964-II, and on quarterly averages of the private nonfarm average hourly earnings index, seasonally adjusted, from 1964-III to 1975-IV.

Source: U.S. Department of Labor, Bureau of Labor Statistics.

temporary triggered persistent inflation trends and if a protracted period of market slack were required to regain stability, the costs of regaining stability (measured in reduced output and employment) could be weighed against the less visible costs of inefficiency from misallocation of resources that might result from direct intervention. Remedial measures intended to improve labor cost stability (either by limiting the initial impact of a price level disturbance or by fostering more rapid readjustment toward stability) included proposals and policies such as export limitations, commodity agreements, "guideposts," "wage-price review boards," or more formal wage and price control procedures.

Relationships between Wages, Labor Costs, and Prices

Wage measures are typically expressed in money wages per hour of work. Wages paid under piece-rate arrangements are usually expressed as hourly rates and premium rates for overtime are averaged with straight-time rates for most industries. Levels and costs of non-wage benefits are not generally available in hourly wage terms. In addition, most measures of hourly wages pertain to production and nonsupervisory workers. For many purposes measures of hourly wages are therefore most appropriately treated as indices of hourly labor costs.

Several elements must be taken into account when hourly labor cost changes are compared with changes in prices. Some of these involve payments to other factors of production, and several show pronounced cyclical behavior. While labor costs comprise the dominant share of all costs, other factor costs include payments to capital in the form of depreciation allowances, interest, and profits. Costs of imported factors (such as oil), prices of farm products, and prices of other material inputs are usually quickly reflected in prices of related and final products. As a result, price changes in these sectors often influence the price level during relatively short periods independently of hourly labor cost trends.

The productivity of labor—output per hour of work—is subject to cyclical influences that must be taken into account in translating labor costs per hour of work into labor costs per unit of output. Labor costs expressed per unit of output are commensurate with units in which prices are measured. While output per hour of work has risen at an annual rate averaging about 2.5 percent since World War II, increases have been larger than average in the early stages of cyclical expansions and smaller (or there have been temporary reduc-

Figure 2
WAGES, LABOR COSTS, AND PRICES, 1950–1975

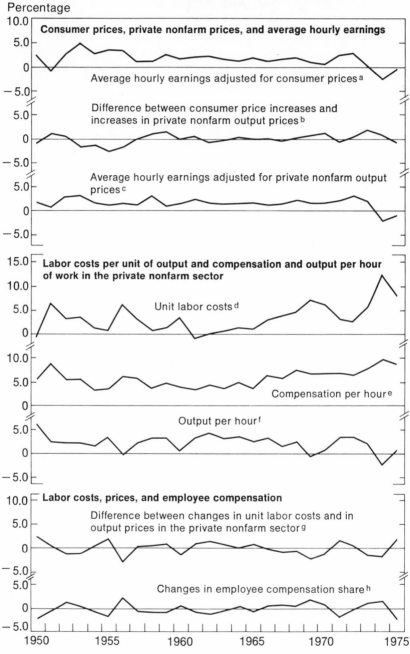

tions) when the pace of business activity has tapered off or declined. In addition, the employee compensation share of the value of output has usually risen during cyclical expansions, a movement usually offset in large part by opposite changes in the profits share.

Several features of the relationship between prices and labor costs during the years from 1950 through 1975 are illustrated in Figure 2. The relationship between average hourly earnings changes on the one hand and two measures of prices on the other is illustrated in the first panel. Increases in average hourly earnings of workers in the private nonfarm sector are compared with the prices of products they consume (as measured by the consumer price index) and with the prices of products they produce (the price deflator for private nonfarm output). The rate of increase in real average hourly labor costs for private nonfarm workers (measured in terms of the prices of output produced in that sector) has been more stable than real average hourly earnings (measured in terms of consumer prices), with food price behavior accounting for much of the difference. The pronounced decline in real average hourly earnings in 1973–1974 (measured on both bases) reflects the surge in prices of energy and basic materials during that period, but it also reflects an unusually sharp reduction in productivity or output per hour. Changes in productivity, compensation, and unit labor costs are shown in the second panel. Cyclical changes in productivity growth, combined with the more

Notes to Figure 2
a Annual percentage change of the ratio of the private nonfarm average hourly earnings index to the consumer price index.
b Annual percentage change of the ratio of the consumer price index to the private nonfarm implicit price deflator.
c Annual percentage change of the ratio of the private nonfarm average hourly earnings index to the implicit price deflator for the private nonfarm sector.
d Annual percentage change of unit labor costs in the private nonfarm sector.
e Annual percentage change of compensation per hour in the private nonfarm sector.
f Annual percentage change of output per hour of all persons in the private nonfarm sector.
g Annual percentage change of the ratio of the private nonfarm implicit price deflator to private nonfarm unit labor costs.
h Annual percentage change of the estimated labor share of output in the private nonfarm sector computed by dividing total compensation of employees minus compensation of government employees, plus nonfarm proprietors' income by Gross Domestic Product minus production in the farm sector minus compensation of government employees.
Source: *Economic Report of the President, 1976* (Washington, D.C.: U.S. Government Printing Office, January 1976), Appendix B, Statistical Tables Relating to Income, Employment and Production.

gradual changes in compensation trends, produced sharp peaks in the rate of increase in unit labor costs. High rates of increase in compensation per hour of work from 1966 through 1975, combined with the interruptions in productivity growth during the two most recent recessions, produced very large increases in unit labor costs during those periods. As shown in the bottom panel of the figure, however, the impact of temporary changes in productivity on unit labor costs was not fully reflected in price changes, since there were short-term shifts in the employee compensation share of the private nonfarm output.

In summary, labor costs are by far the largest component of total costs. Significant shifts in the growth of output per hour of work and in the labor share within cycles have frequently resulted in significant short-term differences between the rate of price inflation and the rate of increase in hourly labor costs. Changes in the prices of other factors of production, which also tend to be cyclical (at least in part), contributed to short-term differences between price and hourly labor cost trends. Variation over several cycles in productivity growth trends and in factor shares has been relatively small, even though significant shifts within cycles have occurred. Consequently, in the absence of secular trends in the prices of other factors of production, there is a strong long-term tendency for price inflation to proceed in parallel with wage inflation at a rate that is less than the rate of increase in hourly labor costs by a margin approximately equal to the average rate of increase in output per hour of work. Another way of stating this proposition, of course, would be to say that real income tends to rise over the long term by about the same rate as output per hour of work, apart from any changes in labor force participation and average hours of work.

Determinants of Wages

An analysis structured to examine differences in rates of wage and price increase and to account for labor cost and other components of price change presents descriptive information on the timing and magnitude of different elements in the wage-price adjustment process. A description of historical experience given in these terms will, however, give only limited insight into the way market forces have influenced wage and price trends or the way the character and speed of market adjustments have been conditioned by institutional features in relevant markets. To trace wage and price trends to significant causal factors it is necessary to make use of a conceptual framework derived from general principles of price formation and adjustment, to elaborate institutional determinants of wage and price levels, or to combine elements of both. This discussion draws upon an extensive literature on labor markets to sketch some of the main elements of a conceptual framework for (1) an examination of recent experience, (2) a discussion of institutional features of the labor market that significantly influence the wage adjustment process, and (3) an assessment of policy problems posed by recent experience and current conditions. Price developments, even in the short term, depend on the extent to which cost and price increases are validated by the monetary authority, of course, and longer-term inflation trends can be sustained only through corresponding rates of monetary expansion. However, the short-term responsiveness of inflation to aggregate demand changes and the real output and employment effects of such changes are conditioned by wage behavior in the labor market, and this discussion is addressed to issues concerning short-term wage behavior.

Basic Concepts. In neoclassical wage theory, wages offered by employers are based on the value of marginal increments of labor as an input into the production process, and these depend on the contribution to production that the worker can make and on the value of the output produced.[1] With a conventionally shaped demand curve derived on this basis and with a labor supply curve, the equilibrium wage and employment level is determined by the intersection of the two curves in the same manner as for any economic good. Aggregate counterparts of curves derived in this way are used to describe an economy-wide equilibrium in the labor market.

This simple analysis must obviously be extensively elaborated in order to be applied to actual labor market behavior. Two major aspects of actual labor markets that are not addressed in this simple framework are the lack of homogeneity of labor inputs and the process by which adjustment to change occurs. Extension of the framework to deal with productive contributions and availability of different types of skills is relatively straightforward. In hiring decisions the employer will take into account his production requirements and the appropriateness and quality of the workers' skills, as well as relative wage costs. The worker, on the other hand, will search for the employment he prefers in which his skills are valuable. Some segmentation occurs, both on the demand and supply sides, and by skills, geographically, and according to other characteristics. A range

[1] See, for example, Alfred Marshall, *Principles of Economics*, 8th ed. (New York: Macmillan Company, 1948), Book VI.

of substitution possibilities in production and multiple skill capabilities lends continuity to most distinctions between categories and permits flux between them, however. Moreover, mobility across boundaries is facilitated by investment in the form of geographic moves, skill development by workers, and training by employers. Nevertheless, heterogeneity implies the need for some matching of workers with jobs, and it produces a structure of relative wages that reflects skill scarcities, investment costs, and the value of different productive contributions.

To deal with the manner in which adjustment to change occurs is more complex. Attainment of equilibrium for all product and labor markets has traditionally been described at an abstract theoretical level in terms of an auction process. While this paradigm may be considered a reasonably realistic representation of the way prices are established in some markets, it is nevertheless true that in many markets prices are set by sellers and adjusted only periodically, with markets cleared over time through a combination of inventory, production, and price adjustments. It is clear from only casual observation that wage-setting arrangements and price formation in competitive auction markets differ markedly. Workers seeking jobs do not normally explicitly bid down wages by offering their services at lower-than-prevailing rates, and employers usually do not continuously vary offers for new employees and rates of pay for existing employees. Job vacancies and unemployment, frequently over substantial periods, are characteristic features of the labor market in which wages are not continuously adjusted to market-clearing levels.

Many of the labor market issues of the greatest practical interest and greatest policy importance are those involving wage and employment adjustments. There is also an extensive literature of analyses that have been explicitly addressed to labor market adjustment issues. The analytical approaches that have been developed have drawn primarily on work in three broad areas: the institutional characteristics of labor markets, theoretical models of the adjustment process, and analysis of empirical relationships between wages and related economic data.

The role of collective bargaining has received the most attention in analyses examining the way the institutional features of labor markets influence wage adjustment. The extent to which union bargaining may alter behavior (either through raising the relative wages of union members or introducing an upward bias into overall wage increases) has been debated throughout the period after World

War II.[2] The issue has not been resolved conclusively on the basis of the empirical studies carried out or on the basis of bargaining models. However, analyses framed in terms of union acceptance of somewhat lower employment as the counterpart of somewhat higher wages have made it difficult to dismiss the possibility that normal unemployment rates are influenced by collective bargaining. Whatever the influence of bargaining practices, contracts establishing wage rates may contribute to wage rigidity, and contracts incorporating deferred wage adjustments and those extending over more than one year may introduce rigidity or inertia into rates of wage increase. Of course, even in the absence of contractual agreements establishing wage rates, there are other factors that foster wage rate rigidity. These factors—related to the desirability of mutually satisfactory and productive long-term relationships between employers and employees—introduce an element of inertia into rates of wage increase in an inflationary environment.

Empirical analyses of forces influencing wage levels and changes in average wages have concentrated heavily on relationships between wage changes and unemployment. Analyses following this approach are of particular significance, both for the manner in which policy choices came to be framed as a result of the approach and for the influence of the approach on public perception of the effects of alternative policies. The inverse relationship between wage inflation and unemployment in historical data gave rise to extensive research efforts to refine estimates of "Phillips curves," and some form of the relationship was incorporated into most econometric models used as forecasting tools for policy planning. The credibility of this approach to short-term forecasting and policy analysis and to analyzing the longer-term consequences of alternative policy choices for attainable combinations of employment levels and inflation rested almost exclusively on a discernible empirical regularity in historical data.[3] Eco-

[2] The major work on relative wage effects of unions is H. Gregg Lewis, *Unionism and Relative Wages in the United States* (Chicago: University of Chicago Press, 1963). Essays on the influence of unions on inflation are published in Philip D. Bradley, ed., *The Public Stake in Union Power* (Charlottesville, Va.: University Press of Virginia, 1959) and David McCord Wright, ed., *Impact of the Union* (New York: Harcourt, Brace and Co., 1951).

[3] The habit of looking at policy choices in terms of an unemployment-inflation trade-off was introduced into economics through an analysis by A. W. Phillips, "The Relationship between Unemployment and the Rate of Change of Money Wages in the United Kingdom, 1861-1957," *Economica*, vol. 25, no. 100 (November 1958), pp. 283-99. The empirical relationship had been noted much earlier by Irving Fisher, "A Statistical Relation between Unemployment and Price Changes," *International Labour Review*, vol. 13, no. 6 (June 1926), pp. 785-92; reprinted in *Journal of Political Economy*, vol. 81, no. 2, part 1 (March/April 1973), pp. 496-502.

nomic theory, however, provided strong grounds for questioning the interpretation of such an observed regularity as a "menu for policy choice," while the reasoning advanced to support this interpretation was fragile.[4] Thus, economic theory formed a basis for judgments that policy choices based on deliberate attempts to induce higher employment by aiming the sights of aggregate demand toward higher inflation targets would be frustrated after only limited and temporary effects.

Analyses of the process of wage adjustment that made use of the influence of expectations provided a more realistic appraisal of the linkages between short-term inflation and unemployment relationships and longer-term developments. The role of price expectations in the wage adjustment process was described by Friedman, who developed for the labor market an analogy of the influence of expected price changes on nominal interest rates.[5] Phelps and others introduced expectations into more formal models of the dynamics of wage adjustment.[6]

These analyses of the influence of expectations on wage adjustment were significant contributions both for the insight they provided into short-term stabilization policy choices and for the framework they employed for labor market analysis. In these analyses, the formation of price and wage expectations on the basis of experience pointed toward a conclusion that only transitory employment gains might be achieved at the expense of a higher target rate of inflation. With respect to the process of wage adjustment, these analyses took into account relationships between a particular wage decision and other wages and prices. That is, the extent to which a particular nominal wage increase would be translated into a real wage increase depended on increases in prices and other wages in the system. Although this approach may have been introduced mainly for analytical convenience, it highlights the economic role of relative wage relationships and introduces allocative aspects of the structure of

---

[4] See Albert Rees, "The Phillips Curve as a Menu for Policy Choice," *Economica*, vol. 37, no. 147 (August 1970), pp. 227-38, in which elements of supporting rationale are summarized, and for an early analysis that contains elements of the basic reasoning underlying grounds for questioning this view see William Fellner, "Demand Inflation, Cost Inflation, and Collective Bargaining," in Bradley, ed., *The Public Stake in Union Power*, pp. 225-54.

[5] Milton Friedman, "The Role of Monetary Policy," *American Economic Review*, vol. 58, no. 1 (March 1968), pp. 1-17.

[6] Edmund S. Phelps, "Money Wage Dynamics and Labor Market Equilibrium," *Journal of Political Economy*, vol. 76, no. 4 (August 1968); reprinted along with related essays in Edmund S. Phelps, ed., *Microeconomic Foundations of Employment and Inflation Theory* (New York: W. W. Norton and Company, Inc., 1970).

wage differentials into formulations of the dynamics of wage adjustment.[7] Thus pressures for maintenance or restoration of equilibrium in the structure of relative wages can exercise an influence on specific wage decisions that is to some extent independent of other conditions of demand or supply in the sector concerned.

The heterogeneity of labor as an input in the production of economic goods and services arises from the wide diversity of skills, ability, training, and experience of members of the work force. This diversity provides the basis for a pattern of wage differentials or a structure of relative wages based on a productivity theory of wage determination. Development of analytic approaches to take past and expected price increases into account represented an integration of the role of wage differentials with the process of wage adjustment. In this study the behavior of wage trends is discussed in terms of these basic economic determinants of wages together with those institutional features of the labor market that influence the timing and size of wage adjustments.

Wages and the Market. The issue of the extent to which wages are responsive to market forces has frequently been collapsed into the issue of the sensitivity of rates of wage increase to the unemployment rate. This tendency to identify the influence of the market with the degree to which changes in the average wage level respond to unemployment has been encouraged by (1) the way in which theoretical macroeconomic models have been designed, (2) the development and widespread use of economy-wide econometric models, and (3) the formulation of policy problems in terms of an unemployment-inflation trade-off. The extent to which excess demand is adequately represented by the unemployment rate has frequently been questioned. Labor economists and industrial relations specialists have also expressed skepticism about the direct influence of unemployment on the terms of collective bargaining settlements or on the size of other wage adjustments. This skepticism is in part based on the observation that unemployed workers do not ordinarily engage in wage-cutting to secure jobs and that in most instances substitution of unemployed workers at lower wage rates for existing employees is not a realistic option for employers. Labor economists have instead tended to identify the decisive particular circumstances surrounding a wage adjust-

---

[7] See, in particular, Edmund S. Phelps, "Money Wage Dynamics and Labor Market Equilibrium," and Dale T. Mortenson, "A Theory of Wage and Employment Dynamics," in *Microeconomic Foundations of Employment and Inflation Theory,* pp. 124-66 and 167-211.

ment at a specific time and location and in a specific industry sector, even though these circumstances might often not be easily made part of a general model of wage determination.

Many of the economic factors that have been identified as influencing the size of wage increases tend to be associated with general unemployment conditions. For example, a significant increase in employment in a major sector or geographic area is frequently accompanied by a reduction in overall unemployment. Downward pressure on prices and profit margins is more likely when demand is weak and unemployment is high or rising than at low or declining unemployment. Rising profit margins and high productivity growth, on the other hand, are likely to accompany low or declining unemployment rates. Steeper rates of increase in consumer prices have typically occurred during periods of strong demand and low unemployment. Unemployment may not therefore be the primary channel of influence on rates of wage increase in spite of statistical evidence of a systematic relationship.

A systematic relationship between unemployment and overall rates of wage increase is weakened to the extent that forces working through other channels have a stronger direct influence on specific wage adjustments than does unemployment. For example, a large increase in food prices that boosted consumer prices could significantly raise wage increases even though the unemployment rate was relatively high. Strong price competition from steel imports could keep profit margins under pressure and wage increases moderate in that sector even though the unemployment rate was relatively low. Also, wage settlements are sometimes influenced by political or economic rivalry within or between unions. Effects on wages from these sources may disturb customary or traditional wage differentials within firms or between industries or skill classes, and pressures for realignment of relative wages can exert an influence on wages in sectors far removed from the sources of the initial disturbance. The influence on wage increases through these channels detracts from the stability of short-term relationships between wage increases and unemployment and affects the path of adjustment over time even in the absence of changes in price expectations. Price level changes introduce additional distortions in a labor market with diverse wage-setting practices and arrangements. For these reasons, the short-term relationship between unemployment and wage increases reflects only in a crude and inadequate way the degree to which wage increases are sensitive to market forces.

Wage decisions that reflect the outcome of forces working through several channels of influence may show a relationship to any particular factor that depends heavily on the strength of the other forces at work. For example, wage increases negotiated in collective bargaining situations in 1970 were unusually large even though profits had declined sharply and unemployment had risen to a level higher than had been experienced for several years. Smaller wage increases were negotiated in 1973 even though unemployment had declined and profits had risen during the cyclical recovery. Changes in relative wage positions and in rates of price increase may provide the explanation for much of this difference. Similarly, the size of new wage increases emerging during the period of unusually high unemployment in the wake of the 1973 recession could be expected to depend to a considerable degree on the influence of forces working through channels other than unemployment.

Measures of the extent to which available labor resources are fully utilized (measures such as the unemployment rate) can in general be expected to capture only some aspects of the influence of labor market forces on wage adjustments. There are in addition some features of the labor market that attenuate the short-term effects of economic forces on wages, and other features that produce wage adjustments representing further steps toward completion of a process set in motion by earlier market or institutional circumstances. These features operate to dilute, to delay, and generally to obscure the influence of relevant market forces and they reduce the applicability of an instantaneous automatic price-adjustment model to the labor market.

Relatively small changes in market conditions, or larger changes that may be only temporary, may not be reflected by wage changes because equilibrium wage levels are in some instances only defined within a range. A range of possible equilibrium wage levels is implied by the use of concepts from capital theory in analyzing hiring and training costs incurred by employers and in analyzing work experience valuable only to the firm in which it is acquired (firm-specific human capital). The value of firm-specific training and of work experience with a particular employer—which is to say, the existence of firm-specific human capital—drives a wedge between the wage a worker could expect to earn from another employer and the higher wage his own employer would be willing to pay to retain him. The employer presumably expects that his investment will on average be recouped over time through payment of wages that, while higher than could be earned elsewhere, are lower than the value of the worker's current contribution to production. So long as the equilibrium wage level remains within this range, the wage will not be sensitive to labor market changes. Changes in market conditions that shift the relevant range may be accompanied by a change in wage position within the range instead of by a wage adjustment or by such a change in position in addition to any actual wage adjustment that occurs.[8]

Models of the collective bargaining process are usually framed in terms of bilateral monopoly analysis in which equilibrium solutions for the wage level span a range of possible outcomes.[9] Collective bargaining introduces additional elements that influence the range of outcomes besides those elements dealt with in analyses based on human capital concepts. These elements include the cost of a strike to an employer, earnings foregone by workers during a strike, and effects of alternative wage levels on union membership and employment. The predictability of the timing and size of wage adjustments in response to changes in economic forces in the labor market depends in part on the width of the ranges of wage levels consistent with equilibrium that are derived from these concepts.

Wage adjustments taking place at any time include not only those with a range of possible outcomes in response to current labor market conditions, but also those that reflect the diffused effects of earlier labor market changes. The primary channel through which the effects of earlier changes are diffused is the possibility for substitution in the labor market. Employers are induced to match wage levels for comparable workers in other firms or industries in order (1) to attract or retain workers, (2) to foster a constructive industrial relations climate, and ultimately (3) to encourage a productive work force. Similar considerations induce employers to maintain a set of wage differentials appropriate to differences in experience, skills, and job classifications. Workers can move to jobs for other employers similar to those they hold and often they can shift to other kinds of work as well. Segmentation of the labor market—either geographically, occupationally, or by levels of skill—operates to retard diffusion, but marginal changes that take place when the degree of segmentation is low or when threshold levels are reached limit the size of maintainable wage differentials.

A significant role has been attributed to social and institutional factors as a channel through which diffusion occurs in the labor

---

[8] See Gary S. Becker, *Human Capital: A Theoretical and Empirical Analysis with Special Reference to Education* (New York: Columbia University Press for the National Bureau of Economic Research, 1964).

[9] See George de Menil, *Bargaining: Monopoly Power versus Union Power* (London, England, and Cambridge, Mass.: The MIT Press, 1971).

market.[10] Peaceful industrial relations and high productivity depend in part on the workers' acceptance of wage patterns as fair and equitable. Although principles such as "equal pay for equal work" may be well established, it is difficult to establish a basis in equity for the size of wage differentials for different kinds of work. Wage relationships or comparisons that have acquired the status of customary or normal patterns therefore foster the acceptability of continuing similar differentials or of only a gradual adjustment to new relationships. The development of relationships that became customary, of course, presumably took place in a market context in which wage differentials were in large part shaped by productivity differences. Institutional factors that tend to knit wage relationships into recognizable patterns include wage-setting on the basis of historical tandem relationships, linkages with prices or other wages, and periodic surveys to establish a basis for wage adjustments.

Short-Term Wage Adjustments and Labor Market Equilibrium. Changes in average wage levels realized in the short term reflect not only the effects of new wage decisions but also the effects of contracts and practices based on earlier decisions. To consider the significance of the timing of wage decisions, it is useful to distinguish between two broad channels of influence on wage decisions. Labor market conditions such as the extent to which qualified workers are readily available, the strength of hiring demand, inflation trends, and cost and profits conditions can be included in one broad channel. A second broad channel of influence includes those forces that assert themselves to maintain equilibrium in patterns of wage differentials or to compensate for departures from equilibrium that may have built up. New wage decisions are likely to be affected primarily by current labor market conditions working through both of these channels. Current wage adjustments are rooted in conditions that prevailed in the past in two important ways, however. New wage decisions are made in the context of a structure of relative wages that itself reflects the cumulative effects of past decisions. And wage adjustments resulting from earlier wage decisions primarily reflect the labor market conditions prevailing when these decisions were reached.

The most straightforward and obvious way in which wage decisions reached in the past influence current wage adjustments is through the provisions of previously negotiated multi-year contracts. The size of

[10] For example in J. R. Hicks, *The Crisis of Keynesian Economics* (New York: Basic Books, 1974). See also, Arthur M. Okun, "Inflation: Its Mechanics and Welfare Costs, *Brookings Papers on Economic Activity*, 1975(2), pp. 351-90.

wage adjustments under these contracts may in addition be influenced to some extent by current conditions—if, for example, the contracts contain cost-of-living escalator provisions. Current labor market conditions can also influence wage adjustments under long-term contracts through provisions for reopening the terms of the contracts or, more generally, by variations in the manner in which the terms are administered. Wage adjustments under "comparability" practices based on regular periodic surveys (an example being the procedures for wage adjustments for federal employees) are also mainly influenced by adjustments in other wages that have occurred in the past. The influence of the past is likewise reflected in wage adjustments for which local labor market surveys provide a basis, but the influence of the wage-survey approach on new wage decisions cannot be sharply distinguished from a more general influence of relative wage relationships.

Past adjustments also influence current wage decisions through their effects on the structure of relative wages. The current structure of relative wages may represent an equilibrium pattern of wage differentials, but it is also possible that disturbances were introduced by earlier wage adjustments. Moreover, short-term equilibrium patterns of wage differentials may themselves depend on labor market conditions; dispersion in relative wages has been relatively wide during extended periods of relatively high unemployment and narrow during periods of low unemployment. The effect on new wage adjustments of the structure of relative wages reflects forces working through the second channel of influence described above. The importance of influences working through this channel depends on the extent to which the pattern of wage differentials that has evolved represents an equilibrium pattern under current labor market conditions. If departures from equilibrium have built up, the effects on current wage adjustments depend (1) on the size of the departures from equilibrium, (2) on whether the departures represent wages below or above equilibrium levels, and (3) on whether new wage decisions will be reached in the sectors in which the departures occur.

New wage decisions can be expected to reflect current general labor market conditions that assert themselves through the first broad channel of influence (including conditions specific to firms or industries) to a greater extent than wage adjustments under the terms of existing contracts or adjustments based primarily on survey information. But new wage decisions will be conditioned by the evolving pattern of wage differentials because economic forces will influence the size of maintainable differentials, and the forces of custom or tradition may limit the size and speed of changes. Both the pattern of wage differentials and the conditions for equilibrium will in general be in flux as wage adjustments under contracts reached earlier and wage increases under new decisions are put into effect, and as general labor market conditions change.

For full equilibrium in the labor market, the overall rate of wage increase should be consistent with productivity and price trends and, in addition, an equilibrium pattern of relative wage relationships should prevail. The short-term rate of increase in wages will reflect increases under wage decisions reached earlier (as for example deferred increases under collective bargaining agreements) and new wage decisions influenced by current economic forces in the labor market (including pressures for maintenance or restoration of an equilibrium structure of relative wages). The sensitivity of the average rate of wage increase to a change in aggregate demand will in general depend on the sensitivity to such a change of wages in sectors where new decisions are reached, and also on whether the structure of relative wages would be brought closer to equilibrium by a change in the size of wage increases from new decisions made in response to general economic conditions. That is, if their response would bring the pattern of relative wages closer to equilibrium, short-term wage increases can be expected to show a larger response to a reduction in aggregate demand growth and a rise in unemployment than they would if their response would produce further distortion of the structure of relative wages.

Collective Bargaining, Inflation, and Wage Trends

Collective bargaining and inflation have been two of the major forces influencing short-term wage trends during the decade from 1965 to 1975. Collective bargaining has been important in part because of the occurrence of high and variable rates of inflation that have influenced short-term wage changes by introducing lags in wage adjustments under multi-year contracts. Moreover, the influence of collective bargaining on short-term wage changes in an inflationary environment is amplified insofar as negotiated wage increases are less sensitive to changes in aggregate demand and more sensitive to the structure of relative wages than are wage increases in sectors in which collective bargaining is not an important factor.

The distinction between union and nonunion wage increases represents an oversimplification in discussing the likely influence of relative wage patterns on wage increases compared to other channels of influence in the labor market. For unions that are normally able to negotiate a "wage premium" relative to wages for comparable workers there is likely to be a particularly strong influence from relative wage patterns. This is also likely to be the case (1) for sectors in which payment of wage differentials sufficient to attract highly qualified workers is of paramount importance, (2) for situations in which the maintenance of relative wage parity is considered essential for minimizing the threat of unionization, and possibly also (3) for sectors in which government rate regulation based largely on cost increases is coupled with the maintenance of a protected position in product markets. In other sectors, however, prices and union wages both may be strongly buffeted by current competitive pressures, or the ability of unions to achieve a favorable relative wage position may be limited by low rates of unionization or weak bargaining power. Consequently, there may be significant differences among unions and also among nonunion situations in the relative influence of aggregate demand changes and wage structural pressures on wage increases.

Unionism. It has sometimes been regarded as an implausible proposition that unionism could play a significant role in influencing the size of overall wage changes or in fostering wage rigidity and inertia in the U.S. economy. The main reasons usually given for the implausibility of this view are (1) that only a small fraction of the work force is accounted for by workers who belong to unions (one out of four or five) and (2) that bargaining is so highly fragmented that no individual settlement or small group of large settlements can be viewed as establishing anything approaching a national pattern for wage increases. While these points are valid, and while they limit the direct influence of unionism on overall wage trends, both union influence on wage increases and union-related inertia may be more significant than would be suggested simply by these observations.

The fact that union membership is heavily concentrated among production and nonsupervisory workers is relevant in an assessment of union influence. White collar workers, supervisory personnel, and clerical workers employed in the same firms as production workers covered by collective bargaining agreements are frequently granted wage increases proportionate to or closely patterned after negotiated wage settlements. Some indication of the importance of this can be obtained from data on employment in manufacturing. According to estimates based on surveys by the Bureau of Labor Statistics, about 10.3 million production and related workers were employed in union manufacturing establishments in 1974, compared to 3.5 million in nonunion establishments. Since manufacturing employment averaged about 20 million in 1974, over 4 million additional nonproduction workers may have been employed in union establishments. In many cases, these workers are likely to receive wage increases directly related to those granted under union contracts. For the entire private nonfarm sector in 1972, the ratio of reported union members to production and nonsupervisory workers was about 37 percent (see Table 9). While this ratio should not be regarded as an accurate and unbiased measure of the extent of unionization, it does provide another perspective on the possible influence of unions on wages.

Moreover, many nonunion establishments have wage policies that are closely aligned with wage developments under union contracts. Nonunion establishments have in some instances adopted a policy of following the pattern of union wages in order (1) to avoid the need for developing an independent approach, or (2) to promote healthy industrial relations, or (3) to simplify personnel policies and recruitment efforts. In other cases, wage patterns very similar to those established under union agreements have been adopted to reduce the threat of unionism or else nonunion firms have developed alternative practices, such as merit-based systems under which pay scales compare favorably with union wages, to foster flexibility in promotion policy or work rules changes.

Bargaining in the U.S. economy is highly fragmented—that is, negotiations are carried out separately in different geographic areas, different industries, and frequently in different firms in the same industry. Moreover, negotiations typically do not occur simultaneously for any significant group of bargaining situations or industries. Rather, major negotiations are ordinarily spread out over time with contract expirations and new negotiations occurring at intervals generally ranging between one and three years.

However, it does not follow from this degree of fragmentation in bargaining arrangements in the U.S. economy that the outcome of particular wage negotiations can be regarded either as dependent primarily on factors specific to the sector in which bargaining takes place or on general market conditions prevailing at the time the settlement is reached. The terms of collective bargaining settlements are influenced both by comparisons with wages under other contracts negotiated earlier and with wages in other sectors that may reflect changes in the market environment since expiring contracts were negotiated. It is possible that wage rigidity and inertia are enhanced by fragmented bargaining with individual new wage settlements covering only a relatively small share of the wages set under collective bargaining agreements (and a much smaller share of all wages), and with overlapping contract periods and expiration dates staggered over time. Pressures for restoration or maintenance of equilibrium relationships within the network of wage differentials in the economy—in order to offset departures from equilibrium that have accumulated over the duration of expiring agreements or to improve alignment with projected patterns of other wages in the future—could contribute strongly to wage-trend inertia. Thus, the influence of unionism on inertia in wage trends depends in large part on the quantitative importance of wage comparisons (or the strength of pressures toward equilibrium in the structure of relative wages) rather than on the importance of such other factors as general labor market conditions or conditions specific to the sector in which wage negotiations are taking place.

Contract Provisions. For a significant proportion of union workers, periodic wage adjustments are made under the provisions of long-term multi-year contracts. The size of the wage adjustments and the extent to which they reflect changing circumstances in the economy depend on the characteristics of the contract provisions. While reopening of contracts under specified conditions is sometimes provided for, the most common and quantitatively significant provisions reflecting changing conditions are cost-of-living escalators. The prevalence and design of cost-of-living escalators has varied over time, apparently partly in response to the experience of high and variable inflation. After declining during the 1960s, the proportion of workers under major agreements with escalator provisions rose from about 20 percent in 1966 to 58 percent at the beginning of 1976.[11]

There is a great deal of diversity in the ways that cost-of-living escalator provisions are applied, but in recent years these provisions have in general been revised to produce increments in wages more closely proportionate to increases in the consumer price index. In some instances more frequent adjustments have been scheduled, escalator provisions have been applied to fringe benefits in addition to wages, or upper limits on wage increments have been raised or removed. The influence of changes in the price index on wages during the early 1970s has been estimated to be in the range of .5 to .6 (the measurement being the ratio of average percentage wage increases resulting from escalator provisions to percentage increases in the

[11] See H. M. Douty, *Cost-of-Living Escalator Clauses and Inflation*, Staff Report of the Council on Wage and Price Stability, Executive Office of the President, August 1975, for an extensive discussion of the prevalence and characteristics of escalator provisions.

Table 1
WAGE CHANGES UNDER MAJOR COLLECTIVE
BARGAINING SETTLEMENTS, 1970–1975
(percentage)

	1970	1971	1972	1973	1974	1975
Wage settlements						
First-year wage changes	11.9	11.6	7.3	5.8	9.8	10.2
Average over life of contract[a]	8.9	8.1	6.4	5.1	7.3	7.8
Percentage of workers affected by new settlements[b]	43	38	23	52	50	28
Effective wage rate changes[c]						
Total	8.8	9.2	6.6	7.0	9.4	8.7
Adjustment resulting from						
Current settlement	5.1	4.3	1.7	3.0	4.8	2.8
Prior settlement	3.1	4.2	4.2	2.7	2.6	3.7
Escalator provisions	0.6	0.7	0.7	1.3	1.9	2.2
Escalator coverage						
Percentage of workers covered by escalators[d]	26	28	41	39	39	50

Note: Data relate to collective bargaining situations covering 1,000 or more workers in private nonfarm industries.

[a] Averages over life of contracts do not include wage increases under cost-of-living escalator provisions.

[b] Percent of estimated workers covered in major collective bargaining situations for which new wage settlements were negotiated during the year.

[c] Effective wage rate changes are wage rate changes actually placed into effect during the year for workers covered in major collective bargaining situations. They include wage increases under new settlements, deferred increases under previously negotiated contracts, and increments under cost-of-living escalator provisions.

[d] Estimated percentage of workers under major collective bargaining agreements as of the beginning of the year. By January 1976 the percentage had risen to 58 percent.

Source: U.S. Department of Labor, Bureau of Labor Statistics.

consumer price index).[12] But these estimates may be understated for several reasons. In the data on which they are based, guaranteed increments (frequently a feature of escalator provisions) are treated as fixed wage increases rather than as payments attributable to escalators up to the threshold rate of price increase. In many of the most recently negotiated contracts, escalator formulas provide larger proportionate wage increases than previously. Also, fewer recent con-

---

[12] Ibid., Table 8, p. 29.

tracts include limits on the size of wage increases under escalator provisions, and where limits are included they are usually higher than previously.

The data shown in Table 1 for increments in wages for workers under major collective bargaining agreements show a rise in the size and proportion of overall wage increases attributable to escalator provisions. This rise reflects an increase in the proportion of workers covered, a rise in the rate of price increase, and, in addition, a rise in the overall payoff ratio. The data in Table 2 show the average size of wage increases under escalator provisions since 1968. The influence of wage increments linked to cost-of-living increases by escalator formulas, but guaranteed even if consumer prices rise by a very small amount, is shown in Table 3. Differences in escalator payoffs are shown for broad aggregates and for an aggregate of five major industry sectors. Part of the pronounced rise in the apparent payoff ratio between 1974 and 1975 may be attributed to the lagged influence of large price increases in 1974. While average wage increases under escalators for the five major sectors do not diverge significantly from those for broader industry classifications during the period 1973–1975, there were significant differences among industries. Payoff ratios

Table 2

CONSUMER PRICE INCREASES AND WAGE INCREASES UNDER COST-OF-LIVING ESCALATOR PROVISIONS OF MAJOR COLLECTIVE BARGAINING AGREEMENTS, 1968–1975
(percentage)

	1968	1969	1970	1971	1972	1973	1974	1975
Percentage increase in consumer price index (December to December)	4.7	6.1	5.5	3.4	3.4	8.8	12.2	7.0
Wage increases under cost-of-living escalator provisions (mean percentage increases during the year)								
All industries	1.6	1.6	3.7	3.1	2.0	4.1	5.8	4.8
Manufacturing	1.8	1.7	3.8	3.7	1.8	4.0	7.2	5.2
Non-manufacturing	1.1	1.4	2.6	1.8	2.2	4.7	2.0	4.1

Note: Data on wage increases under cost-of-living escalator provisions relate to all workers covered by escalator provisions under collective bargaining situations covering 1,000 workers or more in private nonfarm industries.
Source: U.S. Department of Labor, Bureau of Labor Statistics.

Table 3

WAGE INCREASES ATTRIBUTABLE TO COST-OF-LIVING ESCALATOR PROVISIONS AND FORMULA-BASED GUARANTEED COMPONENTS, 1973–1975

(mean percentage increases)

	1973	1974	1975
Wage increases under cost-of-living escalator formulas, including guaranteed increments			
All industries			
Total	4.1	6.2	5.2
Excluding guarantee	4.1	5.8	4.8
Manufacturing			
Total	4.0	7.4	5.3
Excluding guarantee	4.0	7.2	5.2
Non-manufacturing			
Total	4.7	2.8	4.9
Excluding guarantee	4.7	2.0	4.1
Five major industry sectors[a]			
Total	4.7	6.9	5.4
Excluding guarantee	4.7	6.6	5.2

Note: Data relate to wage increases under cost-of-living escalator provisions for all workers covered by escalator provisions under collective bargaining situations covering 1,000 workers or more in private nonfarm industries. Averages excluding formula-based wage increments that were guaranteed irrespective of actual consumer price increases correspond to those normally reported by the Bureau of Labor Statistics and reported in Table 2.

[a] The five major sectors included in these averages are: Bituminous Coal and Lignite Mining (SIC-12), Primary Metal Industries (SIC-33), Transportation Equipment (SIC-37), Trucking and Warehousing (SIC-42), and Communication (SIC-48). During the 1973-1975 period, some contracts in these sectors had no escalator provisions and "caps" as well as guaranteed components were included in escalator provisions in some sectors. The averages for each year include only situations in which escalators were present.

Source: U.S. Department of Labor, Bureau of Labor Statistics.

under current contracts for some industries were in the neighborhood of 80 percent.[13]

[13] The ratio of percentage increases in wages under escalator provisions to percentage increases in the consumer price index has been estimated at about 80 percent under the current wage contract in the basic steel industry. Michael L. Wachter, "The Wage Process: An Analysis of the Early 1970s," *Brookings Papers on Economic Activity*, 1974(2), p. 515.

Effects of Escalator Provisions. The direct and indirect effects of cost-of-living escalator provisions on the structure and trend of wage rates depend to a considerable extent on the kinds of economic changes that take place. The cyclical influence of escalators, for example, differs according to the stage of the cycle. If few workers are covered by escalators and payoff ratios are low during an expansionary phase of the cycle, wage increases under long-term contracts may be delayed. Wage trends may accordingly rise less steeply than they would if long-term contracts were not present or if the long-term contracts contained escalator provisions. In addition, more rapid adjustment of other wages will influence relative wage rates, as wage differentials are altered by differences in the timing of wage adjustments. Such short-term distortions in the structure of wage rates may in turn create pressures for restoration of "normal" differentials subsequently when long-term contracts expire.

This pattern is illustrated by wage developments in the late 1960s and during the 1970 recession. Rising inflation led to a gradual rise in union wage increases, particularly for workers under expiring long-term contracts, followed by very large newly negotiated union

Table 4

WAGE CHANGES FOR MANUFACTURING PRODUCTION WORKERS IN UNION AND NONUNION ESTABLISHMENTS, 1969–1974

(percentage change)

	1969	1970	1971	1972	1973	1974
Mean general wage change put into effect						
Union	5.3	6.4	7.1	5.4	6.4	8.7
Nonunion	4.6	4.7	4.0	4.4	6.0	7.7
Mean first-year wage change under new general wage decisions						
Union	7.3	7.6	9.2	5.7	6.0	8.1
Nonunion	4.6	4.6	3.9	4.4	5.9	7.5

Note: Wage changes put into effect during the year include those resulting from current decisions, prior decisions, cost-of-living adjustments, or any combination of these. First-year wage changes for union workers include all changes negotiated during the period and scheduled to go into effect during the first twelve months of the agreement, and for nonunion all changes under decisions during the period.
Source: U.S. Department of Labor, Bureau of Labor Statistics.

wage increases during and immediately after the recession. Wage increases put into effect in the manufacturing sector rose more significantly for union workers than for nonunion workers from 1969 to 1971 (see Table 4). However, increases under new wage decisions for union workers exceeded those for nonunion workers by an even larger margin. Wage increases for nonunion workers in manufacturing declined somewhat from 1969 and 1970 to 1971 and 1972. First-year wage increases negotiated under major collective bargaining agreements greatly exceeded deferred wage increases put into effect during the same year, except for the construction industry (see Table 5). While it has not been uncommon to have front-loaded agreements with first-year wage increases larger than those scheduled to be put into effect during the rest of the term of multi-year contracts, it is clear from the comparisons of average hourly earnings increases for selected sectors (Table 6) that they became much more common and pronounced for contracts negotiated during the period from 1969 to 1971.[14]

During the recession phase of the cycle and in the early stages of a moderate cyclical recovery in which price inflation is still subsiding, the presence of escalator provisions in long-term wage agreements contributes more toward reducing inflation than would fixed wage increments negotiated on the basis of expectations that the inflation rate would remain stable or rise. The increased use of escalator provisions during the period 1973–1975 resulted in a rise in wage increases for union workers in 1973–1974 with less delay than would have been likely in the absence of escalator provisions. There were less pronounced differences in the average size of union and nonunion wage increases during 1974 and 1975 than in the previous recession, partly because escalators reduced the buildup of wage imbalances. Widespread use of escalator provisions also contributed to shortening the delay in translating the decline in the inflation rate during 1975 into smaller wage increases for union workers under long-term collective bargaining agreements.

The influence of escalator provisions on labor costs, margins, and prices in the economy also depends on the character of the price increases that take place. The surge in inflation that began in 1973 was characterized by disproportionately large increases in the prices of farm and food products and in the price of imported products, particularly oil. The rise in inflation was thus accompanied by large inter-

---

[14] See Marvin Kosters, Kenneth Fedor, and Albert Eckstein, "Collective Bargaining Settlements and the Wage Structure," *Labor Law Journal*, vol. 24, no. 8 (August 1973), pp. 517-25, for an analysis of wage increases under collective bargaining agreements during this period.

Table 5

PERCENTAGE INCREASE IN HOURLY EARNINGS AND NEGOTIATED WAGE
INCREASES UNDER MAJOR COLLECTIVE BARGAINING SETTLEMENTS, 1968–1976
(mean percentage change)

	1968	1969	1970	1971	1972	1973	1974	1975	1976[a]
Average hourly earnings, private nonfarm	6.3	6.6	6.6	7.1	6.5	6.4	8.2	8.9	
Wage increases under major collective bargaining agreements[b]									
All industries									
First year	7.4	9.2	11.9	11.6	7.3	5.8	9.8	10.2	5.4
Deferred	4.6	5.4	5.8	7.7	6.0	4.8	5.1	5.2	
Construction									
First year	8.7	13.1	17.6	12.6	6.9	5.0	11.0	8.0	8.1
Deferred	n.a.	n.a.	10.1	13.1	11.6	7.3	5.3	8.0	
Manufacturing									
First year	7.0	7.9	8.1	10.9	6.6	5.9	8.7	9.8	4.8
Deferred	3.9	4.0	4.6	4.8	4.5	4.4	4.6	4.4	
Nonmanufacturing (excluding construction)									
First year	7.6	9.6	14.2	12.2	8.2	6.0	10.2	11.9	4.9
Deferred	n.a.	n.a.	5.2	7.6	7.3	5.0	5.6	5.1	

a Deferred wage increases for 1976 are estimates of wage increases scheduled to be put in effect during the year, excluding increases that may occur under cost-of-living escalator provisions.

b Data on wage increases relate to collective bargaining situations covering 1,000 workers or more in private nonfarm industries. First-year wage changes include all changes negotiated during the year and going into effect during the first twelve months of the agreement. Deferred wage increases are increases put in effect during the year, excluding cost-of-living escalator increases.

Source: U.S. Department of Labor, Bureau of Labor Statistics.

Table 6

CHANGES IN AVERAGE HOURLY EARNINGS FOR SELECTED INDUSTRY SECTORS, 1961–1975

(percentage change at annual rate) [a]

	1961	1962	1963	1964	1965	1966	1967
Private nonfarm index [b]	3.1	3.3	2.9	2.8	3.7	4.1	4.8
Manufacturing [c]							
Steel (331)		3.3	**0.9**	**0.9**	0.8	**4.0**	2.2
Metal cans (341)		3.7	**1.0**	1.0	**3.4**		2.4
Farm machinery (352)		**2.8**		4.0	**1.1**	4.3	
Motor vehicles (371)		**2.9**		3.3	**2.8**	4.4	
Aerospace (372)	**2.3**	3.0	**3.3**	2.9	**2.7**		5.1
Meat products (201)	1.8	**3.5**	2.3		**1.6**	3.2	
Tires and inner tubes (301)		**3.5**	3.5	**1.9**	3.8	**2.7**	1.6
Nonmanufacturing [d]							
Bituminous coal (12)		0.7			**7.1**	2.9	**4.7**
Trucking (421)					**4.4**	2.1	
Telephone communication (481)	**4.5**	4.4		**2.4**	3.2		**3.8**

Notes: Numbers in bold face are percentage changes for six-month averages from six-month averages a year earlier. The six-month interval between months included in these averages spans the period during which wage increases under newly negotiated contracts were put in effect. The percentage changes in bold face accordingly correspond roughly to first-year wage increases under newly negotiated contracts and they reflect wage increases under new contracts negotiated during the calendar year preceding the year in which the bold face figures appear. The percentage changes not in bold face are annual rates of change from the six-month period following major wage negotiations to the six-month period prior to new contract negotiations.

In each of the sectors included, a large share of the workers was directly affected by major contract negotiations, multi-year contracts were prevalent, and it was possible to identify the timing of wage negotiations affecting a significant portion of the workers. It should be recognized, however, (1) that some fraction of the workers in most of these sectors received wage adjustments under contracts with expiration dates not coincident with those covering a majority of the workers, (2) that in some instances wages may have been influenced by contract reopenings or other factors that are not reflected in formal expiration and renegotiation dates, (3) that in other instances wages for a significant portion of workers may have been set through arrangements other than collective bargaining agreements.

1968	1969	1970	1971	1972	1973	1974	1975
6.3	6.6	6.6	7.1	6.5	6.4	8.2	8.8
	6.6	5.1		**14.4**		9.4	**14.3**
	8.4	4.7		**12.6**		7.3	**12.8**
5.4	5.7		**8.3**	5.7		**11.0**	13.4
6.9	5.6		**11.1**	6.3		**10.6**	10.7
	7.6	**6.8**		5.9	**7.5**	7.6	**11.0**
5.7	5.7		**8.0**	5.2		**7.5**	11.7
5.2	4.4		**7.6**	6.1		**3.7**	6.8
1.3	**9.5**		7.6	**10.3**		7.8	**14.9**
5.6	5.0		**13.8**	10.7		**7.0**	7.3
2.3	**8.5**		3.8	**18.0**		9.2	**13.6**

[a] For private nonfarm index, percentage change in annual average from preceding year. For selected sectors, percentage change in six-month averages from earlier six-month averages.
The specific six-month intervals on which the computations are based are:
Steel, bituminous coal, meat products, aerospace, trucking: January to June
Farm machinery, motor vehicles and equipment: April to September
Metal cans: June to November
Tires and inner tubes: July to December, 1959-1965 and January to June, 1965-1975
Telephone communications: July to December, 1958-1959 and January to June, 1959-1975
The six-month intervals for tires and inner tubes and telephone communications were shifted during the period under consideration because there were significant changes in the time of the year when contract negotiations took place.
[b] Index of private nonfarm average hourly earnings, adjusted for overtime (in manufacturing only) and interindustry employment shifts.
[c] Average hourly earnings, adjusted for overtime.
[d] Average hourly earnings, not adjusted for overtime.
Source: U.S. Department of Labor, Bureau of Labor Statistics.

sectoral and international income transfers. The price index for products consumed rose more sharply than the prices of products produced by workers in the nonfarm sector where cost-of-living escalator provisions are concentrated. Indexation of wages, together with indexation of other income payments such as social security, operated to support the real wage and income levels of some of those affected by the rise in prices. However, the uneven character of the inflation resulted in major income shifts; rising relative prices of imports were having an adverse effect on overall real income levels, and there was a major shift in income toward the agricultural sector. Even though these shifts might subsequently be at least partly reversed, wages rose under escalator provisions, and the rise in labor costs from escalators created pressure for further price adjustments. Because the rise in prices that began in 1973 was so uneven, the series of adjustments that was set in motion worked toward a higher overall rise in inflation than would have been triggered by an initial rise in inflation distributed more evenly across the sectors of the economy. Strong pressures for further price increases were created by rising labor costs at a time when there were narrow limits on the degree to which processing and distribution margins could be squeezed in those sectors where price increases had accounted for a disproportionately small share of the rise in inflation. Labor cost increases that were triggered by disproportionately large price increases in a narrow range of sectors were transmitted in part through cost-of-living escalators, and through this process were widely diffused through the economy.

Relative Wages and Their Cyclical Behavior

The dispersion of relative wages has shown a cyclical pattern during the period since World War II, although the pattern does not conform closely to the brief and pronounced unemployment cycles associated with recessions. Instead, after a significant rise in dispersion during the early postwar period, wide dispersion in relative wages has been associated with periods of persistently high unemployment and dispersion has been narrowed during a period of persistently low unemployment (see Figure 3). Even though these statements are cautious, they must be further qualified in view of the behavior of construction wages during the latter half of the 1960s. Wage increases in the high-wage construction sector were larger than average wage increases during this period in which unemployment was low and wage differentials were generally compressed for sectors from which construction wages are excluded.

Figure 3
CHANGES IN RELATIVE EARNINGS AND UNEMPLOYMENT

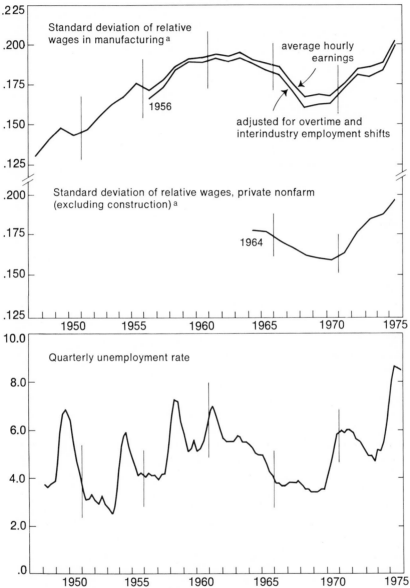

a Standard deviation of natural logarithms of average hourly earnings
for the industry sectors included.
Source: U.S. Department of Labor, Bureau of Labor Statistics.

143

The implications of this broad cyclical pattern of relative wage dispersion depend to a considerable degree on the way the pattern is interpreted. Different interpretations of the main market mechanisms or of the economic forces that gave rise to the cyclical behavior shown by relative wages follow from significantly different views of the process of wage adjustment. The critical question in interpretation is whether the observed changes in wage differentials should be regarded as representing equilibrium patterns of wage differentials, given the degree of slack in the labor market and given other conditions associated with the level of aggregate demand.

Any observed pattern of relative wages, of course, presumably represents at least a temporary equilibrium position reached through the operation of time lags before contract revision or of other factors. However, this temporary equilibrium position may not be maintainable without further adjustments. A pattern of relative wages that cannot be maintained can be viewed as representing a disequilibrium pattern compared to a full long-term equilibrium pattern that could be maintained in the absence of new disturbances.

One possible interpretation of the observed changes in dispersion in relative wages is that they represent full equilibrium positions that could be maintained along with the levels of real economic activity and unemployment levels that brought them about. This appears to correspond closely to the interpretation that has been placed on these changes by Okun and Holt.[15] A slightly different view of the nature of the equilibrium positions represented by different levels of relative wage dispersion is that the pattern of wage differentials prevailing when unemployment was low *could* be maintained, provided that wage premiums negotiated by strong unions could be kept small and unemployment kept low by sufficiently expansionary aggregate demand policies. This view is similar to that suggested by Hall.[16]

Alternatively, short-term variations in relative wage patterns may reflect temporary departures from full equilibrium in the labor market. That is, neither the patterns of relative wages nor the aggregate demand and unemployment conditions giving rise to them can be maintained—particularly at the lowest observed unemployment rates, but also possibly at the highest rates of unemployment experienced.

---

[15] Arthur M. Okun, "Upward Mobility in a High-Pressure Economy," *Brookings Papers on Economic Activity*, 1973(1), pp. 207-52, and Charles C. Holt, "Job Search, Phillips' Wage Relation, and Union Influence: Theory and Evidence," *Microeconomic Foundations of Employment and Inflation Theory*, pp. 53-123, especially pp. 106-07.

[16] Robert E. Hall, "The Rigidity of Wages and the Persistence of Unemployment," *Brookings Papers on Economic Activity*, 1975(2), pp. 301-35, especially pp. 321-25.

Such a view is consistent with the accelerationist interpretation of "Phillips curve" relationships articulated by Friedman, Phelps, and others.[17] The influence on short-term wage trends of wage adjustments under long-term collective bargaining agreements with changing rates of inflation and the various linkages between wages discussed in earlier sections of this paper also fit into this disequilibrium interpretation.

Empirical studies in which attempts have been made to explain overall rates of wage increase through the use of measures of relative wage dispersion have apparently been based (implicitly) on a disequilibrium interpretation of short-term cyclical variations in relative wages.[18] The conceptual basis for including relative wages as an independent variable in equations explaining wage changes has not always been carefully developed, either in terms of its economic role or in terms of the econometric implications of its inclusion, although it has been recognized that overall rates of wage increase and changes in relative wage dispersion jointly reflect the influence of underlying institutional and economic forces.[19] The somewhat ad hoc use of measures of relative wage dispersion in empirical studies is reflected by the fact that some studies show a negative relationship between dispersion of relative wages and rates of wage increase, and at least one study shows a positive relationship between dispersion in past rates of wage increase and the current overall rate of wage increase. In some instances, the influence on rates of wage increase of the measure of dispersion has been attributed to distortions in relative wage relationships, but in another case the dispersion measure has been regarded as a proxy for unemployment.[20]

---

[17] Friedman, "The Role of Monetary Policy," Phelps, "Money Wage Dynamics and Labor Market Equilibrium," and numerous references in two recent surveys; "Inflation: a Survey," by D. E. W. Laidler and J. M. Parkin, Economic Journal, vol. 85, no. 340 (December 1975), pp. 741-809; and John Rutledge, "The Unemployment Inflation Tradeoff: A Review Article," Claremont Economic Papers, paper number 141, The Claremont Colleges, Claremont, Calif.

[18] Arnold H. Packer and Seong H. Park, "Distortions in Relative Wages and Shifts in the Phillips Curve," Review of Economics and Statistics, vol. 55, no. 1 (February 1973), pp. 16-22; D. Q. Mills, "Explaining Pay Increases in Construction: 1953-1972," Industrial Relations, vol. 13, no. 2 (May 1974), pp. 196-201; and M. L. Wachter, "The Wage Process: An Analysis of the Early 1970s," Brookings Papers on Economic Activity, 1974(2), pp. 507-24.

[19] This is recognized by Wachter, "The Wage Process," pp. 513-14.

[20] The analyses by Packer and Seong and by Wachter show a negative relationship between measures of relative wage dispersion and rates of wage increase in manufacturing, while the Mills study shows a positive relationship between the dispersion of the size of wage increases among trades during preceding three-year spans and the average wage increases in construction.

The disequilibrium interpretation of cyclical variation in relative wages has its basis in the influence that can be attributed to institutional and economic factors at work in the labor market. Institutional factors include long-term collective bargaining agreements, the force of customary wage differentials, and the survey methods to establish a basis for wage adjustments—all of which influence the timing of wage adjustments and the pattern of relative wage relationships. One of the main elements in the economic rationale for cyclical changes in relative wage relationships is the influence of changes in relative labor demand that occur in association with changes in total labor demand and employment. The distinction between general and firm-specific investment in human capital establishes a presumption of shifts in relative employment demand along with more general cyclical changes.[21]

A cyclical expansion of final product demand raises the derived demand for labor inputs. Such a cyclical rise in labor demand is likely to be expected to be partly temporary, and therefore potentially at least partly reversible. Firms will accordingly attempt to accommodate their short-term production requirements by hiring workers with appropriate skills and investing little in firm-specific training, because a period of employment attachment is necessary to recoup the return on firm-specific investment in human capital. The increase in relative demand for workers with skills appropriate for general production operations, workers for whom firm-specific training is not initially contemplated, tends to raise their relative wages. Lower hiring costs for relatively low-paid workers who can be used temporarily to raise production also augments relative demand for workers in these skill categories. A temporary reduction in final product demand, on the other hand, will reduce relative demand for workers with low hiring costs, because rehiring these or similar workers may be necessary in the future, and layoffs will be concentrated among workers with relatively low firm-specific investment.

In addition to the relative short-term demand shifts expected to be larger for certain categories of workers than for other workers, wages can be expected to be relatively more flexible for these same workers. For workers with low firm-specific investment in human capital the wedge between the current marginal product of labor and wages that could be earned in other firms is small, which means that changes in the marginal product of these workers should be more

---

[21] This framework was introduced by Walter Y. Oi, in "Labor as a Quasi-fixed Factor of Production," *Journal of Political Economy*, vol. 70, no. 6 (December 1962), pp. 538-55.

quickly translated into pressures for wage adjustments than they would for other workers. Flexibility for changes in relative wages may, of course, be limited to a significant extent by an interest on the part of both workers and management in maintaining a degree of stability in wage schedules and differentials. The consequences of such a tendency toward relative wage stability include layoffs that are more pronounced in the relevant skill categories and demographic groups than for groups with more firm-specific human capital, as well as attempts through the hiring and layoff practices of firms to offset some of the short-term changes in marginal productivity by up-grading or relaxing worker quality standards.

It is also possible to point to supply-side labor market factors that supplement and operate in concert with demand-side factors to influence relative wages. To the extent that unions are able to nego-tiate premium rates relative to wages of comparable nonunion workers, nonunion wages will be reduced relative to those that would prevail in the absence of unionism, and queues will tend to form. Workers in the queue will include not only unemployed workers, but also new job entrants and employed workers responding to job availability. An expansion in demand and employment tends to reduce the number of workers willing to take the relatively low-wage jobs, so that wage differentials are narrowed as wages for these jobs are bid up. Occu-pational licensing and minimum wages also tend to influence wage differentials in part through their effects on supply.[22]

Assessment

Short-term inflation rates have varied over a wider range during the past decade than during peacetime periods earlier in the century. In recent years swings in the rate of increase in prices have been par-ticularly wide for farm and food products, and these swings have had a pronounced influence on both wholesale and consumer price indices. Large increases in the prices of energy products and other basic materials have also contributed more to variation in inflation rates in recent years than at any time since the time of the Korean War. This short-term variation in inflation rates has not been accompanied by as large a variation in wages and hourly labor cost increases, but

---

[22] For an analysis of the uneven effects on demographic groups of cyclical move-ments and the influence of the federal minimum wage on the demographic pattern, see Marvin Kosters and Finis Welch, "The Effects of Minimum Wages on the Distribution of Changes in Aggregate Employment," *American Economic Review*, vol. 62, no. 5 (June 1972), pp. 323-32.

higher average inflation rates have been accompanied by larger hourly wage increases. The relationship between rates of price and hourly labor cost increases has accordingly varied markedly over short periods.

During 1974 and 1975, hourly labor costs rose at about a 9 percent rate, higher than the 6 to 7 percent range that prevailed from 1968 through 1972 (see Table 7). The sharp rise in labor costs per unit of output during the recession of 1973–1975 was reversed when the recovery began; peak rates of increase—over 10 percent—during 1974 were followed by a 3 percent decline in the third quarter of 1975. These short-term changes in the rate of increase in unit labor costs reflected short-term productivity changes, but partially offsetting changes in income shares blunted the extent to which unit labor cost changes were translated into price changes. Similar patterns of short-term change have historically accompanied sharp cyclical swings in economic activity, and historical experience serves as a guide to the longer-term relationship that can be expected between rates of increase in hourly labor costs and prices.

During the period since World War II output per hour of work has increased at an average rate of approximately 2.5 percent. This rate represents the approximate margin by which the rate of wage increase can exceed the rate of price increase on a sustainable basis. A margin near the upper end of this range, or even a temporary higher margin, can reasonably be expected during the course of a steady cyclical recovery. While such a temporary higher margin can facilitate adjustment toward a less inflationary wage-price path, it cannot remove the need for smaller wage increases as a condition for achieving reduced inflation nor can it alter the basic relationships that define sustainable rates of wage and price increase. Consequently, the rate of increase in wages and the factors influencing wage trends are of critical importance in assessing prospects of inflation.

Recent Conditions. Several measures of rates of increase in hourly labor costs are available as guides in making judgments about recent and current trends. One of the most comprehensive is compensation per hour of work, which includes benefits and which is available for major sectors of the economy. The measure that corresponds most closely to an index primarily reflecting changes in wage schedules is the average hourly earnings index. Measures of changes in union wages are also available, with the broadest measures being those for major collective bargaining situations. Considerable sectoral detail is available for components of these broad summary measures, and

Table 7
ANNUAL WAGE INCREASES AND SETTLEMENTS, 1966–1975
(annual percentage change)

	1966	1967	1968	1969	1970	1971	1972	1973	1974	1975
Compensation per hour										
Private nonfarm	6.1	5.7	7.3	7.0	7.3	7.0	6.9	7.4	8.8	9.0
Manufacturing	4.7	5.1	7.0	6.5	6.8	6.6	5.6	7.0	9.9	10.4
Nonfinancial corporations	5.3	5.3	7.2	7.0	7.1	7.1	6.3	7.3	9.4	10.0
Average hourly earnings index [a]										
Private nonfarm	4.1	4.8	6.3	6.6	6.6	7.1	6.5	6.4	8.2	8.9
Manufacturing	3.3	4.6	6.1	5.9	6.2	6.6	6.4	6.1	8.6	9.9
Construction	5.1	5.7	7.2	8.6	9.3	8.5	5.9	5.6	6.0	7.1
Collective bargaining settlements [b]										
Wage increases under major agreements [c]										
All industries										
First year	n.a.	n.a.	7.4	9.2	11.9	11.6	7.3	5.8	9.8	10.2
Over life of contract	n.a.	n.a.	5.9	7.6	8.9	8.1	6.4	5.1	7.3	7.8
Manufacturing										
First year	n.a.	n.a.	7.0	7.9	8.1	10.9	6.6	5.9	8.7	9.8
Over life of contract	n.a.	n.a.	5.2	6.0	6.0	7.3	5.6	4.9	6.1	8.0

Table 7 (continued)

	1966	1967	1968	1969	1970	1971	1972	1973	1974	1975
Construction										
First year	n.a.	n.a.	8.7	13.1	17.6	12.6	6.9	5.0	11.0	8.0
Over life of contract	n.a.	n.a.	8.6	13.1	14.9	10.8	6.0	5.1	9.6	7.5
Wage and benefit increases										
All industries (5,000 workers or more)										
First year	6.1	7.4	8.7	10.9	13.1	13.1	8.5	7.1	10.7	11.4
Over life of contract	4.1	5.1	6.5	8.2	9.1	8.8	7.4	6.1	7.8	8.1
Construction (1,000 workers or more)										
First year	n.a.	n.a.	n.a.	n.a.	19.6	14.1	7.5	5.8	10.8	8.3
Over life of contract	n.a.	n.a.	n.a.	n.a.	15.6	12.0	6.6	5.6	9.2	7.7

[a] Average hourly earnings adjusted for overtime (in manufacturing only) and interindustry employment shifts.
[b] First-year wage changes include all changes negotiated during the year and going into effect during the first twelve months of the agreement. Averages over life of contracts do not include wage increases under cost-of-living escalator provisions.
[c] Data on wage increases relate to collective bargaining situations covering 1,000 workers or more in private nonfarm industries.
Source: U.S. Department of Labor, Bureau of Labor Statistics.

more detailed wage information is available in many instances for specific crafts, occupations, and localities, although this information is not easily integrated with the broader wage measures.

According to these various measures, wages were increasing at peak rates in the 10 percent range during the year beginning with the second quarter of 1974 (Table 8). Although most measures show rates of wage increase somewhat lower since the first part of 1975, new first-year wage increases under collective bargaining agreements have shown only a slight reduction below the 10 percent range. Measures of compensation per hour and adjusted average hourly earnings show a significant slowdown beginning during 1975 when compared to rates of increase prevailing during the last three quarters of 1974. The most pronounced reduction by the first quarter of 1976 from rates of increase prevailing in both 1974 and 1975 is shown by the comprehensive indices of average hourly earnings.

The timing of the rise to significantly higher rates of wage increase in 1974 was apparently influenced in part by the termination of wage and price controls at the end of April 1974, and the controls may have had a marginal influence on overall wage trends after August 1971. Construction wages, which were subject to controls after March 1971, showed the most pronounced reduction from earlier rates of increase. Increases in construction wages have also been smaller than average increases in other wages since mid-1974—perhaps in large part because of the depressed levels of industrial and multi-family housing construction activity—and there have been significant differences in rates of increase among other sectors as well.

Changes in overall rates of wage increase and differences in rates of increase among sectors have in part been attributable to the timing of wage negotiations in collective bargaining situations and to the numbers of workers affected. First-year wage increases under major collective bargaining agreements have averaged about 10 percent since mid-1974, with the range of increases reflecting differences in sectoral conditions, terms of expiring agreements, and other factors. The influence of newly negotiated wage increases on average wage increases has been sensitive to the number of workers affected, which was at a low point in the three-year cycle in 1975, and to the size of deferred wage increases under multi-year agreements. The size of deferred wage increases under multi-year agreements during 1974 and 1975 was influenced to an unusual extent by cost-of-living escalator provisions because a large proportion of workers under long-term contracts were covered by escalator provisions and price increases (which set the escalators in motion) were large.

Table 8

QUARTERLY WAGE INCREASES AND SETTLEMENTS, 1941-I–1976-I

(quarterly percentage changes at annual rates)

	1974				1975				1976
	I	II	III	IV	I	II	III	IV	I
Compensation per hour									
Private nonfarm	8.8	11.8	11.6	10.7	9.1	6.8	8.7	6.5	7.8
Manufacturing	6.3	15.6	12.1	15.0	10.2	8.0	6.5	6.1	8.8
Nonfinancial corporations	8.9	11.7	11.2	11.4	11.8	7.3	7.3	7.3	n.a.
Average hourly earnings index [a]									
Private nonfarm	6.8	10.1	10.7	9.6	8.6	7.5	8.7	8.3	6.0
Manufacturing	6.9	11.3	12.0	11.2	9.5	8.9	8.5	8.3	7.0
Construction	3.7	8.8	12.5	6.3	6.3	8.1	6.6	4.6	n.a.
Collective bargaining settlements [b]									
First-year wage increases									
All industries	7.1	9.2	11.2	10.3	12.1	9.0	9.7	11.0	8.8
Manufacturing	6.7	8.5	10.2	9.0	10.9	10.0	8.7	9.2	9.8
Construction	6.4	9.1	15.1	12.9	6.0	8.2	8.1	9.1	6.4

KOSTERS ON WAGES AND PRICES

Effective wage increases									
All industries	5.3	12.6	14.3	6.6	7.0	8.7	13.9	6.1	4.5
Manufacturing	5.7	14.8	12.6	8.2	7.4	8.7	11.7	6.6	n.a.
Construction	2.4	18.3	13.4	3.2	3.2	19.3	8.7	2.4	n.a.
First-year wage and benefit increases									
All industries (5,000 workers or more)	6.9	9.2	11.9	14.6	12.9	8.9	11.3	14.0	9.5
Construction (1,000 workers or more)	6.7	9.0	14.8	11.5	6.7	8.1	8.1	9.8	6.7

a Average hourly earnings adjusted for overtime (in manufacturing only) and interindustry employment shifts.

b Data on wage increases relate to collective bargaining situations covering 1,000 workers or more in private nonfarm industries. First-year wage changes include all changes negotiated during the year and going into effect during the first twelve months of the agreement. Effective wage increases are wage rate changes actually placed into effect during the year for workers covered by major collective bargaining situations. They include wage increases under new settlements, deferred increases under previously negotiated contracts, and increments under cost-of-living escalator provisions.

Source: U.S. Department of Labor, Bureau of Labor Statistics.

153

Incomes Policy Issues. Proposals for an "incomes policy" have become commonplace. Essentially, these are proposals for some form of wage-price controls designed to contain the inflationary effects of expansionary policies pursued too aggressively or too long in a quest for high employment. Most of these proposals have not been specific about the sectors to which selective controls might be applied or about their standards and administration. The way in which controls would impinge on economic relationships has also usually been left vague, except for the exercise of what is an essentially political rhetoric in which they are portrayed as an instrument for "standing up to" segments of the economy commonly perceived as capable of wielding extensive market power (with references to big business more typical than references to large labor organizations). Nevertheless, on the basis of this analysis of the labor market, several issues can be identified that would need to be addressed in considering any serious wage-price control initiative.

Wage adjustment in the labor market has been characterized here as a process in which continuous equalization of values of marginal products seen by firms with wages at which workers are willing to offer their services is attenuated by several factors. Equilibrium at any point in time is influenced by factors such as the force of custom in the degree to which wage differentials can be varied, the range of wages that may be consistent with equilibrium, and costs of information. Moreover, the timing and size of wage changes that represent moves toward equilibrium relationships are influenced by contract expiration dates and normal pay review practices as well as by changes in related wages and prices in intervals between wage decisions. An analysis attributing a quantitatively significant role to these and other factors that attenuate the market forces pushing wage patterns toward equilibrium might be interpreted as suggesting a corresponding (and quantitatively significant) scope for some form of wage controls. That is, this interpretation of labor market adjustment might be viewed as providing scope for the exercise of wage controls to curb the overall rate of wage increase with consequences that would be no more deleterious to efficient labor resource allocation than the wage patterns that would emerge in the absence of controls.

Labor resources do not generally move to new uses in response to changing wage differentials as quickly as, for example, uses of money are altered by changes in interest rate differentials or internationally traded goods move in response to price differentials. For these reasons, losses through inefficient labor resource allocation could be kept within tolerable limits under a system of wage controls, at least in the short run, although of course it has usually been necessary (for purposes of formal balance in wage-price policy) to couple price controls with wage controls. Price controls have a greater potential for undermining efficiency than wage controls, even in the short run, (1) because there are frequently strong pressures to limit particular price increases despite the deleterious effects of such stringent limits on efficiency, (2) because it is only over a period of time that the effects on capital formation of a squeeze on profit margins became apparent, and (3) because there are overwhelming technical difficulties in administering controls on prices in a way that maintains continuous and complete alignment in all relative prices.

While the technical problems of avoiding serious short-term inefficiency are less unmanageable for controls on wages than for controls on prices, wage-setting is not exclusively a technical process of establishing wage levels and differentials reasonably consistent with efficiency. The mutual acceptability of wage patterns to workers and firms is crucial to the viability of these wage patterns and the productivity of the workers. Since wage patterns are neither fixed indefinitely nor in continuous equilibrium, conditions for acceptability are as a technical matter incapable of being established on analytical grounds. Moreover, in addition to the relative wage positions that actually emerge, the process by which they emerge is normally a critical element in generating acceptability. Wages and other circumstances surrounding conditions of employment have generally been viewed by the parties to wage-setting as properly the subject of bargaining and negotiation rather than of a governmental administrative process, and the history of incomes policies is replete with examples of failure to achieve acceptability for wages set under such an administrative process. Prospects for success of an incomes policy are accordingly critically dependent on the extent to which the policy deals effectively with the problem of gaining acceptability for wage patterns that are generated and the procedures that give rise to these patterns.

The large number of workers whose wages are closely linked to prices through cost-of-living escalator provisions in multi-year wage contracts has introduced a significant new dimension into the labor market environment for wage controls. Although the rise in wages attributable to escalator provisions is only one component of overall labor cost increases, it is the component often likely to be at issue when wage adjustments are measured against an incomes policy standard. Reducing overall wage increases by limiting payoffs under escalator provisions is likely to be generally infeasible and perhaps

155

undesirable. A broad range of key wage increases will accordingly be conditional for the most part on price behavior. Accordingly, consideration of an incomes policy approach premised on the idea of reducing wage increases indirectly by influencing price behavior should include a realistic appraisal of the limited potential for even a marginal effect of controls on prices in any given market environment. Moreover, the fact that wage behavior for a significant proportion of workers is already closely linked to actual price performance reduces the potential for a contribution to stability by a "temporary" incomes policy oriented toward influencing inflation expectations.

The fact that a disproportionate number of workers in the upper part of the wage distribution is under escalator provisions also raises questions about the distributional incidence of wage controls. If wage adjustments under the terms of existing contracts were not modified by controls, the burden of wage restraint induced by controls would presumably fall disproportionately on workers at the lower end of the wage distribution—who include a disproportionate number of workers not under wage contracts with escalator provisions. Special treatment or complete exemption from controls, however, has always been provided for low-wage workers, and it is reasonable to suppose that a similar approach would be followed in any new wage control initiative. For example, a "substandard earnings" level of $3.50 per hour was established in the stabilization legislation in April 1973, a level which at that time was higher than 90 percent of private nonfarm average hourly earnings. Under these circumstances any restraining effect of wage controls would be concentrated on an extremely limited segment of the wage distribution.

Both special treatment for wages at the low end of the wage distribution and the practical effects of escalator provisions under a wage control system limit the range of wages that could presumably be influenced by an incomes policy. In addition, new wage decisions would be the basis for wage adjustments for only a fraction (although for a substantial fraction) of the remaining workers. Consequently, only a limited impact on wage cost trends could reasonably be expected from an incomes policy without significant disturbance in patterns of wage differentials, without overriding the terms of existing wage contracts, or both—which of course has implications too obvious to require elaboration for the acceptability of wages set on this basis.

Comparisons with Circumstances in the Early 1970s. There are several differences between current labor market circumstances and the situation during and shortly after the 1970 recession. These differences are significant both for the interpretation of recent trends and for future labor market developments. The main differences concern cost-of-living escalator provisions and dispersion in the structure of relative wages, differences that are closely interrelated.

In most sectors (other than construction) in which long-term collective bargaining agreements were a significant factor, the large first-year wage increases that were negotiated during the period 1969–1971 appear to have been generally consistent with the restoring of positions in the wage structure existing before the late 1960s acceleration of inflation. That is, these large first-year wage increases can be viewed as "catch-up" increases negotiated to restore an earlier balance in relative wages. These circumstances were followed by a major expansion of cost-of-living escalator coverage after 1970, both in the number of workers under contracts with escalator provisions and in the degree to which increases in consumer prices were translated into proportionate wage increases. Widespread introduction and upgrading of escalator provisions apparently took place partly in reaction to the experience of the late 1960s and partly in response to the new surge in inflation that began in 1973.

Although hourly wage rate increases did not initially rise sharply when price increases accelerated in 1973, several factors contributed to the sharp rise in 1974. After the termination of controls in April 1974 there were a number of instances in which wage increases were put in effect to compensate for limits imposed by the controls. In other instances wage adjustments intended to compensate in part for the surge in prices and to accommodate pressures for wage realignment built up during the controls may have been delayed until the stabilization program no longer provided a basis for holding back on wage increases.[23] In addition, much of the direct impact of escalators on wages as a result of the rise in the rate of inflation that began in 1973 came after considerable delay. Wage increases under escalator provisions also influenced related wages by raising standards for the comparisons that normally serve as one of the bases for wage adjustments.

The pervasive influence of escalators since 1973 has in general reduced erosion in relative wage positions of workers under multi-

---

[23] For a discussion of the design of the wage and price controls and an assessment of its influence on wage and price trends, see Marvin Kosters, *Controls and Inflation: The Economic Stabilization Program in Retrospect* (Washington, D.C.: American Enterprise Institute, 1975). See also Daniel J. B. Mitchell, "The Impact and Administration of Wage Controls," in J. Kraft and B. Roberts, eds., *Wage and Price Controls: The U.S. Experiment* (New York: Praeger Publishers, 1975), pp. 36-69.

year contracts, as compared to what happened in the late 1960s. In some situations, where there were no escalator provisions or only limited payoffs under escalator formulas, relative wage positions have, of course, declined. But since 1971 large first-year increases under heavily front-loaded agreements have been less frequently required to compensate for increases during the term of expiring contracts smaller than those received on average by other workers. Even though first-year wage increases under major collective bargaining agreements in 1974–1975 have been in a range similar to those in 1969–1971, wage increases over the term of expiring contracts have been significantly larger, and in many instances cost-of-living escalator payments have been received throughout the term of expiring contracts (see Table 6).

The structure of relative wages has been closely related to what has happened under major collective bargaining agreements. Since 1973 wage increases under major agreements, including portions of wage increases attributable to escalator provisions, have been a significant factor maintaining (and in some cases increasing) wage differentials. Both the coverage of major agreements and the presence of escalator provisions are disproportionately concentrated in relatively high-wage sectors of the economy (see Tables 9 and 10). These circumstances operated to raise dispersion in relative wages outside the construction sector and produce wider differentials in 1975 than in 1969–1970. Against this background, a reduction in the average rate of wage increase will need to be accompanied by slower wage increases in the relatively high-wage sectors (including many in which collective bargaining is the predominant influence) unless wage differentials are to widen further. Moreover, 1975 wage differentials were already relatively wide by historical standards, although not wider than has been the case during periods of persistently high unemployment.

Up to this point developments in the construction sector have by and large been excluded from the discussion of union wage increases and relative wage dispersion. Construction wage developments in 1974–1975, however, differed substantially from construction wage developments in the late 1960s. Before 1971, large construction wage increases and the high relative wages that emerged were widely regarded as giving rise to spillover effects for wages in other sectors. But construction wages have recently increased at rates below the average for other wages, and this decline in relative wages in construction can be expected to limit upward wage structural pressures from this source. Thus, while wage trends in many of the

Table 9
UNION MEMBERSHIP AND WORKERS COVERED BY MAJOR AGREEMENTS AND ESCALATOR PROVISIONS IN THE PRIVATE NONFARM SECTOR
(percentage)

	Ratio of Number of Union Members to Number of Production and Nonsupervisory Employees (1972)[a]	Ratio of Number of Workers Covered by Major Collective Bargaining Agreements to Number of Production and Non-supervisory Employees (1974)	
		All workers under major agreements	Workers under major agreements with escalators
Total, private nonfarm	37.3	20.4	11.8
Quartiles of private nonfarm distribution			
I Highest ($4.92–$7.17)	81.4	54.7	36.4
II Upper middle ($3.91–$4.92)	47.4	19.3	10.9
III Lower middle ($3.74–$3.91)	19.9	2.7	0.9
IV Lowest ($2.33–$3.74)	14.7	13.6	4.7
Construction	94.6	51.7	5.3
Private nonfarm, excluding construction	33.7	18.2	12.3
Quartiles of private nonfarm distribution excluding construction			
I Highest ($4.59–$6.24)	73.3	48.2	41.4
II Upper middle ($3.81–$4.59)	45.4	17.6	9.9
III Lower middle ($3.74–$3.81)	19.9	2.8	0.9
IV Lowest ($2.33–$3.74)	14.7	13.6	4.7

Note: Quartiles were derived by ranking average hourly earnings levels for forty-three industry sectors and applying the 1967 weights that are used in constructing the private nonfarm average hourly earnings index.

[a] A similar method of ranking was used in establishing quartiles for union membership, but rankings were based on slightly different levels of aggregation.

Sources: For union membership, *Directory of National Unions and Employee Associations* (Washington, D.C.: Bureau of Labor Statistics, 1973), p. 80. For workers under major agreements and for workers under major agreements with escalators, Peter Kuhmerker, "Scheduled Wage Increases and Escalator Provisions in 1976," *Monthly Labor Review,* vol. 99, no. 1 (January 1976), p. 44. For the number of production and nonsupervisory employees, *Employment and Earnings,* February 1975.

relatively high wage sectors—sectors in which major union agreements with escalator provisions are heavily concentrated—may operate through wage-structural linkages to retard and limit a reduction in the average rate of wage increase, this influence may be

Table 10
THE DISTRIBUTION OF WORKERS COVERED BY MAJOR AGREEMENTS AND ESCALATOR PROVISIONS BY QUARTILES OF PRIVATE NONFARM AVERAGE HOURLY EARNINGS
(percentage)

	Distribution of Workers under Major Collective Bargaining Agreements	Distribution of Workers under Major Collective Agreements with Cost-of-Living Escalator Provisions	Fraction of Workers under Major Collective Bargaining Agreements with Cost-of-Living Escalator Provisions
Total, private nonfarm	100.0	100.0	58.1
Quartiles of private nonfarm distribution			
I Highest ($4.92–$7.17)	60.1	68.8	66.5
II Upper middle ($3.91–$4.92)	20.6	19.9	56.1
III Lower middle ($3.74–$3.91)	4.5	2.6	33.2
IV Lowest ($2.33–$3.74)	14.7	8.7	34.3
Construction	—	—	10.3
Private nonfarm, excluding construction	100.0	100.0	67.6
Quartiles of private nonfarm distribution, excluding construction			
I Highest ($4.59–$6.24)	55.5	70.4	85.8
II Upper middle ($3.81–$4.59)	21.8	18.1	56.2
III Lower middle ($3.74–$3.81)	5.0	1.7	33.6
IV Lowest ($2.33–$3.74)	17.6	9.0	34.1

Note: Quartiles were derived by ranking average hourly earnings levels for 43 industry sectors and applying the 1967 weights that are used in constructing the private nonfarm average hourly earnings index.
Source: Kuhmerker, "Scheduled Wage Increases and Escalator Provisions in 1976," p. 44.

somewhat offset by the recent tendency for the high relative wages in construction to subside.

Implications. The rate of increase in wages and hourly labor costs is closely linked (with a margin of flexibility related to short-term developments) to the rate of inflation sustainable over the longer term. Rates of wage increase, particularly in recent years, have shown a considerable degree of stability over short periods of time, and adjustments to new rates of increase have proceeded more gradually for wages than for prices. Both economic and institutional factors are at work in this adjustment process, and the relative importance of particular forces differs with changes in circumstances.

One current element of major significance in the labor market is the widespread use of cost-of-living escalators in collective bargaining agreements. The prevalence of escalator provisions contributes toward mitigating pressure for large newly negotiated wage increases to "catch up" for developments in the past, and slower price increases are translated relatively promptly into slower wage increases. However, the operation of escalator provisions in multi-year agreements also produces moving targets for wage comparisons that will influence the terms of new wage settlements and other wage adjustments. The sensitivity of wage increases to price increases (a sensitivity increased by cost-of-living escalator provisions) strengthens the link between currently realized inflation and the conditions it creates for inflation in the future.

The close linkage of wage increases in major sectors of the economy with consumer price increases (operating through a series of agreements with overlapping durations and staggered expiration dates) sets a pattern in which wage increases tend to be diffused through the labor market as a result of wage comparisons. Since the influence of collective bargaining agreements with escalators is concentrated in high-wage sectors of the economy, slower average wage increases than those produced by strong escalator provisions in multi-year agreements can occur only in conjunction with a widening of wage differentials (even if only a temporary one). Moreover, any tendency for acceleration in the rate of consumer price inflation must intensify pressures in the labor market for higher average wage increases or wider differentials in relative wages.

Current labor market conditions give rise to a situation in which the influence of changes in consumer price inflation on wage rates can be expected to be relatively prompt and quite pervasive. These circumstances strengthen the influence of a reduction in inflation on labor cost stability at the same time as they raise the risk that an increase in inflation will lead to adverse changes in conditions for stability. Policies that lead to stable or lower consumer price inflation will have a favorable secondary influence on labor cost trends. On the other hand, policies that lead to higher inflation will set in motion a process through which this higher inflation will be quickly translated into unfavorable labor cost and price prospects. Any significant rise in the rate of wage increase in high-wage sectors of the economy (in the context of the current pattern of wage differentials) is likely to give rise to a tendency for larger wage increases to spread throughout the economy as a result of pressures from wage comparisons.

The increased sensitivity of overall wage trends to actual price behavior has come about, in part, through institutional adaptation to the experience of high and variable inflation. The rise in the probability that higher realized inflation will create conditions encouraging higher subsequent inflation has raised the risk of policies that could result in even a temporary rise in inflation. Consequently, during the current recovery, it would seem appropriate to have more cautious demand-management policies than those that might have been defended in earlier periods of cyclical recovery—unless decreased importance is attached to a durable move toward regaining price level stability.

EMPLOYMENT, UNEMPLOYMENT, AND THE INFLATION-RECESSION DILEMMA

Geoffrey H. Moore

Summary

An alternative way of viewing the unemployment/inflation trade-off yields more sensible and more decisive results than the customary way. It uses the ratio of employment to population of working age, instead of the unemployment rate, as the variable that measures the utilization of the potential labor force. This measure avoids the problem of variation in labor force participation rates, which to some degree respond to conditions of demand. It avoids the problem of discouraged workers who are not counted as unemployed because they are not seeking work, even though they "want" work in some sense; obviously they are not employed. It avoids such definitional problems as the degree to which a person must actively be seeking work to be considered unemployed or whether he has realistic ideas about his employability, wage aspirations, and so on.

The record for the postwar period shows a fairly close relationship between movements in the employment/population ratio and in the rate of wage or price inflation. This is not the case with the unemployment rate, at least in its raw form. It appears that one of the factors explaining the persistence of inflation during the 1973–1975 recession, despite the high unemployment rate, was that the percentage of persons employed held up relatively well, and that provided support for wage income and consumer demand. In this regard the moderate decline in the inflation rate since 1974 was about in line with previous experience.

The implication is that policy makers and others concerned about the state of the labor market and its bearing on wage and price inflation should pay closer attention than they have to the percentage of the population employed. Wider reporting of this statistic on a current basis, along with the reporting of the unemployment rate and other labor market information, would make it easier for it to be given that closer attention.

Employment and Unemployment during Recession

One of the clichés of the times is that the 1973–1975 recession was the longest and deepest since the Great Depression of the 1930s. Such an appraisal is commonly based on the fact that the unemployment rate averaged 8.5 percent during 1975, higher than in any year since 1941. But the employment ratio, which is the percentage of the population employed, gives a contradictory verdict. In so doing, it may help solve an economic puzzle—why, in the face of this "worst recession," wages and prices have continued to advance at near-record rates.

Admittedly, history will probably continue to record the 1973–1975 recession as the worst since the 1930s, particularly since it was worldwide. Yet in several significant respects it was in the same family with the three recessions that occurred in the United States between 1948 and 1958, and not at all in a class with the Great Depression. For example, the decline in nonfarm employment lasted nine months (September 1974 to June 1975) and came to 3 percent, compared to declines of fourteen months and 4 percent in 1957–1958; sixteen months and 3 percent in 1953–1954; and thirteen months and 4 percent in 1948–1949. In 1929–1933 the drop in nonfarm employment lasted forty-three months and reached 32 percent. Industrial production fell 13 percent in 1973–1975, 12 percent in 1957–1958, but 53 percent in 1929–1932. Real gross national product dropped nearly 7 percent in 1973–1975, 4 percent in 1957–1958, but 33 percent in 1929–1932.[1]

A large part of the reduction in output in 1973–1975 was attributable to a reduction in inventory investment, which was what happened in the earlier postwar recessions but not in 1929–1932. This

[1] In general, measures of activity obtained by deflating dollar values by price indices (such as real GNP) showed 1973-1975 declines sharper in relation to those in previous recessions than did measures of activity expressed in physical units (such as man-hours, units sold, and so on). Hence it is possible that the deflation procedure, which is especially hazardous when prices are rising rapidly and forcing extensive adjustments in spending habits, contract terms, and accounting procedures, has exaggerated the recent declines in the deflated (constant dollar) aggregates of sales, output, inventories, and incomes.

MOORE ON EMPLOYMENT AND UNEMPLOYMENT

probably contributed to the brevity of the decline in employment, since inventory movements are usually quickly reversed and do not have the longer-run implications of a decline in basic demand. The pecuniary volume of business scarcely declined at all in 1973–1975, nor did personal income, whereas they declined slightly in the earlier postwar recessions and dramatically in 1929–1932.

The unemployment rate and the employment ratio for the low years of each of the six recessions since 1949 are given in Table 1. According to the unemployment rate, the latest recession was by far the worst. According to the percentage of the population that continued to be employed, it was next to the mildest. Which of these characterizations is more accurate can be a matter of argument, but there is no question that they are different.

The two measures give more nearly similar verdicts when the lows are compared with the previous highs. The rise in unemployment in the first three recessions was larger than in the next two, and the decline in the employment ratio also was larger in the first three than in the next two. Moreover, the rise in unemployment and the decline in the employment ratio both were larger in the 1975 recession than in any of the previous five. This measurement of the severity of recession depends, of course, partly on the degree to which the economy enjoyed full employment when the recession began,

Table 1
EMPLOYMENT AND UNEMPLOYMENT IN RECESSION YEARS, 1949–1975
(percentages)

Business Cycle Low (1)	Unemployment Rate (2)	Employment Ratio (3)
1949	5.9	54.6
1954	5.5	53.8
1958	6.8	54.2
1961	6.7	54.2
1970	4.9	56.1
1975	8.5	55.3

Sources: Column (1) Business cycle trough years, National Bureau of Economic Research, Inc.; column (2) Unemployment as percentage of civilian labor force, U.S. Bureau of Labor Statistics; and column (3) Civilian employment as percentage of population sixteen years old and over, U.S. Bureau of Labor Statistics.

and not only on the amount of slack there was when the economy hit bottom. Nevertheless, even by this measure, the unemployment rate puts the 1975 recession well in front of the others, whereas the employment ratio does not. According to the decline in the employment ratio, the 1973–1975 recession barely exceeded the worst of the earlier postwar recessions; according to the rise in the unemployment rate, it was much worse.

The Inflation Trade-off

These alternative ways of looking at the employment situation are of more than academic concern. Not only do they tell us how people are faring in the job market, but also they have a bearing on the way we interpret the inflation that has accompanied the recession. If the percentage of the population employed is high, the total earnings of the population are likely to be higher than would otherwise be the case, and the same holds true for spending capacity. Under these circumstances, wage rates and prices are likely to remain higher than they otherwise would. If the unemployment rate is high, on the other hand, one might expect the opposite conditions: greater downward pressure on wages because of the large numbers seeking work, and hence lower cost-pressure on prices. Both propositions must of course be qualified because many other factors besides employment and unemployment influence wages and prices. Moreover, the propositions do not tell what we should expect if employment and unemployment are *both* at relatively high levels.

In 1975, in fact, we had both a high unemployment rate and a moderately high employment ratio. The employment ratio seems more consistent with the inflationary conditions that existed than does the unemployment rate. Neither the rate nor the ratio can explain the whole situation, but the employment ratio does give a clue, which the unemployment rate alone does not, to determining why inflation persisted in 1975. Unemployment was a serious problem, but at the same time a relatively high percentage of the population continued to be employed, and the fact that they were employed helped to sustain demand, wages, and prices. If we ignore this fact, and thereby treat employment and unemployment merely as opposite sides of the same coin, we may overlook one of the factors that can help explain the current dilemma of high unemployment and persistent inflation.

This dilemma has been growing more and more serious since World War II. Although reductions in the rate of inflation have continued to accompany recessions (sometimes with a short lag), each succeeding recession (with a partial exception in 1961) has left the rate of inflation in both prices and wages higher than it was left by the recession before. As Table 2 shows, the steady upward progression in the rate of increase in hourly compensation, from less than 1 percent at the trough of the 1949 recession to nearly 8 percent at the trough of the 1975 recession, has been matched by a similar progression in the rate of increase in consumer prices.

If the figures on prices and wages in Table 2 are compared with those on employment and unemployment in Table 1, one can see why it is important to look at both measures. If the unemployment rate is taken as the measure of slack in the economy at business cycle lows, one would have to say it bears virtually no relation to the rate of increase in either prices or wages. If, on the other hand, the employment ratio is taken as the measure of the degree to which there is full employment in the economy, the figures fall more nearly into place. The high rates of price and wage inflation in 1970 and 1975 correspond with relatively high employment ratios.

Data for years other than the six recession years covered in these tables support these results (see Figures 1 and 2). The two diagrams on the left hand side of each figure relate unemployment to wage changes (Figure 1) and to price changes (Figure 2). The two

Table 2

PRICES AND WAGES IN RECESSION YEARS, 1949–1975

(percentages)

Business Cycle Low (1)	Rate of Change in:	
	Consumer prices (2)	Hourly compensation (3)
1949	−1.8	0.6
1954	−0.5	3.1
1958	1.8	3.5
1961	0.7	4.3
1970	5.5	6.3
1975	7.0	7.7

Sources: Column (1) Business cycle trough years, National Bureau of Economic Research, Inc.; column (2) Percentage change in consumer price index, December of preceding year to December of current year, U.S. Bureau of Labor Statistics; column (3) Percentage change in average hourly compensation, fourth quarter of preceding year to fourth quarter of current year, private nonfarm sector, U.S. Bureau of Labor Statistics.

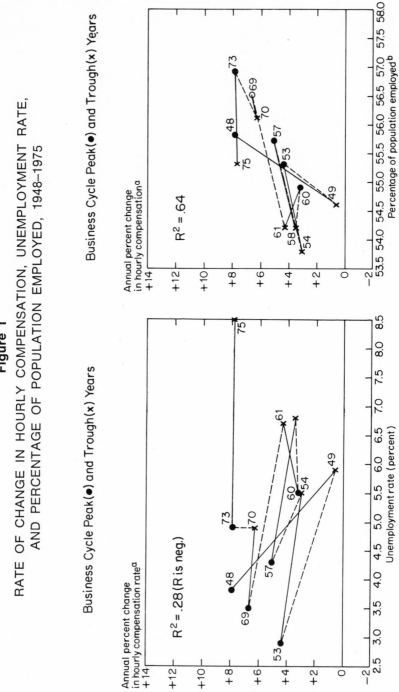

Figure 1

RATE OF CHANGE IN HOURLY COMPENSATION, UNEMPLOYMENT RATE, AND PERCENTAGE OF POPULATION EMPLOYED, 1948–1975

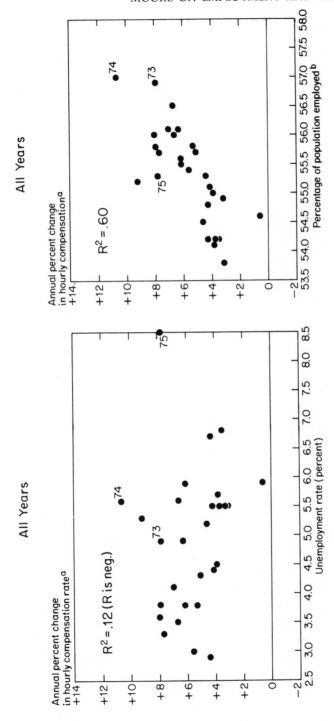

Note: The correlation (R^2) is based on data ending with 1974.
[a] Fourth quarter of preceding year to fourth quarter of current year, private nonfarm sector.
[b] Civilian employment as percent of noninstitutional population sixteen years of age and over.
Source: Table 5.

Figure 2

RATE OF CHANGE IN CONSUMER PRICE INDEX, UNEMPLOYMENT RATE,
AND PERCENTAGE OF POPULATION EMPLOYED, 1948–1975

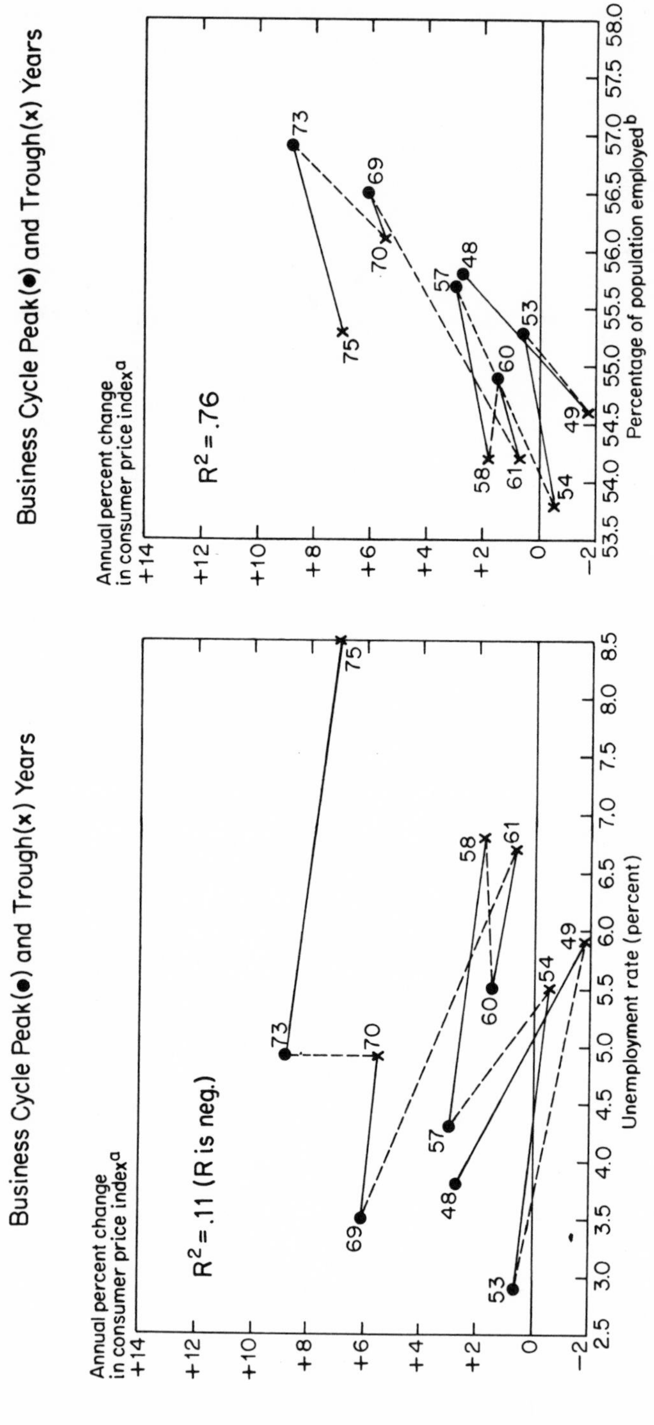

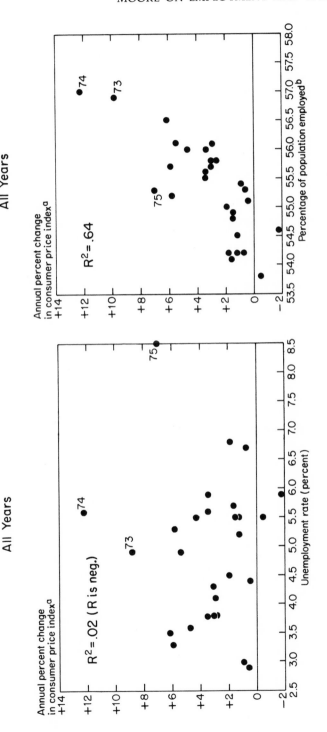

All Years

All Years

Note: The correlation (R^2) is based on data ending with 1974.
[a] December of preceding year to December of current year.
[b] Civilian employment as percent of noninstitutional population sixteen years of age and over.
Source: Table 5.

on the right relate the employment ratio to the same wage and price data. One would expect diagrams using unemployment to show a scatter of points sloping downward to the right, in accordance with the so-called Phillips curve. It takes a close look to find any trace of this, though most of the lines connecting the peaks and troughs of the business cycles do slope downward. On the other hand, the diagrams using the employment ratio show a much tighter relationship, with the scatter of points clearly sloping upward to the right. The correlation coefficients, which are nearly zero for unemployment but moderately high for employment, confirm this impression. (For further discussion, see Technical Note 1.)

Another way to depict the relation between employment, unemployment, and the rate of inflation is shown in Figure 3. The employment ratio and the rate of change in the consumer price index have followed nearly parallel courses. The unemployment rate (plotted on an inverted scale) has deviated from both, notably in the early 1950s and again in recent years. Especially noteworthy is the moderate decline in the employment ratio during the recent recession and the similarly moderate decline in the rate of inflation, in sharp contrast with what was happening to the unemployment rate.

One cannot deduce cause and effect from these or any other sets of numbers: they merely make one or another hypothesis more or less plausible. In this instance, since alternative measures of slack in the economy behave quite differently, and one (the employment ratio) bears a plausible and fairly consistent relationship to rates of price and wage inflation while the other (the unemployment rate) does not, we would be well advised to reconsider our hypotheses about the way slack in the economy affects the rate of inflation. The employment ratio shows that sometimes there may be less slack than would meet the eye of one who looks only at the unemployment rate.

This is indeed the case during the present recovery, which at present writing (May 1976) is about one year old. The unemployment rate in April 1976 was 7.5 percent. By historical standards, such a rate suggests an enormous amount of slack in the economy, more than in any previous postwar recession year except 1975. It is more than one and a half times as high as the average unemployment rate during 1948–1974, which was 4.8 percent. The employment ratio, on the other hand, was 56.2 percent in April 1976. It is well above the average ratio for 1948–1974, which was 55.3 percent. It is also well above the level of any postwar recession year, and indeed higher than in four of the six peak years in the business cycle (1948, 1953, 1957, and 1960). The economy, after a year of recovery, is providing

Figure 3
UNEMPLOYMENT RATE, EMPLOYMENT RATIO, AND THE RATE OF CHANGE IN THE CONSUMER PRICE INDEX, 1948–1976

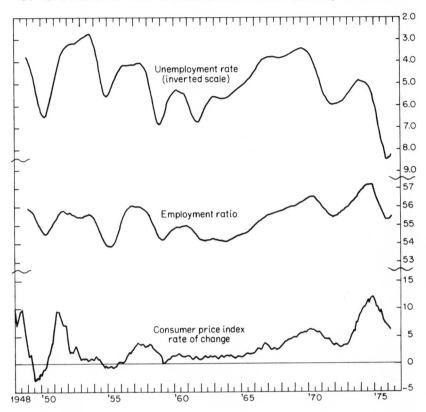

Note: The unemployment rate and employment ratio are twelve-month moving averages; the rate of change in the consumer price index is the percent change over twelve months. All series are plotted at end of the twelve-month period.
Source: U.S. Bureau of Labor Statistics. For annual data see Table 5.

employment for a relatively large fraction of the population of working age, though many are still seeking work. Under these conditions, judging from past experience, we should not find it surprising that the pace of wage and price inflation is still a worrisome problem.

Nature of the Employment Ratio

The employment ratio used in this paper is not the only available measure of employment, nor even the only employment ratio. It takes the total population sixteen years of age and over as the potential labor supply, ignoring the fact that there are many in the population who—because of age, illness, affluence, or preoccupation with other duties—are not likely to become employed under any circumstances. It does not count those who are in the armed forces as employed, but does count them in the population. By using "civilian employment" in the numerator it conforms to customary usage in reports of the number employed. By using total population in the denominator it makes a simple allowance for the trend in the population of the country or, more specifically, the trend in the number of persons (apart from children under sixteen) who are largely supported by those who are employed. Since the size of the armed forces is subject to noneconomic considerations, the alternative treatments (either adding the armed forces to the employed or subtracting them from the population) do not seem to yield as satisfactory a ratio for economic analysis as the one adopted, though opinions may differ on this point. (For further discussion, see Technical Note 2.)

The employment ratio avoids some of the definitional questions that beset measures of unemployment. For example, the so-called "discouraged worker," who is not counted as unemployed because he is not seeking work, even though he wants work, is obviously not counted as employed. Young people whose principal activity is going to school, but who are counted as unemployed if they are seeking part-time work, are not counted as employed unless they actually have a job. Unlike the unemployment rate, the employment ratio does not depend implicitly on the degree to which a person must actively seek work to be considered unemployed nor does it depend on whether his ideas are realistic or unrealistic as to employability, earning capacity, the suitability of working conditions, and so on. If he does not have a job, he is not counted as employed. Hence it is both a more objective and a more neutral measure (as well as being, one hopes, less controversial) than the unemployment rate. For example, when the definitions of employment and unemployment were revised in 1967 in response to the recommendations of the Gordon Committee (which in turn arose out of a controversy regarding the measurement of unemployment), the revisions altered the unemployment count in 1966 by 3.4 percent but altered the employment count by only 0.06 percent.[2]

---

[2] See Robert L. Stein, "New Definitions for Employment and Unemployment," *Employment and Earnings and Monthly Report on the Labor Force*, U.S. Bureau of Labor Statistics, February 1967, Table 1.

If the employment ratio is to receive due attention, however, it must be reported promptly and prominently, together with other statistics on the employment situation. At present, it is not so reported. The Bureau of Labor Statistics does not refer to it in its monthly press release, though it does report both the numerator and the denominator. The bureau does show an employment ratio (the ratio of civilian employment to civilian population) in its monthly *Chartbook on Prices, Wages and Productivity* and in its monthly *Employment and Earnings*. Although such notices are helpful, they are not likely to receive much public attention, because they do not appear as promptly as the figures in the monthly press releases.[3]

Implications

The principal implication of the findings described above is that, in the conduct of economic policy, careful attention should be paid to the level and change in the percentage of the population employed. This is not to say that unemployment should be ignored. It is simply to say that evaluations of the labor market based upon employment data are not always consistent with those based upon unemployment data and it is therefore essential for us to analyze the difference and its implications for wage and price trends.

A high level of unemployment not accompanied by a low level of employment (relative to population) may not imply a deficiency of demand. It may, on the contrary, imply that large numbers of workers are seeking jobs, or seeking to change jobs, because employment opportunities are plentiful. The existence of numerous vacancies, satisfactory wage levels, and good working conditions induce persons to seek jobs, or to leave jobs they have in order to search for better ones, or to take more time than they might otherwise take to find the best job they can. For example, many persons, particularly married women with small children, and young people who are attending school, can accept only part-time employment. The fact that there are many more part-time jobs available today than there were twenty or thirty years ago, partly because of the growth of service industries, induces many to enter the labor force who would not otherwise have done so. Initially, they are likely to be counted as unemployed. Such changes in both supply and demand have tended to raise the unem-

---

[3] A useful analysis of the employment ratio in comparison with the unemployment rate and related measures is Julius Shiskin (commissioner of labor statistics), "Employment and Unemployment: the Doughnut or the Hole?" *Monthly Labor Review*, vol. 99, no. 2 (February 1976).

ployment rate, but they are not a symptom of inadequate demand and they do not necessarily call for measures to stimulate demand. More appropriate policies in such instances may be those that help to place people in jobs or to train them for jobs that are available, or those that improve productivity and reduce costs, increasing incentives to employ people without at the same time putting upward pressure on prices. By means of such policies the employment ratio may be raised and unemployment reduced without the usual inflationary consequences.

Technical Note 1: Long-run Changes in Employment, Unemployment, and Inflation Rates

In the unemployment diagrams (left hand panels of Figures 1 and 2), there is clear evidence that the unemployment rate associated with a given rate of wage or price inflation has become higher in recent years than it was formerly. This is one way of accounting for the apparent lack of association between the two: the Phillips curve has shifted to the right. This means, of course, that some factor has caused the unemployment rate to drift *upward* relative to the rate of wage or price change. The employment ratio diagrams (right hand panels of Figures 1 and 2) show some evidence of a similar shift, but to the left. This shift is much less pronounced than for unemployment, but insofar as it is present it means that some factor has caused the employment ratio to drift *downward* relative to the rate of wage or price change.[4]

The employment ratio has tended to drift downward because of the declining proportion of adult men in the population and the rising proportion of adult women and teenagers. Since the adult men have

---

[4] Linear regressions fitted to the annual data used in the charts, 1948-1974, show that a time trend (T) has a significant positive influence on the relationships with the unemployment rate (UR), and a positive but not significant influence on those with the employment ratio (E/P):

$$\Delta HC = \quad 1.11 \; - \; 0.52 \, UR \; + \; 0.11 \, T \quad R^2 \; = \; .25$$
$$\qquad\qquad (0.38) \, (-1.61) \qquad (2.57)$$

$$\Delta CPI = \quad -7.33 \; - \; 0.62 \, UR \; + \; 0.22 \, T \quad R^2 \; = \; .35$$
$$\qquad\qquad (-1.81) \, (-1.36) \qquad (3.51)$$

$$\Delta HC = \quad -86.57 \; + \; 1.64 \, E/P \; + \; 0.02 \, T \quad R^2 \; = \; .58$$
$$\qquad\qquad (-4.87) \quad (4.87) \qquad (0.60)$$

$$\Delta CPI = \quad -134.35 \; + \; 2.39 \, E/P \; + \; 0.09 \, T \quad R^2 \; = \; .68$$
$$\qquad\qquad (-5.73) \quad (5.37) \qquad (1.84)$$

The unemployment rate is not significant in either equation though it has the appropriate sign; the employment ratio is significant in both equations.

much higher employment ratios than either adult women or teen-agers, a decline in their relative numbers tends to reduce the overall employment ratio. For example, between 1948 and 1973 (both prosperous years in the business cycle), the proportion of adult males in the working age population fell from 45 percent to 42 percent, while adult women and teenagers rose from 55 to 58 percent (see Table 3). The percentage of adult males employed in 1948 was 84 compared to 33 for adult women and teenagers; by 1973 the former had dropped to 76, and the latter had risen to 43. As a net result of these offsetting changes the overall employment ratio rose from 56 to 57 percent, but other things equal it would have risen to 58 percent had the composition of the population remained the same. The shift in composition caused a downtrend of one percentage point in twenty-five years. This factor, incidentally, cannot bear any respon-sibility for the positive correlation between the employment ratio and the rate of inflation, since the latter has moved *upward* over the years.

The unemployment rate was affected not only by these demo-graphic changes but also by the changing propensity of different groups to enter or leave the labor force. Adult men comprised 67 percent of the labor force in 1948, but only 56 percent in 1973; adult women and teenagers, entering the labor force in large num-bers, increased from 33 to 44 percent. These were much larger shifts than those in the population and they had a substantial effect on the overall unemployment rate, which rose from 3.8 to 4.9 percent from 1948 to 1973. Without the shift in labor force composition the rate would have risen only half as much, to 4.4 percent. The higher unemployment rates for adult women and teenagers (4.9 percent in 1948 and 6.9 percent in 1973) than for adult men (3.2 percent in both years), coupled with their sharp rise in the labor force, added about half a percentage point to the unemployment rate over the twenty-five-year period. This was a much bigger proportionate shift than in the employment ratio, since the unemployment rate is a much smaller figure.

This points to one of the merits of an unemployment *ratio* (unemployment as a percentage of population of working age) as compared with the unemployment *rate* (unemployment as a per-centage of labor force): the population is less affected than is the labor force by changes in age-sex composition. Short-run as well as long-run changes in labor force participation affect the behavior of the unemployment rate. In the population the long-run changes dominate; they are generally smaller than in the labor force; and some of them

Table 3
EMPLOYMENT AND UNEMPLOYMENT, 1948 AND 1973

	Noninstitutional Population, Sixteen and Over		Civilian Employment		Unemployment		Civilian Labor Force		Armed Forces		Not in Labor Force	
	1948	1973	1948	1973	1948	1973	1948	1973	1948	1973	1948	1973
	Number (in thousands)											
Males, 20 and over	46,958	62,843	39,382	47,946	1,305	1,594	40,686	49,539	1,041	1,901	5,231	11,404
Females, 20 and over	48,716	69,289	14,937	29,228	564	1,485	15,500	30,713	16	40	33,200	38,536
Teenagers, 16–19	8,853	16,130	4,028	7,236	407	1,226	4,435	8,461	402	386	4,016	7,283
Total	104,527	148,263	58,344	84,409	2,276	4,304	60,621	88,714	1,459	2,326	42,447	57,223
	Percent of total											
Males, 20 and over	44.9	42.4	67.5	56.8	57.3	37.0	67.1	55.8	71.3	81.7	12.3	19.9
Females, 20 and over	46.6	46.7	25.6	34.6	24.8	34.5	25.6	34.6	1.1	1.7	78.2	67.3
Teenagers, 16–19	8.5	10.9	6.9	8.6	17.9	28.5	7.3	9.5	27.6	16.6	9.5	12.7
Total	100.0	100.0	100.0	100.0	100.0	100.0	100.0	100.0	100.0	100.0	100.0	100.0
	Percent of noninstitutional population											
Males, 20 and over	100.0	100.0	83.9	76.3	2.8	2.5	86.6	78.8	2.2	3.0	11.1	18.1
Females, 20 and over	100.0	100.0	30.7	42.2	1.2	2.1	31.8	44.3	0.0	0.1	68.2	55.6
Teenagers, 16–19	100.0	100.0	45.5	44.9	4.6	7.6	50.1	52.5	4.5	2.4	45.4	45.2
Total	100.0	100.0	55.8	56.9	2.2	2.9	58.0	59.8	1.4	1.6	40.6	38.6

Note: The unemployment *rates* (percent of civilian labor force), 1948 and 1973, are: total, 3.8, 4.9; males, twenty and older 3.2, 3.2; females, twenty and older, 3.6, 4.8; teenagers, 9.2, 14.5.

Source: U.S. Bureau of Labor Statistics.

are predictable. Some consideration might well be given, therefore, to more extensive use of the unemployment ratio (see also Technical Note 2, below).

Technical Note 2: Correlation Analysis of Employment, Unemployment, and Inflation Rates

Some of the factors underlying the fact that the employment ratio is more closely associated with inflation rates than is the unemployment rate are illuminated by a correlation analysis involving both measures.

The total population aged sixteen and over can be divided into the following groups: (1) civilian employed, (2) armed forces, (3) unemployed, and (4) not in the labor force. If we divide each of these by the population sixteen and over and multiply by 100, the four ratios, which we designate E/P, A/P, U/P and NL/P, add to 100. The employment ratio, E/P, is equal to 100 minus $(A/P + U/P + NL/P)$. When the rate of change in prices or wages is regressed upon these variables, we can determine what each contributes to the result.

The simple correlation matrix, based upon annual data, 1948–1974, is given in Table 4.

From this we learn that the employment ratio is more highly correlated with the rate of change in consumer prices or hourly

Table 4

CORRELATION MATRIX

	$\triangle CPI$	$\triangle HC$	E/P	A/P	U/P	NL/P
Consumer price index $(\triangle CPI)$[a]	+1.0					
Hourly compensation $(\triangle HC)$[b]	+0.8	+1.0				
Employment ratio (E/P)	+0.8	+0.8	+1.0			
Armed forces ratio (A/P)	−0.3	−0.2	−0.2	+1.0		
Unemployment ratio (U/P)	−0.1	−0.3	−0.4	−0.6	+1.0	
Not-in-labor-force ratio (NL/P)	−0.7	−0.6	−0.8	0.0	0.0	+1.0

[a] Percent change from December to December.
[b] Percent change from fourth quarter to fourth quarter.

compensation than are any of the other ratios. The armed forces ratio has a slight *inverse* correlation with the price and wage variables. The unemployment ratio is slightly correlated inversely with the price and wage variables.[5] The not-in-the-labor-force ratio has a substantial *inverse* correlation with the price and wage variables. In terms of these simple correlations, therefore, it appears that the ratios involving the armed forces, unemployed, and those not in the labor force belong together in that each appears to be (if anything) inversely correlated with the rates of change in prices and wages.

This is confirmed by multiple regressions using the three variables simultaneously (fitted to annual data, 1948–1974):

$$\Delta HC = \begin{array}{cccc} 88.17 & - & 2.28 \, A/P & - & 2.05 \, U/P & - & 1.81 \, NL/P \\ (5.04) & & (3.59) & & (4.04) & & (4.11) \end{array}$$
$$R^2 = .62 \qquad (1)$$

$$\Delta CPI = \begin{array}{cccc} 143.51 & - & 2.98 \, A/P & - & 1.66 \, U/P & - & 3.39 \, NL/P \\ (7.11) & & (3.92) & & (2.75) & & (6.43) \end{array}$$
$$R^2 = .73 \qquad (2)$$

The regression coefficients are all negative and statistically significant. The regressions were also computed with a time trend variable, but the time trend variable was not significant. Since the regression coefficients are substantially similar in magnitude, the multiple correlations are not greatly different from those obtained from the employment ratio alone:

$$\Delta HC = \begin{array}{cc} -100.77 & + & 1.92 \, E/L \\ (5.78) & & (6.09) \end{array} \qquad R^2 = .60 \qquad (3)$$

$$\Delta CPI = \begin{array}{cc} -149.89 & + & 2.76 \, E/L \\ (6.45) & & (6.58) \end{array} \qquad R^2 = .63 \qquad (4)$$

The multiple regressions indicate that the reason the employment ratio is more highly correlated with price and wage changes than is the unemployment rate is that the employment ratio implicitly takes account of two other factors that contribute to the relationship, these being the percentage of the population not in the labor force and the percentage in the armed forces. The influence of the not-in-the-labor-force ratio is, on the whole, more powerful than that of the unemployment ratio, as the following regressions testify:

---

[5] The unemployment ratio differs from the unemployment rate in that the latter uses labor force (employment plus unemployment) as the denominator rather than population. Nevertheless, the ratio and the rate are highly correlated because of the dominant influence of the numerator upon their fluctuations.

$$\Delta HC = \underset{(3.95)}{84.24} - \underset{(2.00)}{1.02\ U/P} - \underset{(3.56)}{1.92\ NL/P} \qquad R^2 = .41 \qquad (5)$$

$$\Delta CPI = \underset{(5.44)}{143.38} - \underset{(0.51)}{0.32\ U/P} - \underset{(5.29)}{3.52\ NL/P} \qquad R^2 = .54 \qquad (6)$$

The armed forces ratio contributes significantly (and inversely) to the correlation, when treated as one of the three sectors outside civilian employment, as is shown by a comparison of equations (5) and (6) with (1) and (2). On the other hand, treating the armed forces as a sector to be included with civilian employment does not significantly improve the correlation, as the following regressions show:

$$\Delta HC = \underset{(5.34)}{-98.22} + \underset{(5.76)}{1.89\ E/P} - \underset{(0.51)}{0.27\ A/P} \qquad R^2 = .60 \qquad (7)$$

$$\Delta CPI = \underset{(5.96)}{-140.06} + \underset{(6.29)}{2.63\ C/P} - \underset{(1.54)}{1.07\ A/P} \qquad R^2 = .67 \qquad (8)$$

The persistence of the negative sign on the armed forces ratio is puzzling, and it is not clear what the reason for it may be. But it does suggest that nothing is to be gained in interpreting price and wage behavior by using an employment ratio defined to include the armed forces, which of course would then be counted *positively*. Similarly, from this point of view, nothing is to be gained by using an employment ratio defined to exclude the armed forces from the population, since this also would have the opposite effect to what the regressions suggest (compare columns 3 and 4 of Table 5).

Table 5
ANNUAL DATA ON EMPLOYMENT, UNEMPLOYMENT
AND INFLATION RATES, 1948–1975
(percentages)

Year	E/P (1)	A/P (2)	E+A P (3)	E P−A (4)	U/P (5)	UR (6)	NL/P (7)	ΔCPI (8)	ΔHC (9)
1948	55.8	1.4	57.2	56.6	2.2	3.8	40.6	2.7	7.9
1949	54.6	1.5	56.1	55.4	3.4	5.9	40.4	−1.8	0.6
1950	55.2	1.5	56.8	56.1	3.1	5.3	40.1	5.8	9.2
1951	55.7	2.9	58.5	57.3	1.9	3.3	39.6	5.9	7.7
1952	55.4	3.3	58.7	57.3	1.7	3.0	39.6	0.9	5.6
1953	55.3	3.2	58.5	57.1	1.7	2.9	39.8	0.6	4.4
1954	53.8	3.0	56.8	55.5	3.2	5.5	40.0	−0.5	3.1
1955	55.1	2.7	57.9	56.7	2.5	4.4	39.6	0.4	4.1
1956	56.1	2.5	58.6	57.5	2.4	4.1	39.0	2.9	7.0
1957	55.7	2.4	58.1	57.1	2.5	4.3	39.4	3.0	5.1
1958	54.2	2.3	56.4	55.4	4.0	6.8	39.6	1.8	3.5
1959	54.8	2.2	57.0	56.0	3.2	5.5	39.8	1.5	4.2
1960	54.9	2.1	57.0	56.1	3.2	5.5	39.8	1.5	3.2
1961	54.2	2.1	56.3	55.4	3.9	6.7	39.8	0.7	4.3
1962	54.2	2.3	56.5	55.5	3.2	5.5	40.3	1.2	3.7
1963	54.1	2.2	56.3	55.4	3.3	5.7	40.4	1.6	3.8
1964	54.5	2.2	56.6	55.7	3.0	5.2	40.4	1.2	4.6
1965	55.0	2.1	57.1	56.2	2.6	4.5	40.3	1.9	3.9
1966	55.6	2.4	57.9	56.9	2.2	3.8	39.9	3.4	6.2
1967	55.8	2.6	58.4	57.3	2.2	3.8	39.4	3.0	5.3
1968	56.0	2.6	58.6	57.6	2.1	3.6	39.3	4.7	8.0
1969	56.5	2.5	59.1	58.0	2.1	3.5	38.9	6.1	6.7
1970	56.1	2.3	58.4	57.4	2.9	4.9	38.7	5.5	6.3
1971	55.5	2.0	57.5	56.6	3.5	5.9	39.0	3.4	6.1
1972	56.0	1.7	57.7	57.0	3.3	5.6	39.0	3.4	6.6
1973	56.9	1.6	58.5	57.8	2.9	4.9	38.6	8.8	7.9
1974	57.0	1.5	58.5	57.8	3.4	5.6	38.2	12.2	10.6
1975	55.3	1.4	56.7	56.0	5.1	8.5	38.2	7.0	7.8
Average, 1948–1974	55.3	2.3	57.6	56.6	2.8	4.8	39.6	3.0	5.5

Definitions:
- P = Noninstitutional population sixteen years of age and over
- E = Civilian employment
- A = Armed forces
- U/P = Unemployment ratio (percentage of population)
- UR = Unemployment rate (percentage of civilian labor force)
- NL = Not in labor force
- CPI = Percent change in consumer price index, December of preceding year to December of current year
- HC = Percent change in average hourly compensation, private nonfarm sector, from fourth quarter of preceding year to fourth quarter of current year

Source: U.S. Bureau of Labor Statistics.

INTERNATIONAL INTERDEPENDENCE AND THE U.S. ECONOMY

Marina v. N. Whitman

Summary

The Keynesian income-expenditure analysis that dominated economic thinking and policy analysis in this country over most of the postwar period and the monetarist "counterrevolution" that challenged this neo-Keynesian orthodoxy are both fundamentally analyses of a closed economy and pay little attention to economic interdependence among nations. Their point of view is the natural outgrowth of the long-prevailing belief that the United States was too large and too self-sufficient to be much affected by economic developments in the rest of the world. But since 1950 the gradual decline in the share of world economic activity accounted for by the United States and the gradual increase in the share of the foreign trade sector in our own economy have tended to modify the view that the United States can be considered as a closed economy. And the economic upheavals of the past few years—the end of the Bretton Woods system, the depreciation of the dollar, commodity shortages, and the effect of OPEC's policies on petroleum prices and supplies—have driven home the reality of interdependence. Reflecting all these developments, much of the recent analytical work in international economics has moved away from closed-economy models to models based on the fundamental assumption of a highly integrated world economy. Reality doubtless lies somewhere in between.

As the existence of two-way interdependence has been increasingly recognized, some Americans have been having second thoughts about it. While the economic benefits of international trade and investment continue to be acknowledged, greater emphasis has recently been placed on another aspect of such international integration: the

183

increased vulnerability to external influences and the reduced impact of government policies on the domestic economy that accompanies it. The tension between growing international integration in the sphere of private transactions and the continuing desire for national autonomy in the sphere of public policy is sharpened by the increased responsibility for achieving a variety of domestic economic goals that has devolved on the U.S. government—as well as on the governments of other industrialized nations—in the period since World War II.

Concern about the international transmission of economic disturbances, and their magnification in the transmission process, has grown in recent years. The United States, which was regarded during much of the postwar period as an "island of stability" in a generally volatile economic sea, has more recently come to be viewed as a major exporter of inflation to other nations. The shift in perception was due partly to the accelerating inflation in the United States after 1965. It was also due partly to the implications of the monetary approach to balance-of-payments theory, and of recent empirical work on the purchasing-power-parity theory, regarding the international transmission and magnification of inflation by a reserve-currency country like the United States. At the same time, the foreign sector of the U.S. economy shifted from being a stabilizing influence on the domestic price level to being a major source of inflationary disturbance. Indeed, in the early 1970s, the intensity of the inflationary pressure on the U.S. economy originating in the foreign trade sector did much to change the view that this country was an essentially closed economy to the view that this country is a large open economy. The integrated-world model of the monetary approach to balance-of-payments theory yields much larger estimates of the impact of external disturbances—in particular, of the depreciation of the dollar—on the U.S. price level than does the Keynesian closed-economy analytical framework. Recent empirical studies incorporating a variety of channels for the international transmission of inflation suggest that the actual influence of external disturbances on domestic inflation lies somewhere between the extremes implied by the contrasting analytical models.

In general, one would expect that increased economic openness or interdependence, by expanding the channels of transmission through both trade and capital flows, would have brought about some convergence of economic fluctuations among the participating nations. A survey of recent empirical investigations indicates some convergence—or reduction of dispersion—of price movements among major industrialized countries when the period encompassing the mid-1960s through the early 1970s is compared with the earlier post-war years. On the question whether there has been convergence of fluctuations in real economic activity, the evidence is inconclusive. The shift from fixed to flexible exchange rates in the early 1970s appears to have been accompanied by some increase in the dispersion of both price movements and fluctuations in real economic activity, but to a much smaller extent than might have been expected. The reason may be partly the importance of the common shock that hit all countries studied at the same time—the OPEC oil price increase—and partly the fact that the new exchange-rate regime is one of managed rather than one of free flexibility. The shift in analytical focus already mentioned is also important. According to conventional closed-economy models, exchange-rate flexibility can be expected to enhance national economic autonomy in three ways: by abolishing balance-of-payments disequilibrium as a policy problem; by eliminating the "leakage" into the balance of payments of the domestic multiplier effects of stabilization policies; and by insulating the domestic economy against imported inflation. The open-economy assumptions of much recent analysis imply, in contrast, that each of these three aspects of flexibility has important limitations, so that the economic independence provided by flexibility is correspondingly limited.

Whereas the share of the United States in global real economic activity has been declining gradually over the past two decades, its central role in the international financial sphere shows no such down-trend. Even the recent upheavals in the international monetary system have only slightly affected the key international functions, both private and official, performed by the dollar under the Bretton Woods system. Indeed, one can even argue that the world is today more firmly on a "dollar standard" than it was before. The recent move from pegged exchange rates to managed flexibility has of course had important effects on the relationship between the U.S. economy and the international monetary system. In addition to alleviating the difficulties and instabilities created by cumulative overvaluation of the dollar, this change in the exchange-rate regime has reduced some of the asymmetry in behavior and influence between the United States and other industrialized countries that arose under pegged exchange rates from the dollar's reserve-currency status. And this reduction in asymmetry has made financial interdependence between the United States and other countries, like the interdependence on the real side, more a two-way phenomenon than it was.

185

In addition to economic developments, a changing climate of foreign relations has affected our economic relationships with other nations. For most of the postwar period, economic relations among Western nations tended to be governed by an overriding concern for mutual security in the face of threatened Communist aggression. Today, the diffusion of cold war concerns has contributed to the development of a growing impatience, both in this country and abroad, with the special position of the United States in the international economy. The formulation of economic policies in the face of declining hegemony and increasing interdependence has produced in this country, as well as elsewhere, a rise in defensive economic nationalism: the desire to retain or regain domestic economic autonomy.

The shift to flexible exchange rates was one aspect of the search for buffers with which to strengthen national autonomy in the economic sphere. But the insulation provided by rate flexibility, although essential in preventing widespread resort to much more damaging insulating barriers in the form of piecemeal restrictions on trade and capital flows, has turned out to be more limited than many anticipated. The establishment of an effective international adjustment mechanism in the form of exchange-rate flexibility was long overdue, but greater coordination among governments is also essential to relieve the persistent strains imposed by the vulnerability resulting from interdependence. The United States has generally taken a lead in promoting negative coordination (or the avoidance of explicit beggar-my-neighbor policies), but today positive coordination (or the cooperative setting of macroeconomic targets and policies) is also required to help minimize the tension between market integration and the continuing desire for national self-determination in the sphere of public policy. If we are to reap the full benefits of international economic integration, some globalization of the management of macroeconomic policy problems is required.

The American Economy: From Independence to Interdependence

Whereas the idea of economic interdependence among nations has always lain at the heart of the pure theory of international trade, it was virtually ignored in the development of macroeconomic analysis and the theory of economic policy in the United States during the two decades immediately after World War II. The Keynesian income-expenditure analysis developed and refined on this side of the Atlantic is fundamentally the analysis of a closed economy, into which "foreign repercussions" are introduced as second-order effects that can alter the magnitude but not the direction of impact of policy measures or other exogenous disturbances on the national economy. The quantity-theory "counterrevolution" that challenged this neo-Keynesian ortho-doxy was equally strongly rooted in closed-economy assumptions, substituting domestic monetary policy for domestic fiscal policy as the key macroeconomic variable. And the major survey of inflation theory published by two American economists in the mid-1960s relegated discussion of the influences of foreign prices on domestic inflation to a single footnote.[1]

Today, in contrast, the term "interdependence" is on almost every tongue, and it is scarcely possible to hold—or to read—a serious discussion of any aspect of contemporary major economic problems in the United States, or of the policy responses to those problems, without incorporating the international dimensions of the problems themselves and of the policies proposed to deal with them. This shift in perception and attitude is undoubtedly due in part to the dramatic events of the past few years: the upheavals in the international mone-tary system, the emergence of the OPEC cartel with its dramatic economic and political effects, the simultaneous development first of explosive inflation and then of severe recession in a large number of countries. But the shift is also rooted in some important changes in the international economic position of the United States—changes that have been taking place gradually over a much longer period of time— as well as in the emergence of new developments in economic theory that have significantly affected the analytical perspective from which economists view the problems confronting economic policy making. These theoretical developments are of course related to and in part stimulated by changes in economic realities—in the data, so to speak. But in their impact on policy analysis, these expansions and shifts in analytical framework tend to take on a life of their own, becoming an independent influence on the way problems and issues are per-ceived, in addition to the influence that is exerted by changes in the underlying quantitative data.

The Changing Nature of Interdependence. Among the important developments in the underlying data is the change in the real (as opposed to the financial) position of the United States in the world economy over the past quarter century. The United States remains

---

[1] Martin Bronfenbrenner and F. D. Holzman, "Survey of Inflation Theory," *American Economic Review*, vol. 53, no. 4 (September 1963), pp. 593-661.

the world's largest national economy, with a gross national product accounting for nearly half that of all the OECD countries combined, and more than three times as large as that of Japan, the second largest non-Communist country. But the U.S. share of world GNP has fallen by more than one-third since 1950: from 39 percent in that year to 25 percent in 1975. In certain important industrial sectors, the U.S. share of world production dropped even more sharply between 1950 and 1970: from 76 percent to 31 percent in the case of motor vehicles and from 46 percent to 20 percent in the case of steel—while, concomitantly, our share of world consumption of industrial materials fell from 42 percent to 27 percent. In international trade, our share of world exports fell more gradually, from 16 percent in 1950 to 12 percent in 1975.[2]

There are exceptions to this pattern of a declining world share in at least two important areas: the United States is today a more important agricultural exporter than ever before, and in the early 1970s continued to hold nearly 70 percent of the total direct investment claims of the world's major capital-exporting nations, about the same proportion as a decade earlier, despite the introduction during the intervening years of several programs designed to limit outflows of capital from the United States.[3] But the drop in the U.S. share of international reserves, at first deliberately encouraged by U.S. policies to help other nations rebuild their war-depleted stocks and then the increasingly troublesome result of an overvalued dollar, was the most precipitous of all: from 50 percent in 1950 to 7 percent in 1974.[4]

Actually, to emphasize the declining share of the United States in the world economy may be to put an unwarranted negative emphasis on a phenomenon that is in large part a result of the rapid recovery and subsequent healthy growth of the economies of other industrialized nations since World War II. Perhaps it would be better to talk, instead, about the growing share of the rest of the world in the global economy. But, however one describes it, there is no question that this shift in relative importance in the "real" side of the global economy has affected the nature of the interactions between

---

[2] *International Economic Report of the President*, various issues; International Monetary Fund, *International Financial Statistics*, various issues; *Materials, Needs and the Environment Today and Tomorrow*, Final Report of the Commission on Materials Policy (1973), Table 9.1, p. 9-4; Peter G. Peterson, *The United States in the Changing World Economy*, vol. 2: *Background Material* (Washington, D.C.: U.S. Government Printing Office, 1971).

[3] International Monetary Fund, *Balance of Payments Yearbook*, various issues.

[4] These proportions refer to gross reserves. The net reserves of the United States (international reserves minus liabilities to foreign official agencies) have been negative in nine of the past ten years.

the United States economy and the rest of the world. It has been significant particularly because the shift in relative importance has been accompanied by an increase in the openness of the United States economy, and therefore in its sensitivity to influences from abroad. The ratio of imports to GNP in the United States has grown from 4.4 percent in 1950 to 8.3 percent in 1975, and that of exports to GNP from 4.6 percent to 9.8 percent over the same period.[5] Of course, the openness of other industrialized nations has also increased substantially over the same period, and the United States still remains the least open economy in the non-Communist world. The point is simply that the United States is today more deeply involved in two-way interdependence than ten or twenty years ago. It used to be said that "when the United States sneezes, Europe catches pneumonia." Today, it is increasingly clear that we can all catch the flu from each other and that we are mutually dependent on each other for economic health.

The continuing importance of the United States in the world economy, along with the increased sensitivity of the domestic economy to external influences, creates a channel through which developments and policies in the United States have an additional indirect impact on our own economy through their effects on the economies of the rest-of-the-world. In recent years, the most dramatic example of such feedback was the substantial and greater-than-anticipated impact that the depreciation of the U.S. dollar had on the acceleration of domestic inflation, a phenomenon analyzed in greater detail in a later section of this paper. A less dramatic example of such feedback, in an entirely different area, can be observed for domestic corporate profits. The share of foreign earnings in the profits of U.S. corporations has roughly tripled since 1950.[6] At the same time, the share of sales of local affiliates of U.S. firms in the GNP of such important partner countries as Canada, the United Kingdom, West Germany, and France has been increasing steadily.[7] The circular flow from economic developments in this country through the activities of U.S. affiliates to other economies and then back again to domestic corporate profits through the earnings of those affiliates clearly has had a growing impact on real economic activity in the United States.

---

[5] *Economic Report of the President*, January 1976, Table B-1, p. 171.
[6] U.S. Bureau of the Census, *Statistical Abstract of the United States*, 1974, Table 802, p. 488, and *Survey of Current Business*, various issues.
[7] *Implications of Multinational Firms for World Trade and Investment and for U.S. Trade and Labor*, Report to the Senate Committee on Finance, 93rd Cong., 1st sess. (1973) and Organization for Economic Cooperation and Development, *National Accounts of OECD Countries*, 1960-1971 (Paris: Organization for Economic Cooperation and Development, no date).

In contrast to the declining relative importance of the United States on the real side of the world economy in the years since World War II, the international financial position of the United States and the U.S. dollar (which are not always identical) has generally grown stronger throughout most of this period. Under the Bretton Woods system, the dollar came to serve a number of unique international functions, both private and official, and even the major upheavals in international financial markets associated with the termination of that system and the somewhat ambiguous transitional situation that has prevailed since have at most impinged marginally on the international financial status of the dollar.

Oddly enough, while the declining share of the United States in the world economy has been associated with increasing openness of the domestic economy on the real side, the continued or even increasing international importance of the U.S. dollar in the financial sphere has also been associated with an increase in two-way interdependence between the United States and the rest of the world. One result of the very rapid growth of the Eurodollar market, for example, has been that the assets of foreign branches of U.S. banks grew at an average annual rate of nearly 30 percent between 1960 and 1974,[8] much more rapidly than those banks' domestic assets. The most important exposure of U.S. financial markets to influences from abroad, however, has probably come through the dramatic increase in foreign ownership of the U.S. public debt. The proportion of the privately held portion of the U.S. gross public debt held by foreign and international investors—a proportion which ranged between 5 and 9 percent over the period 1958–1970—leaped to the range of 20 to 21 percent in 1971–1973.[9] In flow terms, the massive accumulations of dollars by foreign central banks during the monetary turmoil of 1971–1973 meant that some 70 percent of the estimated total federal unified-budget deficit of $66 billion during that period was financed by foreigners, and more than 75 percent of the estimated $30 billion increase in marketable debt outstanding was acquired by foreign holders.[10] Even though econometric evidence suggests that, before 1972, changes in foreign central bank holdings of U.S. Treasury bills had only small, short-term effects on Treasury bill rates,[11] foreign

---

[8] Gregory Schmid, "Interdependence Has Its Limits," *Foreign Policy*, no. 21 (Winter 1975), p. 189.

[9] *Federal Reserve Bulletin*, various issues.

[10] Richard V. Adams, "Foreign Activity in United States Treasury Securities in Fiscal Years 1971-1973," in *Issues in Federal Debt Management*, Proceedings of a Conference Sponsored by the Federal Reserve Bank of Boston, June 1973, p. 195.

[11] Thomas D. Willett, "Discussion" [of Adams's paper] in ibid., pp. 201-02.

ownership of such a substantial portion of the public debt cannot but expose this important segment of U.S. financial markets to significant influences from abroad.

Even more significant, in the minds of most Americans, than the broad general trends described so far is the rapidly increasing dependence of the United States on other countries for imports of certain specific critical materials—especially on third-world countries for petroleum and a number of important raw materials. Of the thirteen basic industrial raw materials required by a modern economy, for example, the United States was dependent on imports for more than half of its supplies of four of these in 1950, six in 1970, and the number is projected to rise to nine by 1985 and to twelve by the end of the century.[12] The influence of the producing countries on the U.S. economy that these projections imply will be enhanced substantially if the countries that produce these materials are successful in their efforts to create imitations of the OPEC cartel in order to exploit their potential oligopoly power.

Integration, Vulnerability and National Autonomy. Partly as the result of some of the developments just described, both policy makers and the public in the United States appear currently to be having some second thoughts about interdependence. For the first two decades after World War II, the rapid growth of international trade and investment was perceived essentially in classical terms: as a development that enhanced specialization, efficiency, and competition, thus raising output, income, and standards of living in the participating countries. More recently, however, another aspect of this growth of interdependence has been increasingly emphasized: the growing sensitivity of national economies to events and policies originating outside their borders and therefore beyond their control.

This fundamental tension between the rapid increase of international market integration in the sphere of private transactions and the continuing desire for national autonomy in the sphere of public policy is not new. It was stated succinctly in 1968 by Richard Cooper in his now-classic book, *The Economics of Interdependence:* "The central problem of international economic cooperation—and of this book—is *how to keep the manifold benefits of extensive international economic intercourse free of crippling restrictions while at the same time preserving a maximum degree of freedom for each nation to*

---

[12] Lester Brown, *World Without Borders* (New York: Random House, 1972), p. 194.

pursue its legitimate economic objectives." [13] Most nations have been seriously concerned with this tension for some time. If it has come to prominence in the United States rather later than elsewhere, it is partly because our perceptions of the "dark side" of interdependence have been heightened by a number of dramatic events in the past few years, and partly also because it is only recently that Americans have come to recognize that interdependence has increasingly become a two-way phenomenon.

The reduction in national economic autonomy, or self-determination, that is the concomitant of increasing openness has several aspects. The most obvious of these is the increased vulnerability or sensitivity of the domestic economy to influences originating abroad. The larger the export sector relative to GNP, the more important will shifts in foreign demand be as a source of domestic economic fluctuations. The more dependent a country is on imported oil, the more will domestic prosperity be affected by foreign decisions regarding its supply or price. Such vulnerability is not absolute, of course; it "is a matter of degree and varies with the costs and time involved in developing alternatives. This implies hard policy choices about acceptable degrees of dependence and how willing we are to sacrifice the economic benefits of cheaper foreign supplies" [14]—or, more generally, of international specialization and exchange for the sake of reduced vulnerability. Such problems may ring hollow in the ears of those countries whose vulnerability is far greater and whose available alternatives are far more restricted than ours, but they are real problems nonetheless.

Probably no government has ever regarded a loss of autonomy with equanimity, but the problem is today exacerbated by the fact that, in the years since World War II, the governments of industrialized nations have taken upon themselves (or had thrust upon them by their electorates) responsibility for an increasingly ambitious list of domestic macroeconomic goals. With our own Employment Act of 1946 as a prototype, governments have become responsible for the achievement and maintenance of high levels of employment, for a reasonable degree of price stability, and for an acceptably rapid rate of economic growth. These increased responsibilities are critical to an assessment of the benefits and costs of increased economic interdependence. For, as Cooper has noted, the efficiency implications

---

[13] Richard N. Cooper, *The Economics of Interdependence* (New York: McGraw Hill, 1968), p. 5. Emphasis in original.

[14] Joseph S. Nye, Jr., "Independence and Interdependence," *Foreign Policy*, no. 22 (Spring 1976), p. 133.

of pure trade theory argue that, for private transactions, the boundaries of the nation-state should have no significance—that is to say, for private markets in both goods and factors of production, the optimum size of the integrated area is the world. The economic justification for nation-states, then, lies in the existence of public or collective goods—including stabilization targets, the distribution of income, and the regulatory climate—and of differences in the consumption preferences for such goods among the citizens of different nations.[15] The greater the divergences among countries with respect to the transformation curve or the indifference map for public goods, and the greater the weight of such goods in the nation's welfare function, the greater will be the welfare costs of international economic integration that must be set off against the efficiency gains from the integration of private markets.[16]

The increased responsibility for the achievement of collective macroeconomic goals brings into sharp relief another aspect of the reduced autonomy resulting from increased economic openness (under pegged exchange rates): the attenuated effectiveness of domestic policy instruments in achieving these goals. For example, an increase in the marginal propensity to import that generally accompanies international integration of commodity markets reduces the domestic multiplier impact of fiscal policy by increasing the proportion of the impact that leaks into imports, affecting the level of aggregate demand abroad rather than at home. Capital-market integration similarly attenuates the impact of monetary policy on the level of domestic economic activity, as flows of interest-sensitive capital across national boundaries offset the desired change in domestic interest rates or credit-market conditions.

Another characteristic of the governments of industrialized nations in the postwar era is their increasing concern with questions of equity (perceived in terms of the actual distribution of income) rather than simply with questions of efficiency (or the maximization of total potential income). Because the costs and benefits of economic integration tend to fall unevenly on different regions, different factors of production, different industries, and different individuals, and

---

[15] Richard N. Cooper, "Worldwide vs. Regional Integration: Is There an Optimal Size of the Integrated Area?" (Paper presented at the Fourth World Congress of the International Economic Association, Budapest, 1974; processed), and *Economic Mobility and National Economic Policy*, Wicksell Lectures 1973 (Stockholm: Almqvist & Wiksell International, 1974), pp. 58-59.

[16] For an example in terms of the trade-off between inflation and unemployment, see Marina v. N. Whitman, "Place Prosperity and People Prosperity: The Delineation of Optimum Policy Areas," in Mark Perlman et al., eds., *Spatial, Regional and Population Economics* (New York: Gordon & Breach, 1972), pp. 359-93.

because it often proves difficult in practice to tax the gainers to compensate the losers, interdependence becomes a political issue, to be approached with caution by a democratically elected government.

Finally, by increasing the importance to the domestic economy of what happens in the world outside its borders, interdependence creates an enhanced need for the coordination of national economic policies in order to increase the probability of each nation's achieving its own economic goals. For example, the failure of governments to coordinate their macroeconomic policies at least to the extent of knowing what course of action is proposed in one's partner countries and taking this information into account in one's own policy formulation (an iterative process, obviously) is likely to result in macroeconomic overkill—a collective excess of stimulative measures leading to inflationary pressures or of contractionary measures leading to recession and unemployment. Thus, paradoxically, in an interdependent world, "autonomy may at times be increased by yielding some 'sovereignty' in the freedom to formulate economic policy with apparent (but often illusory) independence of other nations' actions." [17] At present, the institutions and instrumentalities for the coordination of national economic policies are relatively undeveloped and inadequate to the expanding tasks being thrust upon them, and neither the United States nor any other industrialized nation is experienced in making the international coordination of economic policies politically acceptable.

Analytical Developments and Recent Experience

Transmission of Economic Disturbances. Concern about the transmission of economic disturbances between the United States and other industrialized nations, and the magnification of these disturbances in the transmission process, has been growing over the past decade, with a tremendous acceleration in the most recent few years. From the post-Korean War period to the mid-1960s, in contrast, the general view in this country, and to a considerable extent in other countries as well, was that the United States was an "island of stability" whose presence helped damp the waves of economic fluctuation in partner countries. Our rate of inflation was well below those generally experienced in other industrialized countries, and our cyclical fluctuations in real economic activity had been growing steadily milder in amplitude and duration. Our balance on goods and services

---

[17] Cooper, *The Economics of Interdependence*, pp. 4-5.

was positive throughout the period, representing a net transfer of U.S. output to the rest of the world, and rose irregularly from $0.5 billion in 1953 to $8.5 billion in 1964.[18]

If the situation is looked at from the other direction, the foreign sector also appeared as a stabilizing influence on the domestic price picture in the United States. Over the period from 1954 to 1970, the rate of price increase for the import component of the GNP deflator was far below the aggregate rate of increase. The same was true, although to a lesser extent, of the export component.[19]

Between the mid-1960s and the end of the Bretton Woods system in mid-1971, the general view of the role of the United States changed substantially: the former "island of stability" came to be regarded as a major exporter of inflation to other countries. One reason for this shift was the change in our domestic rate of inflation. Domestic inflation began to accelerate substantially in 1966, and in 1968–1970 actually rose above the average rate for nine other major industrialized countries.[20] Over the period from 1964 to 1972, furthermore, our balance on goods and services underwent a negative shift of more than $14 billion (from a surplus of $8.5 billion to a deficit of $5.9 billion).[21] This means that a significant share of the excess demand pressure that would otherwise have exerted still greater upward pressure on the domestic price level spilled over instead into foreign markets.

In addition to the changes just described in certain key economic parameters for the U.S. economy, several important analytical developments contributed to the changing perception of our role in the transmission process. A growing body of empirical evidence tended to verify Balassa's 1964 reappraisal of the purchasing-power-parity doctrine, which suggested that the relationships among different price indices vary systematically among countries with different economic characteristics.[22] Specifically, the proposition is that countries with a

---

[18] *Economic Report of the President*, January 1976, Table B-89, p. 274.

[19] Ibid., Table B-3, p. 175.

[20] David I. Meiselman, "Worldwide Inflation: A Monetarist View," in Meiselman and Arthur B. Laffer, eds., *The Phenomenon of Worldwide Inflation* (Washington, D.C.: American Enterprise Institute, 1975), pp. 86-87.

[21] *Economic Report of the President*, January 1976, Table B-89, p. 274.

[22] Bela Balassa, "The Purchasing Power Parity Doctrine: A Reappraisal," *Journal of Political Economy*, vol. 72, no. 6 (December 1964), pp. 584-96; Gottfried Haberler, "International Aspects of U.S. Inflation," in *A New Look at Inflation: Economic Policy in the Early 1970s* (Washington, D.C.: American Enterprise Institute, 1973); Ronald McKinnon, *Monetary Theory and Controlled Flexibility in the Foreign Exchanges*, Essays in International Finance No. 84 (Princeton, N.J.: Princeton University Press, 1971).

relatively high real-growth rate based on a rapid rate of productivity increase tend to experience a more rapid rise in the consumer price index relative to the rise in the prices of traded or tradeable goods than do slower-growing countries. According to this theory, rates of increase in the consumer price indices can be considerably greater in fast-growing countries—such as Germany and Japan—than in slower-growing countries—such as the United States and Great Britain—and still be consistent with equal or even slower rates of increase in the indices of tradeable goods prices (such as the wholesale price index or, even more, an index of export prices)—an implication strikingly borne out by the data for the countries just mentioned. This view implies that "inflation in the United States, whether zero or positive, is transmitted in magnified form to some other countries . . ." and "that the United States is capable of 'exporting inflation' to some countries, even if it has no inflation (in terms of the CPI) at home." [23]

Second, recent work on the monetary approach to balance-of-payments theory has stressed a basic asymmetry of the Bretton Woods gold exchange standard: that the United States, by virtue of its reserve-currency status, was alone free to determine its rate of inflation domestically, free of any direct balance-of-payments constraint, while the money supplies and thus the inflation rates in other countries were determined primarily by their balance-of-payments positions and the resulting changes in the international reserve component of the domestic monetary base.[24] Harry Johnson has gone so far as to argue that, if foreign central banks recognize the inevitability of importing inflation from the reserve-currency country, they may go ahead and expand the domestic component of the monetary base in advance, and thus prevent any actual reserve inflow. He thus implies that the price-specie flow mechanism may operate to transmit inflation internationally even in the absence of significant observable flows of international reserves.[25] Obviously, the end of the dollar-based gold-exchange standard in mid-1971 and the shift to generalized floating

[23] Gottfried Haberler, "Inflation as a Worldwide Phenomenon—An Overview," in Meiselman and Laffer, The Phenomenon of Worldwide Inflation, p. 16. Haberler notes (p. 17) that European complaints about the United States exporting inflation antedated the inflation which started in this country in 1965.

[24] For a survey of this literature (which is to be distinguished from the "domestic monetarism" associated above all with the name of Milton Friedman), see Marina v. N. Whitman, "Global Monetarism and the Monetary Approach to the Balance of Payments," Brookings Papers on Economic Activity, 1975(3), pp. 491-536. The point is a controversial one, and the evidence on the extent to which countries are actually able to sterilize the impact of reserve flows on their money supplies is not conclusive (Whitman, pp. 522-26).

[25] Harry G. Johnson, "Secular Inflation and the International Monetary System," Journal of Money, Credit, and Banking, vol. 5, no. 1, pt. 2 (February 1973), p. 516.

shortly thereafter significantly reduced (if they did not entirely eliminate) this particular mechanism of transmission.

The erosion of the stabilizing position of the United States in the world economy was well under way by the second half of the 1960s; the parallel shift in the role of the foreign sector in the U.S. economy came somewhat later, though more suddenly. No longer did the prices of exports and imports rise less rapidly than the aggregate domestic price level. On the contrary, between 1970 and 1975, the export component of the GNP deflator rose nearly twice as fast, and the import component nearly three times as fast, as the aggregate index.[26] By 1975, several years after the shift to an exchange-rate regime that presumably increased the ability of countries to insulate themselves from external disturbances, both the United States and the other industrialized nations appeared paradoxically to be importing inflation from each other to a much greater extent than ever before in the postwar period.

There can be little doubt that during 1971–1974 the intensity of the inflationary pressure on the U.S. economy from the foreign trade sector did much to stimulate the shift in the view of this country from an essentially "closed economy" to a "large open economy." For one thing, the apparent impact of the dollar depreciation on the domestic price level took many Americans by surprise. Initial predictions of the magnitude of this inflationary impact were in general far too low. They were underestimates because most of them were based implicitly on the assumptions of the conventional Keynesian model, that elasticities of substitution between domestic and foreign goods are low and that domestic wages and prices are stable (in terms of the home currency) up to the point of full employment. Under these assumptions, depreciation of the dollar in the presence of unemployment would affect the domestic price level only through raising the prices of imported inputs or finished goods. Since imports constituted about 7.5 percent of GNP during 1971–1973, an effective dollar depreciation of 10 percent, for example, could have been expected to raise the domestic price level (in terms of the GNP deflator) by about three-quarters of 1 percent. Furthermore, this represented an upper-bound estimate, inasmuch as the relatively large size of the United States in world markets made it unlikely that the full amount of the depreciation would be passed through in the form of increased dollar prices of imports.

During the past five or six years, however, analyses of devaluation have increasingly incorporated the fundamental assumption of a

---

[26] *Economic Report of the President*, January 1976, Table B-3, p. 175.

highly integrated world economy, in contrast to the Keynesian view of the world as consisting of relatively closed national economies. And the assumptions underlying this so-called "monetary approach" have very different implications from those of the Keynesian model regarding the impact of an exchange-rate change on the domestic price level. Specifically, this approach holds that high elasticities of substitution prevail among countries for most tradeable goods and that, because world markets today are highly integrated, a single price must prevail in all markets for goods that are close substitutes for one another. The implication of this view is that competitive forces will produce offsetting changes in domestic prices, thereby quickly eliminating the initial shift in relative prices arising from an exchange-rate change.[27] Under the assumptions of such a perfectly competitive model, the upper bound on the increase in the domestic price level (as elasticities of substitution between foreign and domestic goods approach infinity) would be the amount of the effective depreciation itself.

Several recent empirical investigations have incorporated at least some of the additional effects of depreciation on the domestic price level that are implied by the analytical approach described here. In general, they have yielded estimates of the price level impact of exchange-rate changes much higher than crude ex ante calculations based on the conventional Keynesian view, but still well below the long-run upper bound implied by the monetary approach. Making use of regression results for the period 1950–1971, on the basis of Phillips curve equations that incorporate an import-price term, Kwack, for example, estimated that the U.S. price level (as measured by the consumer price index) would rise by about 20 percent of an effective devaluation of the U.S. dollar, or by two percentage points in the case of an effective devaluation of 10 percent.[28] Nordhaus and Shoven reached roughly consistent results: using an input-output approach to estimate the transmission of the price effects of depreciation, they concluded that the 10 percent effective depreciation of the dollar between November 1972 and August 1973 accounted for between 1.9 and 2.3 percentage points of inflation over that period.[29]

---

[27] For references, see Whitman, "Global Monetarism."

[28] S. Y. Kwack, "The Effects of Foreign Inflation on Domestic Prices and the Relative Price Advantage of Exchange Rate Changes," in Peter B. Clark, Dennis Logue, and Richard J. Sweeney, eds., The Effects of Exchange Rate Adjustment (U.S. Department of the Treasury, forthcoming 1976).

[29] William Nordhaus and John Shoven, "Inflation 1973: The Year of Infamy," Challenge, May-June 1974, pp. 14-22.

Such studies as these may still not capture the total indirect effects of depreciation on prices in industries producing exportable and import-competing goods and, through effects on wages, even in sectors producing nontradeable output. In particular, the sharp improvement in our net balance on goods and services over the year 1973 (from a deficit of $0.8 billion in the fourth quarter of 1972 to a surplus of $11.6 billion in the fourth quarter of 1973, both in 1958 dollars) represented 38 percent of the total increase in our real GNP that year. At a time when important segments of the economy were straining against capacity limitations, this diversion of nearly 40 percent of the real increase in domestic output from domestic to foreign absorption must have had pervasive effects on the domestic price level.

Still another recent study attempts to take just such a broad view of the external effects on inflation in the United States over the period from mid-1971 to mid-1974, not only encompassing the general aggregate-demand effects but also attempting to decompose the external impact into two parts: the portion of domestic inflation resulting from the effective depreciation of the dollar and the portion due to other "extraordinary" increases in the prices of U.S. exports and imports over the period.[30] Some notion of the magnitude of the indirect effects of depreciation-induced demand pressures can be gleaned from a comparison of the two estimates of the price impact of depreciation that the authors derive by two different techniques. The first, using an input-output approach similar to that of Nordhaus and Shoven, takes account of the dispersion throughout the economy of depreciation-induced cost increases originating in the import sector, but does not take account of the effects of any increase in aggregate demand for U.S. output as the result of stimulus to the export- and import-competing sectors. The second estimate comes from simulating the Federal Reserve Board's quarterly econometric (FRB) model which (in contrast to the input-output approach) takes explicit account of increases in export prices and the demand shift from traded to nontraded goods, and allows wages to respond endogenously to the increase in consumer prices. Clearly, the incorporation of these indirect effects makes a substantial difference: whereas the first (input-output) results implied that just over 4 percent of the 18.6 percent increase in prices, or less than one percentage point (as measured by the personal consumption deflator) over the period from the second quarter of 1971 to the second quarter of 1974 was attributable

---

[30] Richard Berner et al., "International Sources of Domestic Inflation," Joint Economic Committee, *Studies in Price Stability and Economic Growth*, no. 3 (94th Cong., 1st sess.), August 5, 1975.

to the 13 percent effective depreciation of the dollar over the same period, the simulation of the FRB model yielded a comparable estimate of 15 percent (or something under three percentage points).

The reason that this study yielded lower estimates of the inflationary impact of depreciation than those described just previously is that, rather than attributing the initial unusual price increases in U.S. exports and imports to the change in the dollar's exchange rate, it attributed the bulk of these increases to other exogenous disturbances affecting world commodity markets, of which the OPEC-induced increase in prices of petroleum products was the most dramatic example. Here, in contrast to what is the case with depreciation, the higher exogenous prices are associated with a decline in *real* GNP, so that there is no additional inflationary pressure arising from aggregate demand. For this reason, the estimate based on the input-output model and the estimate based on the FRB model simulation yield approximately the same results: that some 24 percent, or nearly one-quarter of the three-year rise in the personal consumption deflator is attributable to these "extraordinary" increases in the prices of U.S. exports and imports.[31]

As the authors are careful to point out, their assumption that increases in U.S. export and import prices between 1971 and 1974 were exogenously determined cannot be entirely valid. In reality, "developments within the United States clearly have influenced both the course of the dollar's exchange rate vis-à-vis other currencies, as well as movements in the prices of the commodities that the U.S. imports and exports."[32] Thus their results are best regarded as estimates of an upper limit for the contribution of foreign developments to domestic price increases. Nevertheless, despite the fact that they undoubtedly fail to catch some of the external influences on domestic inflation in the United States and overestimate others, studies such as the ones described here serve to drive home two points. The first is that the foreign sector is an important transmission belt for inflationary impulses, even in such a relatively closed economy as the United States, and that the actual channels of transmission are more varied and complex than those encompassed by the conventional Keynesian analysis. The second is that, in an economy like ours, shifts in *relative* prices, which in recent years appear to have been caused at least as much by fluctuations and disturbances on the supply

---

[31] The authors caution that, because the model is non-linear, "the 15 and 24 percent figures cannot be added to obtain a combined effect for both the depreciation and the exogenous price increases." Ibid., p. 20.

[32] Ibid., p. 2.

side as by the vagaries of demand usually stressed in modern economic analysis, are likely to have a substantial and prolonged (although ultimately transient) inflationary effect on the general price level, even in instances where their *real* effects are deflationary.

Interdependence, Transmission and Convergence. The discussion so far has focused on trends in interdependence, on the mechanisms for international transmission of inflation, and on their implications for the economy of the United States. More generally, however, one would expect that an increase in economic openness or interdependence, by widening the channels of transmission on both trade and capital account, would have brought about some convergence or synchronization of economic fluctuations among the participating countries. A priori considerations suggest such convergence not only for price movements under pegged exchange rates, but also for fluctuations in real economic activity as sensitivity to external disturbances increases. The fact that such convergence can occur for a number of reasons other than an increased tendency toward international transmission—such as a common response to some common exogenous disturbance, for example [33]—confuses the statistical evidence but does not alter the basic relationship. Furthermore, the shift from pegged to flexible exchange rates in the period from 1971 to 1973 would be expected to have increased the dispersion among national rates of inflation and among cycles in real economic activity as well. That is, theory suggests that such a shift should reduce the channels of transmission and thus enable countries both to insulate themselves at least partially from disturbances originating abroad and to increase the domestic impact of their own macroeconomic policies.

In recent years quite a number of empirical investigations into various aspects of this convergence-divergence question have been conducted, primarily by inquiring whether the dispersion across industrialized countries of various quantitative measures of both prices and real economic activity has increased or decreased over time. The largest number of such studies has been conducted on the dispersion among national rates of inflation.[34] Unfortunately, because of differ-

[33] For a detailed analysis of the interrelations between dispersion of national inflation rates and international transmission, see Walter S. Salant, "The International Transmission of Inflation," paper prepared for the Brookings Conference on World Inflation, Washington, D.C., November 21-23, 1974, pp. 5-21.

[34] W. H. Bruce Brittain, "Have Flexible Exchange Rates Caused World Inflation?" (First National City Bank, 1975; processed); J. Marcus Fleming, "International Aspects of Inflation," paper presented at the International Economics Association [IEA] Conference in Inflation Theory and Anti-Inflation Policy, Saltsjöbaden, Sweden, August 28-September 3, 1975; Hans K. Genberg and Alexander K. Swo-

ences among the various studies in the selection of price indices, of time periods for comparison, of the number and mix of industrialized countries, and of the particular measure of dispersion (in particular, whether the standard deviation, the coefficient of variation,[35] or both were used), the various results are not directly comparable, and the picture that has emerged is somewhat ambiguous. Some of these studies have shown no clear trend in the dispersion of national inflation rates over the postwar period spanned by the Bretton Woods system. Others, utilizing different price indices, time periods, or country samples, have found some degree of convergence—that is, reduction in dispersion—for the period from the mid-1960s through the early 1970s as compared with the earlier postwar years before about 1963 or 1965. Most of them, however, have found some increase in the standard deviation among national inflation rates beginning in 1971 or 1972 or (at the latest) in 1973—that is, after the end of the Bretton Woods system in mid-1971 or after the move to generalized floating early in 1973. Because the average rate of inflation for all countries in the sample increased markedly during this most recent period, the use of the coefficient of variation as the measure of dispersion reintroduces some ambiguity into the pattern and makes any general conclusion regarding the expected increase in dispersion less certain than it appeared when the standard deviation was used. One study also found an increase in dispersion in 1971–1975 (and even more markedly for 1973–1975) over the average for the 1960s not only for three different price indices but also for an index of stock prices and for representative interest rates.[36]

In a few cases, investigators have gone behind the rates of national price inflation to look at what happened to money supply growth rates in major industrialized countries. Here the results have been somewhat surprising: there is no evidence of increased dispersion among the rates of money supply growth in the flexible-rate period

---

boda, "Causes and Origins of the Current Worldwide Inflation," paper presented at the IEA Conference; H. R. Heller, "International Reserves and Worldwide Inflation," International Monetary Fund, *Staff Papers*, vol. 23, no. 1 (March 1976), pp. 61-87; Organization for Economic Cooperation and Development, "The International Transmission of Inflation," *Economic Outlook*, no. 13 (July 1973), pp. 81-96; Charles Pigott, R. J. Sweeney and Thomas D. Willett, "Some Aspects of Behavior of Flexible Exchange Rates," paper presented at the Conference on Monetary Theory and Policy, Konstanz, Germany, June 1975; Salant, "The International Transmission of Inflation"; Ronald L. Teigen, "Interpreting Recent World Inflation," *American Economic Review*, vol. 65, no. 2 (May 1975), pp. 129-32.

[35] Teigen argues (p. 130) that the standard deviation is the more appropriate measure.

[36] Pigott et al., "Some Aspects of Behavior."

as compared with earlier years.[37] In one of the most detailed of the statistical studies, the author reported that, although he observed an increase in quarter-to-quarter divergences among the money supply growth rates in ten major industrialized countries beginning in 1972, no such change was observable for longer periods. In fact, the monetary policies of the nine other industrialized nations appeared to be closer to those of the United States in the flexible-rate period than they were before the move away from pegged rates. Such evidence led the investigator to conclude that the nature of monetary interdependence has remained fundamentally unchanged in the face of a substantial change in the international monetary system because countries have apparently chosen to continue behaving as if exchange rates were fixed—that is, except for very short-period divergences, to maintain as close coordination of monetary policies as they did before.[38]

In looking at changes in the degree of dispersion of cycles in real economic activity, there is a wide variety of potential proxy variables to choose from. The fact that such cyclical fluctuations take place around underlying growth trends, which themselves differ among countries, complicates the interpretation of the results. And, in fact, two of the three empirical investigations of this question found no particular trend in the dispersion of real GNP growth rates or of "potential output gaps" among major industrial countries over the postwar period, even when the pegged and flexible-rate periods were compared.[39] The most detailed and exhaustive of the empirical studies, however, did discern the sort of changes in dispersion among the potential output gaps of twelve major industrial countries that had been anticipated on a priori grounds.[40] That is, there appears to have been some decline in the dispersion—or increase in the synchronization—of real cycles between 1952–1957 and 1964–1970, presumably as the result of increasing economic integration, and then a decrease in synchronization from the latter period to 1971–1974. The author noted that the decrease in synchronization as a result of greater flexibility in exchange rates was presumably moderated considerably

---

[37] Brittain, "Have Flexible Exchange Rates Caused World Inflation?"; K. S. Sri-Kumar and W. H. Bruce Brittain, "Have Flexible Exchange Rates Really Mattered?" (First National City Bank, November 1975; processed).

[38] Brittain, "Have Flexible Exchange Rates Caused World Inflation?" p. 10.

[39] J. Marcus Fleming, "International Aspects of Inflation"; OECD, "The International Transmission of Inflation."

[40] Duncan Ripley, "Cyclical Fluctuations in Industrial Countries" (International Monetary Fund, 1976; processed).

by the impact of a major exogenous shock common to all the countries in the sample: the oil price increases of 1973–1974.[41] She noted, too, that

> the United States' pattern of cyclical movement relative to that of its trading partners . . . is quite different from that of most other industrial countries. It shows reasonably high levels of covariation during periods when external shocks were hypothesized to have harmonized cyclical movements across countries, and practically no covariation when it was thought that fluctuations should have been transmitted through the current account.[42]

This last observation is consistent with the relatively small size of the external sector relative to total GNP in the United States, but it is not fully consistent with some recent National Bureau of Economic Research (NBER) findings on the relationship between the U.S. trade account and business cycles here and abroad. The authors of the NBER study found that there has indeed been a common international growth cycle for nine major industrial countries over the period 1953–1973 and that, perhaps surprisingly, in terms of the degree of association, the United States occupies an intermediate rather than a dominant position.[43] In addition, monthly trade data for the period 1958–1973 show a close connection between movements in the U.S. trade balance and differences in the timing and severity of cycles here and abroad. U.S. exports to four of its major partner countries grew about six times as fast when those countries were in the expansion phase of their own cycles as they did when those countries were in the contraction phase, whereas U.S. imports from these same four countries grew more than three times as fast during cyclical upswings in this country as they did during downswings.[44] Once again, the United States has not always appeared as the cyclical leader: rather, the pattern has been "for other countries to lead the United States into growth recession and for the United States to lead other countries into recovery"—that is, the postwar evidence "provides no support for the popular misconception that the

[41] Ibid., p. 15.

[42] Ibid., pp. 8-9.

[43] Geoffrey H. Moore, "The State of the International Business Cycle," *Business Economics*, vol. 9, no. 4 (September 1974), pp. 21-29.

[44] Geoffrey H. Moore and Philip A. Klein, "Impact on U.S. Trade Performance of Business Cycle Movements in Major Industrial Countries" (National Bureau of Economic Research, 1975; processed).

contagion runs in a dominant way from the United States to the other major industrialized nations." [45]

Finally, the various studies described in the previous paragraphs shed little or no light on the question why, despite some tendency toward increased dispersion under flexible rates, a considerable common element remains—in other words, why certain channels of international transmission appear to persist, even under flexible rates.[46] Why do flexible rates appear to provide only limited insulation of national economies one from another, rather than the high degree of insulation implied by simple models focused on the trade balance? One immediate answer is, of course, that the present system is far from the freely floating rates of the textbooks; it is rather a system of managed floating wherein governments still undertake substantial intervention in foreign-exchange markets. But this does not seem to be the whole story.

Most textbook models of the adjustment process under either pegged or floating rates are based on the assumption of instantaneous adjustment in all markets. Most also assume, implicitly if not explicitly, the prevalence of totally inelastic price expectations (that is, actual prices are expected to continue unchanged forever). In fact, however, the existence of adjustment lags in both goods and asset markets and different assumptions about the formulation of price expectations may create channels for the international transmission of inflation under flexible rates in the short run, so that a rise in foreign prices may cause upward pressure on domestic prices before the domestic currency appreciates to its new equilibrium level in the foreign-exchange markets. Furthermore, certain institutional features common to most industrialized economies tend to serve as transmis-

---

[45] Geoffrey H. Moore and Philip A. Klein, "New International Business Cycle Indicators System: Applying the NBER Indicator Approach to International Growth Cycles" (National Bureau of Economic Research, 1975; processed), pp. 26 and 29. For a more detailed discussion of the "sneeze hypothesis," see Philip A. Klein, *Business Cycles in the Postwar World* (Washington, D.C.: American Enterprise Institute, 1976), pp. 27-43.

[46] This author used analysis of variance to check for significant differences in the behavior of three indices among the Group of Ten countries over three periods: from the second quarter of 1955 to the third quarter of 1965, from the fourth quarter of 1965 to the second quarter of 1971, and from the third quarter of 1971 to the third quarter of 1974. The F-ratios turned out to be significant (at the 95 percent level) for quarterly changes in all three indices—the wholesale price index (WPI), the consumer price index (CPI), and the index of industrial production (IP)—for the first period; they were significant for the CPI and the IP, but not for the WPI, in the second period; and they were not significant for any of the three indices for the third or flexible-rate period, when one would have expected experiences among countries to be most divergent.

sion channels for world inflation: among these are (1) the tendency of monetary authorities to "accommodate" imported inflation by preventing a fall in nominal incomes in the face of a real-income decline caused by worsening terms of trade, and (2) the demand-shift inflation caused by the uneven sectoral impact of a rise in foreign prices and the resulting change in the exchange rate.[47]

More fundamental, however, is the fact that flexible exchange rates cannot be expected to abolish interdependence in an integrated world economy. According to conventional Keynesian closed-economy models, in which the balance of payments is generally equated with the balance on goods and services, exchange-rate flexibility can be expected to strengthen national economic autonomy in three ways. First, by making possible permanent improvement in the balance of payments, such rate flexibility would eliminate the need to use macroeconomic policies for the elimination of balance-of-payments disequilibria as well as for the achievement of domestic targets. Second, by eliminating the "leakage" of domestic multiplier effects through the balance of payments, flexible rates would directly enhance the domestic impact of stabilization policies. And, finally, rate flexibility would insulate the domestic economy against imported inflation by eliminating, through an appreciation of the domestic money, both the direct-cost and the aggregate-demand inflationary pressures caused by a rate of price increase higher abroad than at home.

In a different analytical framework, however, each of these characteristics is seen to have important limitations. The monetary approach to the balance of payments implies that exchange-rate changes can cause only a temporary change in the balance of payments; in the long run, according to this view, the conditions for equilibrium in all markets require that the balance of payments revert to its original level. The applicability of the assumptions underlying the monetary approach and the relevance of stationary-state equilibrium conditions to policy analysis are important issues, but there is no doubt that the insights this approach offers have posed significant questions about the conditions under which an exchange-rate change can be counted on to effect a durable improvement in the balance of payments.

Similarly, the use of a model that focuses on the conditions for money-market equilibrium implies that, if capital is highly mobile internationally in response to interest-rate differentials, a shift from pegged to flexible rates will weaken rather than strengthen the

[47] J. David Richardson, " 'Imported Inflation' under Variable Exchange Rates: Some Transmission Channels" (University of Wisconsin, 1975; processed).

domestic effectiveness of fiscal policy (while the effectiveness of monetary policy will be enhanced). The reasoning is essentially an extension to the open economy of the idea of "crowding out," according to which the interest-rate rise caused by an increased government deficit with an unchanged money supply (or an unchanged rate of money growth) will discourage private investment and thus offset the stimulative effect of the deficit. In the open economy case, the rise in domestic interest rates resulting from stimulative fiscal policy will attract capital inflows, cause the currency to appreciate, and thus lead to a deterioration in the goods and services account which again offsets the desired stimulative effect. Again, the extent to which the assumptions of the model are met and the extent to which such offsetting actually occurs are unsettled issues. But the very possibility that such effects may operate introduces a cautionary note into our expectations about what happens to the domestic efficiency of fiscal policy as the result of a move from pegged to flexible rates.

Finally, there is the fact that flexible exchange rates provide only limited insulation against foreign disturbances in a world of capital mobility. If there are internationally mobile securities and investors sensitive to interest-rate differentials among countries, a change in monetary policy abroad will affect domestic as well as foreign interest rates and will thus impinge on the domestic level of economic activity even under flexible rates. In fact, the impact of certain kinds of disturbance abroad may actually be aggravated rather than lessened by rate flexibility. As an example, Cooper has cited an exogenous shift in asset preferences that increases the foreign demand for domestic securities at constant rates of interest. The result of such a shift would be an appreciation of the domestic currency leading to a current-account deficit and a reduction of domestic aggregate demand and income.[48] Furthermore, even if the foreign disturbance were monetary in origin (the case in which the insulation provided by flexible rates is supposed to be most effective), the existence of capital mobility might still, under certain circumstances, magnify the international transmission process more under flexible than under fixed rates. This could happen if an increase in the foreign price level (together with an accompanying equiproportional appreciation of the domestic currency that would leave the current account exactly unchanged) were to lead to an increase in the net capital outflow from the appreciating country—an increase such as might occur, for example, if the increasing foreign price level were to create expanded

[48] Richard N. Cooper, "Monetary Theory and Policy in an Open Economy," *Scandinavian Journal of Economics* (forthcoming, 1976).

profit opportunities abroad. In this case the maintenance of overall equilibrium in the foreign exchange market would cause the domestic currency to appreciate less than in proportion to the rise in the world price level, leading to an improvement on current account and thus an inflationary increase in aggregate demand at home.[49] Thus, the degree (and even the direction) of insulation provided by flexible exchange rates depends both on the type of disturbance that is assumed to dominate in the international arena and on the particular nature of the domestic response.

The U.S. Role and the Policy Environment

The United States and the Dollar in the International Monetary System. The foci of the discussion so far have been the gradually declining share of the United States in the world economy, the concomitant gradual increase in the openness of the U.S. economy to two-way economic interdependence, and some changing perceptions of the way in which these developments affect the economic inter-relationships between the United States and the outside world. In the financial sphere, however, the picture is one of a continuing central role for the United States and the dollar, a position relatively unaffected by the recent upheavals in the international monetary system.[50] And this continuing role, along with some new developments in the analytical framework within which its function and implications are analyzed, has major implications for the U.S. economy and the conduct of U.S. economic policy.

The legal foundations of the Bretton Woods system, the Articles of Agreement of the International Monetary Fund (IMF), provided for formal symmetry in the rights and obligations of the member countries, after an initial period of transition. But even before the postwar transition period was over, it had become clear that the actual international monetary arrangements were developing in a significantly asymmetrical fashion, with the U.S. dollar serving a number of unique functions. Because it was backed by the world's largest and strongest economy and because it was, until 1958, the only major currency that enjoyed market convertibility, the dollar came to serve as the major vehicle currency in private international transactions

---

[49] Richardson, "Imported Inflation," p. 20, and Salant, "The International Transmission of Inflation," p. 52.

[50] This discussion draws heavily on Marina v. N. Whitman, "The Current and Future Role of the Dollar: How Much Symmetry?" *Brookings Papers on Economic Activity*, 1974(3), pp. 539-83.

(even those transactions in which no American was involved), as well as the main medium in which private balances of liquid international assets were held. Because of the unique commitment of the United States to maintaining the parity of the dollar by buying and selling gold for monetary purposes at a fixed price, the dollar became the primary medium of exchange-market intervention through which other countries maintained their parity obligations as their currencies gradually became convertible. The dollar also became the *numéraire* of the IMF system—the currency in terms of which most other currencies were defined—as well as the major medium of international reserve growth in the postwar period. Finally, because of its special place in the system, the United States played a passive role in the exchange-rate adjustment process; other countries from time to time changed the par values of their currencies against the dollar, but the value of the dollar remained fixed in relation to gold, and therefore to other currencies collectively, between 1945 and 1971.

The United States formally terminated the Bretton Woods system partly because both we and others had become increasingly dissatisfied with our special role. Other nations wanted to curb the freedom of the United States to print international money—what General de Gaulle had once termed our "exorbitant privilege"—while we wanted the freedom to control our own exchange rate and thus alleviate the difficulties resulting from an increasingly overvalued dollar. Reflecting these desires, most of the proposals put forth for the comprehensive reform of the international monetary system provided for symmetrical treatment of the dollar and other currencies, reducing or eliminating much of the special position occupied by the United States under the Bretton Woods system.[51] But a survey of recent developments suggests, ironically, that the international monetary system is at present more firmly rooted in an international "dollar standard" than before, and that the quest for symmetry is likely to prove as unsuccessful today as it was thirty years ago. In any viable international monetary system the dollar and the United States are almost certain to continue to play special roles, and this fact will continue to be an important determinant of the international framework within which U.S. economic policies are formulated and carried out.

A year or so after the dramatic termination of the Bretton Woods system, a leading international economist predicted that "at the end of the decade the position of the dollar will not be very different from

---

[51] See Whitman, "The Current and Future Role of the Dollar," pp. 543-50.

what it is now." [52] There have been some modifications, some chipping away around the edges in certain areas, but on the whole that prediction appears to be holding up quite well. In the late 1960s, somewhere between one-quarter and one-third of world trade is thought to have been invoiced and transacted in dollars, even though the U.S. share of world trade was only about 15 percent. The limited evidence we have suggests that, at least as of 1973, the quantitative importance of the dollar as a vehicle currency for international transactions remained essentially unchanged. [53]

The dollar also remains the major medium for private international liquidity, despite the modest growth of foreign private holdings of American dollar balances (that is, liabilities of U.S. residents) over the past decade, as a result of the explosive growth since 1964 of Eurodollar holdings—dollar-denominated deposits held outside the United States, primarily in London. The growth was particularly rapid during the latter part of the decade: estimates of the net size of the Eurocurrency market (net of interbank deposits) suggest that it expanded from $50 billion at the end of 1969 to $240 billion in October 1975, with Eurodollars accounting for some 84 percent of this total in the earlier year and 76 percent in the latter year. [54] To what extent these Eurodollar deposits, which arose partly in response to U.S. monetary policy (in particular to the imposition of controls on capital outflows in 1964) and partly from the worldwide expansion of the U.S. banking system, reflect a specific demand for *dollar* liquidity is uncertain, but there are a number of reasons for regarding them

---

[52] Richard N. Cooper, "The Future of the Dollar," *Foreign Policy*, no. 11 (Summer 1973), p. 4.

[53] Benjamin J. Cohen, *The Future of Sterling as an International Currency* (New York: St. Martin's Press, 1971), ch. 1; Sven Grassman, "A Fundamental Symmetry in International Payments Patterns," *Journal of International Economics*, vol. 3, no. 2 (May 1973), pp. 110-16; Stephen P. Magee, "U.S. Import Prices in the Currency-Contract Period," *Brookings Papers on Economic Activity*, 1971(1), pp. 126-27. In the spring of 1975, however, the International Air Transport Association and OPEC announced that international airline fares and petroleum prices would thereafter be established in terms of SDRs rather than U.S. dollars.

[54] Morgan Guaranty Trust Company of New York, *World Financial Markets*, various issues and private correspondence with the author. Sweeney and Willett argue, however, that a much smaller fraction of gross Eurocurrency deposits (about $30 billion as of early 1974) can legitimately be regarded as "world money" additional to national monetary aggregates, and that even this portion is more comparable to such broad aggregates as M-4 or M-5 in the United States than to such a narrow aggregate as M-1. Richard J. Sweeney and Thomas D. Willett, "Eurodollars, Petrodollars and World Liquidity and Inflation," paper presented at Carnegie-Rochester Monetary Conference, Pittsburgh, November 1975.

primarily as a substitute for foreign holdings of American liquid dollar assets.[55]

Some thirteen years ago, Charles Kindleberger suggested that the integration of long-term capital markets in Europe was taking place not directly but indirectly, through the United States.[56] He predicted, further, that this trend would continue, with the Euromarket taking the place of the New York bond market. This is precisely what happened. The introduction of U.S. capital controls in 1964 closed the New York market to most foreign borrowers for a decade, but the (then-embryonic) Eurobond market offered an alternative source of dollar-denominated bonds. The proportion of all Eurocurrencies represented by Eurodollars, the dollar-denominated portion of international bond issues, and the dollar-denominated share of total private international liquidity have all dropped somewhat since the late 1960s, with the Deutsche mark and the Swiss franc experiencing the greatest concomitant increase in importance. Despite the diversification implied by these changes, however, dollar-denominated assets still accounted for some three-quarters of the world's private international liquidity in 1974.[57]

Since 1971 the most significant erosion of the dollar's official international position has occurred in its role as an international numéraire or unit of account. Symbolically, the IMF, which had always defined par values of currencies in terms of U.S. dollars (as well as gold content), began in June 1972 to express them also in terms of its own Special Drawing Rights (SDRs); at about the same time, it began to value reserve holdings and other financial data in SDRs. Of more substantive importance was the change in the valuation of the SDR itself, which increased its practicality as an alternative to the dollar as an international unit of account. SDRs had been valued in terms of monetary gold when they were introduced in 1970; in June 1974 the IMF adopted an experimental valuation of the SDR in terms of a "basket" of sixteen leading currencies, in which the U.S. dollar has a weight of 33 percent, and in the 1976 draft amendments to the IMF's Articles of Agreement, the SDR was formally substituted for gold as the IMF's own unit of account. A number of countries have

---

[55] Raymond F. Mikesell and J. Herbert Furth, *Foreign Dollar Balances and the International Role of the Dollar* (New York: Columbia University Press for the National Bureau of Economic Research, 1974), p. 17.

[56] Charles P. Kindleberger, "European Economic Integration and the Development of a Single Financial Center for Long-Term Capital," *Weltwirtschaftliches Archiv*, vol. 90, no. 2 (July 1963), pp. 189-210.

[57] International Monetary Fund, *Annual Report of the Executive Directors for the Fiscal Year Ended April 30, 1974*, p. 44.

recently shifted from a dollar peg for their currencies to one based either on the SDR "basket" or some other trade-weighted basket of currencies in order to hedge against abrupt shifts in the international value of a single currency peg. In 1975, the member nations of the European Economic Community (EEC) abandoned the dollar in favor of the SDR as their common unit of account, while Iran and several Arab oil states severed the traditional link between their own currencies and the dollar.

Far less change has occurred in the dollar's other official functions. As part of their effort at monetary integration, the EEC countries have experimented with multicurrency intervention as a substitute for dollar intervention, and the Committee of Twenty's blueprint for international monetary reform contained suggested schemes for multicurrency or SDR intervention. But such little evidence as we have suggests that any reduction in the dollar's position as the universal medium for official intervention in foreign exchange markets has been at most marginal. Any alternative system, it should be noted, would have to overcome the very substantial margin of efficiency, convenience, and simplicity enjoyed by the mechanism of dollar intervention.

The U.S. dollar has dominated international reserve growth throughout the postwar period, accounting for about 80 percent of the increase since 1950. In recent years there has been some diversification of reserves away from direct claims on the United States, partly into Eurodollars and partly into new reserve currencies, primarily the Deutsche mark. But dollar-denominated international assets (including Eurodollar holdings) still accounted for about three-quarters of all foreign exchange reserves at the end of 1974 and for more than half of international reserves in all forms.[58]

The primary reason for the continued importance of the dollar in the international monetary system is, as Cooper has put it, that "there is at present no clear, feasible alternative." [59] No other medium of exchange possesses the advantages the dollar derives from the economic size of the United States, the depth, breadth and efficiency of our capital markets, and the absence of exchange controls limiting the international usability of the dollar. It is true that rapid inflation in the United States and substantial fluctuations in the value of the dollar against other major currencies in the years immediately following the end of the Bretton Woods system have reduced the attractive-

---

[58] International Monetary Fund, *Annual Report of the Executive Directors for the Fiscal Year Ended April 30, 1975*, p. 39.
[59] Cooper, "The Future of the Dollar," p. 5.

ness of the dollar as a guarantor of stability in asset values. There is, however, a strong argument for regarding the relatively large fluctuations of the dollar as being in part a transitional phenomenon associated with the long-delayed accomplishment of a substantial shift in the desired composition of reserve assets—a shift caused by the previous prolonged period of cumulative disequilibrium in external positions. Indeed, since late 1974, the demand for dollars to make oil payments appears to have substantially reduced the magnitude of the "dollar overhang" problem in the eyes of other industrialized countries, and the substantial reduction in the fluctuations of the dollar over the past year or so lends credence to the belief that the turbulent transition period may now be behind us. The fact that over the past year this country has reestablished an inflation performance superior to that of most other major industrialized countries, even while the process of economic recovery began sooner and proceeded faster in this country than elsewhere, should also help to restore the relative position of the dollar as a store of value—despite the persistence here, as elsewhere, of rates of inflation uncomfortably high by historical standards.

All of this strongly suggests that the United States and the U.S. dollar will continue to occupy a key position in the international monetary system. Furthermore, several of the components of the piecemeal evolutionary process of monetary reform that has taken place over the past few years have tended to enhance rather than reduce the importance of these special functions. Specifically, the progress toward demonetization of gold, the unlikelihood of any further allocations of SDRs in the near future, and the failure so far of the reform effort to endow SDRs with any important additional attributes of international money have all tended to place the international monetary system on a dollar standard more exclusively than ever before, whatever the expressed intentions to the contrary of the participants in the reform process.

At the same time, the significant alteration in the exchange-rate adjustment process, from a system of pegged rates in which the United States was essentially passive to a system of managed floating in which the dollar participates, has had important effects. For one thing, it has contributed to slowing the rapid increase in foreign reserves associated with the very large U.S. deficits on the official reserve transactions basis in 1970–1972, an increase which many analysts argue contributed significantly to worldwide inflation. The abandonment of parity obligations has substantially modified a major source of the asymmetry characterizing the Bretton Woods system:

the fact that U.S. monetary policy had a much larger impact on the world money stock than the monetary policy of any other country (or other countries combined), not merely because of our larger size, but also because the money that flowed out of this country as ordinary money entered other countries as "high-powered money"—that is, as part of their monetary base. To put it another way, the United States was able to offset the impact of payments deficits on its domestic money supply, and therefore to exercise a disproportionate influence on the money supplies of other countries, partly because of the "automatic sterilization" that occurred whenever other countries held their foreign exchange reserves in the form of U.S. Treasury bills or in the form of deposits in U.S. commercial banks.[60] Today such automatic sterilization still takes place to some extent, but it arises from the voluntary actions of those surplus-country central banks that regard liabilities of the U.S. government or of the U.S. banking system as desirable components of their asset portfolios. It does not now occur as a by-product of exchange-market intervention conducted by nations in the fulfillment of their parity obligations under the IMF Articles of Agreement.

In addition to its effect on the process of automatic sterilization, the shift in exchange-rate regime has affected the nature of financial interdependence between the United States and other countries in more subtle ways. The most direct link among national money markets over the past decade has been the Eurodollar market and, until recently, it was generally believed that "the degree of independence of the Eurodollar market from New York [was] limited," [61] owing partly to the dominant position of U.S. banks in the Eurocurrency market. Recently, however, this interdependence, like that on the real side, has become more of a two-way phenomenon than it had been. There are a number of reasons: the substantial increase in foreign holdings of the U.S. public debt in 1971–1972, the growing importance of non-U.S. participants in the Eurocurrency market and of Eurodeposits denominated in currencies other than dollars, and the increased effect of foreign money market conditions and foreign regulations on Eurodollar rates since the repayment (in 1970 and 1971) of large borrowings by U.S. banks from their overseas branches. But there is another reason as well, much more directly linked than these to the change in the international monetary system. It has generally been believed that, until 1971, the key currency role of the

---

[60] Genberg and Swoboda, "Causes and Origins."

[61] Geoffrey Bell, *The Euro-Dollar Market and the International Financial System* (New York: John Wiley, 1973), p. 42.

United States enabled it to exert a powerful influence on monetary conditions and prices abroad precisely because it was "the only country that [did] not (or [could] afford not to) care seriously about the effect of its price level on its external position." [62] Today, however, with exchange rates more responsive than before to supply-demand relationships in commodity, asset, and money markets, matters are reversed: it is now a question of the degree to which the United States, as well as other countries, must worry about the effect of changes in its external position, reflected in changes in its exchange rate, on its domestic price level. And, although the relatively small size of the foreign sector in the United States reduces this kind of sensitivity, there is considerable evidence from recent history to indicate that this country neither is nor feels immune to the impact of exchange-rate changes on its own price level. In this respect, the shift to managed floating has probably somewhat reduced the asymmetry of responses to external pressures as between the United States and non-reserve-currency countries.

The aspect of the changed international adjustment mechanism with the most immediate and direct impact on the United States was the dramatic correction (some would argue overcorrection) of the long-term cumulative overvaluation of the dollar, the resulting change in the composition of the U.S. payments balance, and the effect this change had in turn on the domestic U.S. economy. Between June 1970 and April 1976, the dollar underwent an effective (trade-weighted) depreciation of 12.5 percent against the currencies of fourteen other major industrialized countries. [63] Although the exact degree of causal relationship will remain endlessly controversial, the fact is that this country's balance on goods and services improved substantially from a deficit of nearly $6 billion in 1972 to a surplus of roughly $4 billion in 1973 and 1974 (deteriorating by only $350 million between the latter two years, despite an estimated increase of some $16 billion in our oil-import bill) and a surplus of more than $16 billion in 1975. [64] The domestic impact of this shift varied, of course, according to the overall cyclical position of the domestic economy. In 1973, when many industries were straining against capacity limitations, it almost

[62] William D. Nordhaus, "The Worldwide Wage Explosion," *Brookings Papers on Economic Activity*, 1972(2), p. 459.

[63] Morgan Guaranty Trust Company of New York, *World Financial Markets*, various issues. The effective depreciation of the dollar reached a maximum of 20 percent (from pre-June 1970 parities) in early 1975.

[64] Differences in the timing of the business cycle in the United States and our major partner countries were also a major factor in the improvement in the balance on goods and services.

certainly aggravated inflationary pressures. In 1975, in contrast, when the economy was suffering widespread excess capacity as a result of the steepest recession in our postwar history, the nearly $13 billion improvement in net exports made a welcome contribution to the substantial recovery in real growth that got under way in the second half of the year.

Along with this dramatic improvement in the balance on goods and services, the more realistic valuation of the dollar against other currencies has (along with other factors) created pressures for retarding the growth of American direct investment abroad and accelerating foreign direct investment in this country. Although a slowdown is just beginning to appear in the aggregate figures on foreign direct investment (complete data for 1975 are not yet available), it can be clearly discerned in the recent data and projections for capital expenditures abroad by foreign affiliates of U.S. firms. Such expenditures increased by 3 percent in 1975 and are projected to increase by only 2 percent in 1976, as contrasted with an increase of 25 percent in each of the preceding two years. They are actually expected to fall slightly in Europe in 1976 over the 1975 level, the first time since the 1950s that such a drop has occurred.[65] The rate of foreign direct investment in this country has already accelerated substantially, albeit from a very small base. Such investment averaged $3.5 billion in 1973 and 1974, as contrasted with an annual average of less than $1 billion in 1967–1972.[66]

Underlying these developments on both current and capital account is a fundamental improvement in the international competitive position of the U.S. economy. Over the period from 1965 to 1970, unit labor costs in manufacturing increased more rapidly in the United States than in four out of five major competitor countries (the only exception being Italy, whose rate of increase was fractionally higher than ours).[67] In 1970–1975, in contrast, although the average rate of increase in unit labor costs in this country was higher than in the previous period in absolute terms (6.4 percent as compared with 4.7 percent), the average rates of increase in the other five countries, measured on a U.S. dollar basis, were between two and three times as great as ours.[68] Part of this shift in relative position was the result of a difference in national experiences between the two periods (that is, the U.S. rate of increase was lower in 1970–1975 than those of the

---

[65] U.S. Department of Commerce, *News*, March 31, 1976.
[66] *International Economic Report of the President*, March 1976, p. 162.
[67] The five are France, West Germany, Italy, Japan, United Kingdom.
[68] Ibid., pp. 76-77.

other countries even when the latter are measured on a national currency basis), but part of it is also the result of the fact that the overvaluation of the dollar, increasing throughout the first period, was corrected during the second. Today, in 1976, it is clear that the United States is once again leading other industrialized nations in economic recovery. At the same time, our relatively superior inflation performance in the past year [69] gives reason to hope that, with good economic management, the United States may once again regain its historic position as an "island of stability" in the international economy.

Changing Perceptions of the International Framework and U.S. Policy Responses. In addition to strictly economic developments, a rapidly changing climate of foreign relations has affected our economic relationships with other nations.[70] From the end of World War II until relatively recently, the international economic policy of the United States was primarily a stepchild of our overriding national security objectives. The desire to enhance the economic strength of free-world nations as a bulwark against the perceived threat of worldwide Communist aggression underlay the American initiative for Marshall Plan aid and for subsequent mutual security arrangements in Europe, and helped create domestic support for economic assistance to developing nations. This same concern buttressed U.S. support for the formation and growth of the European Economic Community and helped to determine our leading role in multilateral trade negotiations. And the free-world nations accepted chronic U.S. payments deficits and a dollar-centered international monetary system as yet another aspect of the wide-spreading U.S. security umbrella.

With the thawing of the cold war, U.S. foreign economic policy has not been dominated by national security considerations to the same extent as before. And whatever becomes of the increasingly controversial idea of "détente," we are not likely to return in the near future to such a simple bipolar view of the world and our relationships within it. In the past, the United States was frequently willing to subordinate its short-term economic interests, narrowly conceived, to the long-term political and economic advantages of strengthened economies in other free-world nations and of a viable trading and monetary system linking those nations. Other countries, in turn, were willing to accord the United States certain special privileges

---

[69] Ibid., pp. 138-39.
[70] See Marina v. N. Whitman, "Leadership without Hegemony: Our Role in the World Economy," *Foreign Policy*, no. 20 (Fall 1975), pp. 139-40.

(primarily that of printing international money) as a concomitant of the special responsibilities we undertook for the military security and economic stability of the non-Communist world.

More recently, however, as cold war concerns have diffused and domestic economic problems have become more urgent, the United States and other major countries have both (albeit for somewhat different reasons) grown impatient with our special position, especially in the monetary sphere. Other countries have increasingly urged a system in which the United States behaves and is treated "just like everyone else." And we, disillusioned with our role as "world policeman" and increasingly reluctant to sacrifice immediate economic interests at home for the sake of international stability, have at times given disturbing indications that we might be only too glad to comply. For reasons already discussed, a viable international economic system that is also genuinely symmetrical seems unlikely to materialize. And the abandonment of economic leadership by the United States would carry a high political and economic cost: just as the worldwide economic agonies of the 1930s were almost certainly aggravated and prolonged by our reluctance to assume the responsibilities of economic leadership that Britain could no longer carry, so the economic problems of the 1970s and 1980s could very well be exacerbated by our premature abandonment of our present responsibilities in the absence of international institutions adequate to the task of mobilizing collective economic leadership. But to maintain such responsibilities means a willingness and ability to exercise leadership in an economic environment we no longer dominate, in which many other participants share economic power although they do not always willingly share responsibility, and yet in which (as was made clear at the Rambouillet meeting in November 1975) other countries still look to the United States as a primary source of, as well as solution to, their own economic difficulties.[71]

---

[71] The United States does not appear entirely comfortable with this position. In a recent speech, one member of the Board of Governors of the Federal Reserve System noted that "for every one percent increase in U.S. GNP, German GNP rises by something like 0.04 to 0.05 percent, i.e., four or five hundredths of one percent." Henry C. Wallich, "The American Economy, Europe, and the Federal Republic of Germany," *Remarks at the Bicentennial of German-American Relations*, Eicholz, Germany, February 19, 1976, p. 5. The study on which Wallich's remarks were based is Dean A. De Rosa and Gary L. Smeal, "The Transmission of Economic Activity Between the Major Industrial Countries" (U.S. Treasury, 1976; processed). This same study found evidence of an increase in interdependence of national (nominal) incomes among major industrialized countries between 1960 and 1974.

The formulation of economic policies in the face of declining hegemony and increasing interdependence has led to the rise in this country, as well as elsewhere, of what has been termed defensive economic nationalism—a nationalism based not on the desire to extend national power beyond one's own borders but rather on the desire to retain or regain control over economic developments within one's own borders in an environment of increased vulnerability to disturbances originating abroad and expanded governmental responsibility for the fulfillment of a variety of economic objectives at home. Barriers to insulate the domestic economy from foreign "disturbances" have historically taken the form of restrictions on imports. More recently, as concern with the international transmission of economic disturbances has broadened, the United States and other countries have resorted to a wider variety of insulating devices. The shift to floating exchange rates primarily represented an effort to create a buffer between national economies. Our plans for reduced dependence on imported energy—to the extent that they are translated from words into action—represent a very different kind of insulation against imported disturbances, this time on the supply side. And, with the acceleration of worldwide inflation and the increasing concern about "stagflation," countries have sought to avoid importing (or perhaps even to export) inflation by erecting barriers to exports just as they have long sought to ward off (or export) unemployment by restricting imports. The short-sightedness and ultimate ineffectiveness of such policies should be particularly apparent under a regime of flexible exchange rates (where export restrictions of any significant magnitude must exert downward pressure on the domestic currency and thus, *ceteris paribus*, upward pressure on the domestic price level), and our own experiments with export controls in 1972–1974 were both limited and short-lived.[72] But it was enough to make our foreign customers nervous and to lend support to those protectionist forces in Western Europe and Japan that had long been urging reduced dependence on U.S. agricultural exports through the promotion of greater domestic self-sufficiency at substantially increased cost.

Part and parcel of this heightened concern for control over the domestic economic environment is the increasing politicization of issues relating to foreign economic policy. This politicization has a number of root causes. One is the increasing inadequacy of the

---

[72] The administration prepared an export-control program for cattle hides in mid-1972 which was never implemented because it was determined that the requisite legislative authority did not exist. The export of soybeans was embargoed briefly in the summer of 1973, and controls were imposed on the export of ferrous scrap in July 1973 and discontinued in 1974.

international ground rules governing economic behavior, an inadequacy which is both cause and effect of the desire for reduced vulnerability. This inadequacy has taken the form of gradual erosion in the case of the international trading system grounded in the General Agreement on Tariffs and Trade (GATT) and of dramatic breakdown in the case of the international monetary system based on the Articles of Agreement of the International Monetary Fund. A second root cause is the fact that the policies associated with economic interdependence, unlike those associated with the maintenance of mutual security in the 1950s and 1960s, have an exceedingly uneven impact at home, benefiting some groups and geographic regions and harming others. Given a growing concern with distributional equity, and the absence of adequate mechanisms for implementing the compensation principle (that is, for insuring that the gainers from economic integration or the society as a whole adequately compensate those who must bear the burden of adjustment), the pressure for buffers against interdependence are bound to persist. The important questions for policy are, first, how to provide these buffers in such a way as to create minimum interference with the acknowledged benefits of market integration and, second, to what extent policy coordination can be used to reduce the remaining tension between market integration and the desire for national economic self-determination.

The first question lies at the heart of the argument in favor of retaining flexible exchange rates. Although the degree of insulation provided by managed flexibility is somewhat more limited than had been generally anticipated—partly because of the high degree of integration of international financial markets and partly because of the magnitude of the common exogenous shocks which occurred shortly after the shift to floating rates—there is no question that the insulation provided is far more efficient and disrupts market integration less than the alternative of pegged rates and piecemeal restrictions on trade or capital flows (or both). This is particularly true if one takes the view, which has much wider acceptance in the United States than in Western Europe and Japan, that freedom of international transactions in capital markets tends to promote the maximization of world income and world welfare on the same basis as does such freedom in commodity markets. Experience indicates strongly that, whereas it may be possible under favorable circumstances to support the liberalization of trade transactions even under pegged rates, the pressures for restrictions on capital flows are likely to prove irresistible as external disequilibria build up and speculative pressures increase. It is no coincidence that the United States felt itself free to remove its "temporary" programs restricting capital exports (programs introduced a decade before) only after the move to generalized floating. More broadly, the avoidance of a wholesale retreat from a liberal international trading system into competitive protectionism in the face of the oil crisis and subsequent widespread recession was doubtless made possible by the shift from pegged rates to managed floating.

The Question of Coordination: What and How? In considering the extent to which coordination among governments can relieve the vulnerability resulting from interdependence, it is first important to sort out what is meant by "policy coordination." In fact, it is possible to talk about several different levels of policy coordination. At the lowest level, the phrase can simply mean the avoidance of explicit beggar-my-neighbor policies, such as trade barriers or exchange-rate manipulation, in the solution of domestic economic problems. Although our own record has not been spotless, the United States has tended to take the lead in promoting negative coordination of this sort during the postwar period. This country took the initiative in promoting trade liberalization through successive rounds of multilateral trade negotiations, the latest of which is currently under way in Geneva. Since the successful avoidance of beggar-my-neighbor policies requires that countries eschew inconsistent targets for such variables as the current account or the exchange rate, the United States has throughout the discussions and negotiations on international monetary reform stressed the importance of insuring such consistency. To that end, we initially urged a larger role for "objective indicators," or guidelines on balance-of-payments and reserve targets, than most other industrialized countries were willing to accept. The general concept has carried over into the floating-rate context in the suggested guidelines for floating in the Committee of Twenty's "Outline of Reform." [73]

The theoretical insights provided by the monetary approach to balance-of-payments analysis imply that, in a world of managed floating, rules for exchange-market intervention are inadequate to insure that inconsistent targets and exchange-rate manipulation will

---

[73] See *Economic Report of the President,* January 1973, Appendix A, Supplement to ch. 5; "Quantitative Indicators from the Point of View of the Overall Operation of the System" (memorandum submitted by the U.S. deputies of the Committee of Twenty to the secretary, International Monetary Fund, May 17, 1973; processed). Also, International Monetary Fund, "Outline of Reform," "Annexes" 1 and 4, "Reports of Technical Groups: On Indicators," all in *International Monetary Reform: Documents of the Committee of Twenty* (Washington, D.C.: International Monetary Fund, 1974).

be avoided, since there is more than one means of pursuing such targets. And, in fact, the recent history of managed floating is replete with instances of countries' supporting their currencies indirectly through foreign borrowing rather than directly in the exchange markets. Fundamentally, in this view, the avoidance of inconsistent external targets requires not merely rules governing exchange-market intervention but rules guaranteeing the compatibility of national monetary policies with each other, and the compatibility of fiscal policies to the extent that they are financed by money creation or affect the demand for money.

The degree of coordination just described is, of course, much more demanding than would be the mere avoidance of restrictive commercial policies and of explicit beggar-my-neighbor behavior. It means positive coordination, not merely in the sense that each country take account of the probable macroeconomic policies of others in setting its own and thus avoid global stimulative or deflationary "overkill," but in the sense that countries actually set macroeconomic targets and plan the policies to achieve them cooperatively, including the coordination of timetables for implementing the policies. And the history of past efforts along these lines is not encouraging. In the early 1960s, for example, efforts to establish guidelines for international cooperation on stabilization policies among OECD countries foundered on disagreement between the United States and the European countries as to how formal and restrictive the agreed principles should be. Fifteen years later, at the Rambouillet meeting in November 1975, this country was not receptive to urgings that the U.S. government increase its stimulative measures in order that faster recovery in this country (and the consequent expansion of our import markets) could provide the basis for an export-led recovery in our partner countries. In retrospect, however, it seems that the differences of views on this issue may have been less the result of uncooperativeness on the part of the United States than of the failure of the other participants to recognize how stimulative our policies were already or how rapid a rate of real growth we had actually achieved in the second half of 1975.

The somewhat discouraging experience of the European Economic Community in trying to establish an economic and monetary union shows how difficult it is for nations to make the transition from negative coordination (in the sense of abolishing explicit barriers to international transactions) to positive coordination of national economic policies. But both the logic of analysis and the evidence from recent experience suggest that there is no alternative; the dynamics of tension between the vulnerability created by increasing integration at the market level and the persistence of fragmentation at the policy level suggest that if we do not find ways to make progress on the latter we will inevitably slip backward away from the former. The shift to managed flexibility of exchange rates has alleviated the burden by providing a partial buffer against external disturbances, but the buffer is only partial and the need to take a global approach to macroeconomic policy problems remains.

CORPORATE TAXES AND FINANCING UNDER CONTINUING INFLATION

George M. von Furstenberg

Summary

High rates of inflation can subvert the normal workings of our tax and financing systems, and this is nowhere more evident than in the case of businesses, particularly nonfinancial corporations. If the prices of products sold are determined by current market conditions, but the expenses incurred in producing them are all determined on an historical-cost basis, tax liabilities will be raised in real terms as a result of inflation even if the margin of return over replacement costs has not risen at all. In the long run, however, the tax-raising effects of inflation may be reversed, and other effects that can cause balance sheet deterioration and a significant reduction in the investment incentives for nonfinancial corporations may increase in importance.

There are two factors that together may produce a decline in the effective tax rate. First, under current tax laws corporations are free to use the last-in first-out (LIFO) method of inventory valuation, which allows them to charge current cost against book profits for those inventories they continue to buy. To this extent inflationary revaluations are not taxed. Second, like other borrowers, corporations may expense not only "real" interest but also the inflation premium in their interest payments. Once the inflation premium in interest rates is fully reflected in the average rate on outstanding debt, the deductibility of that premium can be worth more to the average corporation than the loss in deductions stemming from the continued

I am indebted to Burton G. Malkiel of the Council of Economic Advisers (CEA) and to William J. Fellner of the American Enterprise Institute (AEI) for help and advice. Useful suggestions were received also from Robert W. Kilpatrick of the Office of Management and Budget, David C. Munro of CEA, and Marvin Kosters and Dan Larkins of AEI, but the views expressed are solely my responsibility.

use of historical-cost depreciation on fixed assets. The effective tax rate for most LIFO companies may thus be lower in the long run than it would be with complete indexing or in the absence of inflation. However, it takes well over a decade of higher inflation for this result to emerge for LIFO companies, and companies remaining on the first-in first-out (FIFO) method would face higher effective tax rates as a result of inflation, even in the long run. Whether the tax squeeze from inflation continues indefinitely thus depends on the specific assumptions made.

There is, however, another hidden tax that corporations must bear under inflationary conditions. Even at high rates of inflation corporations require the services of non-interest-bearing monetary assets. Once inflation has settled at its higher level, corporations cannot allow the real value of these assets to fall year after year. However, the funds committed to maintaining the real value of monetary assets may have to be raised externally unless investment is cut back. The resulting balance-sheet deterioration, if continued for long, would first shut corporations out of the market for new equity issues and then curtail their access to the bond market. Hence, even if the effective tax rate on profits is not raised permanently by inflation, higher rates of inflation may well lower the rate of investment in the nonfinancial corporate sector.

Introduction

A number of authors have recently described how inflation has raised the effective tax rate of corporations.[1] For nonfinancial corporations, particularly those using the FIFO method of inventory accounting, inventory profits have boosted the tax base even though they do not increase a firm's real net worth when they are the result of general price inflation. Furthermore, historical-cost depreciation has fallen increasingly short of replacement-cost depreciation as the price of new plant and equipment has continued to rise faster than in earlier

---

[1] See William J. Fellner et al., *Correcting Taxes for Inflation* (Washington, D.C.: American Enterprise Institute, 1975); William D. Nordhaus, "The Falling Share of Profits," *Brookings Papers on Economic Activity*, 1974(1), pp. 169-208; J. J. Siegfried, "Effective Average U.S. Corporation Income Tax Rates," *National Tax Journal*, vol. 27 (June 1974), pp. 245-59; Charles W. Stewart, Jr., "Taxation and the Crisis of Capital," *Tax Review*, vol. 35 (August 1974), pp. 31-34; George Terborgh, "Inflation and Profits," Machinery and Allied Products Institute, Memoranda G-70, Washington, D.C., January 1975; and Norman B. Ture, "Capital Needs, Profits, and Inflation," *Tax Review*, vol. 36 (January 1975), pp. 1-4.

periods. On the other hand, since nonfinancial corporations are net debtors, untaxed capital gains have accrued to the extent that the level of inflation was higher than anticipated, and once inflationary expectations were reflected in interest rates, the tax savings from deducting interest payments have been raised.[2] The net result has been that (so far at least) the annual net return on capital—defined as the sum of inflation-adjusted profits and the actual net interest paid—has been subject to higher effective corporation income tax rates the higher the rate of inflation.[3]

While this result has been documented conclusively for the past, the functional relationships have not been expressed in a way that would allow one to state by how much a given rate of inflation maintained for t years would change the effective tax rate and alter future financing ratios. This paper attempts to develop the systematic relationships necessary for appraising what will happen to capital formation and taxation under inflationary conditions, once normal levels of capacity utilization have been restored.

Effective corporate tax rates and the development of financial flows can be compared systematically over time only if the annual estimates are adjusted for cyclical effects. So that the data for our model will be consistent with the 1973 level of capacity utilization, this paper assumes a 3.7 percent growth in all real variables each year after 1973.[4] With this assumption, the model predicts inventory

---

[2] See John B. Shoven and Jeremy I. Bulow, "Inflation Accounting and Nonfinancial Corporate Profits: Physical Assets," *Brookings Papers on Economic Activity*, 1975(3), pp. 557-611, and the forthcoming sequel "Inflation Accounting and Nonfinancial Corporate Profits: Financial Assets and Liabilities," by the same authors.

[3] The real cost of the interest payments is lowered by the inflation premium because the inflation premium is treated as a deductible business expense instead of being treated as a partial repayment of debt equal to the reduction in the real indebtedness to the lender. The lenders, on the other hand, may be taxed on the inflation premium in interest payments received, even though this premium merely offsets the reduction in the real value of their claim. However, since the majority of the holders of corporate debt are taxed very little (insurance companies) or not at all (pension funds), the tax treatment is strongly asymmetrical between borrowers and lenders. Hence, additional inflation lowers the after-tax cost of debt, even if greater inflation is fully anticipated, provided the expected variability of rates of inflation does not change. For further discussion see Martin S. Feldstein, "Inflation, Income Taxes and the Rate of Interest: A Theoretical Analysis," Harvard Institute of Economic Research, Discussion Paper No. 414, May 1975.

[4] Fixed nonresidential business capital has grown by 3.7 percent from 1960 to 1970, or by less than the over 4 percent annual rate of growth in the potential output of the corresponding sector (mainly nonfinancial corporations). However, the decline in the ratio of capital to capacity output appears to have halted in the late 1960s.

profits, underdepreciation, and net interest payments at different infla-tion rates. Since book profits are derived by adding inventory profits and underdepreciation to the net return on capital, and subtracting net interest paid, these are the only items that can cause the effective tax rate to vary in the model, given that the statutory tax rate on book profits is fixed. After estimating each component in turn, we calculate the profits tax liabilities of nonfinancial corporations. Next, dividend pay-out is specified to obtain retained earnings exclusive of inventory profits and underdepreciation. Finally, the growth of both internal and external financial resources is compared to the projected growth in the replacement value of assets, in order to determine the effect of inflation on the adequacy of financing and (by implication) on the required rate of return on investment.

Inventory Profits

As a first step in identifying the tax effects of inflation, we estimate the corporate inventory valuation adjustment (IVA). The IVA is equal to inventory profits with the sign reversed because it is used as an adjustment to book profits. If s is the share of the total stocks held by nonfinancial corporations that are subject to FIFO accounting in figuring the cost of goods sold, if INV_{-1} is the book value of all inventories held by nonfinancial corporations at the end of last year and at last year's prices, and if $\dot{p}$ is the percentage rise in the whole-sale price index for industrial commodities from year to year, then inventory profits (IVA) can be estimated as follows: [5]

$$IVA = a[s(INV_{-1})\dot{p}] \qquad (1)$$

If the chosen fixed-weight price index correctly mirrors the aver-age appreciation rate of inventories, the regression coefficient a should

---

[5] The real value of stocks held by nonfinancial corporations was estimated by the Bureau of Economic Analysis, U.S. Department of Commerce, which also provided estimates of s. This variable appears to have remained approximately constant at 89 percent from 1954 through 1973 before falling to 76.8 percent by the end of 1974. The value of inventories was converted from 1972 dollars to current dollars by using the wholesale price index for industrial commodities, rebased from 1967 to 1972. Annual inventory profits are estimated in the national income accounts by the change in the book value of inventories within a year less the change in real stocks valued at that year's prices. The result is the change in the value of inventories held at the end of the preceding year, which results from the change in the average price level from the preceding to the current year, given that inventories then in stock were acquired from zero to twelve months earlier.

be unity. Inventory profits occur under the LIFO method of inventory accounting only when the real stocks purchased are smaller than the lower-priced old stocks used up over some period in any category. In that case (taxable) inventory profits arise on the net reduction in real stocks during the current year. Since the annual level of stocks declined only twice during the 1954–1975 estimation period, in 1958 and in 1975, inventory profits realized by firms on LIFO are likely to be small. Even though the aggregate experience is not duplicated by every firm using LIFO and inventories in some pools are reduced while inventories in other pools are growing, such profits are ignored in the estimate below (unsigned t-values in parentheses):

$$IVA = -0.8979 \, s(INV_{-1})p; \, \overline{R}^2 = 0.881;$$
$$(14.56) \tag{2}$$
$$D.W. = 1.44; \, S_c = 3.02 \, (\$ \text{ billion})$$

Since the regression coefficient is not significantly less than unity at the 5 percent level, equation (2) shows that inventory profits can be expressed as the product of FIFO stocks at the end of last year and the rate of inflation. From 1957 to 1973, the real value of stocks held by nonfinancial corporations grew nearly in proportion to the real gross product of these corporations. If proportional growth continues and if inventories were approximately in equilibrium in 1973, the nominal value of inventories can be projected for later years of high capacity operation by assuming 3.7 percent real growth per annum and using the rates of inflation in wholesale prices specified in Table 1. The implied IVA can then be obtained once the declining percentage of FIFO inventories, s, has been projected for future years.[6]

Underdepreciation

If the actual service lives of depreciable assets and the time distribution of the services they yield are reflected in depreciation allowances and if depreciation is calculated on a replacement-cost basis, we will obtain the correct write-off for capital resources used up during the current production period. Underdepreciation will result if inflation causes the historical-cost depreciation actually claimed by non-

---

[6] The percentage of FIFO inventories, s, is estimated to decline from 76.8 percent in 1974 to 72 percent in 1975. It is then assumed to fall by four percentage points each year through 1990, so that s is 52 percent in 1980, 32 percent in 1985, and 12 percent in 1990.

financial corporations (tax depreciation) [7] to fall short of replacement-cost depreciation. This can occur even with the use of shorter tax lives and more accelerated methods in tax depreciation than would be given by the actual experience reflected in replacement-cost depreciation.

After 1954, new investment could be depreciated with accelerated methods, and tax service lives were shortened in 1962 and again in 1971. The 1962 *Guidelines* reduced tax service lives for new equipment by about 30 to 40 percent from the lives prescribed in the 1942 edition of Bulletin F but did not change the tax lives for structures. Further reductions of about 20 percent in tax lives for equipment were permitted through adoption of the asset depreciation range (ADR) system in 1971. If actual depreciation has not accelerated as much as depreciation for tax purposes and if actual service lives have not fallen as much as tax service lives, replacement-cost depreciation must be estimated on more realistic assumptions than are used for tax depreciation.

Robert Coen has recently concluded that the tax service lives for equipment prescribed in the Treasury's 1962 *Guidelines* were on average in line with service lives revealed by investment behavior in manufacturing, but that the average life of structures was somewhat shorter.[8] Thus his findings would support using 60 to 70 percent of Bulletin F service lives for equipment and perhaps 90 percent for structures. However, according to Allan Young, 85 percent of Bulletin F service lives represents a reasonable approximation for both types of assets.[9] Several studies have suggested that the actual service yielded by capital assets may not decline significantly until shortly before the asset is discarded.[10] If this "one-hoss-shay" pattern

---

[7] The depreciation tabulated by the Internal Revenue Service from tax returns filed by businesses is not precisely equal to historical-cost depreciation in the national income accounts (NIA), which is here called tax depreciation. NIA depreciation includes an allowance for accidental damage to fixed capital, and, moreover, it is charged on certain short-lived assets which are included in business fixed investment on an NIA basis, but expensed in the year of acquisition by businesses.

[8] Robert M. Coen, "Investment Behavior, the Measurement of Depreciation, and Tax Policy," *American Economic Review*, vol. 65 (March 1975), pp. 59-74.

[9] Allan H. Young, "New Estimates of Capital Consumption Allowances in the Benchmark Revision of GNP," *Survey of Current Business*, vol. 55 (October 1975), pp. 14-16, 35.

[10] See, for instance, Zvi Griliches, "Capital Stock in Investment Functions: Some Problems of Concept and Measurement," in Carl F. Christ et al. (eds.), *Measurement in Economics: Studies in Mathematical Economics and Econometrics in Memory of Yehuda Grunfeld* (Stanford: Stanford University Press, 1963), pp. 115-37; Zvi Griliches, "Production Functions in Manufacturing: Some Pre-

230

is approximately correct, replacement-cost depreciation is correctly charged on a straight-line basis to prevent intertemporal distortions in profit accounting.[11] Hence, straight-line replacement-cost depreciation with 85 percent of Bulletin F service lives will be compared to tax depreciation in an attempt to identify any past or future under-depreciation. The difference between tax depreciation and replacement-cost depreciation yields the capital consumption adjustment to profits (CCA) that was introduced into national income accounting during the 1975 benchmark revisions.

To estimate the capital consumption adjustment for future years, we must project both tax depreciation and replacement-cost depreciation. Under given depreciation rules, the current tax depreciation (D) claimed by nonfinancial corporations can be expressed as a function of past depreciation and a two-year average of the most recent gross fixed investment (I). The latter yields the base for the first full year of depreciation on new assets.[12]

$$D = bD_{-1} + c[(I + I_{-1})/2] \tag{3}$$

In the stationary state with zero rates of inflation and net investment, the coefficients b and c would necessarily sum to unity. Assuming straight-line depreciation, the fraction $(1 - b)$ represents the reduction in depreciation charges on previous years' investment resulting from the fact that some assets were discarded or fully depreciated

---

liminary Results," in Murray Brown (ed.), *The Theory and Empirical Analysis of Production* (New York: Columbia University Press for the National Bureau of Economic Research, 1967), pp. 275-322; and Helen S. Tice, "Depreciation, Obsolescence, and the Measurement of the Aggregate Capital Stock in the United States, 1900-1962," *Review of Income and Wealth*, vol. 13 (July 1967), pp. 119-54.

11 Depreciation rules that stabilize the annual flow of profits used in macro-economic comparisons differ from those designed to maintain equality between the book value and the market value of assets, but stability in profits is intended here. For instance, if an asset yields a constant annual stream of services until the end of its useful life, the market value of the asset would decline at the increasing rate implied by the annuity method of depreciation. See Paul A. Samuelson, "Tax Deductibility of Economic Depreciation to Insure Invariant Valuations," *Journal of Political Economy*, vol. 72, no. 6 (December 1964), pp. 604-06, and Young, "New Estimates," p. 35.

12 Since only a half-year of depreciation can be claimed on groups of assets acquired in the most recent year, depreciation for the first year of asset life is determined by investment in both the current and in the previous year. An exception to this rule is provided under current law mainly for the benefit of small businesses. Under this provision, depreciation equal to 20 percent of the value of new investment up to a maximum of $2,000 per annum can be claimed in the current year no matter when assets (up to $10,000 for corporations and individuals not filing a joint return, up to $20,000 on joint returns) were acquired during that year.

a year ago. The coefficient c indicates the first-year depreciation rate on new investment; aside from composition effects it is a function of the depreciation rules used. If fixed investment is growing rapidly in nominal terms, the coefficient b approaches unity at the limit since the original cost of the oldest classes of assets that are dropping out of the depreciable base is then very small compared to the original cost of depreciable assets purchased in later years on which depreciation continues to be charged.[13] While faster growth in I raises b towards unity, accelerated methods of depreciation or reductions in service lives increase c and lower b.

The two opposing forces operating on b appear to have been roughly offsetting until 1971 inasmuch as estimates for the subperiods 1955–1961 and 1963–1970 before and after adoption of the 1962 *Guidelines* yield coefficients not significantly different from those shown for the 1954–1971 period as a whole.

$$D = 0.9464\,D_{-1} + 0.0954\,[(I + I_{-1})/2]$$
$$\quad\;(14.54)\qquad(2.08)\qquad\qquad\qquad (4)$$
$$\bar{R}^2 = 0.998;\,D.W. = 2.42;\,S_c = 0.62\ (\$\ \text{billion})$$

The roughly 20 percent reduction in tax service lives in 1971 combined with the subsequent acceleration of inflation may have left the first regression coefficient, b, again roughly unchanged at 95 percent, but the second coefficient, c, is assumed to have risen to 11 percent after 1971. Should the average annual rate of inflation in fixed asset prices rise substantially above the 7–8 percent rate that prevailed from 1971 to 1975, b would have to be raised towards unity, while it would have to be lowered towards 0.89 if the rate of inflation declined.[14]

Replacement-cost depreciation can be estimated in the same way as tax depreciation, except that the lagged depreciation term is multiplied by p/p_{-1} (or one plus the annual rate of growth in the implicit deflator for the fixed investment of nonfinancial corporations) to convert to a replacement-cost basis. In the specification below first-year depreciation is assumed to remain unindexed.

$$DR = b'\,(p/p_{-1})DR_{-1} + c'[(I + I_{-1})/2] \qquad (5)$$

---

[13] If b approaches unity at high but steady rates of growth of nominal investment, equation (3) implies that the ratio of current investment to current tax depreciation approaches the ratio of the nominal rate of growth of investment (which equals the rate of growth of depreciation under steady growth conditions) to the first-year depreciation rate, c.

[14] Given a c of 0.11, the lowest possible value of b with zero inflation and no growth is 0.89, with b and c summing to unity.

The regression coefficients b' and c' are invariant to inflation and stable over time since the depreciation method and service lives used to calculate replacement-cost depreciation are held fixed throughout. With annual data for 1954 through 1975, the regression estimate for replacement-cost depreciation (DR) is

$$DR = 0.8291 \; (p/p_{\text{-}1}) \; DR_{\text{-}1} + 0.1532[(I + I_{\text{-}1})/2]$$
$$(27.41) \qquad\qquad (6.86) \qquad\qquad\qquad (6)$$
$$\overline{R}^2 = 0.999; D.W. = 1.20; S_c = 0.53 \; (\$ \text{ billion})$$

On a priori grounds (which require that the sum of the two regression coefficients be no less than unity), both coefficients were raised slightly for forecasting replacement-cost depreciation by using [15]

$$DR = 0.84(p/p_{\text{-}1})DR_{\text{-}1} + 0.16[(I + I_{\text{-}1})/2] \qquad (7)$$

The ratio of tax depreciation to replacement-cost depreciation will stabilize after one replacement cycle if the rate of growth of investment (g) and the inflation rate (i) are steady, but the size of this ratio is a function of both of these factors. From equations (3) and (5) the ratio that will eventually emerge is [16]

$$D/DR = \frac{c(1+i)(1+g-b')}{c'[(1+g)(1+i)-b]} \qquad (8)$$

With the values $g = 0.037$, $b' = 0.84$, $c' = 0.16$, and $c = 0.11$, and the combinations of i and b shown in the columns below, equation (8) yields

i	0%	2.5%	5%	7.5%	10%
b	0.92	0.93	0.94	0.95	0.96
D/DR	1.158	1.044	0.955	0.884	0.824

Because accelerated methods are used, tax depreciation thus exceeds replacement-cost depreciation by almost 16 percent if there is no inflation; but this excess turns into a shortfall at steady rates of

---

[15] The implicit deflator for the fixed investment of nonfinancial corporations is not entirely suitable for converting depreciation to a replacement-cost basis since it is weighted by the current rather than by the past composition of investment. However, it is the closest proxy available. If this deflator overtakes effective price increases, the regression coefficients b and c may sum to less than unity. Furthermore, the degree of collinearity between $DR_{\text{-}1}$ or $D_{\text{-}1}$ and $(I+I_{\text{-}1})/2$ is very high so that the sum of the two coefficients is more reliable than the parts.

[16] Under steady growth conditions, equations (3) and (5) can be rewritten as follows to yield (8):

$$(3) \quad D = c[(I + I_{\text{-}1})/2] \; [1 + b(1 + g)^{-1} (1 + i)^{-1}$$
$$+ b^2(1 + g)^{-2} (1 + i)^{-2} \ldots] ,$$
$$(5) \quad DR = c'[(I + I_{\text{-}1})/2] \; [1 + b'(1 + g)^{-1} + b'^2(1 + g)^{-2} \ldots]$$

inflation between 3 and 4 percent per annum. At 10 percent inflation, tax depreciation is eventually almost 18 percent less than replacement-cost depreciation.

Net Interest Paid

The net interest paid by nonfinancial corporations can be expressed as the product of the net interest-bearing debt outstanding and the interest rates applicable to the debt issued over the years. Both the net debt outstanding each year (which can be calculated from the flow of funds accounts) and the level of interest rates are influenced by inflation. The effect of inflation on each of these will be dealt with in turn.

In the absence of aggregation and composition problems, the change in the annual amount of net interest paid (*DNIP*) by nonfinancial corporations could be deduced from an identity. As shown below, *DNIP* would be equal simply to the interest rate on new issues, *n*, multiplied by the year-to-year change in the net debt outstanding, *DD*, plus the difference between the new issue rate and the rate previously applicable to the debt that is being refinanced in the current year, *Dn*, multiplied by the amount of such refinancing, *REF*.

$$DNIP = k(n)DD + h(Dn)REF \qquad (9)$$

In practice, equation (9) is not an identity, in part because of the heterogeneity of the debt that is netted against interest bearing assets.[17] More important, the change in net interest paid by nonfinancial corporations reported in the national income accounts is little larger than the product of *n* and *DD*,[18] and the extra interest costs

---

[17] Corporate bonds, mortgages, bank loans not elsewhere classified, open-market paper (commercial paper and acceptances), finance company loans, and U.S. government loans outstanding reported in the flow of funds accounts are treated as interest-bearing liabilities which are netted against the corresponding assets. These assets are U.S. government and state and local government securities held by nonfinancial corporations, commercial paper, consumer credit, and time deposits (mainly CDs). In recent years the interest-bearing liabilities have tended to exceed the interest-bearing assets by a factor of six. Corporate bonds, mortgages and bank loans constitute the bulk of the interest-bearing liabilities of nonfinancial corporations.

[18] The change in net indebtedness is calculated from the Board of Governors of the Federal Reserve System, *Flow of Funds Accounts 1945-1972* (Washington, D.C.: Federal Reserve System, August 1973), pp. 85-87, and subsequent tabulations. Since the consolidated balance sheet data are for year-end, the net interest-bearing debt outstanding during the year is calculated as a simple average of two adjacent year-end figures, and differences in the resulting averages yield *DD*.

from refinancing at higher rates could not be quantified successfully.[19] However, the change in net interest paid appeared to be a stable fraction of the additional interest payments on the change in net debt outstanding, as shown below.[20]

$$DNIP = 1.1976(n)DD; \overline{R}^2 = 0.855; D.W. = 1.82;$$
$$(14.53) \hspace{4cm} (10)$$
$$S_e = 0.73 \text{ (\$ billion)}$$

Since the new issue rate reflects the average interest rate on AAA-rated new debt, the value of k exceeds unity—in part because of the lower quality of and higher interest rates on other debt. On the assumption that the desired real indebtedness at least would not fall as a result of inflation, the effect of inflation on net interest paid by nonfinancial corporations can be estimated once the effect on the new issue rate has been determined.

In the literature nominal interest rates have frequently been treated as a function of a real rate and lagged rates of inflation and this procedure will be followed here. However, such a treatment is troublesome because it implies (1) that the information used to form expectations and contract prices is limited to past inflation and interest rates, (2) that the elasticity of expected rates of inflation with respect to deviations of the current rate from the weighted average of past rates is low and completely insensitive to new information about government policy intentions, and (3) that nominal interest rates, no matter how determined, do not influence future policies and rates of inflation.[21] In spite of misgivings about the validity of all these assumptions, we will employ a regressive process to generate interest rate forecasts at full capacity on the basis of given inflation rates.

Following Fisher, nominal interest rates (n) are assumed to be a composite of the constant equilibrium rate of interest as it would be

[19] Because the net debt outstanding has doubled every six or seven years in the postwar period, the amount of refinancing of long-term debt has been quite small in relation to the annual change in total debt outstanding. An attempt was made to represent the annual amount of refinancing (REF) by an index growing at a fixed compound annual rate and to construct interest rate differences (Dn) from rates eight to ten years back. However, this procedure failed to yield a product whose coefficient (h) was positive and statistically significant in any of the experiments with several alternative growth rates of refinancing centered around 9 percent per annum.

[20] Because net interest paid by nonfinancial corporations was very small (less than \$2 billion per annum) until the mid-1950s, the regression is for annual data from 1957 through 1975, with lagged data input reaching back to the end of 1955.

[21] For a discussion of related specification issues, see Eugene F. Fama, "Efficient Capital Markets: A Review of Theory and Empirical Work," *Journal of Finance*, vol. 25, no. 2 (May 1970), pp. 383-417.

in the absence of inflation (r), and of the rate of inflation (i). Expected rates of inflation may be derived as a Koyck weighted average lag of present and past rates of inflation. Hence, with the adjustment coefficient, a, and the exponentially declining lag weight, w, we obtain

$$n = r + a(i + wi_{-1} + w^2 i_{-2} \ldots), \text{ or} \tag{11}$$

$$wn_{-1} = wr + a(wi_{-1} + w^2 i_{-2} \ldots). \tag{12}$$

Substituting from (12) into (11) yields:

$$n - n_{-1} = dn = (1 - w)r + ai - (1 - w)n_{-1} \tag{13}$$

Using year-to-year changes in the CPI to represent the rate of inflation of most concern to lenders and First National City Bank's rate on new issues of high-grade corporate bonds for n,[22] the regression estimated for 1954–1975 is

$$dn = 1.2008 + 0.2605i - 0.3351n_{-1}; \overline{R}^2 = 0.439, D.W. = 1.82,$$
$$(3.15) \quad (4.29) \quad (3.49)$$
$$S_e = 0.45 \text{ (percentage points)} \tag{14}$$

The coefficient of n_{-1} shows that $(1 - w)$ equals 0.3351. Substituting this into the constant term, $(1 - w)r$, and solving yields 3.58 percent for r. Because an interest rate between 3 and 4 percent does not seem unreasonable for corporate bonds in the absence of inflation, the regression results are consistent with the a priori specification.[23]

The real interest rate r^* that emerges after a long period of inflation at the rate i may be distinguished from the constant equilibrium rate r that would prevail in the absence of inflation. The rate r^*, defined as $n - i$ once n has ceased to change ($dn = 0$), is derived from equation (13) using the values estimated in (14). Since the coefficient a is estimated to be less than $(1 - w)$, r^* is lower under secular inflation than under noninflationary conditions, as shown below.

$$r^* = r - i[1 - a/(1 - w)] = 3.58 - 0.223i \tag{15}$$

A lower real interest rate at higher and more variable expected rates of inflation may be explained by borrowers' requiring a larger risk

---

[22] Estimates beginning April 1972 are computed by Data Resources, Inc.

[23] Similar coefficient estimates with smaller standard errors were obtained using Moody's yields on AAA corporate bonds, on BAA corporate bonds, and on all industrial corporate bonds. However, the yield on new issues seemed most consistent with the initial specification. An increase in the annual rate of growth of the money supply was not found to be statistically significant in lowering the average annual yield of corporate bonds, though changes in M_1 growth probably affect movements in these rates over shorter periods since the inflation rate and inflationary expectations do not adjust immediately.

premium than is required by lenders as real interest rates and the real value of indebtedness become increasingly uncertain. Borrowers risk bankruptcy if the real rate turns out higher than expected while lenders merely have a disappointingly small return in the opposite case.

In 1973, nonfinancial corporations paid net interest of $24.5 billion on an estimated average net debt of $407 billion outstanding, up $46 billion from the year before. Each year thereafter, the change in net interest will grow at the following rate from the preceding year, assuming 3.7 percent growth in real net indebtedness per annum.[24]

$$dDNIP/DNIP_{-1} = 1.037(1 + i)[1 + dn/n_{-1}] - 1 \qquad (16)$$

Since dn is given by equation (14), equation (16) can be used to estimate the development of net interest paid by nonfinancial corporations from 1974 on for specified inflation rates and the chosen rate of growth.[25] Once interest rates have stabilized after a prolonged period of steady inflation at the rate i, the change in net interest paid grows at the rate of $i + 0.037$ $(1 + i)$ and the growth in net interest as a whole also converges to this rate. Ultimately, therefore, net interest paid grows at the same rate as the net debt outstanding.

Effective Corporate Income Tax Rates

With the relations just estimated, net interest paid, tax depreciation, replacement-cost depreciation, and the IVA can be calculated from 1973 on, given the specified growth rates of net debt, gross fixed investment, and inventories. To derive the base of the corporate income tax (book profits), we must first project the annual net returns on capital. These returns, before deducting net interest paid and taxes, but after deducting replacement-cost depreciation and inventory profits, are assumed to grow each year after 1973 by the same 3.7 percent real growth rate as all other input variables and by the rate of inflation shown in the first column of Table 1. Thus, their

---

[24] Differencing equation (10) yields:
$$dDNIP = 1.1976[(dn)DD + (n_{-1})dDD].$$
Using $DD = 1.037(1 + i)DD_{-1}$, $dDD = [1.037(1 + i) - 1]DD_{-1}$, and
$$DNIP_{-1}/DD_{-1} = 1.1976(n_{-1})$$ then yields equation (16).

[25] In the projections, the coefficient 1.1976 in equation (10) was set equal to unity because the excess over unity may, in part, be a transitional phenomenon resulting from refinancing at higher rates and because multiplicative projection of the risk premium over AAA rates is of dubious validity in experiments with different inflation rates.

Table 1
DERIVATION OF THE RATIO OF THE CORPORATION INCOME TAX
TO THE NET RETURN OF NONFINANCIAL CORPORATIONS,
1973–1990, AT 1973 CAPACITY UTILIZATION RATES
($ billion)

Year	Year-to-Year Change in Consumer Price Level (%)a	New Issue Rate (%)	Net Interest Paid	Tax Depre- ciation	Replace- ment Cost Depre- ciation	CCA	IVA
1973	6.2	7.65	24.5	70.3	68.7	1.6	−18.4
1974	11.0	9.15	30.1	77.7	79.6	−1.9	−41.5
1975	9.1	9.66	36.0	86.4	95.8	−9.4	−25.5
1976	6.0	9.19	40.8	96.4	107.5	−11.1	−14.5
1977	5.0	8.61	45.3	107.3	119.0	−11.7	−12.5
1978	5.0	8.23	49.9	119.0	131.4	−12.4	−12.8
1979	5.0	7.97	54.8	131.7	144.6	−12.9	−13.0
1980	5.0	7.80	60.0	145.3	158.8	−13.5	−13.2
1985	5.0	7.51	92.9	231.9	249.0	−17.1	−12.4
1990	5.0	7.47	142.9	362.0	384.1	−22.1	−7.1

a This rate of price increase is used in calculating the new issue rate, net interest paid, and the net returns on capital after 1973. To calculate the IVA, the actual rate of inflation in the WPI for industrial commodities is used for 1974 and 1975. Thereafter, all prices are assumed to change at the same rate as the CPI. The actual rate of change in the implicit deflator for the fixed investment of nonfinancial corporations is used in calculating investment and depreciation in 1974 and 1975.

ratio to GNP is fixed at the 1973 level and their share of national income is also approximately fixed.[26] Adding inventory profits and underdepreciation (by subtracting the IVA and CCA) and subtracting net interest paid from annual net returns will yield the book profits projected at 1973 capacity utilization rates.

Corporate profits tax accruals for all levels of government combined are then projected as 38 percent of book profits. This rate would apply if the provisions of the Tax Reduction Act of 1975 were in force throughout the estimation period and state and local profits tax rates were constant at their 1975 average level of about 5.5 per-

[26] Replacement-cost depreciation and indirect business taxes in particular may not grow in proportion to GNP though replacement-cost depreciation will do so eventually under the specified conditions.

Net Returns on Capital	Book Profits[b]	Corporation Income Tax at 38% of Book Profits	Gross Cash Flow[c]	Ratio of Tax to Net Return on Capital (%)	Tax Ratio With 0% Inflation from 1980[d]	Tax Ratio With 10% Inflation from 1980[d]
100.5	92.8	35.3	109.4	35.1	35.1	35.1
115.7	129.0	49.0	116.2	42.4	42.4	42.4
130.9	129.8	49.3	141.4	37.7	37.7	37.7
143.9	128.7	48.9	161.7	34.0	34.0	34.0
156.7	135.6	51.5	178.9	32.9	32.7	33.9
170.6	145.9	55.4	196.7	32.5	31.1	33.8
185.8	156.9	59.8	215.8	32.2	30.0	33.8
202.2	168.9	64.2	236.8	31.8	28.9	33.8
309.6	246.2	93.6	372.1	30.2	26.9	30.9
473.8	360.1	136.8	578.2	28.9	26.0	28.2

[b] Book profits are calculated by subtracting the (negative) IVA and CCA and the (positive) net interest paid from the annual net returns on capital.
[c] Cash flow, gross of dividends, is equal to book profits minus corporation income taxes plus the actual depreciation allowances and IVA.
[d] Inflation rates are adjusted towards these levels from 1977 on to avoid discontinuity.
Source: see text. Simulation carried out by author.

cent. Dividing the tax accruals by the annual net return on capital yields the effective tax rates shown in the third-to-last column of Table 1.

Under the provisions of the 1975 law, the effective tax rate is found to decline consistently from 1974 on as inflation and the share of inventory profits in book profits decline. Within five years the effective tax rate is projected to decline by ten percentage points from its 1974 high of 42.4 percent. The decline occurs because the rise in the ratio of deductible net interest to the net return on capital and the decline in the relative importance of inventory profits outweigh the effect of rising underdepreciation (CCA) on book profits and hence on taxes. The effective corporate tax rate continues to decline gradually toward 28.9 percent in 1990. It would subsequently remain near that level if the rate of inflation were constant at 5 percent. By 1990 almost 90 percent of all inventories are assumed to be held by companies using LIFO. Hence taxable inventory profits cannot be reduced much further by companies' switching to LIFO after 1990. Furthermore, by that year, the rates of growth in net interest, in the CCA, and hence in book profits and taxes, no longer differ significantly from the rate of growth of the net return on capital, so that steady long-term relationships are approached by the end of the next decade.

While the decline in the rate of inflation from the level of recent years lowers the effective tax rate, the passage of time also lowers the tax rate at given rates of inflation as depreciation allowances and net interest paid adjust gradually to steady-state relationships. For instance, if the rate of inflation were to decline from 6 percent in 1976 to 4 percent in 1977, and then to 2 and 1 percent, with price stability prevailing from 1980 on, the effective tax rate (shown in the second-to-last column of Table 1) would be lower from 1977 on than it would if the inflation rate stabilized at 5 percent. Furthermore, it would continue to decline until 1990 even though inventory profits would have ceased to occur in 1980.

If the rate of inflation is 10 percent per annum in the next decade, after rising in equal annual steps from 6 percent in 1976 to 10 percent in 1980, the effective tax rate also declines over time. As shown in the last column of Table 1, the decline is at first much slower than with 5 percent inflation but is faster subsequently. During an extended transition period, the growth in net interest paid exceeds the growth in the net return on capital—and the higher the projected rate of inflation relative to the rate expected in the past, the more the growth in net interest paid will exceed the growth in the net return on capital. In addition, the ongoing shift to the LIFO method of inventory accounting helps reduce the tax rate.

Hence, while it is true that tax rates are initially higher the greater the rate of inflation projected from a common take-off point such as 1976, this relationship may not be maintained in the presence of debt finance once the difference in the rates of inflation between two alternative paths has been constant for an extended period. The fact that by 1990 the effective tax rate with 10 percent inflation is below the effective tax rate with 5 percent inflation under the conditions reflected in Table 1 is a case in point.

The conditions under which a higher steady rate of inflation would actually imply an effective tax rate lower than that implied by a lower steady rate of inflation can be defined precisely for the very long run. This may be done first by using a highly simplified example to point out the critical relationships. Assume that the total capitalization of a corporation using LIFO is $100 (million) and that it has $25 of debt outstanding and a 10 percent depreciation rate per annum. Furthermore, assume the rate of inflation jumps from zero to 10 percent and the interest rate rises immediately by 10 percentage points on all outstanding debt. Then tax depreciation would be $10, replacement-cost depreciation $11, and interest payments would rise by $2.50. Clearly, the increased deductions from higher interest payments would far outweigh the loss in deductions from the $1 of underdepreciation generated by inflation. Conversely, with complete indexing, this corporation would clearly pay higher taxes since it would lose $2.50 in deductions for a $1 gain. Furthermore, the conclusion that the effective tax rate would be lowered by inflation under present law is quite robust, inasmuch as it would continue to hold unless the depreciation rate were much higher, the percentage of debt financing much lower, or the increase in interest rates stemming from inflation much smaller than assumed in this example.

Having identified the critical elements of the argument, let us return to the projections based on the 1973 relationship to see whether nonfinancial corporations as a group would, in the long run, be better off under the present tax system, provided they use LIFO, than they would under complete indexing. In all previous experiments the ratio of gross investment to net debt outstanding was held constant at its 1973 level of 25 percent. Furthermore, the ratio of replacement-cost depreciation to gross investment approaches 80 percent.[27] Hence the ratio of replacement cost depreciation to net debt outstanding tends towards 20 percent. However, previous calculations showed that the ratio of tax depreciation to replacement-cost depreciation falls from 1.158 to 0.824, or by 33.4 percent of replacement-cost depreciation, if the steady rate of inflation is 10 percent rather than zero percent. Hence, the deductions lost on account of underdepreciation amount to the product of 20 percent and 33.4 percent, or about 6.7 percent of net debt. The interest deduction gained from the 10 percent inflation exceeds this amount, even though the nominal interest rises by only 7.8 percentage points, or by less than the full amount of inflation according to equation (15). However, even after the new issue rate has risen to within ten basis points of its ultimate equilibrium level,

---

[27] From equation (5), footnote 16, the ratio of DR to I is found to be 79.0 percent with 10 percent inflation and 14.07 percent growth in I, and 82.7 percent with zero percent inflation and 3.7 percent growth in I. This variation occurs because the first nominal depreciation charge on new investment is not assumed to be adjusted for inflation.

a rise accomplished after six years of steady 10 percent inflation, it still takes many more years before net interest paid approaches the product of the new issue rate and net debt outstanding—this because of the existence of older debt contracted at lower rates.[28] Hence, only in the very long run would the effective tax rate be lower at 10 percent than at zero percent inflation, given the assumed percentages of debt financing and LIFO.

For corporations using FIFO, this result is not possible in the aggregate since the ratio of inventories to net debt outstanding tends to 67 percent in all the previous experiments with differing inflation rates. With inventory profits—equal to 6.7 percent of outstanding debt—added to taxable profits in the case of 10 percent inflation and with another 6.7 percent for underdepreciation as before, the sum of 13.4 percent exceeds the increase in deductions from higher net interest payments—an increase equal to 7.8 percent of net debt. Individual FIFO corporations with exceptionally high levels of debt financing could, of course, still escape the tax-raising effects of inflation in the long run.

The effect of inflation on the effective tax rates of corporations is therefore very different from its effect on individual income taxes. If the individual income tax schedules and the levels of personal exemption and maximum standard deduction are fixed in nominal terms, the tax consequences of inflation are irreversible and the real tax burden will increase as long as inflation persists.[29] For corporations, higher rates of inflation imply higher tax rates only during a transition period, and tax rates may ultimately be lower than they would be in the absence of inflation without any indexation other than that implied by the LIFO method of inventory accounting. However, these lower rates would emerge only after a very long period of steady 10 percent inflation. Furthermore, tax rates would be higher at inflation rates of 6 percent or less than they would with no inflation. While the relationship between nominal interest rates and inflation is linear, the relationship between the ratio of tax depreciation to

[28] The previous estimate of the change in net interest paid [equation (10)] made no provision for refinancing at higher or lower rates, the result being that net interest paid on new debt grows only gradually relative to the net interest paid on old debt as growth proceeds. The speed with which the average interest rate on the net debt outstanding converges to the new issue rate is positively related to the inflation rate.

[29] See Fellner et al., *Correcting Taxes for Inflation*; Joseph A. Pechman, "Responsiveness of the Federal Individual Income Tax to Changes in Income," *Brookings Papers on Economic Activity*, 1973(2), pp. 385-421, esp. 405-11; and George M. von Furstenberg, "Individual Income Taxes and Inflation," *National Tax Journal*, vol. 28, no. 1 (March 1975), pp. 117-25.

replacement depreciation and inflation is nonlinear. The higher the rate of inflation, the less this ratio falls with each percentage-point increase in the inflation rate. Hence, as inflation rises, the growth in underdepreciation slows while the growth in interest rates is constant. The beneficial tax effects of the latter begin to exceed the harmful effects of the former at a 3 percent inflation rate so that the steady-state tax rate falls from a maximum of 28.5 percent at 3 percent inflation to 27.5 at 6 percent inflation, the same as with no inflation.[30] The steady-state tax rate then falls to 25.9 percent when the permanent rate of inflation is 10 percent (as shown in Figure 1).

Financing Relationships

The effect of inflation on the effective corporate tax rate has been calculated on the assumption that the growth in real indebtedness and in the net return on capital matched the 3.7 percent annual rate of growth in real gross investment. If this assumption holds true, then eventually replacement-cost depreciation and the replacement value of the net capital stock will also grow at this 3.7 percent rate. Furthermore, in our calculations, we allowed relative price changes among inventories, fixed investment, and consumer goods only for past periods; from 1976 on all prices were assumed to change at the same rate. Hence the experiments with different inflation rates all implied asymptotically constant ratios of net debt outstanding to the replacement cost of the net capital stock and of inventories.[31]

The marginal debt ratios shown in Table 2 indicate that about 50 percent of the annual change in the value of depreciable assets and inventories can be financed through debt without causing the amount of net debt outstanding to grow faster than the replacement cost of these two types of assets. One is then led to ask whether the debt

---

[30] It can be calculated from Table 1 that without inventory profits the effective tax rate would be 27 percent with 10 percent inflation and 26 percent with no inflation in 1990. However, the latter rate rises to 27.5 percent in the very long run when net interest paid is down to 3.58 percent of net debt outstanding, while the former falls to 25.9 percent when net interest paid is up to 11.35 percent of net debt outstanding. The tax rate with steady 5 percent inflation would ultimately settle at 27.9 percent.

[31] It can be shown that the replacement value of the year-end net capital stock grows at the same nominal and real rates as net debt outstanding if

$$NK/I = (1 - DR/I)(1 + g)/g$$

The ratio of replacement-cost depreciation (DR) to gross investment (I) eventually stabilizes at 0.827, 0.808, and 0.790 if the steady rate of inflation is zero, 5, and 10 percent, respectively. Hence, with $g = 0.037$, NK/I would approach 4.85, 5.38, and 5.89, respectively.

Figure 1

EFFECTIVE INCOME TAX RATES OF NONFINANCIAL
CORPORATIONS AFTER COMPLETE ADJUSTMENT
TO STEADY RATES OF INFLATION

(in percent)

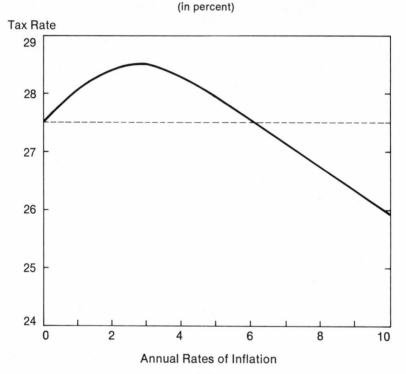

Annual Rates of Inflation

Note: Includes combined federal, state, and local profits taxes under 1975 law, shown in percent of the net return on capital.

financed portion (the "debt" ratio) plus the internally generated portion (the "internal" ratio) are consistent with the assumed growth in the nominal value of these assets. Since an average future rate of inflation of around 5 percent may represent the most likely outcome among the alternatives presented, the components required for the calculations are again shown only for this case. Thereafter we investigate how changing the inflation rate affects the balance between the projected sources and uses of funds and whether a financing squeeze would develop at higher inflation that could jeopardize the assumed investment program.

With 3.7 percent annual growth in real gross investment, with the specified rates of inflation, and with the estimate of replacement-cost depreciation shown in Table 1, the annual net investment in both fixed assets and inventories can be readily calculated from 1973 on. Since replacement-cost depreciation and inventory profits were subtracted from gross returns to obtain net returns and since retained earnings are also adjusted to exclude the effects of inflation-produced revaluations, the nominal appreciation in the value of inventories and depreciable assets is treated as entirely unrealized.[32] The balance sheet will then be based on historical cost and the income statement will reflect replacement-cost accounting. To achieve consistency, in Table 2, the unrealized nominal capital gains are added to net investment to obtain the change in the replacement value of assets (and liabilities). Thus, the specified change in net debt outstanding and the sum of retained earnings and nominal appreciation, both divided by the change in the value of assets, will yield the debt ratio and the internal ratio, respectively.

To estimate the appreciation component, we must first specify an initial value of the replacement cost of the net capital stock. To do this we assume that the ratio of the net capital stock to gross fixed investment was 5.26 in 1964, a multiple suggested by equation (7).[33] Multiplying the net capital stock each year by the annual inflation rate from that year then yields the unrealized capital gains (appreciation) on depreciable assets. This appreciation is added to the capital stock along with net investment (after replacement-cost depreciation) to obtain the replacement cost of depreciable assets in the next year. Thus, if the inflation rate is i percent per year and the real growth rate is g percent, the appreciation component of the change in the replacement cost of the net capital stock is defined as i percent and the net investment component as $g(1 + i)$ percent.[34] With the net

---

32 Whatever realization is required for tax purposes is, of course, reflected in the estimate of corporate profits tax accruals.

33 Footnote 16 suggests that the replacement value of the investment surviving from last year is equal to the fraction $b'/(1 + g)$ of this year's investment. Hence NK/I approaches $1/[1 - b'/(1 + g)]$, or 5.26, if we ignore the complication introduced by the fact that the first term of equation (5) is an average of two years of investment. If we do not ignore that complication, as in footnote 31, the same multiple would be found with an inflation rate just below 4 percent, which may represent the average rate of inflation reflected in the 1964 net capital stock. Nevertheless, since investment has varied considerably from year to year, the value chosen for NK/I in any one year is to some extent arbitrary.

34 The decomposition of $(1 + i)(1 + g) - 1$ into i and $g(1 + i)$ is, of course, not the only algebraic resolution of the percentage change in the replacement-cost of the net capital stock into its inflation and growth components. Alternatively, one could use $i(1 + g)$ and g, but expressing the growth component in current prices and appreciation as a revaluation of last year's net capital stock seems preferable.

Table 2

DERIVATION OF ACTUAL AND PROJECTED COVERAGE RATIOS OF NONFINANCIAL CORPORATIONS, 1965–1990

($ billion)

Year	Net Investment			Appreciation			
	Fixed assets (1)	Inven- tories (2)	Sum (3) = (1) + (2)	Fixed assets (4)	Inven- tories (5)	Sum (6) = (4) + (5)	Change in Assets (7) = (3) + (6)
1965–68	81.9	38.9	120.8	31.5	10.3	41.8	162.6
1969–73 a	111.0	37.0	148.0	102.0	40.9	142.9	290.9
1974	31.9	11.0	42.9	48.6	54.0	102.6	145.5
1975	36.1	12.8	48.9	89.2	35.4	124.6	173.5
1976	37.5	14.0	51.5	45.5	21.4	66.9	118.4
1977	38.9	15.2	54.1	42.0	19.6	61.6	115.7
1978	40.5	16.6	57.1	46.1	21.3	67.4	124.5
1979	42.6	18.1	60.7	50.4	23.2	73.6	134.3
1980	45.0	19.6	64.6	55.1	25.3	80.4	145.0
1985	63.0	30.1	93.1	84.4	38.7	123.1	216.2
1990	93.4	46.1	139.5	128.0	59.2	187.2	326.7

a The actual tax amount of $39.1 billion rather than $35.3 billion shown in Table 1 under 1975 law is used in calculating cash flow for 1973. The provisions of the Tax Reduction Act of 1975 are assumed to be in effect thereafter.

b Retained earnings are shown with IVA and CCA. They are obtained by subtracting replacement-cost depreciation and dividends from the gross cash flow shown in

capital stock estimate built up in this fashion from 1964 levels, the ratio of the net capital stock to investment rises to 5.8 in 1976 and then remains in the range from 5.65 to 5.95 in all the experiments through 1990.

To estimate unrealized capital gains on inventories we find the product of the real value of last year's inventories multiplied by last year's wholesale price index for industrial commodities and the percentage change in that index from last year. The numerator of the internal ratio shown in Table 2 is then obtained by adding retained earnings to unrealized capital gains. We calculate retained earnings from Table 1, assuming that dividends from 1974 on are equal to 49 percent of after-tax book profits, the same ratio as in 1965–1968.

Summing the debt and internal ratios yields the "coverage" ratio in the last column of Table 2, which is used to indicate the adequacy

Retained Earnings[b] (8)	Retained Earnings Plus Appreciation (9) = (6) + (8)	Change in Net Debt (10)	Internal Ratio (11) = (9)/(7)	Debt Ratio (12) = (10)/(7)	Coverage Ratio (13) = (11) + (12)
83.8	125.6	96.1	0.772	0.591	1.363
54.8	197.7	185.7	0.680	0.638	1.318
−2.6	100.0	61.5	0.687	0.423	1.110
6.2	130.8	57.0	0.754	0.329	1.083
15.1	82.0	52.2	0.693	0.441	1.134
18.7	80.3	54.0	0.694	0.467	1.161
21.0	88.4	58.9	0.710	0.473	1.183
23.4	97.0	64.0	0.722	0.477	1.199
26.7	107.1	69.7	0.739	0.481	1.220
48.3	171.4	106.7	0.793	0.494	1.287
84.7	271.9	163.2	0.832	0.500	1.332

Table 1. Dividends in turn are assumed to be 49 percent of after-tax book profits from 1974 on. After-tax book profits are equal to 62 percent of the book profits shown in Table 1.
Source: see text. Simulation carried out by author.

of the specified sources of funds to meet the projected uses. This ratio averaged well over 1.3 from 1965 through 1973. Because a number of non-interest-bearing monetary assets and non-depreciating real assets have been omitted from the asset side, while new equity issues represent the only major omission on the liability side, the coverage ratio would be expected to be greater than unity. However, it cannot be stated precisely by how much it must exceed unity to be consistent with the projected increase in the replacement value of depreciable assets and inventories, since some of the omitted items that represent an additional use of funds (such as foreign direct investment by U.S. nonfinancial corporations net of foreign branch profits) [35] are difficult

---

[35] Foreign branch profits were not included in the sources of funds projected and they can therefore be netted against the use of funds for foreign direct investment.

to forecast. Hence, we can conclude only that if the annual coverage ratios are consistently projected to be less than 1.3 at 1973 capacity utilization rates, they would probably not be sufficient to allow investment to grow as much as projected. Since, in competitive equilibrium, the market value of a firm tends to be equal to the replacement cost of its assets, economic forces would tend to counteract persistent deviations of the projected coverage ratio from past levels. If the coverage ratio were too low, it could be raised for a time by an increase in indebtedness and a reduction in dividends. But since both balance-sheet deterioration and divided reduction raise the cost of capital to the firm, there would eventually be a decline in the rate of investment and a rise in net returns on capital from the projected levels.

From Table 2 it does in fact appear that with 5 percent inflation the coverage ratio would remain well below its 1965–1973 level until at least 1985. Thus, for a time, there may be insufficient incentives for corporations to follow the investment path projected. Since the coverage ratio rises above 1.3 by 1990, the outlook for investment would gradually improve. However, if a greater-than-projected debt burden were contracted in the lean years up to 1985 to maintain investment, net interest paid would also be higher than projected in 1990. Under such conditions it is doubtful whether increased equity issues could be used to bring the debt back to projected levels.

It is interesting to contrast these results with those expected if the rate of inflation settled at either higher or lower rates than the 5 percent annual rate used in Table 2. Table 3 shows that the coverage ratio would at first be even lower than at 5 percent inflation if the rate of inflation dropped to zero percent by 1980. The reason for this is that the average interest rate reflected in net interest paid falls only gradually towards the 3.58 percent equilibrium level of the new issues rate. Soon after 1980, however, net interest paid begins to grow distinctly less rapidly than the net return on capital. Furthermore, tax depreciation catches up with and subsequently exceeds replacement-cost depreciation. Hence, the coverage ratio rises rapidly. By 1990, the internal ratio alone exceeds unity and the coverage ratio approaches 1.6. Whether the projected investment is feasible in earlier years therefore depends on whether investors look far enough ahead to see the dramatic improvement in the coverage ratio that ultimately results under conditions of price stability. If investors recognize that the marginal productivity of investment is much greater than its average productivity (because the coverage ratio increases), they may be willing to look beyond the period of low average profitability and of low internal ratios that would last until the early 1980s.

Table 3
INTERNAL, DEBT, AND COVERAGE RATIOS AT DIFFERENT INFLATION RATES

Year	No Inflation[a]			5 Percent Inflation[b]			10 Percent Inflation[c]		
	Internal ratio	Debt ratio	Coverage ratio	Internal ratio	Debt ratio	Coverage ratio	Internal ratio	Debt ratio	Coverage ratio
1976	0.693	0.416	1.109	0.693	0.441	1.134	0.693	0.492	1.185
1977	0.668	0.399	1.067	0.694	0.467	1.161	0.720	0.499	1.219
1978	0.640	0.417	1.057	0.710	0.473	1.183	0.739	0.505	1.244
1979	0.634	0.412	1.046	0.722	0.477	1.199	0.752	0.508	1.260
1980	0.628	0.470	1.098	0.739	0.481	1.220	0.760	0.492	1.252
1985	0.880	0.516	1.396	0.793	0.494	1.287	0.764	0.495	1.259
1990	1.041	0.533	1.574	0.832	0.500	1.332	0.780	0.497	1.277

a The inflation rate is assumed to fall from 6 percent in 1976 to 4 percent in 1977, 2 percent in 1978, 1 percent in 1979, and to be zero percent thereafter. Because the debt outstanding at the end of 1976 is taken to be the average of the average debt outstanding in 1976 and 1977, the change in debt outstanding during 1976 differs even though the 6 percent inflation rate from 1975 to 1976 is common to all experiments and inflation rates diverge only from 1977 on.

b The inflation rate is 5 percent in every year after 1976.

c The inflation rate is 7 percent in 1977, 8 percent in 1978, 9 percent in 1979, and 10 percent each year thereafter.

Source: see text. Simulation carried out by author.

Moreover, later in the 1980s, there should be a ready market for new equity issues that could be used to retire any indebtedness above projected levels that was necessary to supplement the low financial coverage projected for earlier years.

With 10 percent rather than zero percent inflation starting in 1980 the results are just the opposite: better first and worse later than with 5 percent inflation. Here the coverage ratio is initially shored up because the average net interest rate on outstanding debt rises only gradually towards the 11.35 percent level of the new issue rate ultimately expected with 10 percent inflation. In addition, it takes several years for tax depreciation to decline to its eventual level of 82.4 percent of replacement-cost depreciation. Because of these factors the coverage ratio is at first higher but then much lower than with zero percent inflation. From 1985 on, it would also be lower than with 5 percent inflation and would remain continuously below 1.3. Under such conditions, new equity issues that are as great or greater in relation to gross investment than in 1965–1973 are likely to be dilutive. Such issues would not constitute a feasible means of supplementing the projected coverage ratios.[36]

As was the case with taxes, it may again be rewarding to go beyond the simulation period and to use higher inflation rates than hitherto assumed to determine the durability and significance of the results. Table 4 shows that even after a very long period of 10 percent inflation the coverage ratio would remain close to its 1990 level and would remain permanently below 1.3. It would improve somewhat further at lower inflation rates, particularly if there were no inflation at all. This strengthens the conclusion that the coverage ratio is negatively related to the rate of inflation in the long run.

The reasons for this can be explained if we first ignore the contribution of retained earnings to the numerator of the coverage ratio. Outstanding debt and the replacement value of assets both grow by $i + g(1 + i)$ percent. In the long run, the marginal debt ratio equals the average ratio of outstanding debt to the sum of the replacement values of depreciable assets and inventories. In previous experiments this ratio was roughly 50 percent.[37] As a result, the coverage ratio, including the appreciation component in both numerator and denominator, would tend to $0.5 + i/[i + g(1 + i)]$, or 1.46 at high inflation rates, if retained earnings are ignored.

---

[36] Stock issues are deemed dilutive if the market value of a firm is below the replacement value of its assets.

[37] From 1976 on DO/I and INV/I are 4.02 and 2.70 in all experiments, respectively. Hence the average debt ratio, $DO/(NK + INV)$, is equal to one-half if NK/I equals 5.34 (see footnote 31).

Table 4

DERIVATION OF THE COVERAGE RATIO IN THE STEADY
STATE WITH DIFFERENT INFLATION RATES

(components are in 100 percent of gross fixed investment)

	No Inflation	5 Percent Inflation	10 Percent Inflation
Net fixed investment	17.3	19.2	21.0
Inventory investment	9.6	9.6	9.6
1. Total net investment	26.9	28.8	30.6
Appreciation of fixed assets	0	24.7	51.6
Inventory appreciation	0	12.4	23.7
2. Total appreciation	0	37.1	75.3
Book profits (under LIFO)	71.8	72.9	67.6
Less taxes	27.3	27.7	25.7
Less dividends	21.8	22.1	20.5
Plus CCA	13.1	−3.6	−13.9
3. Retained earnings	35.8	19.5	7.5
4. Change in debt	14.6	34.2	53.0
5. Change in specified liabilities (2 + 3 + 4)	50.4	90.8	135.8
6. Change in specified assets (1 + 2)	26.9	65.9	105.9
7. Coverage ratio (5/6)	1.87	1.38	1.28

Source: see text. Simulation carried out by author.

In fact, however, retained earnings (excluding inventory profits
and underdepreciation) become negative at high rates of inflation.
Furthermore, book profits also turn negative eventually because the
ratio of net interest payments to the annual net return on capital rises
progressively with the rate of inflation. Hence, with taxes and dividends (other than "return of capital" dividends) zero, retained earnings after replacement-cost depreciation are simply equal to the net
return on capital (which, after 1976, is a constant 99 percent of annual
gross investment (I) in all experiments) less net interest paid. Net
interest paid in turn is the product of the new issue rate (n) and the
average net debt outstanding during the year (DO). Using equation
(15) we find

$$n = i + r^* = 3.58 + 0.777i \text{ (percent)} \tag{17}$$

Hence, with book profits zero or negative, retained earnings are

$$RE = [0.99(I/DO) - (0.0358 + 0.777i)] DO \qquad (18)$$

The ratio of gross fixed investment to net debt outstanding, I/DO, is 0.25 and independent of i, so that RE equals $(0.2117 - 0.777i)DO$. The sum of the change in outstanding debt and retained earnings is only $[0.2117 + 0.223i + g(1 + i)]DO$ since, of the part of the change in net debt that provides for the maintenance of the previous real value of that debt (iDO), about 78 percent is needed to cover the inflation premium in interest payments. Hence, with g of 0.037 as before, the coverage ratio (CR), instead of being 1.46, is found to be only about 1.09 as the inflation rate goes to infinity in the equation below, and CR is higher at lower inflation rates.

$$CR = [0.5(0.2117 + 0.223i + g(1 + i)) \\ + i]/[i + g(1 + i)] \qquad (19)$$

Furthermore, if, contrary to equation (15), the real interest rate (r^*) does not fall as inflation rises so that the coefficient of i is unity in equation (17), the coverage ratio also approaches unity. In that case no funds can be committed to maintain the real value of non-interest-bearing monetary assets or to invest in anything other than depreciable assets and inventories without balance-sheet deterioration.[38] Corporations cannot allow the share of these other assets to decline indefinitely. Hence the higher the inflation rate and the more complete the inflation adjustment in nominal interest rates [39] the more the coverage ratio is depressed and the less likely it becomes that the real investment of nonfinancial corporations can continue to grow at the projected rate of 3.7 percent per annum and keep up with the growth in real GNP in the long run.

---

[38] For this reason John Lintner has concluded that "the relative dependence on external financing necessarily varies directly with realized inflation rates" and inflation thus produces "a deadweight dilution of the real returns on owning equities over the period." See Lintner, "Inflation and Security Returns," *Journal of Finance*, vol. 30, no. 2 (May 1975), pp. 273-74.

[39] A number of reasons have been given in the theoretical literature why nominal interest rates would not be expected to rise by the full amount of inflation even in the long run. See, for instance, Thomas J. Sargent, "Anticipated Inflation and the Nominal Rate of Interest," *Quarterly Journal of Economics*, vol. 86 (May 1972), pp. 212-25; Sargent, "Rational Expectations, the Real Rate of Interest, and the Natural Rate of Unemployment," *Brookings Papers on Economic Activity*, 1973(2), pp. 429-801; and Ignazio Visco, "Anticipated Inflation and the Nominal Rate of Interest: Some Further Results," *Quarterly Journal of Economics*, vol. 89 (May 1975), pp. 303-10. However, even if the nominal interest rate rises by only 78 percent of any increase in the inflation rate as assumed in the projections presented in this paper, balance-sheet deterioration would still tend to result.

Conclusion

This paper has focused not on cyclical developments but on the long-term effects of continuous inflation on the taxes and investment incentives of nonfinancial corporations. The financial resources available to corporations were estimated on the assumption that the real net returns on capital, gross investment, and net debt all grow at the same 3.7 percent rate from 1973 levels, but that the rates of inflation diverge in alternative simulations from 1976 on. Under these conditions, the short-run effects of inflation were found to differ considerably from the effects remaining in the long run.

Higher rates of inflation at first raise the effective corporate tax rate because net interest paid adjusts only slowly to the growing inflation premium embodied in the rate on new debt issues, whereas the ratio of tax depreciation to replacement-cost depreciation falls more rapidly towards its steady-state level. However, once inflation has stabilized at a rate of 6 percent or more for a sufficiently long period, corporations on LIFO actually face lower effective tax rates than they would in the absence of inflation. As far as corporate income tax accruals are concerned, high inflation rates thus need not permanently raise the ratio of taxes to the net return on capital (including net interest paid), though they do so initially.

While increasing inflation raises the effective corporate tax rate in the short and intermediate run but not necessarily in the long run, its effect on the financial resources of corporations is quite the reverse. This effect becomes more rather than less adverse over time as inflation continues, and deadweight dilution is likely to be more severe the higher the rate of inflation. Hence it appears that the emphasis on the profits tax effects of inflation has been somewhat misplaced. While these tax effects are initially worrisome, they do not by themselves permanently threaten the viability of the investment growth projected in this paper, since effective corporate tax rates are lower the longer inflation is maintained at any high level. This result, however, affords little comfort to the corporations (or to those concerned with the economy) since it is due to the declining share of book profits in the net return on capital—the net return being increasingly preempted by interest payments.

In the long run, the wages of inflation are paid by corporations and their owners not in the form of profits taxes but through the implicit taxes on cash balances and through the balance-sheet deterioration associated with persistently high rates of inflation. The consequences of this deterioration may be severe. Unless the annual rate of inflation is kept to 5 percent or less, on the average, the net return on capital will eventually have to be raised through reduced growth in investment. Slower growth in the productivity of labor and in potential output would result, and distributional tensions could add to the loss of output and detract from social well-being and economic welfare.[40] However, since these corrosive effects may not become apparent until the next decade, the damage done by allowing inflation to continue at a higher rate than up to the mid-1960s may not be recognized in time to muster the political will to prevent it.

[40] If the elasticity of factor substitution is below unity, the increasing scarcity of capital would lower the share of labor in the corporate product. If this reduction is resisted, both increased unemployment and higher prices could result from attempts to maintain past rates of growth in real wages in spite of lesser capital formation in the nonfinancial corporate sector. However, general equilibrium effects for the economy as a whole cannot be inferred from a discussion restricted to the corporate sector, especially since no attention has been paid to the aggregate supply of private saving and public dissaving.

THE PROBLEM OF STAGFLATION

Gottfried Haberler

Summary

The recession that bottomed out in spring 1975 was longer and probably somewhat more severe than any of the earlier recessions in the postwar period. Although it was mild in comparison with the deep depressions of the interwar period, it had a feature that made it perplexing and disturbing from the theoretical as well as from the policy point of view: it was a highly inflationary recession—a pronounced case of stagflation. Stagflation, the coexistence of substantial unemployment and rising prices, can occur in business cycle downswings (inflationary recession) as well as in upswings. Stagflation on the recent scale—deepening recession with inflation accelerating to the two digit level (1974) and then a cyclical recovery starting with 6 to 8 percent inflation (1975)—is a new phenomenon, although there have been earlier cases of shortlived mild stagflation.

The theoretical problem is how to explain rising prices when supply exceeds demand in labor markets (unemployment) and commodity markets (underutilization of capacity and growing inventories). The policy problem is that expansionary monetary-fiscal policies designed to reduce unemployment intensify the inflation while anti-inflationary contractive monetary-fiscal measures accentuate unemployment.

The solution of the theoretical problem is this: In a truly competitive economy, stagflation would be impossible. If supply exceeds demand, prices and money wages would fall under competition and not rise as they often do now, in the aggregate as well as in particular industries. True, a perfectly competitive economy is an ideal which has never been fully realized. But the point is that the deviations

255

from the competitive ideal have multiplied, especially since the 1930s. Labor unions have made money wages almost totally rigid downward and they often push wages up even if there is considerable unemployment. And government policies in many ways have intensified the trend. Minimum wages, generous unemployment benefits, and welfare payments create unemployment and have greatly strengthened the power of unions to push wages up under the threat of crippling strikes. Agricultural policies push farm prices up. Outside the public utility area few business monopolies or oligopolies could survive without government protection through import tariffs, quotas, "voluntary" restrictions imposed on foreign exporters, "antidumping" duties on imports, and other similar measures. But why, it may be asked, did stagflation suddenly reach such a high level in 1974–1975? The answer is to be found in the inflationary history of the postwar period, which has given rise to inflationary expectations. If the public expects prices to go on rising at (say) 15 percent and the actual price rise is then reduced to (say) only 7 percent, disappointments, losses, retrenchment, and unemployment are the unavoidable consequence, even in a more competitive economy than the one we now have. But the stagflation would not have become so serious and intractable if it were not for the multitude of restrictions on the free-market economy that have piled up in recent years.

Every inflation, including cost push inflation and stagflation, is a monetary phenomenon in the sense that it would be impossible without monetary growth. And no inflation can be stopped without restraint on monetary growth. In other words macroeconomic measures of demand management are necessary conditions for a successful stabilization policy. But in the stagflation case macroeconomic policies are not sufficient. If we rely on monetary-fiscal policy alone to subdue inflation we create so much unemployment that the fight against inflation will be given up before inflation has been eliminated. If we apply strong monetary-fiscal measures to push the economy quickly to full employment, we create an economically and politically unsustainable inflation. An economically efficient and politically acceptable policy requires that macroeconomic monetary-fiscal measures be supported by microeconomic measures—that is to say, by a structural reform designed to make the economy more competitive and flexible than it now is. Such a reform would make macro-policies more effective; it would make sure that (so long as there is unemployment and slack), a monetary expansion would result to a large extent in a growth of employment and output rather than a rise in prices, and that a curb on monetary growth would result to a large extent in falling prices rather than in lower output; or in monetarist terms, that an increase in money GNP would go to a greater extent than at present into quantities than into prices and a decrease in money GNP (or a decrease in its rate of increase) to a greater extent into prices than into quantities.

The structural reform would to a large extent consist of phasing out or changing the various existing policies that restrict competition, raise costs, and reduce output. Examples are the deregulation of industry, the phasing out of numerous restrictions of agricultural production and price supports (including government sponsored and enforced private marketing boards), freer trade, and so on. The most difficult but crucially important problem will be how to restrain the monopoly power of labor unions. Several measures are suggested, short of radical changes in collective bargaining. The paper cites examples of measures that would make the economy more competitive and flexible.

If nothing is done along these lines the ongoing expansion is bound sooner or later to accelerate the inflation, probably before anything like full employment has been reached. The consequence will be either a step on the monetary brake followed by another (inflationary) recession or, perhaps more likely, an irresistible call for wage and price controls despite the complete failure of all earlier experiments with controls. Since the people will remember from the last time how to anticipate and evade controls the system will run its course fast the next time around. The controls will quickly become ineffective, merely disrupting the economy and saddling it with a new bureaucracy—or, perhaps more likely, they will be followed by consumer rationing and allocation of means of production, thus leading into a regimented economy under the guise of economic planning.

Structural reform is a slow process at best. What are our policy options in the meantime? The only safe policy is, I believe, to let the ongoing expansion proceed slowly in the hope that inflation will not accelerate too much. It would be a capital mistake to try to push the economy quickly to full employment by additional expansionary monetary-fiscal measures, in the attempt to reduce unemployment to a low level in a hurry. In the absence of structural reform, such a course would—in a hurry—produce unsustainable inflation followed by a new inflationary recession. To say, as some do, that a policy of forced draft would reduce prices by increasing output and supplies is like saying that one can make a drunk sober by forcing whisky down his throat to pep him up. True, if the poison is withdrawn too quickly a situation may arise where one must increase the dose

257

of the stimulant temporarily to forestall an imminent collapse. But the economy does not face that danger now. The ongoing expansion has gathered momentum and will continue for quite a while without any additional monetary-fiscal stimulation.

Introduction

About a year ago, in March or April 1975, the American economy passed the trough of the sixth postwar recession (not counting the mini-recession of 1966, nor the February-October recession of 1945, the latter being clearly not a cyclical recession but a period of physical changeover from war to peace). The last recession was the longest and most economists would say the severest of the six.[1] The contrast between the last and the earlier recessions was much greater in Europe and Japan than in the United States. This was, in fact, the first truly worldwide recession in the postwar period. But it was a recession and not a depression, if by depression we mean a slump of the order of magnitude of the Great Depressions of the 1930s (1929–1933 and 1937–1938) and the (so-called first post-World War I) depression of 1920–1921. However, the 1974–1975 recession had a feature that made it perplexing and disturbing from the theoretical as well as from the policy point of view: it was a highly inflationary recession, a pronounced case of stagflation.

Stagflation and inflationary recession are usually used as interchangeable terms. But it is better to make a distinction. Stagflation can be defined as the coexistence of significant inflation and substantial general unemployment and slack over a considerable period. Inflationary recession is a cyclical recession characterized by rising unemployment and declining output combined with significant inflation. The *rate* of inflation may go up as was the case in the last recession until about the end of 1974, or it may decline as was the case in the last three or four months of the recession in 1975. Stagflation is the wider concept; it covers inflationary recessions as well as those cyclical upswings (or phases of cyclical upswings), like the present one, that are characterized by substantial general unemployment and inflation. The rationale of this definition is, as we shall see presently, that the coexistence of high general unemployment and inflation poses the same problems for economic theory and economic policy in recessions as well as in recoveries.

---

[1] Geoffrey Moore doubts, however, that it was the severest recession. See his contribution to this volume.

Stagflation of the present scale and duration is a new phenomenon. It has not happened before that a long and severe recession was accompanied by rapid and for some time even accelerating inflation on a two-digit level; and no earlier cyclical recovery has started with 6 to 8 percent inflation with which the present one started. It is true that faint symptoms of the new disease had been noticed in some of the earlier postwar recessions when prices failed to decline or even continued to rise although at a much lower rate than in the last recession. Moreover, it is significant that the cyclical recoveries in the postwar period have shown a tendency to start from successively higher inflation rates. (See Table 2 in Geoffrey Moore's contribution to this volume.)

An earlier episode resembling the current stagflation was the price rise that occurred after the great contraction of 1929–1933 and before the short but very sharp depression of 1937–1938. The price rise was deliberately brought about by the various New Deal measures—NRA, AAA, the Wagner Act and dollar devaluation. But after a while it caused great alarm although, compared with our recent inflation rates, the price rise was modest. It was a case of cost-push inflation and stagflation. Although the expansion from 1933–1937 was fairly rapid and long (fifty months), unemployment was still very high (14.3 percent at the upper turning point of the cycle in 1937). In the following depression unemployment rose again to 20 percent and there was a mild decline in the price level in 1938 and 1939.

Theoretical and Policy Problems Posed by Stagflation

The coexistence of substantial unemployment and rising price and wage levels is a puzzling phenomenon for the economic theorist and it confronts economic policy, and more precisely macroeconomic ("Keynesian") policies of demand management, with a nasty dilemma.

The theoretical puzzle is well expressed by the repeated rueful complaints by Arthur Burns that the economy does not seem to behave as it used to. How is it possible that in the face of substantial unemployment and excess capacity—in other words, that despite excess supply in labor and commodity markets—wages and prices continue to rise sharply? The answer is that in an ideal fully competitive economy stagflation would be impossible and that in moderately competitive economies as we had them in the not too distant past stagflation would be mild and confined to short periods.

The policy dilemma of stagflation is this: If macroeconomic monetary and fiscal policies try to counteract inflation, they increase unemployment; if they try to reduce unemployment they intensify inflation. In the "classical" recessions (depressions) and booms of the past the dilemma did not exist or existed only to a small extent and in an ideal competitive economy there would be no such dilemma. The policy conclusion is obvious: To eliminate the dilemma or to reduce it to more tolerable proportions, the economy must be made more competitive by removing at least the most serious restraints and restrictions on free competitive markets.

The crucial importance of the fact that the economy has increasingly deviated from the competitive ideal can perhaps be most clearly demonstrated if we analyze the impact of the so-called "special factors" on inflation, recession, and stagflation under alternative assumptions about the competitive structure of the economy.

Let us take as an example the enormous rise in the oil price decreed by OPEC. First, let us ask how an ideal fully competitive economy would react to a levy (deterioration in the terms of trade) imposed by the foreign oil cartel. If the price of oil (and of oil-related products) were forced up and the price level were to remain stable other prices would have to decline. If full employment were to be preserved, this would require that money wages (more generally, money incomes) go down. In an ideal competitive economy where wages were flexible downward (as well as upward) a suitably tight monetary policy would bring about the necessary wage and price adjustments without creating more than temporary, frictional unemployment.[2] The resulting decline in *real* wages would reflect the unavoidable decline in real national income.

Second, let us assume money wages to be entirely rigid downward—a quite realistic assumption indeed. In that case, keeping the price level stable by monetary policy would cause unemployment (a recession). That is what Arthur Burns told Congress; the Federal Reserve System, he said, could have prevented inflation, despite the oil price rise, but only by forcing down other prices and thereby creating an intolerable amount of unemployment. It was therefore necessary to allow prices to rise in order to bring about the unavoidable reduction in *real* wages by inflation. The argument is unexceptionable.[3] But it should be observed that with wages rigid downward

---

[2] For our purposes it is not necessary to discuss how the money supply would have to be managed to keep the price level stable.

[3] It is in effect an application of the theorem formulated by F. A. Hayek and Charles Schultze that says downward wage rigidity (even without any wage push upward) is inflationary as a consequence of *shifts* in demand. Wages and cost of production rise where demand has increased, but fail to decline where demand has decreased. See F. A. Hayek, "Inflation from Downward Inflexi-

(without any wage-push upward) the rise in the price of imported oil, representing a burden of about $20 to $22 billion for the $1.5 trillion U.S. economy, would merely cause a once-for-all price rise of about 1.4 percent. In other words, only a small fraction of the inflation that actually occurred from 1973 to 1975 could be explained—and justified—in this manner. To say that only a small degree of inflation can be "justified" merely means that with rigid money wages the oil price rise would create some unemployment if the price level were kept stable. It is not intended to prejudge the question whether the inflationary reaction to the oil price rise would reduce the *real* burden of the oil price rise—something which depends on the reaction of OPEC. If the nominal price of oil (in dollar terms) remained unchanged, the *real* burden of the oil price rise would be reduced by inflation in the importing countries, because the terms of trade would be better than they would be if the importing countries kept the price level stable. But it is probably realistic to assume that OPEC would react by raising the nominal price of oil so as to keep the real price at some preassigned level.

It is true, there were other "special factors" at work (there always are): the rise in domestic energy prices, the Russian wheat sale, a moderate crop shortfall not to mention the temporary disappearance of the anchovies from the Peruvian coast, a disappearance that caused a sharp rise in soybean prices. The result of all these changes was an *internal* income transfer from the urban sector to energy producers and farmers. This, in turn, had an inflationary impact through the Hayek-Schultze effect. But all special factors combined in conjunction with money wage rigidity can explain only a fraction (perhaps a fourth) of the two-digit inflation. The comparative unimportance of the special factors in the inflation picture has been acknowledged by Arthur Burns. In a recent speech he said: "The truth is that, for many years now, the economies of the United States and many other countries have developed a serious underlying bias toward inflation. This tendency has simply been magnified by the special influences that occasionally arise—such as a crop shortfall that results in higher farm prices, or the action of a foreign cartel that raises oil prices." [4]

---

bility of Wages" in *Problems of U.S. Economic Development*, ed. by Committee for Economic Development (CED), (New York: The Committee, 1958), vol. 1, pp. 147-52. Reprinted in F. A. Hayek, *Studies in Philosophy, Politics and Economics* (Chicago: University of Chicago Press, 1967), and Charles L. Schultze, *Recent Inflation in the United States* (Study Paper No. 1, Joint Economic Committee, 86th Congress, 1st session, Washington, September 1959).

[4] Speech at the University of Georgia, Athens, Georgia, September 19, 1975 (reproduced from typescript).

Third, downward rigidity of money wages is unfortunately not the only nor the most important present deviation from the competitive ideal. As William Fellner, Friedrich Hayek, and others have pointed out, labor unions, like everyone else, have become "inflation conscious"—in other words, money illusion has largely disappeared and "real wage resistance" (in the phrase of Sir John Hicks) has developed. The same is true of other pressure groups that manage by political means to force the government to raise the price of their products and the incomes of their members. Organized agriculture is the best and most important example. The resistance to real-income reductions finds its expression in aggressive wage contract bargaining and widespread indexation. Furthermore, labor unions and other pressure groups are in general not satisfied with preserving their real incomes but wish to increase them. The recent wage contract won by the teamsters' union under pressure of a nationwide strike in an election year is a perfect example. It provides for a substantial (10 percent) annual increase in money wages for the next three years plus full indexation. The precise magnitude of the real wage increase is not quite clear. But there can be no doubt that the terms of the contract greatly exceed the annual increase in overall productivity and that the contract must, therefore, be judged to be highly inflationary. If, under these circumstances, an attempt is made to hold the lid on inflation by monetary restraint, unemployment develops. This is stagflation.

Enough has been said to make clear that in an ideal, fully competitive market economy stagflation would be impossible. The spectacle of wages rising rapidly in the face of heavy unemployment, both overall and in particular industry, could not be seen in a free-market economy.

But why has stagflation suddenly reached such a high level in 1974–1975? There has been no sudden burst but rather a gradual (though since the 1930s rapidly accelerating) rise in restrictions on the competitive market economy. The answer is to be found in the inflationary history of the postwar period. Prolonged inflation, whatever its origin, was bound to erode money illusion and to generate inflationary expectations. If most people expect an inflation of (say) 15 percent and the actual rate is then reduced to 7 or 8 percent, losses, retrenchment and some unemployment must be expected even in a much more competitive economy than the one we actually have. But it is still true that the resulting stagflation, unemployment, and slack would never have become so serious and intractable if so many restrictions, rigidities, and deviations from the competitive ideal had not piled up over the years, (especially since the 1930s).

How about the monetary factor? The monetarists are, of course, right that stagflation, like any other kind of inflation, is a monetary phenomenon in the sense that it would be impossible without monetary growth. But we must keep in mind that what monetarists have established is a close relationship between monetary growth and the growth of *money* GNP. The relationship between monetary growth and *real* GNP is a different matter. In the words of a prominent monetarist "we still know very little about the division of short-run changes in nominal GNP between changes in output, on the one hand, and changes in prices, on the other. This is a deficiency of both the Keynesian and the monetarist analyses." [5] It is true that macroeconomic theories of the monetarist or Keynesian type cannot tell us how a change in money GNP will be divided between price change and quantity change. To solve that problem microeconomic considerations are needed. But Meiselman underestimates what we know about that problem. In particular he is much too pessimistic when he says that we do not know why the recovery after 1933 was so slow and why the "revival was aborted in 1937." [6] I find Milton Friedman's microeconomic explanation of "why [in 1933 to 1937] so large a part of the growth in nominal national income was absorbed by prices" entirely convincing. It was "the cost push" he said, from the "NIRA, AAA, Wagner Labor Act and the associated growth of union strength" that was responsible. [7] In 1937 the alarming price rise induced the Federal Reserve System to raise reserve requirements in order to remove excess reserves. This, in turn, led the banks to contract credit and brought on the depression. This explanation should be acceptable for Keynesians as well as for monetarists. Alvin Hansen, for example, was fully aware of the danger that an "increase in aggregate demand [may be] unnecessarily dissipated on higher prices with corresponding

---

[5] David I. Meiselman in *Answers to Inflation and Recession: Economic Policies for a Modern Society* (New York: National Industrial Conference Board, 1975), p. 23. Friedman, too, notes that the highly aggregated macro-models of the monetarist and Keynesian type have nothing "to say about the factors that determine the proportions in which a change in nominal income will, in the short run, be divided between price change and output change." See Robert J. Gordon, ed., *Milton Friedman's Monetary Framework: A Debate with His Critics* (Chicago: University of Chicago Press, 1974), pp. 49–50 and 135.

[6] Meiselman, *Answers to Inflation and Recession*, p. 23.

[7] Milton Friedman, "What Price Guideposts?" in George P. Shultz and Robert Z. Aliber, eds., *Guidelines, Informal Controls and the Market Place* (Chicago: University of Chicago Press, 1966), p. 22.

less effect on output and employment." [8] And Keynes himself did mention the importance of downward flexibility of *relative* wages, of prices, and of exchange rates for the smooth functioning of the economy and the effectiveness of macro-policies.[9]

There exists a substantial modern literature on the "Microeconomic Foundations of Employment and Inflation Theory." [10] This theory is essentially one of frictional or structural unemployment, inasmuch as it describes and analyzes in detail the search for suitable jobs on the part of employees who have lost their previous job and the search for suitable candidates for job openings on the part of employers. Stress is laid on the cost (both money and opportunity cost) of gathering information about jobs, including the income foregone by not accepting second- or third-best options that may present themselves. One aim of most contributors to this literature is to explain unemployment without reference to labor unions and money illusion. It is unquestionably true that the picture of a perfectly competitive labor market in which wages immediately adjust to the market-clearing level does not correspond to reality. Even if there were no unions and no money illusion, workers who have lost their jobs would not immediately accept wage cuts in their old employment (if that were an option) or inferior job offers elsewhere. They would take their time and invest time and money to search for acceptable openings. What is true of labor markets is also true of many commodity markets, especially of the market in durable manufactured goods where seller-buyer and manufacturer-customer relationships are important. In these markets prices are sticky and respond sluggishly to changes in demand, even in the absence of monopolies and oligopolies. This stickiness implies that in the short run quantity adjustments resulting in ups and downs of employment and of capacity utilization play a great role. All that is well described in Okun's paper.[11]

This analysis of frictional or structural unemployment is an extremely useful exercise. It has greatly enriched our knowledge of

[8] Alvin H. Hansen, *A Guide to Keynes* (New York: McGraw-Hill, 1953), p. 193.
[9] J. M. Keynes, *The General Theory of Employment, Interest and Money* (New York: Harcourt, Brace & Co., 1936), p. 270.
[10] See especially a volume of essays under that title edited by Edward S. Phelps (New York: W. W. Norton, 1970). See also the interesting article by Arthur Okun, "Inflation: Its Mechanics and Welfare Costs," in *Brookings Papers on Economic Activity*, 1975 (2), pp. 351-90.
[11] Okun, "Inflation: Its Mechanics and Welfare Costs." Sir John Hicks, too, has stressed the difference between what he calls the "fixprice" and "flexprice" sectors of the economy. See his booklet *The Crisis of Keynesian Economics* (Oxford: Clarendon Press, 1974), passim.

the way the economy works. The perfectly competitive economy in which all prices and wages immediately adjust to any change in the data and in which markets are cleared continuously at the full-employment level is an ideal never fully realized—even in the absence of monopolies or oligopolies in commodity and labor markets.

What I find unfortunate and unacceptable is the tendency in that literature to obliterate the distinction between general depression or recession unemployment (often called Keynesian unemployment) on the one hand and frictional or structural unemployment on the other hand, to play down the importance of labor unions, to ignore the fact that unions have made money wages almost completely rigid downward, to neglect the inflationary implications of the fact that the unions often push up wages even in the face of heavy unemployment.

I find equally unconvincing the reinterpretation of Keynes's theory of involuntary unemployment. It runs as follows: Unemployment is the "consequence of a decline in demand when traders do not have perfect information on what the new market-clearing price will be. No other assumption . . . needs to be relinquished . . . in order to get from the Classical to Keynes' Theory of Markets." [12] If, as Keynes says, workers do not accept a reduction of their real wage when it comes in the form of a reduction of their money wage, while they do accept it in the form of a rise in prices, it is not because unions rule out money wage reductions or because of money illusion. The real reason is said to be different: A rise in the price level "conveys" the information that "money wages everywhere have fallen relative to prices." Workers reject an equal cut in their real wage in the form of a money wage reduction because "a cut in one's own money wage does not imply that options elsewhere have fallen." [13] Tobin offers the same interpretation of Keynes's theory of involuntary unemployment. "Rigidities . . . of money wages can be explained by workers' preoccupation with relative wages and the absence of any central economy-wide mechanism for altering all money wages together." [14]

This interpretation is in my opinion unconvincing. Keynes was confronted with the mass unemployment and misery of the 1930s; he surely did not want to say that workers were unemployed (more or

---

[12] Axel Leijonhufvud, *On Keynesian Economics and the Economics of Keynes* (London and New York: Oxford University Press, 1968), p. 38.

[13] Armen A. Alchian, "Information Costs, Pricing and Resource Unemployment," in *Microeconomic Foundations of Employment and Inflation Theory*, ed. E. Phelps, p. 44.

[14] James Tobin, "Inflation and Unemployment," *American Economic Review*, March 1972, p. 5.

less voluntarily) because they were shopping around for better opportunities or that they were "preoccupied" not so much with their own
plight as with the possibility that if they accepted a lower money
wage other groups might get away with a better bargain. Keynes was,
of course, opposed to *general* wage reduction as a recovery measure.
But even at that time few economists favored that policy.[15]

The upshot of this discussion is that the literature on the micro-
foundations of inflation and employment theory is of little help for
explaining the stagflation dilemma, because it abstracts from the most
important factors—wage rigidity, wage push, real wage resistance
from labor unions, similar activities of other pressure groups, and
the effects of the widespread government regulation of industries.
I find Frank H. Knight's explanation much more convincing. With the
Great Depression in mind Knight wrote in 1941: "In a free market
these changes [in demand and prices of different types of goods]

---

[15] It is true, there can be found passages in *The General Theory* which suggest
that Keynes held the theory criticized here. On p. 264 for example he wrote:
"since there is, as a rule, no means of securing a simultaneous and equal reduction of money wages in all industries, it is in the interest of all workers to resist
a reduction in their own particular case." This could be interpreted to mean that
workers were primarily interested in relative wages. True, no one wants to be
discriminated against, and the invisible hand of free competition would bring
about equal pay for equal work and eliminate any discrimination. But the process
of competition requires that the price be bid down when there is excess supply.
To say that despite the heavy unemployment, wage reductions are refused because
workers are primarily concerned with relative wages—in other words, because
they are unwilling to work at a lower wage than that of workers in some other
industries—implies that the individual workers who become unemployed (as
distinguished from their unions) prefer a zero-wage to a positive wage. That is
not a plausible behavior assumption and it is difficult to believe that Keynes
meant to make it. The situation is, however, quite different if we drop the
assumption of competition and instead assume collective bargaining through a
union. For a union it is perfectly rational to accept a certain amount of unemployment, provided the total wage (of those employed and those unemployed)
is greater than under full employment. Obviously, generous unemployment benefits will make it much easier for the unions to solve the difficult problem of
sharing the burden of unemployment among their members and thus will induce
the unions to accept a larger amount of unemployment than they would otherwise
accept.

In the next sentence after the one quoted above Keynes makes it clear that
he was thinking of general wage cutting: "In fact, a movement by employers to
revise money-wage bargains downward will be much more strongly resisted, than
a gradual and automatic lowering of real wages as a result of rising prices."
There can hardly be a quarrel with that proposition up to the point where money
illusion has been fully eroded by prolonged inflation and real wage resistance
and real wage push have developed. That point marks *The Crisis of Keynesian
Economics* of which Hicks speaks (see footnote 11 above). As was noted earlier,
Keynes favored changes in relative "wages of particular industries so as to
expedite transfers from those which are relatively declining to those which are
relatively expanding." (*The General Theory*, p. 270.)

would be temporary, but even then they might be serious; and with important markets as unfree as they actually are . . . the results take on the proportion of a social disaster." [16] Since 1941 the economy has moved much farther away from the competitive ideal. There are many more powerful unions—for example public employees (including not only bus drivers, subway personnel, garbage men but also teachers, civil servants, firemen, policemen) are now unionized and do not hesitate to use the strike weapon to push up their wages. Many other pressure groups have organized themselves and government regulation of more and more industries has made more prices rigid downward while they remain elastic upward. In addition the public sector has grown enormously—which is bound to slow GNP growth.[17] Slower growth of aggregate supply collides with ever increasing claims on the available national product. This puts heavy pressure on the monetary authorities to make a choice between giving way and financing an inflation or standing firm and bringing on a recession. Monetarists are right when they say that stagflation like any other type of inflation cannot be stopped without an appropriate monetary policy. Monetary restraint is a necessary condition for stopping an inflation but it is not a sufficient condition for an economically efficient and politically feasible anti-stagflation policy. I agree with William Fellner, Herbert Giersch, Friedrich Hayek, Hen-

---

[16] F. H. Knight, "The Business Cycle, Interest and Money," reprinted from *Review of Economics and Statistics*, vol. 23, no. 2 (May 1941), in F. H. Knight, *On the History and Methods of Economics* (Chicago: University of Chicago Press, 1956), p. 335.

[17] This ominous development has gone farthest in Great Britain. *The Economist* of London recently (November 15, 1975, p. 18) reported about a study by two Oxford economists (Robert Bacon and Walter Eltis) which reaches the conclusion that "Britain's [economic] disaster in the past decade . . . has been that . . . in 1961-1973 the numbers of men employed in industry fell by 14%. . . . The emigration has been into the public sector employment, where the marginal productivity of labor is often tiny or nil, with a . . . 53% increase in local government employment . . . and a 14% increase in central government employment." The study by Bacon and Eltis was summarized in three articles in the *Sunday Times* (London), November 2, 9, and 16, 1975, and will be published in full by Macmillan (London) later this year.

The same alarming development threatens Italy. Guido Carli, the former governor of the Italian National Bank, has warned that the government deficits in Italy have now grown beyond the capacity of the economy to absorb them, crushing the economy and cutting living standards. These deficits result from the growth of the bureaucracy, generous social security and health insurance payments, liberal unemployment benefits, and the massive cost of what Carli calls "concealed unemployment"—that is, in many industries workers produce goods, at public expense, for which there is no demand. (See *New York Times*, December 9, 1975.) The United States is rapidly moving in the same direction. See Warren Nutter, *Where Are We Headed?*, AEI Reprint No. 34 (Washington, D.C.: American Enterprise Institute, 1976).

drik S. Houthakker [18] and others that a tight monetary and fiscal policy must be supplemented by measures designed to make the economy more competitive. If we rely on monetary and fiscal restraints alone, we will create so much unemployment that the fight against inflation will be broken off prematurely. This premature breaking off has in fact taken place in country after country. The result will be more inflation and more unemployment, a stop-and-go cycle around a steepening price trend. The great danger is that the cry for comprehensive wage and price controls will become irresistible despite the dismal failure of controls whenever and wherever they have been tried. Since the people will remember from the last time how to anticipate and evade the controls, the next time around the system of controls will run its course rapidly: that is, it will break down, merely disrupting the economy, or (perhaps more likely) will be quickly followed by consumer rationing and allocation, leading straight into a fully planned and regimented economy.

Structural Reform or How to Make the Economy More Flexible and Competitive

In recent years government policies and regulations that restrain competition, protect (or even create) private monopolies, restrict production, and raise or fix prices have come under closer scrutiny. Economists have unearthed and described dozens of such cases.[19] Phasing out these restrictions and changing these policies would go

---

[18] William Fellner, "Lessons from the Failure of Demand-Management Policies: A Look at the Theoretical Foundations," *Journal of Economic Literature*, vol. 14, no. 1 (March 1976), pp. 34-53; Herbert Giersch, "Some Neglected Aspects of Inflation in the World Economy," *Public Finance* (The Hague, 1973), esp. pp. 104-08; F. A. Hayek, "Unions, Inflation and Profits," in *Studies in Philosophy, Politics and Economics* (Chicago: University of Chicago Press, 1967), and "Inflation, the Path to Unemployment," in *Inflation: Causes, Consequences, and Cures* (London: Institute of Economic Affairs, 1974), "Zwölf Thesen zur Inflationsbekämpfung," in *Frankfurter Allgemeine Zeitung*, August 19, 1974; Hendrik S. Houthakker, "Incomes Policies as a Supplementary Tool" in *Answers to Inflation and Recession: Economic Policies for a Modern Society* (New York: The Conference Board, 1975). The title of Houthakker's speech is misleading. He argues that price and wage controls and incomes policies (in the conventional sense) can make only an "extremely modest contribution." His thesis is that macroeconomic policies must be supplemented by "structural reform."

[19] See for example Hendrik S. Houthakker, "Specific Reform Measures for the United States," in *Answers to Inflation*, pp. 83-85; Murray L. Weidenbaum, *Government-Mandated Price Increases: A Neglected Aspect of Inflation* (Washington, D.C.: American Enterprise Institute, 1975), and numerous other AEI publications; and *Annual Report of the Council of Economic Advisers, 1975*, Chapter 5, "Government Regulations."

a long way toward making the economy more competitive and flexible than it is now, thus making macroeconomic recovery and anti-inflation policies more effective. Here only a few examples can be mentioned.

In the field of agriculture, although output restrictions on some basic foodstuffs were belatedly lifted after food prices had exploded in 1973 and 1974, such restrictions still exist on several important products. Furthermore, interregional trade in many agricultural commodities (especially dairy products, fruits, and vegetables) is severely restricted by federal and state marketing orders or by producers privately organized—organizations in restraint of trade that are government-sponsored, government-licensed, government-enforced, and of course exempt from antitrust laws. Imports of many agricultural products from abroad, especially of meats and fruits, are sharply restricted. Such policies freeze and distort prices and reduce output because they prevent a rational interregional and international division of labor. There exist, furthermore, many import restrictions on industrial products, apart from tariffs, including the so-called "voluntary restrictions" imposed on foreign exporters, ranging from exporters of steel to exporters of textiles. These "voluntary" restrictions are especially damaging and costly because they force foreign producers to organize themselves in export monopolies at the expense of the American consumers. There is, furthermore, the Buy American Act which prevents foreign competition and costs the U.S. taxpayer many hundreds of millions of dollars. The field of transportation and energy is full of government-imposed restrictions on competition.[20]

Most difficult to deal with, but crucially important, are restrictions in the labor market imposed by labor unions. The importance of unions has been often questioned on the ground that in the United States only 20-25 percent of the labor force is unionized. But it has been demonstrated many times that, for various reasons that need not be repeated here, nonunion wages tend to follow union wages although at a distance and usually with a lag.[21] Leaving aside far-reaching structural reforms of the present methods of wage determination by industry-wide collective bargaining under the constant threat of crippling strikes, there exist a number of policy changes that could reduce wage pressure, increase competition, and expand output and employment. Houthakker mentions the following: "Unions should be prevented from restricting membership by apprenticeship

---

[20] See especially the CEA report for 1975, Chapter 5, and numerous AEI publications.

[21] See, for example, Gottfried Haberler, *Economic Growth and Stability* (Los Angeles: Nash, 1974), p. 107.

requirements, nomination procedures, or excessive entrance fees; nor should they be allowed to operate hiring halls. The Davis-Bacon Act and similar laws requiring excessive wages to be paid under government contracts have interfered seriously with the performance of the construction market [and cost the taxpayer hundreds of millions of dollars]; they should be phased out not only at the federal but also at the state level." [22] Today, moreover, the government finances strikes by generous unemployment benefits and welfare payments. In some states such benefits go even to the strikers themselves, and in that connection a proposal of Arthur Burns should be mentioned. In an important speech he has recommended that "public employment" be offered "to anyone who is willing to work at a rate of pay somewhat below the Federal minimum wage." Burns stressed that a low rate of pay in such public service employment is essential to prevent "such a program from becoming a vehicle for expanding public jobs at the expense of private industry." [23] Public service employment would largely take the place of the present system of unemployment benefits which have become so generous that they "blunt incentives to work." [24] It has been found that in many cases unemployment benefits and various welfare grants (all of which are tax-free) exceed the income after taxes that a person could earn if he accepted a job for which he was qualified.

Minimum wage laws cause considerable unemployment among teenagers and other underprivileged groups, especially blacks and high-school dropouts. The minimum wage laws deprive thousands of young people of their first crucial on-the-job training and may seriously damage their whole future working career. These laws are a social and economic crime and should be phased out. [25] Unions strenuously object to the phasing out of minimum wage legislation. They even reject a reduction of the minimum wage for teenagers on the grounds that such a change would give employment to some teenagers at the expense of adult workers; "sons would displace their

[22] Houthakker, "Specific Reform Measures for the United States," pp. 83-85.

[23] Speech at the University of Georgia, Athens, Georgia, September 19, 1975 (reproduced from typescript). Britain's economic disaster in the past decade, which was mentioned in footnote 17 to this paper, should serve as a warning not to expand employment without proper safeguards.

[24] Ibid.

[25] Actually there is a strong movement in Congress to raise the minimum wage from $2.30 to $3.00 an hour and henceforth to adjust it automatically for any rise in the consumer price index (indexation). This measure would sharply reduce job opportunities for teenagers and other underprivileged persons, it would magnify and perpetuate, even in boom times, unemployment among such groups and would accentuate the inflation.

fathers on the jobs." This argument completely misses the purpose of policies designed to make the economy more competitive and flexible. Such structural reform is not a zero-sum game: The purpose is not a redistribution of a given pie but the enlargement of the pie. Overall employment and output would increase, and so would real wages, partly because more expansionary and more effective monetary and fiscal policies would be possible if the threat of rekindling inflation were eliminated (or at least sharply reduced) by measures that would make the economy more competitive and flexible.

What about incomes policy? A policy along the lines indicated above, designed to make the economy more competitive, is sometimes called an "incomes policy." Arthur Burns has used that terminology. In earlier publications I have called it "incomes policy II" as distinguished from incomes policy I in the usual sense of wage and price guidelines, price stops, wage freezes, and similar measures. Because of these connotations of the term incomes policy, it is perhaps better not to use it for the policy here recommended.

Keynesians and monetarists alike should be able to agree on the desirability of structural reform for the purpose of making the economy more competitive and more flexible. The Keynesian (or, more precisely, the Phillips-curve advocate) would say that such a reform would improve the terms of the trade-off between unemployment and inflation, while the monetarist would assert that the reform would reduce the level of "natural" unemployment.[26]

Concluding Remarks

I am painfully aware that structural reform along the lines sketched here will be at best a very slow process. Vested interests fiercely resist any attempt at deregulation and liberalization and the beneficiaries of present policies hold on, tooth and nail, to their privileges and monopoly positions. What, then, are the policy options if quick relief through structural reform is beyond our grasp?

There is, I believe, no other choice but to continue the present policy of letting the economic expansion proceed slowly in the hope that inflation will not accelerate too rapidly. In my opinion it would be a great mistake to speed up the expansion in order to reduce unemployment quickly, whatever the political appeal of such a policy

---

[26] Such an agreement would not compel the two groups to forego the pleasure of continuing their quarrels, the monetarist insisting that the trade off cannot be permanent and the Keynesian objecting that the "natural" level of unemployment will never be reached.

may be in an election year. Quick expansion surely would speed up the ongoing inflation. The consequence would be either that the monetary brake would be applied and the expansion give way to a new inflationary recession or (perhaps more likely) that the call for wage and price controls would become so strong that the system of controls would be tried once more despite the dismal failure of earlier attempts. The controls would either soon become ineffective, merely further disrupting the economy and burdening it with a new bureaucracy without preventing a recession, or worse (but perhaps more likely) lead to consumer rationing, compulsory allocation of factors of production, and full regimentation of the economy in the guise of economic planning.

The many Keynesians who argue that large unemployment and slack in the economy make a quick expansion safe at present forget that the experiment has been made: much unemployment and slack has *not* prevented the rapid inflation of the last three years. (The operation of "special" inflationary factors can, as we have seen, "explain" only a fraction of the price rise that has occurred.) To say as some do that a more rapid monetary expansion would reduce the rate of inflation because it would stimulate production and so increase aggregate supply is like saying that one can make a drunk sober by forcing whiskey down his throat to pep him up. True, if the poison is withdrawn from him too rapidly a situation may arise where one must increase the dose of the stimulant temporarily to forestall an imminent collapse. But I do not believe that the economy faces that danger now. The economic recovery that started a year ago has gathered momentum and is likely to continue for a considerable period without any additional monetary or fiscal stimulation.

REDUCING INFLATIONARY PRESSURES BY REFORMING GOVERNMENT REGULATION

Murray L. Weidenbaum

Summary

Government policy makers often tend to ignore the effects of their programs on productivity, capital formation, innovation, and inflation. The result is that numerous government activities generate inflationary pressures or otherwise interfere with the attainment of important national goals unrelated to the activities themselves. Admittedly, government imposition of socially desirable requirements on business through the regulatory process may appear to be an inexpensive way of achieving national objectives. It apparently costs the government little and apparently puts no significant burden on the taxpayer. But the public does not escape paying the cost. Every time that a government agency imposes on a firm a more costly (albeit safer or less polluting) method of production, the cost of the firm's product will tend to rise.

The increasing array of governmental regulatory activities necessitates a new way of looking at the microeconomic effects of government programs. A parallel can be drawn to macroeconomic policy making, where conflicting objectives are recognized, and attempts at reconciliation or trade-off made—such as the attempts made at trade-offs among the objectives of economic growth, employment, income distribution, and price stability. At the microeconomic level, it is necessary to reconcile the goals of specific government programs with other important national objectives that are not now the concern of many of these agencies. Healthy working conditions are an important national objective, but surely not the only one. And society has no

The author is indebted to Roland McKean and Lee Benham for numerous insights and suggestions.

273

stake in selecting the most costly and disruptive methods of achieving a higher degree of job safety. Similarly, we must relate environmental protection, product safety, and other regulatory efforts to costs to the consumer, the availability of new products, and the efficiency of productive activity.

One method of broadening the horizons of government policy makers and administrators is through the device of the economic impact statement. Economic regulatory commissions and other agencies and departments acting as regulators should be subject to the requirement that they consider the costs and other adverse effects of their actions as well as the benefits. Regulations that impose costs on society greater than the benefits they generate should be modified or terminated. But it must be understood that this is not a plea for the general elimination of government regulations. It is a plea for reducing (where possible) their inflationary (and other undesirable) consequences. Government regulation should be carried to the point where the incremental benefits equal the incremental costs, and no further. Overregulation—which can be defined as a situation where the costs exceed the benefits—would thus be avoided.

The budget process should be more effectively used to manage regulatory activities. There are "hidden taxes" imposed on consumers by regulatory agencies, and these should be considered by the Congress when it examines the rapidly rising appropriation requests from these agencies. Moreover, the proliferation of regulatory agencies requires that they be thinned out and consolidated so that their often overlapping or inconsistent objectives can be reconciled within the government. The public should not be subjected to the crossfire of conflicting regulations, nor should it be made to suffer the inefficiency imposed by overregulation.

Introduction

Numerous government activities often unwittingly generate inflationary pressures or otherwise interfere with the attainment of important national goals unrelated to the activities in question. These unwanted side-effects occur in large part because government policy makers frequently tend to ignore the effects of government programs on productivity, capital formation, innovation, employment, and inflation.

For example, government imposition of socially desirable requirements on business through the regulatory process appears to be an inexpensive way of achieving national objectives. This practice apparently costs the government little and represents no significant direct burden on the taxpayer. But the public does not escape paying the cost: every time the Environmental Protection Agency imposes a more costly (albeit less polluting) method of production on any firm the cost of the firm's product to the consumer will tend to rise. Similarly, each time the Consumer Product Safety Commission sets a standard that is more costly to attain than the present standard, product costs will increase.

The monetary authorities could offset the inflationary effects of regulation by attempting to maintain a lower rate of monetary growth than they otherwise would. In practice, however, public policy makers tend to prefer the higher rate of inflation to the additional monetary restraint with its resulting decreases in employment and output. Also, to the extent that real resources are devoted to low-payoff activities, economic welfare is reduced.[1] The loss of the potential increases in productivity as a result of such diversion eliminates one possibility for offsetting ordinary factor cost increases and thus exacerbates the problem of inflation.

It is not inevitable, of course, that every regulatory activity increase inflationary pressures. In those instances where regulation generates social benefits (such as a healthier and thus more productive work force) in excess of the social costs it imposes, inflationary pressures should be reduced. The point being made here is that many forms of governmental intervention in the private sector involve heavy costs—and that, with some care and concern, the regulatory process might be revised so as to achieve much the same benefits as are now achieved at lower costs. Indeed, the central purpose of this paper is not to propose the general elimination of regulatory programs but to indicate some of the more promising approaches to reducing their inflationary and other negative consequences—and at the very least to suggest that Congress might reasonably examine the costs and benefits of regulation when the agencies make their requests.

Adverse Effects of Government Regulation of Business

Regulation and Inflation. There is a variety of ways, direct and indirect, in which the operation of governmental regulatory programs contributes to exacerbating the problem of inflation. Sometimes the

---

[1] For a more extensive discussion, see Murray L. Weidenbaum, *Government-Mandated Price Increases* (Washington, D.C.: American Enterprise Institute, 1975).

impact is direct and visible. A case in point is the passenger automobile, in which the federal government has required the manufacturer to incorporate a wide array of specified safety and environmental features. With the so-called interlock system, the public outcry against this requirement became so intense that the Congress overruled the regulators, eliminating the requirement.

Other varieties of government regulation, though indirect, may be equally costly. Several research efforts examining building regulations have documented repeated instances of increases in the price of housing as a result of building codes. A study at Rutgers University tentatively concluded that overly stringent or outdated codes increase housing costs by somewhere between 5 and 10 percent of total unit costs.[2] Several scholars have estimated the effects of land-use controls on the cost of residential housing, and although the analyses have varied in methodology and data, they have generally concluded that there is a weak to moderate (but uniformly positive) relationship between single-family housing costs and land-use controls in developing areas.[3]

In many other ways, government regulation increases the overhead cost of producing goods and services: the rapidly rising burden of paperwork furnishes a striking example. The Standard Oil Company of Indiana, to take just one instance, is required to file approximately 1,000 reports annually to thirty-five federal agencies, including the Federal Power Commission, the Federal Energy Administration, the Bureau of Indian Affairs, and the Small Business Administration. Duplication inevitably occurs. The company must report its oil and gas reserves, with each report taking slightly different form, to the Federal Energy Administration, the Federal Power Commission, the Federal Trade Commission, and the U.S. Geological Survey. It requires 636 miles of computer tape to store the data that the company must supply to the Federal Energy Administration. In total, Standard of Indiana has 100 full-time employees whose work is centered around

[2] See George Sternlieb and David Listokin, *Building Codes, State of the Art, Strategies for the Future*, Report submitted to the HUD Housing Review Task Force, June 1973 (processed).

[3] See George Sternlieb et al., *The Private Sector's Role in the Provision of Reasonably Priced Housing*, prepared for the San Francisco Federal Home Loan Bank Board, December 11, 1975, p. 22; James G. Coke and Charles S. Liebman, "Political Values and Population Density Control," *Land Economics*, vol. 38 (November 1961), pp. 347-61; Richard F. Muth and Elliot Wetzler, *Effects of Constraints on Single-Unit Housing Costs* (Arlington, Va.: Institute for Defense Analyses, 1968); Lynn Sagalyn and George Sternlieb, *Zoning and Housing Costs: The Impact of Land Use Controls on Housing Prices* (New Brunswick: Center for Urban Policy Research, Rutgers University, 1973).

meeting federal regulations, representing an annual cost of about $3 million.[4]

Employee fringe benefit costs have increased as a result of new pension regulations. Some portion of advertising costs may be traced to the requirements imposed by affirmative action programs. In a more indirect way, it is likely that productivity is adversely affected by the variety of regulations designed to improve the quality of the work environment. On the other hand, to the extent that the regulations reduce accidents and absenteeism they contribute positively to output and thus to economic welfare. One would like to see a cost/ benefit analysis here, but in practice the regulating emphasis is on what are essentially "bureaucratic" concerns. With that emphasis more forms are now filled out; more safety rules are posted; more inspections take place; and more fines are levied. But no significant reduction in industrial accident rates has resulted. Table 1 contains the latest available data on accident rates in U.S. industry. It can be seen that the experience for 1973 (the first year of operation of the Occupational Safety and Health Administration) was not any more favorable than the experience for 1972, the year before the advent of OSHA.

The data on one year's experience should be used with considerable caution. In historical perspective 1973 may not turn out to have been a representative year. Also, more complete reporting of accidents may have resulted from the OSHA procedures. Nevertheless, two separate studies of the OSHA program to date have yielded negative findings. Nicholas A. Ashford concluded that "The OSHAct has failed thus far to live up to its potential for reducing job injury and disease . . . OSHA has had little measurable impact in reducing injuries and deaths."[5] And in a more detailed statistical analysis, Robert S. Smith reported similar findings: "the estimated effects [of OSHA] on injuries are so small that they cannot be distinguished from zero."[6]

In the case of the job safety program, as in numerous other areas where the government has become involved, the original concern of the public and the Congress has been reduced to emphasis upon not violating the rules and regulations. "You won't get into trouble if you don't violate the safety standards," is the response of the bureau-

---

[4] James Carberry, "Red Tape Entangles Big Petroleum Firms In Complying With Federal Regulation," *Wall Street Journal*, September 3, 1975, p. 30.

[5] Nicholas A. Ashford, *Crisis in the Workplace: Occupational Disease and Injury* (Cambridge: MIT Press, 1976), p. 13.

[6] Robert S. Smith, *The Occupational Safety and Health Act* (Washington, D.C.: American Enterprise Institute, 1976), p. 70.

Table 1
INCIDENCE RATES OF OCCUPATIONAL INJURIES AND ILLNESSES FOR SELECTED INDUSTRY GROUPS, UNITED STATES, 1973 AND 1972
(per 100 full-time workers)

Industry	Total Recordable Cases		Lost Workday Cases		Nonfatal Cases without Lost Workdays	
	1973	1972	1973	1972	1973	1972
Private nonfarm sector[a]	11.0	10.9	3.4	3.3	7.6	7.6
Transportation and public utilities[b]	10.5	10.8	4.6	4.5	5.9	6.3
Wholesale and retail trade	8.6	8.4	2.7	2.8	5.9	5.6
Finance, insurance, and real estate	2.4	2.5	.8	.8	1.6	1.7
Services[c]	6.3	6.1	2.0	2.0	4.3	4.1

Note: The incidence rates represent the number of injuries and illnesses per 100 full-time workers, and were calculated as $(N/EH) \times 200{,}000$, where
N = number of injuries and illnesses
EH = total hours worked by all employees during calendar year
200,000 = base for 100 full-time equivalent workers (working 40 hours per week, 50 weeks per year)

[a] Includes oil and gas extraction, which is not a component of the industry divisions listed. Other mining activities are not included.

[b] Excludes railroads (SIC 401).

[c] Includes agricultural services, forestry, and fisheries (SIC 07-09).

Source: U.S. Bureau of Labor Statistics, Department of Labor, *Occupational Injuries and Illnesses by Industry, 1973* (Washington, D.C.: U.S. Government Printing Office, 1975), p. 2.

crats even if as many accidents occur after the rules are established as occurred before. The focus is shifted to such trivia as raising and answering these questions: How big is a hole? When is a roof a floor? How frequently must spittoons be cleaned?[7] The results measured by any improvement in safety are almost invariably disappointing—yet the reaction to this situation is predictable: Redouble the existing effort—more rules, more forms, more inspections, and thus higher costs to the taxpayer and higher prices to the consumer.

[7] Weidenbaum, *Government-Mandated Price Increases*, chapter 5.

Regulation and Innovation. One hidden cost of government regulation is a reduced rate of introduction of new products. The longer it takes for a new product to be approved by a government agency—or the more costly the approval process—the less likely that the new product will be created. In any event, innovation will be delayed.

A recent case is the asthma drug, beclomethasone dipropionate (BD). Although this drug has been used successfully by millions of asthma patients in England, it still has not received the approval of the U.S. Food and Drug Administration. BD is described as a safe and effective replacement for the drugs that are now administered to chronic asthma patients, but without their adverse side effects. Unlike BD, the steroids (such as prednisone) currently prescribed in this country can stunt growth in children, worsen diabetes, increase weight through water retention, and cause bone softening. The delaying procedures of the FDA are preventing Americans from switching to the safer product, BD.[8]

Professor Sam Peltzman of the University of Chicago has estimated that the 1962 amendments to the Food and Drug Act are delaying the introduction of effective drugs by about four years, as well as leading to higher prices for drugs.[9] As a result in large part of the stringent drug regulations, the United States was the thirtieth country to approve the anti-asthma drug metaproterenol, the thirty-second country to approve the anti-cancer drug adriamycin, the fifty-first country to approve the anti-tuberculosis drug rifampin, the sixty-fourth country to approve the anti-allergenic drug cromolyn, and the one hundred sixth country to approve the anti-bacterial drug co-trimoxazole.[10]

The regulators seem to have made the private sector fearful. In August 1975, the National Cancer Institute reported that the solvent trichlorethylene, known as TCE, might be a possible cause of cancer. TCE at the time was used in decaffeinated coffee. It seems that the government used a generous dose of the chemical on the test animals—the equivalent, to be exact, of a person's drinking 50 million cups of decaffeinated coffee every day for an entire lifetime. But

[8] William Franklin and Francis Lowell, "Unapproved Drugs in the Practice of Medicine," *New England Journal of Medicine*, May 15, 1975, pp. 1075-77.

[9] Sam Peltzman, "An Evaluation of Consumer Protection Legislation: The 1972 Drug Amendments," *Journal of Political Economy*, September/October 1973, p. 1090; Sam Peltzman, *Regulation of Pharmaceutical Innovation* (Washington, D.C.: American Enterprise Institute, 1974).

[10] Testimony by Dr. William Wardell, University of Rochester School of Medicine and Dentistry, before the Senate Committee on Labor and Public Welfare, Subcommittee on Health, Washington, D.C., September 27, 1974.

did the industry laugh at this example of governmental nonsense? Hardly. With the cyclamate episode still firmly in mind, one major producer quickly changed to another chemical.[11]

Examples of obvious inefficiencies or of trivia in the regulation of business are not hard to find.[12] Capable, intelligent, and well-meaning administrators delegating decisions to capable, intelligent, and well-meaning subordinates cannot specify in advance all the correct or desirable exceptions to general rules; nor should they. The difficulty comes when the administrators or (especially) the subordinates are not capable, intelligent, or well meaning. The problem of bureaucracy is precisely that it tries to apply general rules to specific situations. Upon examination, the reported examples of regulatory nonsense often do not turn out to be mere flukes, but the almost inevitable result of the rapid expansion of regulatory functions in the United States in recent years.[13]

The adverse effect of regulation on new product introduction may be felt more strongly by smaller firms than by larger firms and thus have an anti-competitive impact. According to Dr. Mitchell Zavon, president of the American Association of Poison Control Centers:

> We've got to the point in regulatory action where it's become so costly and risky to bring out products that only the very largest firms can afford to engage in these risky ventures. To bring out a new pesticide you have to figure a cost of $7,000,000 and seven years of time.[14]

Regulation and Capital Formation. Federal regulation also affects the prospects for economic growth and productivity by levying a claim on a rising share of new capital formation. This effect of regulation is most evident in the environmental and safety areas and its importance can be quite readily observed.

An examination of the flow of capital spending by U.S. manufacturing companies just before the recent recession is revealing. In

---

[11] U.S. Food and Drug Administration, *Trichlorethylene (TCE) and Coffee*, FDA Talk Paper (Rockville, Maryland: U.S.F.D.A., June 27, 1975), p. 1; *Memorandum of Alert; Trichlorethylene*, Memorandum from associate director for carcinogenesis, DCCP, NCI to chairman, DHEW Committee to Coordinate Toxicology and Related Programs, March 21, 1975, p. 1 and attachments; Isadore Barmash, "General Foods Changing Sanka and Brim Solvent," *New York Times*, July 17, 1975, pp. 37, 45.

[12] See Weidenbaum, *Government-Mandated Price Increases*, passim.

[13] See Murray L. Weidenbaum, *Business: Government and the Public* (Englewood Cliffs, New Jersey: Prentice-Hall, forthcoming 1977), Chapter I.

[14] Sheila Rule, "Pesticide Regulations Called Too Stringent," *St. Louis Post-Dispatch*, September 18, 1974, p. 18F.

1969, the total new investment in plant and equipment in the manufacturing sector of the U.S. economy came to $26 billion. The annual totals rose in the following years. But when the effect of inflation is eliminated, it can be seen that four years later, in 1973, total capital spending by U.S. manufacturing companies was no higher than in 1969. In real terms, it was approximately $26 billion in both years.

That is not the end of the story, however. In 1973, a much larger proportion of capital outlays was devoted to meeting government regulatory requirements in the pollution and safety area than had been devoted to that purpose in 1969—$3 billion more.[15] Hence, although the economy and its needs had grown substantially in those four years, the real annual investment in modernization and new capital actually declined. The situation was worsened by the accelerated rate at which existing manufacturing facilities were closed down as a result of the rapidly rising costs of meeting government regulations. About 350 foundries in the United States were closed down from 1971 through 1974 because they could not meet requirements such as those imposed by the Environmental Protection Agency and the Occupational Safety and Health Administration.[16] Such closings may help to explain why the American economy, for a substantial part of 1973, appeared to lack needed productive capacity, despite large nominal annual investments in new plant and equipment in recent years.

The governmental decision-making process can have other adverse effects on capital formation by introducing uncertainty about the future of regulations governing the introduction of new processes and products. An example is furnished in a November 1975 report of a task force of the President's Energy Resources Council dealing with the possibility of developing a new synthetic fuel industry. In evaluating the impact of the Federal Water Pollution Control Act Amendments of 1972, the task force reported, "It would be next to impossible at this time to predict the impact of these requirements on synthetic fuels production."[17] Moreover, in considering the National Environmental Policy Act of 1969, the task force stated that the major uncertainty was not whether a project would be allowed to proceed,

---

[15] Lewis Beman, "Why Business Ran Out of Capacity," *Fortune*, May 1974, p. 262.
[16] Robert E. Curran, *The Foundry Industry* (Washington, D.C.: U.S. Department of Commerce, Bureau of Domestic Commerce, March 24, 1975), p. 20; Raymond E. Walk, "Analysis of Shipment Trends and Foundry Closings in the U.S.," *Modern Casting Market Insight*, No. 739, March 31, 1975, pp. 1-8 plus appendix.
[17] Synfuels Interagency Task Force, *Recommendations for a Synthetic Fuels Commercialization Program*, Report submitted to the President's Energy Resources Council, vol. 1 (Washington, D.C.: Government Printing Office, 1975), p. C-22.

but rather the length of time that it would be delayed pending the issuance of an environmental impact statement that would stand up in court. The task force pointed out, "The cost of such delays (construction financing and inflated raw materials and labor costs) is an obvious potential hazard to any synfuels project."[18]

In evaluating the overall impact of government regulatory activity, the task force concluded, "In summary, some of these requirements could easily hold up or permanently postpone any attempt to build and operate a synthetic fuels plant."[19]

Regulation and Employment. Government regulation, albeit unintentionally, can have strongly adverse effects on employment. The minimum wage has increasingly priced teenagers out of labor markets. One recent study has shown that the 1966 increase in the statutory minimum wage reduced teenage employment in the United States by 320,000 below what it otherwise would have been in 1972: that is to say, as a result of that one increase in the compulsory minimum wage, the youth unemployment rate in 1972 was 3.8 percentage points higher than it would otherwise have been.[20]

In construction labor—where unemployment rates are substantially above the national average—government regulation also acts to price some segments of the work force out of competitive labor markets. Under the Davis-Bacon legislation, the secretary of labor promulgates "prevailing" wages to be paid on federal and federally supported construction projects. A variety of studies has shown that these federally mandated wage rates are often above those that actually prevail in the labor market where the work is to be done.[21]

Moreover, the equal employment opportunity program may tend to increase unemployment by delaying the filling of job vacancies—though there are no data to indicate that this may happen to any important degree. To the extent that employers must undergo protracted job searches before hiring employees, the average length of unemployment is likely to be lengthened. It has been my own experience that a position may remain unfilled despite the presence of an

---

[18] Ibid., p. C-18.

[19] Ibid., p. 134.

[20] James F. Ragan, Jr., *Minimum Wage Legislation and the Youth Labor Market*, Working Paper No. 8 (St. Louis: Center for the Study of American Business, Washington University, 1976), p. 29.

[21] John P. Gould, *Davis-Bacon Act* (Washington, D.C.: American Enterprise Institute, 1971); Armand J. Thieblot, Jr., *The Davis-Bacon Act* (Philadelphia: University of Pennsylvania, The Wharton School, 1975).

adequate labor supply at market prices because the governmental regulatory requirements for advertising have not been met.

Regulation and Entrepreneurial Functions. One of the unmeasurable effects of government regulation is what it does to the basic entrepreneurial nature of the private enterprise system. To the extent that management attention is diverted from traditional product development, production, and marketing concerns to the meeting of governmentally imposed social requirements, a significant (although subtle) socialization of corporate activity may result.

In employee pensions, for example, the recently enacted pension regulation has shifted much of the concern of pension fund management from maximizing the return on the contributions to a more cautious approach of minimizing the likelihood that the fund managers will be criticized for their investment decisions. It thus becomes safer—although not necessarily more desirable to the employees covered—for the pension managers to keep more detailed records of their deliberations, to hire more outside experts (so that the responsibility can be diluted), and to avoid innovative investments.[22]

Because of the difficulty of appreciating the extent of the detail and trivia of the government regulation imposed on private sector activities, it is instructive to examine the *Federal Register*, the official publication that contains the rules and regulations promulgated by federal agencies. The January 16, 1976 issue is dominated by ninety-four pages of tables setting forth the minimum wage rates for federal and federally assisted construction established by the secretary of labor under the Davis-Bacon Act. Next comes a major item on the FDA's orange juice standards, which presents specifications on the types of equipment deemed acceptable for measuring the color of orange juice and on the number of points required (36 to 40) for canned orange juice to qualify as being of "good color." This fascinating portion of the *Register* is followed by lemon regulation 22, which restricts the number of lemons that may be shipped from California and Arizona during the period January 18–24. Another FDA regulation then describes the handling of dried prunes. Admittedly, several of the other items in the January 16 *Register* may be of somewhat greater importance than these. They deal with standards on school bus brakes, procedures for making rural housing loans, advertising for eyeglasses, subsidies for local railroad service, and the

---

[22] Shoya Zichy, "How Small Funds Are Coping With the New Pension Law," *Institutional Investor*, September 1975, pp. 19-20; "Pension Reform's Expensive Ricochet," *Business Week*, March 24, 1975, pp. 144-55.

amount of notice that must be given if a drawbridge is required to be open. But, taken altogether, this issue of the *Register* does at the very least suggest the problems of bureaucratic control.

Approaches to Regulatory Reform

A new way of looking at the microeconomic effects of government programs is needed. A parallel can be drawn to macroeconomic policy making, where important and at times conflicting objectives are recognized and attempts at reconciliation or trade-off made (as among economic growth, employment, income distribution, and price stability, for example). At the microeconomic level, it is likewise necessary to reconcile the goals of specific government programs with national objectives. Healthy working conditions, for example, are an important national objective, but not the only important national objective. And society has no stake in selecting the most costly and disruptive methods of achieving a higher degree of job safety. Similarly, we should relate environmental protection, product safety, and other regulatory efforts to costs to the consumer, the availability of new products, and the employment of the work force.

One device for broadening the horizons of government policy makers and administrators is the economic impact statement. Policy makers should be required to consider the costs (and other adverse effects) of their actions as well as the benefits. Moreover, economic impact statements should be required of procurement and subsidy programs that contain regulatory features, as well as being required of all regulatory commissions and of departments and agencies engaged in regulation. But it must be understood that this is not a plea for the elimination of government regulation. It is a plea for reducing where possible the inflationary and other undesirable consequences of such regulation. The theoretical rationale for this moderate approach has been provided by Professor F. A. Hayek in his *Constitution of Liberty:*

> a free market system does not exclude on principle . . . all regulations governing the techniques of production. . . . They will normally raise the cost of production, or what amounts to the same thing, reduce overall productivity. But if this effect on cost is fully taken into account and it is still thought worthwhile to incur the cost to achieve a given end, there is little more to be said about it. The appropriateness of such measures must be judged by comparing the overall

costs with the gain; it cannot be conclusively determined by appeal to a general principle.[23]

In a more specific way, the same point has been made by a leading liberal legislator. Senator Hubert Humphrey has provided a cogent statement on the shortcomings of the existing regulatory approach:

> The government goes around willy-nilly making decisions of consequence. There was no estimate of the economic impact of the Occupational Safety Act, for example. I happen to be for the occupational safety program, but what were its economic implications? Did anyone think that through? No.[24]

The costs and the benefits should be weighed one against the other. In the process the regulations that generate excessive costs should be modified or eliminated. This much is clear, and even Senator Humphrey might be expected to agree. But, in addition, we need to go beyond the direct impact of the regulations on price and include their impact on productivity, capital formation, and innovation.

Relating Costs to Benefits. In November 1974, President Ford instructed the federal agencies under his jurisdiction to examine the effects of the major regulatory actions they would be taking on costs, productivity, employment, and other economic factors (Executive Order 11821). Although this may be considered a useful step forward, it is nevertheless subject to severe shortcomings. First of all, many of the key regulatory agencies—ranging from the Consumer Product Safety Commission to the Federal Trade Commission—are so-called "independent agencies," which are beyond the President's jurisdiction in these matters.

Second, even in the case of the regulatory activities that come within the President's jurisdiction, the new policy is limited to the regulations that, in the issuing agency's own estimation, are "major." In any event, the agencies covered by the executive order are only required to examine the economic aspects of their actions.[25] A broader

[23] F. A. Hayek, *The Constitution of Liberty* (Chicago: University of Chicago Press, 1960), pp. 224-25.

[24] Hubert H. Humphrey, "Planning Economic Policy," *Challenge*, March-April 1975, p. 22.

[25] Office of the White House Press Secretary, *Executive Order: Inflation Impact Statements*, November 27, 1974, pp. 1-2; U.S. Office of Management and Budget, *Evaluation of the Inflationary Impact of Major Proposals for Legislation and for the Promulgation of Regulations or Rules*, Circular No. A-107, January 28, 1975, pp. 1-4.

approach seems to be warranted, in the fashion of the current environmental impact statements.

Society is now supposed to examine the environmental impact of the various major actions it takes. Would it not also be appropriate to require each federal, state, and local environmental agency to assess the impact of its actions on the society as a whole, and particularly on the economy? This would represent a reasonable and desirable extension of Executive Order 11821. Certainly the nation has no desire to select the most expensive or most disruptive ways of achieving its environmental goals, and should not select them. Of course, much would depend on the "teeth" that would be put into any required economic impact statement. Merely legislating the performance of some economic analysis by an unsympathetic regulator would serve little purpose beyond delaying the regulatory process and making it more costly. But limiting government regulation to those instances where the total benefits to society exceeded the cost would be a major (and desired) departure from current practice. It could significantly slow down—if not reverse—the current expansion of federal regulation of business.

To an economist, government regulation should be carried to the point where the incremental benefits equal the incremental costs, and no further. (Indeed, this is the basic criterion that is generally used to screen proposed government investments in physical resources.) Overregulation—which can be defined as regulation for which the costs exceed the benefits—should be avoided. But if policy makers tend to ignore or downplay the costs of regulation, we are bound to overregulate—as, indeed, we do today.

In making decisions on which regulations to adopt, the governmental decision-making body should pay particular attention to several areas of "overhead" costs that are often neglected—the monitoring costs to the government itself, the information costs imposed on both the public and private sectors, and the related private costs of compliance or avoidance. It is hardly coincidental that, with the recent expansion of governmental regulatory activity, the costs of corporate legal departments and legal services have escalated rapidly.[26]

It is also important to build into the governmental processes those incentives that would encourage government officials to pay increased attention to the costs and other side effects generated by the actions they take. New regulations might be limited to those instances where it can be demonstrated that net benefits accrue to

---

[26] Ernest Dickinson, "Lawyers Proliferate and Prosper," *New York Times*, January 25, 1976, p. F-7.

society as a whole. At the operational level, attention might be given to the use of the budget process as an added tool for managing regulation. In those cases where the cost-benefit analyses produced by an agency did not turn out to be an accurate representation of the effects of a regulation—that is, where an agency's regulations in practice generated more costs than benefits—the agency's budget for the coming year should be reduced.

Budget reviewers, be they examiners in the executive branch or committee staff in the legislature, face the perennial question of how to evaluate the effectiveness of an agency that does not provide marketable outputs. The traditional response is to concentrate on the inputs utilized (as, for example, workload statistics). Benefit/cost analysis, cost/effectiveness analysis, or other quantitative forms of program evaluation may provide useful alternatives in such cases. Unfortunately, because the requested appropriations for the regulatory agencies are relatively small portions of the government's budget, limited attention has been given to these activities during the budgetary process. In view of the large costs they often impose on the society as a whole (the "hidden taxes" shifted to the private sector), greater attention is warranted to the reviews accompanying their appropriation requests than is now given.

The wide dissemination of data on the economic impact of government regulation might serve to alter the balance-of-interest-group forces now exerted on the decision-making process. At present, it often appears that the interest groups that would benefit from the regulation are well aware of that, and thus mobilize their forces in favor of greater regulation. But the information on the adverse consequences of regulation, if widely distributed, might generate countervailing interest-group pressures.[27]

Reorganization of Regulation. The effort to reform government regulation, however, must proceed beyond mere statistical analysis. It should also cover the question of reorganizing the wide variety of regulatory agencies currently established. During the past decade there has been a rapid expansion of federal regulatory agencies, with the newcomers to the federal bureaucracy including the Consumer Product Safety Commission, the Environmental Protection Agency, the Federal Energy Administration, the National Transportation Safety Board, and the Occupational Safety and Health Administration.

---

[27] Roland McKean, "Property Rights within Government, and Devices to Increase Efficiency in Government," *Southern Economic Journal*, October 1972, pp. 177-86.

The expenditures of the major federal regulatory agencies came to almost $2.8 billion in the fiscal year 1976 (see Table 2). This is a 48 percent increase over the costs of these regulatory activities in fiscal 1974. It is apparent that the biggest regulatory budgets are not those for the traditional industry-specific regulatory commissions, such as the ICC ($50 million) or the CAB ($85 million). Rather, the largest proportion of the funds is devoted to the broader regulatory activities of the Department of Labor ($397 million, mainly for wage and hour standards and job safety), Department of Agriculture ($381 million, largely for food inspection), and the Federal Energy Administration ($208 million). These newer programs generally apply to all industries.

A consolidation of the numerous federal regulatory agencies might now be desirable. Each of these regulatory agencies was created to further one specific objective—a cleaner environment, healthier working conditions, safer products, and so on—and they were created at different times under different circumstances. Legislative mandate in hand, each agency pursues its individual tasks as it sees them. Yet increasingly the achievement of one agency's objective may frustrate another. The Environmental Protection Agency encourages the conversion of power plants from coal to less polluting fuels such as natural gas and then the Federal Energy Administration urges the shift back to coal, which is the relatively more plentiful fuel. Examples abound of overlapping jurisdictions and cross-cutting objectives—job safety against elimination of discrimination, a quieter workplace against a cleaner workplace, clean air against clean water, and so on.[28] For example, the desulfurization of coal—to reduce air pollution—requires a combination with lime. But combining coal with lime generates large quantities of solid waste calcium sulfate. Disposing of calcium sulfate in turn creates water pollution. Another example relates to federal food standards that require meat-packing plants to be kept clean and sanitary. Surfaces that are easiest to clean are usually tile or stainless steel. But tile and stainless steel are high reflectors of noise. They may not always meet the standards set for occupational safety and health.[29]

Perhaps an organizational structure can be developed that encourages better communication among the regulators and, especially,

---

[28] "Efforts to clean up the factory may result in polluting the general environment, and, conversely, efforts to 'contain the pollution' may mean increased pollution within the plant." Ashford, *Crisis in the Workplace*, p. 7.

[29] Mitchell R. Zavon, "The Contradictory Impacts of Health and Environmental Regulation on Industry," *Mutation Research*, 1974, p. 350.

Table 2
EXPENDITURES ON FEDERAL REGULATORY ACTIVITIES, FISCAL YEAR 1976
(in millions of dollars)

Area and Agency	Amount
Consumer safety and health	
Department of Agriculture	$ 381
Department of Health, Education, and Welfare	189
Department of Justice	171
Department of Transportation	234
Department of the Treasury	320
Consumer Product Safety Commission	37
National Transportation Safety Board	10
Subtotal	1,342
Job safety and other working conditions	
Department of the Interior	79
Department of Labor	397
Equal Employment Opportunity Commission	60
National Labor Relations Board	70
Occupational Safety and Health Review Commission	6
Subtotal	612
Environment and energy	
Environmental Protection Agency	54
Federal Energy Administration	208
Subtotal	262
Financial reporting, and other financial	
Cost Accounting Standard Board	2
Council on Wage and Price Stability	2
Securities and Exchange Commission	49
Subtotal	53
Industry-specific regulation	
Civil Aeronautics Board	85
Commodity Futures Trading Commission	11
Federal Communications Commission	50
Federal Maritime Commission	8
Federal Power Commission	36
Federal Trade Commission	45
International Trade Commission	10
Interstate Commerce Commission	50
Nuclear Regulatory Commission	198
Renegotiation Board	5
Subtotal	498
Grand total	2,767

Source: *Budget of the U.S. Government for the Fiscal Year 1976* (Washington. D.C.: U.S. Government Printing Office, 1975), various pages.

the reconciliation of conflicting objectives within the governmental mechanism. Such a structure might permit a greater degree of "internalizing" the benefits and costs of the regulatory process. Moreover, an attempt at reconciliation would be performed in the government itself—one hopes before the issuance of regulations— and this could help reduce the number of situations where business firms and individuals are caught in the crossfire of conflicting government regulations.

General Attitudes toward Regulation. Basically, however, it is attitudes that need to be changed, and experience with the job safety program provides a striking example. Although the government's safety rules, regulations, and requirements have resulted in billions of dollars in public and private outlays, the basic goal of a safer work environment has not been achieved, as we have seen.

A more satisfying answer to improving the effectiveness of government regulation of private activities requires a basic change in approach to regulation, and one not limited to the job safety program. (Indeed, that program is used here merely as an illustration.) If the objective of public policy is to reduce accidents, public policy should focus on the reduction of accidents. Excessively detailed regulations often are merely a substitute—the normal bureaucratic substitute— for hard policy decisions. Rather than emphasis being placed on issuing citations to employers who fail to fill forms out correctly or who do not post correct notices, it should be placed on the regulation of those employers with high and rising accident rates, perhaps with the levying of fines on those with the worst safety records. (Variable insurance rates might perform a similar function.) As the accident rates decline toward some sensible average standard, the fines could be reduced or eliminated.

But the government should not be much concerned with the way a specific company achieves a safer working environment. Some companies may find it more efficient to change work rules, others to buy new equipment, and still others to retrain workers. But the making of this choice is precisely the kind of operational business decision making that government should avoid, but that now dominates many regulatory programs. Without diminishing the responsibility of the employers, the sanctions under the federal occupational safety and health law should be extended to employees, especially those whose negligence endangers other employees. The purpose here is not to be harsh, but to set up effective incentives to achieve society's objectives—which is, after all, the purpose of the government. Moreover, any realistic appraisal must acknowledge that important and positive benefits have resulted from some government regulatory activities—less pollution, fewer product hazards, the ending of job discrimination, and the achievement of other socially desirable objectives of our society.

It should also be realized that federal programs were established by the Congress in response to a surge of rising public expectations about corporate performance. Although business executives rarely talk (or write) of the costs and benefits of their actions to society as a whole, they often are aware of the basic societal justification for government intervention. The president of Chrysler furnished a good example in his justification of governmental automobile pollution controls:

> a large part of the public will not voluntarily spend extra money to install emission control systems which will help clean the air. Any manufacturer who installs and charges for such equipment while his competition doesn't soon finds he is losing sales and customers. In cases like this, a Government standard requiring everyone to have such equipment is the only way to protect both the public and the manufacturer.[30]

But the "externalities" generated by federal regulation cannot justify any governmental attempt to regulate *every* facet of private behavior.

Alternatives to Regulation. The promulgation by the government of rules and regulations restricting or prescribing private activity is not the only means of accomplishing public objectives. As Roland McKean has pointed out, codes of behavior adhered to on a voluntary basis may often be effective.[31] Such a "voluntary" approach may have special application at the present time. The recent revelations of misdeeds by corporate executives in their dealings with various government officials have led to pleas for tighter regulation of such business behavior.[32] But given the almost universal public outrage, it is most likely that the prevailing norms of corporate behavior are being

---

[30] John J. Riccardo, "Regulation: A Threat to Prosperity," *New York Times*, July 20, 1975, p. F-12.

[31] See Roland McKean, *Economics of Ethical and Behavioral Codes* (St. Louis: Washington University, Center for the Study of American Business, 1976).

[32] U.S. Senate, Committee on Banking, Housing and Urban Affairs, *Lockheed Bribery* (Washington, D.C.: U.S. Government Printing Office, 1975), pp. 1-57; "New Exxon Policy Bans Political Contributions," *Wall Street Journal*, March 26, 1976, p. 8; Robert M. Smith, "Senators Seek a Law to Curb U.S. Business Bribery Abroad," *New York Times*, May 7, 1976, p. D-1.

changed substantially—and voluntarily—so as to avoid repetition of the episodes which have proven so damaging both to the individuals and to their organizations.[33]

Government itself has available to it various powers other than the powers of regulation. Through its taxing authority the government can provide strong signals to the market. Rather than promulgating detailed regulations governing allowable discharges into the nation's waterways, the government could levy substantial taxes on those discharges. Such sumptuary taxation could be "progressive," to the extent that the tax rates would rise faster than the amount of pollution emitted by an individual polluter. Thus, there would be an incentive for firms to concentrate on removing or reducing the more serious instances of pollution rather than dissipating their environmental clean-up efforts on projects with low pay-offs (that is, with high expense and small improvement in the quality of the environment).

The use of taxation would not be meant to punish polluters, or even to give them a "license" to pollute. Rather it would be meant to make use of the price system by encouraging producers and consumers to shift to less polluting ways of producing and consuming goods and services. The basic point is simple: Most people do not pollute because they get positive pleasure from dirtying the environment. Rather they pollute because it often is easier or cheaper than not polluting. If the government were to change basic incentives through the tax-price mechanism, individuals and organizations (both public and private) would be encouraged voluntarily to alter their economic behavior so as to make it more in keeping with the goals of the society. Perhaps most important would be the shift in public-private relationships from the current adversary position to a more neutral and efficient mode of conduct.

---

[33] "Campaign Gifts: How Much A Guilty Plea Can Cost," *Business Week*, March 24, 1975, p. 32; Byron E. Calame, "Gulf Officers' Ouster Was Boldly Engineered By Mellon Interests," *Wall Street Journal*, January 15, 1976, p. 1; Michael C. Jensen, "Outside Directorships Also Lost in Scandals," *New York Times*, May 7, 1976, p. D-3.

WORLD AND U.S. FOOD TRENDS: A CURRENT PERSPECTIVE FOR POLICY

Harold O. Carter

Summary

The "food crisis" that first emerged around 1972–1973 to replace the "farm problem" has generated considerable debate and concern in the United States and abroad. While the causes of the crisis are generally agreed upon, less consensus exists on its longer-run implication. What some have seen as an ominous trend toward world food shortages and spiraling prices, others see mainly as a large deviation from a relatively steady food-production trend. The purpose of this study is to provide a current perspective on these food and resource trends and to assess the policy directions we might take.

While some gain in world food production relative to population has been documented in the last two decades, serious distributional problems remain between developed and developing countries. Food/ population studies published in the last few years suggest growing cereal grain imbalance between developed and developing countries unless population growth is reduced, or production is expanded at an accelerated pace in the developed countries, or both. The potential exists for expansion of both land base and yield capabilities especially for Latin America and Africa, but substantial financial assistance will be necessary for that expansion. Moreover, the outlook has been considerably improved for obtaining needed fertilizer supplies at prices substantially below their peak 1974 levels. World climate remains a major element of uncertainty, with incomplete evidence available as to sustained detrimental trends for world food production.

Some tentative generalizations are these: (1) the world's food/ population balance is not undergoing a fundamental transformation toward chronic food shortages; (2) rapidly expanding world fertilizer plant capacity has significantly lessened the fertilizer price and supply problems that peaked about two years ago; (3) the agricultural productive capacity of the United States is basically strong and there is potential for expansion in the resource base and for continued productivity growth. One possible problem is that capacity may be developed at a rate faster than the ability of markets to absorb the increased output at acceptable producer prices. The situation for many other developed countries is similar; (4) the real price of grain will remain roughly constant for a few years (depending on the form of the commodity programs and reserve-stocks policy adopted) and then is likely to decline again. Accordingly, food price rises will be more moderate than in the last three years with most of the rise in prices coming from increases in processing and marketing costs.

The major food policy problems are now perceived to be instability of agricultural markets and insecurity of food supplies. The 1973 Agricultural and Consumer Protection Act, to expire in 1977, provides considerable discretionary authority for the secretary of agriculture to cope with a variety of circumstances that would be encountered in changing agricultural market situations. The 1973 act does not deal with the reserve stock question—an omission that needs correcting, especially since there appears little likelihood of moving toward freer world trade. Basically, reserves should be kept at levels only (1) to ensure emergency stocks to meet disastrous shortfalls, particularly for developing countries, and (2) to mitigate wide variations in world grain market supplies and prices.

Introduction

Around 1972–1973 the familiar U.S. "farm problem" disappeared, some say permanently, and the "food crisis" emerged in its place. The emphasis of U.S. agricultural policy shifted from surplus grain disposal (while farm income was propped up through government payments, price supports, and acreage withdrawal) to the encouragement of all-out production to meet rapidly expanding export demand.

The Food Crisis. The causes and events leading to the food crisis of 1973 and 1974 have been reviewed by numerous writers.[1] Explana-

---

[1] See, for example, David Hathaway, "Food, Prices, and Inflation," in *Brookings Papers on Economic Activity*, 1974(1), pp. 63-116; United Nations, World Food Conference, *Assessment of the World Food Situation, Present and Future*, 1974; D. Gale Johnson, *World Food Problems and Prospects* (Washington, D.C.: American Enterprise Institute, 1975); U.S. Department of Agriculture, Economic Research Service, *The World Food Situation and Prospects to 1985*, Foreign Agricultural Economic Report, no. 98 (December 1974).

tions of what underlay this turnabout vary somewhat but the factors commonly cited are (1) poor crops in 1972–1973 attributable to adverse weather in much of the world, (2) large Soviet grain purchases in 1972 to offset production losses in the Soviet Union, (3) shortfalls in the Peruvian anchovy catch in 1972 that significantly reduced animal protein supplies, (4) rising affluence in parts of the world causing significant increases in demand for livestock products and thus for feed grains and concentrates, (5) two devaluations of the dollar that made U.S. exports more a bargain to our foreign customers than they had been, and (6) governmental policies in many countries—policies preventing the price system from rationing the reduced supplies and thus putting much of the burden on the international grain markets.[2]

Less consensus exists on the longer-run implications of the factors noted above than on their particular effect in 1972–1973. Some view the food population trends as suggesting an approaching fulfillment of the Malthusian prophesy,[3] while others see the crisis as only a temporary aberration and believe there are generally ample resources for future generations.[4] Most others fall somewhere in between.[5]

---

[2] Johnson, *World Food Problems and Prospects*, pp. 2-3, argues that this was the major factor accounting for the unparalleled grain price increases.

[3] Lester R. Brown, "The Next Crisis? Food," *Foreign Policy*, no. 13 (Winter 1973-74), p. 3, speaking on the seriousness and permanency of the food crisis, states:

> This year's global food scarcity is often treated by both official Washington and the communication media as a temporary phenomenon, an aberration that will shortly disappear if we will only have patience. But several factors suggest that the world food economy is undergoing a fundamental transformation, and that food scarcity is becoming chronic.
>
> The soaring demand for food, spurred by continued population growth and rising affluence, has begun to outrun the productive capacity of the world's farmers and fishermen. The result has been declining food reserves, skyrocketing food prices, food rationing in three of the world's most populous countries, intense international competition for exportable food supplies, and export controls on major foodstuffs by the world's principal food supplier.

Other well publicized documents that take an alarmist view of trends in resource use, population growth, and food supplies are the familiar Club of Rome reports by D. H. Meadows, D. L. Meadows, J. Randers, and W. W. Behrens III, *The Limits of Growth* (New York: E. P. Dutton and Co., 1972), and M. Mesarovic and E. Pestel, *Mankind at the Turning Point* (New York: E. P. Dutton and Co., 1974).

[4] At the other extreme on the broad issue of resource/food production balance, Colin Clark has argued that the world has the resources, if properly organized, to feed and house 58 billion people. This would be some fifteen to sixteen times current population levels and about nine times that projected for the year 2000. See Colin Clark, *Population Growth and Land Use* (London: Macmillan, 1967).

[5] Other studies and assessments have been made that take a cautiously optimistic view. In general, these studies indicate that while the situation is pre-

Conflicting Goals in Food Policy. Assessment of the many facets of the food situation, as well as our goals and perceptions of the problem, changes with time and as new information unfolds. Conflicting goals of food aid, government costs, and low domestic food prices came into sharp focus in 1974—as noted by the Report of the Council of Economic Advisers.

The U.S. crop shortfall placed two new strains on the capacity to supply food aid. It first raised the opportunity costs of any given quantity of food aid, since any incremental exports would only aggravate the adjustments required in the United States. It also raised the budgetary costs of any given volume of food aid during a period of concerted effort to hold down Federal expenditures. At the same time, however, the immediate benefits to recipient countries from more food aid would be significant. The great difficulties in resolving the conflicting objectives have shown the pitfalls in existing food aid programs, which have been a byproduct of U.S. surplus disposal programs and closely tied to supply conditions for particular commodities.[6]

Indeed, Mayer and Seevers contend, "With the tightening in nearly every conceivable dimension of food markets in the past two years, national food policy must take account of a more complex set of interrelationships."[7] Increasingly, "food power" is being discussed by some as an element in international politics because of the dominance of U.S. grain in world markets, where grain reserves are at record low levels.[8]

This study reviews and evaluates the current agricultural and food situation, not only in looking where we have been, but in assess-

carious enough, food can be produced to meet effective demand provided appropriate action and adjustments are made. These include the assessment paper by the U.S. Department of Agriculture, *World Food Situation and Prospects* (see note 1); a study by the President's Science Advisory Committee, *The World Food Problem* (Washington, D.C.: U.S. Government Printing Office, 1967); an Iowa State University study by L. L. Blakeslee, E. O. Heady, and C. F. Framingham, *World Food Production, Demand and Trade* (Ames, Iowa: Iowa State University Press, 1973); the study by Johnson, *World Food Problems and Prospects;* and a University of California Food Task Force Report, *A Hungry World: The Challenge to Agriculture,* Harold O. Carter, chairman (Berkeley, Calif.: University of California, July 1974).

[6] *Economic Report of the President* (Washington, D.C.: U.S. Government Printing Office, 1975), p. 165.

[7] Leo V. Mayer and Gary L. Seevers, "Food Policy Issues in the United States," *American Journal of Agricultural Economics*, vol. 56, no. 2 (May 1974), pp. 359-63.

[8] Emma Rothschild, "Food Politics," *Foreign Affairs*, vol. 54, no. 2 (January 1976), p. 285.

ing possible future trends and directions. It is our concern that price and income policies based on erroneous assumptions and on interpretations of events often unfolding rapidly and with emotional and political overtones may well exacerbate the food problems of future generations. In a concluding section, we mention the key policy issues, the environment in which these issues must be resolved, and our perceptions of the directions we might take.

World Food Trends and Major Constraints

Because of the complexity of the world food system, the outlook for future food production must be, at best, only an estimate.[9] In this section we review trends in food production and trade and then consider some of the constraints on production in areas where considerable concern has been expressed—namely land, fertilizer, and climate.

Food Production Trends. Food production between 1954 and 1973 declined globally—excluding the People's Republic of China—only once: 1972 production declined 1.6 percent from the previous year. Yet, that single decline seems for some to have deflated high expectations for the "Green Revolution" technologies and thus portended dire consequences for future food balances. However, world food production for the period 1954–1973 increased 2.8 percent annually, whereas population increased at a 2.0 percent annual rate. This combination resulted in an increase in world per capita food production of 0.8 percent (see Table 1). Over these two decades, food production increased at a slightly higher annual rate in developing countries (3.0 percent) than in developed countries (2.7 percent). But because of sharply increasing population growth rates, per capita food production rose at an annual rate of only 0.4 percent in the developing countries, compared to an annual rate of 1.5 percent in the developed countries. Thus, while some gain in world per capita food production has been realized in the past two decades, a serious distributional problem between developed and developing nations remains.

Production data for 1975 and preliminary 1976 reports for the developing countries are encouraging. Total food production gained

---

[9] For a promising modeling approach see G. E. Rossmiller, G. L. Johnson, and M. E. Hanratty, *Global Modeling of Food and Agriculture: Background to a Possible Approach*, Agricultural Sector Analysis and Simulation Project (East Lansing, Mich.: Michigan State University Press, 1975).

Table 1
INCREASE IN FOOD PRODUCTION, POPULATION, AND PER CAPITA FOOD PRODUCTION, 1954–1973
(in percent)

	Increase from 1954 to 1973	Annual Rate of Increase
Food production		
World[a]	69	2.8
Developed countries	65	2.7
Developing countries	75	3.0
Population		
World	44	2.0
Developed countries	22	1.0
Developing countries	61	2.5
Per capita food production		
World	17	0.8
Developed countries	33	1.5
Developing countries	8	0.4

Note: Based on linear trends of indices.
[a] Excludes the Asian centrally planned economies, for which data are lacking.
Source: U.S. Department of Agriculture, Economic Research Service, *The World Food Situation and Prospects to 1985*, Foreign Agricultural Economics Report no. 98 (December 1974), p. 12.

6 percent over 1974 and on a per capita basis the increase was 3 percent—with some South Asian countries realizing even greater gains.[10] Because of the poor crops in the Soviet Union, food production in 1975 declined slightly in the developed countries (1.5 percent total and 2.5 percent per capita). Thus, total world food production gained only slightly and per capita was unchanged.

World Grain Supply and Demand. Since grain is the most important single element in the world's diet (in various direct and indirect uses), changes in production and consumption of grain are accepted barometers of the world food situation.

Table 2 shows world grain production and consumption, the trend values of production and consumption, and deviation of actual production and consumption from their linear trends, for selected periods since 1960–1961. World grain consumption has tended to

[10] U.S. Department of Agriculture, Economic Research Service, working materials, Supply and Foreign Demand Competition Division, May 1976.

Table 2
WORLD GRAIN PRODUCTION AND CONSUMPTION,
DEVIATION FROM 1960/61–1974/75 LINEAR TRENDS
(millions of metric tons)

	Production			Consumption	
	Actual	Trend	Deviation	Trend	Deviation
World total					
1960/61–62/63	810	803	7	805	− 2
1969/70–71/72	1,069	1,066	3	1,073	− 9
1972/73	1,102	1,124	− 22	1,133	− 31
1973/74	1,195	1,152	43	1,163	32
1974/75	1,144	1,181	− 37	1,193	− 49
1975/76	1,151	1,210	− 59	1,223	− 72
World total (excluding U.S.S.R.)					
1960/61–62/63	686	688	− 2	—	—
1969/70–71/72	904	899	5	—	—
1972/73	945	947	− 2	—	—
1973/74	987	970	17	—	—
1974/75	960	993	− 33	—	—
1975/76	1,023	1,016	7	—	—

Note: Grain includes wheat, milled rice, and major coarse grains (corn, barley, rye, oats, and sorghum).
Source: U.S. Department of Agriculture, Economic Research Service, *World Agricultural Situation*, WAS-9 (December 1975), pp. 33, 36.

increase about 30 million tons per year since 1960–1961, while production has increased less than 29 million tons per year. The difference between the two has been taken up by stocks whose initial accumulation began in the 1950s. The 1972–1976 period shows large gaps between trend consumption and actual production. And, because the main factors underlying the consumption trend have been relatively price-inelastic, we have seen large trade and price fluctuations.

Two components make up the consumption trend—food demand and feed demand. Simply maintaining per capita food grain consumption levels with no increased demand from income changes would require over 10 million tons per year (over 1 million tons in developed and 8 to 9 million tons in developing countries). There seems little chance that growth in the food component will lessen appreciably.[11]

[11] U.S. Department of Agriculture, Economic Research Service, *World Agriculture Situation*, WAS-9 (December 1975), pp. 36-37.

The feed component of grain demand has grown more rapidly and is more price-elastic than demand for grain for food. Since 1960–1961 the amount of world grain fed to livestock has increased at a rate of 4.7 percent annually.[12] The United States feeds about one-quarter of the grain being fed annually and U.S. feed consumption has grown at a 2 percent rate. Grain feeding outside the United States (mainly in other developed countries, Eastern Europe and the Soviet Union) has grown at about 6 percent annually. The Soviet Union in particular has expanded grain production rapidly in the last decade, largely for livestock feed, in an attempt to upgrade the diet of the Soviet people. (Note the comparisons between the Soviet Union, United States, and European Economic Community in Table 3.) For the most part, the 1975–1976 shortfalls between production and trend consumption are being made up in reduced livestock feeding levels, as were the 1974–1975 shortfalls. Last year the United States reduced its amount of feed grains fed to livestock by 38 million tons, which is a substantial portion of the production-consumption trend gap. This year, the Soviet Union is apparently making substantial cutbacks in hogs and poultry while attempting to maintain beef and dairy herds.[13]

Hathaway contends that long-run growth in demand for feed grains and oilseeds resulting from increased affluence in both the developed and developing countries has been the major cause of the "food crisis" and is a persistent force not to be overlooked in future assessments.[14] Johnson, however, correctly points out that there was no sudden jump in per capita income in the Soviet Union that would explain the rapid growth in per capita consumption. Thus, the increase must be the result of a deliberate policy change. The Soviet Union has apparently pushed livestock production to the extent that it can now be self-sufficient only in "good" production years. Without Soviet grain stocks of any size, poor crop years require massive imports or livestock liquidation, or both.

World Grain Trade Balances, Past and Projected. The United States is playing a more dominant role than ever before as the supplier for the world's grain importers (see Table 4). During the 1934–1938 period Western Europe was the major net importer while Latin America, the Soviet Union, Eastern Europe, North Africa, the Middle East, and even Asia were among the net exporters. With the possible exception of Latin America, all these regions mentioned as net

[12] Ibid., p. 36.
[13] Ibid., p. 48.
[14] Hathaway, "Food, Prices, and Inflation," p. 95.

Table 3
FEED USE OF GRAIN AND CONCENTRATES, MEAT OUTPUT, AND MEAT CONSUMPTION, IN THE SOVIET UNION, UNITED STATES AND EUROPEAN ECONOMIC COMMUNITY

| | Soviet Union | | | United States | | | | European Economic Community | | |
| | | Meat | | | | Meat | | | Meat | |
Year	Concentrates	Output a	Consumption b	Concentrates	Grain	Output c	Consumption d	Grain	Output e	Consumption f
	million metric tons	million metric tons	(kg/capita)	million metric tons	million metric tons		(kg/capita)	million metric tons	million metric tons	(kg/capita)
1960	—	8.7	40	146.2	110.7	15.7	82	49.1	—	—
1961	59.3	8.7	—	148.4	111.4	16.3	83	50.0	—	—
1962	61.3	9.5	—	147.6	109.7	16.3	84	53.0	—	—
1963	52.3	10.2	—	145.6	107.5	17.2	86	54.8	—	—
1964	48.2	8.3	38	142.8	104.8	18.3	88	57.0	13.0	59
1965	65.3	10.0	41	158.0	118.6	18.0	86	58.8	13.5	59
1966	70.5	10.7	44	158.0	118.8	18.8	89	59.0	13.9	61
1967	75.1	11.5	46	159.9	121.7	19.7	93	63.9	14.4	63
1968	80.3	11.6	48	168.0	127.7	20.1	94	62.8	15.0	63
1969	89.5	11.8	47	177.9	135.2	20.3	95	66.5	15.3	65
1970	103.2	12.3	48	174.9	131.9	21.0	97	66.9	16.2	67
1971	109.7	13.3	50	185.9	143.5	21.8	100	67.4	17.0	70
1972	109.6	13.6	51	186.5	145.7	21.7	99	70.7	16.7	71
1973	117.0	13.5	53	182.5	140.2	20.6	102	70.9	16.9	71
1974	127.9	14.5	55	157.9	117.2	22.1	109	69.0	18.2	73
1975 (preliminary)		15.5				20.6	104		18.0	69

a Slaughter weight. Includes beef, veal, pork, mutton, goat and poultry meat. b Includes fat and poultry meat. c Carcass weight, excluding lard. Includes beef, veal, pork, lamb, mutton and poultry meat. d Includes poultry, game and edible offals. On the basis of retail weight equivalent for red meats and poultry. e Carcass weight. Includes beef, veal, pork, sheep, goat, poultry and horse meat and edible offals. Data from FAS, USDA. f Dressed carcass weight. Includes poultry and horse meat and edible offals. Data from FAS, USDA.
Source: U.S. Department of Agriculture, Foreign Agricultural Service, "Soviet Statistics: The Grain-Livestock Economy," *Foreign Agricultural Circular,* January 1976.

301

Table 4
WORLD NET IMPORTS (−) AND NET EXPORTS OF GRAIN, SELECTED PERIODS, 1934–1976
(million metric tons)

Country	1934–38	1948–52	1960–62	1969–71	1971–72	1972–73	1973–74	1974–75	1975–76
Developed countries									
United States	0.5	14.0	32.8	39.8	42.8	73.6	72.9	65.2	84.1
Canada	4.8	6.0	9.7	14.8	18.3	14.8	12.9	12.8	16.0
South Africa	0.3	.0	2.1	2.5	3.7	3.1	4.0	3.7	3.4
Oceania	2.8	3.7	6.6	10.6	10.8	8.9	9.5	11.3	11.0
Western Europe	−23.8	−22.5	−25.6	−21.4	−18.5	−21.0	−22.5	−19.2	−18.8
Japan	−1.9	−2.3	5.3	−14.4	−15.0	−18.5	−19.2	−18.5	−18.9
Centrally planned countries									
U.S.S.R. & Eastern Europe	4.7	2.7	0.5	−3.6	−13.5	−14.2	−10.5	−8.6	−35.7
China	−1.0	−0.4	−3.6	−3.1	−15.4	−6.3	−5.8	−4.4	−1.7
Developing countries									
Latin America	9.0	2.1	0.8	3.2	−2.0	0.6	−2.5	−3.1	3.7
North Africa and Middle East	1.0	−0.1	−4.6	−9.2	−11.9	−13.7	−13.7	−16.4	−15.7
Asia	2.4	−3.3	−5.6	−11.0	−11.3	−14.8	−15.3	−16.8	−16.0

Note: Grain includes wheat, milled rice, corn, rye, barley, oats, and sorghum.

Source: Data for selected periods 1934-71 and 1972-73 are from *Economic Report of the President* (Washington, D.C.: U.S. Government Printing Office, 1975), p. 172. Data for 1971-72 and 1973-76 are from U.S. Department of Agriculture, Economic Research Service, *World Agricultural Situation*, WAS-9 (December 1975), p. 35.

exporters then are now net importers of a substantial magnitude. The United States now accounts for 47 percent of total world wheat exports and 56 percent of the world's coarse grain exports—and our total share of world exports for all grains has increased in the last four years.[15]

Numerous food/population studies of the past few years have projected growing cereal grain imbalance between developed and developing countries for the 1980s (Table 5). Because of different assumptions on population, income growth rates, and technology, direct comparisons between the studies are difficult. However, there is general agreement in the reports that cereal production in 1985 will balance effective demand for cereals in various uses on a world-wide basis. Projected regional deficits of cereals in the developing countries vary from a low of 22.5 million tons to a high of 118.1 million tons. Much of this extreme variation can be explained by differences in technology changes assumed in the respective reports for the developing countries. To accommodate projected import needs (for most of the estimates shown in Table 5) there must be a substantial change in present world trade patterns. It may, however, be noted that in the early 1970s, however, 57 percent of total world trade and 49 percent of world agricultural trade took place between the developed countries *and these percentages have been rising.*[16]

Current Assessment of Some Major Production Constraints. While it is recognized that a host of factors imposed by nature and man have a profound influence on future world food production, discussion is limited here to intensive and extensive land development, fertilizer, and climate.

Intensive and extensive land development. Continued increases in world production commensurate with projected demand changes— or at least consistent with trends of the past two decades—require that (1) output per unit of land be increased on many soils now used for crops; (2) additional arable soils not now used be developed and their management systems learned; or (3) both.

In recent years the developed world—Europe, North America, the Soviet Union, and most of Oceania—has relied mostly on increased technology to meet expanding production needs. The developing world, particularly Latin America and Africa, has relied more heavily on developing new land area to expand output (Table 6). A com-

[15] U.S. Department of Agriculture, Foreign Agricultural Service, "World Grain Situation: Outlook for 1975-76," *Foreign Agriculture Circular*, December 22, 1975.
[16] U.S. Department of Agriculture, *World Food Situation and Prospects*, p. 18.

Table 5
COMPARISON OF CEREAL PROJECTIONS TO 1985 [a]
(million metric tons)

Item	FAO Base 1969-71	FAO 1985	USDA Base 1969-71	USDA-I[f] 1985	USDA-II[g] 1985	USDA-III[h] 1985	USDA-IV[i] 1985	ISU 1985	UC 1985	IFPRI 1985-86
World										
Demand	1,207	1,725	1,062.6	1,548.5	1,618.7	1,501.8	1,643.9	1,145.5	1,777.2	
Production	1,239	NS	1,081.8	1,550.4	1,620.6	1,503.6	1,645.7	1,187.3 (L) 1,191.7 (H)	1,176.6	
Balance [b]	+32	NS	19.2	1.9	1.9	1.9	1.9	41.8 (L)[i] 46.2 (H)[i]	-0.6	
Developing countries										
Demand	590	929	466.6	691.2	726.2	678.6	743.5		954.5	
Production	585	853	443.1	632.4	648.7	626.2	721.0		917.9	
Balance	-5	-76	-23.5	-58.8	-77.5	-52.4	-22.5		-36.6	
Developing market economies [c]										
Demand	386	629	299.7	479.4	512.6	466.7	529.1	524.7	210.2	534.2 (H)[k] 517.1 (L)[k]
Production	370	544	279.2	424.7	441.0	418.7	513.3	411.0 (H)[i] 406.6 (L)[i]	206.5	451.6
Balance	-16	-85	-20.5	-54.7	-71.6	-48.0	-15.8	-113.7 (H)[i] -118.1 (L)[i]	-3.7	-82.6 (H)[k] -65.5 (L)[k]
Asian centrally planned countries [d]										
Demand	204	300	166.9	211.8	213.6	211.9	214.4		744.3	233.4
Production	215	309	163.9	207.7	207.7	207.7	207.7		711.4	
Balance	+11	+9	-3.0	-4.1	-5.9	-4.2	-6.7		-32.9	
Developed countries [e]										
Demand	617	796	596.0	857.3	892.5	823.2	900.4	403.4	822.7	
Production	654	NS	638.7	918.0	971.9	877.4	924.7	574.0	858.8	
Balance	+37	NS	42.7	60.7	79.4	54.2	24.3	170.6	36.1	

Note: FAO = Food and Agriculture Organization; USDA = U.S. Department of Agriculture; ISU = Iowa State University; IFPRI = International Food Policy Research Institute.

a The data for FAO and USDA are not comparable because FAO carries rice as paddy, USDA carries rice as milled.

b Imbalances for USDA between demand and production in base are due to stock buildup, timing of shipments, and missing data on a number of small importers. Projected equilibrium does not allow for building or reducing stocks.

c UC developing market economies include Africa and Latin America. IFPRI includes Asia, North Africa, Middle East, Sub-Sahara, Africa, and Latin America.

d UC, FAO, and IFPRI Asian centrally planned includes the People's Republic of China and other Asian centrally planned countries (North Korea, North Vietnam, etc). UC also includes Japan.

e Includes the U.S.S.R. and Eastern Europe.

f USDA-I. Assumes economic growth temporarily slowed, but resumes strong expansion in late 1970s. Limited expansion of world trade.

g USDA-II. High world import demand situation. Larger income growth rate than USDA-I in both developing and developed countries.

h USDA-III. Low demand situation that assumes economic stagnation would continue in the late 1970s and recovery does not occur until the 1980s.

i USDA-IV. Developing countries' import needs are reduced. Have assumed that they have increased their investment in food production by increasing the inputs used.

j Projections designated (L) are made under a low variant upper bound on cropland expansion. Those designated (H) are made under a high variant bound on cropland expansion.

k Projections designated (L) are made under a low variant upper bound on income growth. Those designated (H) are made under a high variant bound on income growth.

Source: U.S. Department of Agriculture, Economic Research Service, *The World Food Situation and Prospects to 1985*, Foreign Agricultural Economic Report, no. 98 (December 1974), p. 35; University of California Food Task Force Report, *A Hungry World: The Challenge to Agriculture* (Berkeley: University of California, July 1974); and International Food Policy Research Institute, *Meeting Food Needs in the Developing World: The Location and Magnitude of the Task in the Next Decade*, Research Report No. 1 (Washington, D.C.: International Food Policy Research Report, February 1976).

305

Table 6

PERCENTAGE CONTRIBUTION OF AREA AND YIELD TO CHANGES IN PRODUCTION OF SOME MAJOR CROPS, BY GEOGRAPHIC REGION, 1950–1970

(percent)

Commodity	World	Europe	U.S.S.R.	North America	U.S.	Oceania	Asia	Latin America	Africa
Corn									
1960/50	53.1	82.5	231.1	32.5	35.2	37.2	64.5	51.3	39.5
Area	34.0	13.0	66.0	(19.0)ᵃ	(20.0)	28.0	55.0	77.0	33.0
Yield	66.0	87.0	34.0	100.0	100.0	72.0	45.0	23.0	67.0
1970/60	29.7	64.8	(49.0)	28.1	26.6	39.4	266.6	54.2	88.6
Area	10.0	1.0	—	(53.0)	(60.0)	15.0	58.9	55.0	56.0
Yield	90.0	99.0	—	100.0	100.0	85.0	41.0	45.0	44.0
Soybeans									
1960/50	82.0	(11.5)	62.7	124.0	124.9	—	37.6	423.6	64.7
Area	63.0	—	63.0	78.0	78.0	—	100.0	100.0	0.0
Yield	37.0	—	37.0	22.0	22.0	—	(6.4)	0.0	100.0
1970/60	63.1	408.7	95.6	92.0	92.5	—	12.9	667.4	103.6
Area	73.0	58.0	63.0	76.0	76.0	—	69.6	81.0	100.0
Yield	27.0	42.0	37.0	24.0	24.0	—	30.4	19.0	0.0

Wheat									
1960/50	46.2	32.7	94.2	3.1	10.0	31.6	27.6	6.2	8.1
Area	40.0	9.0	53.0	—	—	56.0	80.2	81.0	100.0
Yield	60.0	91.0	47.0	100+	100+	44.0	19.8	19.0	0.0
1970/60	33.2	37.0	31.8	21.5	19.7	44.2	63.3	38.9	129.0
Area	19.0	(8.0)	1.0	(29.0)	(20.0)	100.0	38.5	20.0	31.0
Yield	81.0	100.0	99.0	100.0	100.0	(18.0)	61.5	80.0	69.0
Rice									
1960/50	48.5	20.2	11.9	28.4	28.4	83.3	38.5	69.3	18.5
Area	35.0	60.0	—	(51.0)	(51.0)	40.0	38.4	89.0	23.0
Yield	65.0	40.0	100+	100.0	100.0	60.0	61.6	11.0	77.0
1970/60	20.0	8.4	476.5	65.4	65.5	76.6	28.5	42.4	134.7
Area	55.0	100.0	52.0	38.0	38.0	40.0	43.2	100.0	37.0
Yield	45.0	(63.0)	48.0	62.0	62.0	60.0	56.8	(12.0)	63.0

a Parentheses denote decrease.

Source: University of California Food Task Force Report, *A Hungry World: The Challenge to Agriculture* (Berkeley: University of California, July 1974), p. 64.

parison of the relative contribution of yield and cropland area to increased production of corn shows that yield increases accounted for 45 percent of gains in Latin America and area accounted for the remaining 55 percent. All increases in the United States between 1950 and 1970 have been attributed to yield increases since area in corn production declined.

In many areas, cultivated lands offer greater potential than new land development for increased short-run food production. A University of California Food Task Force study concluded that the physical and biological potentials of most of the world's land and crops far exceed present performance.[17] Corn, for example, yielded eighty-four bushels per acre in the United States in 1970 and showed a 49 percent yield increase during the 1960–1970 decade (Table 7). World corn yields were forty-one bushels per acre and increased 25 percent during the same period. Latin America, with soils and climate not greatly different from those in the United States and with about the same land area in corn, produced twenty-two bushels per acre in 1970 and showed a yield increase of only 18 percent for the 1960–1970 decade. Similar comparisons can be made for other crops. Although improved technology is not easily transferred, scientific methodology is transferable. If that methodology is systematically applied (and resources are available), yield advances equivalent to those in the United States are possible elsewhere.

Since land areas are finite, concern is often expressed that the world is running out of arable cropland. According to the best statistics available in 1965, about 7.9 billion acres of land were classified as potentially arable.[18] In 1970, only about 46 percent of those 7.9 billion acres was in use for cropland. More than one-half the potentially arable land (over 4 billion acres) is located in the tropics. The largest areas of potentially arable but uncultivated soils are in Africa and Latin America.[19]

Thus, while it seems that the world is not running out of arable land, there are formidable regional distributional problems in mobilizing the necessary technology and financial resources to cope with the problems of expanding the land base. United Nations Food and Agriculture Organization Director-General A. H. Boerma, sum-

---

[17] University of California Food Task Force, *A Hungry World*, Chapter 3.

[18] President's Science Advisory Council, *World Food Problems*, pp. 405-569.

[19] For a discussion of development problems of different soils, see Harold O. Carter, J. G. Youde, and M. L. Peterson, "Future Land Requirements to Produce Food for an Expanding World Population," in *Perspectives on Prime Lands*, U.S. Department of Agriculture Committee on Land Use (Washington, D.C.: U.S. Government Printing Office, 1975).

Table 7

YIELDS FOR CORN, WHEAT, RICE AND SOYBEANS BY
GEOGRAPHIC REGION, 1950–1970

Crop	Year	World	Europe	U.S.S.R.	U.S.	Oceania	Asia	Latin America	Africa
Corn (BU/acre)	1950	25.18	19.76	20.88	39.69	28.69	13.39	17.21	12.43
	1960	32.83	32.51	27.41	56.90	35.70	16.74	18.65	15.30
	1970	41.12	53.23	42.56	84.63	46.86	29.49	22.00	19.29
Wheat (BU/acre)	1950	14.73	22.17	12.50	16.66	16.81	11.45	15.62	8.93
	1960	18.15	28.12	16.07	24.84	18.89	12.05	17.55	8.93
	1970	22.76	39.72	21.27	30.94	17.70	15.92	20.53	14.58
Rice (CWT/acre)	1950	14.55	38.38	12.94	22.85	27.76	14.55	15.17	9.28
	1960	18.57	41.15	18.74	34.10	40.25	17.76	15.89	10.53
	1970	20.00	39.27	32.13	45.52	51.95	20.44	15.26	16.51
Soybeans (BU/acre)	1950	14.88	8.48	6.40	21.27	—	11.90	17.85	7.29
	1960	17.85	10.26	7.44	24.25	—	11.60	17.85	7.44
	1970	19.64	15.47	9.22	27.37	13.39	12.05	19.19	7.29

Source: University of California Food Task Force Report, *A Hungry World: The Challenge to Agriculture* (Berkeley: University of California, July 1974).

marizing results from a country-by-country survey of land-use potentials, has concluded that 138 million acres of new land would be a reasonable target for developing countries to 1985, at a cost of $26 billion.[20] Renovation and improvement of an additional 113.7 million acres would cost another $21 billion, and irrigation schemes for 56.8 million acres would cost $38 billion more. Overall, the investment requirements would exceed $8 billion per year over the next ten years, not including investment requirements for fertilizers, pesticides, and other inputs.

World fertilizer situation.[21] Dramatic changes have occurred in the world fertilizer situation in the last four or five years. After several years of industry overcapacity and declining real fertilizer prices, international fertilizer prices began to climb in late 1971. Export prices of some fertilizer materials had increased two and three times by late 1973 and then climbed still further, peaking in mid-1974. The impact was particularly severe for the developing countries which produce only about 60 percent of the fertilizer they use. Farmers in the United States and elsewhere responded to the higher fertilizer prices by reducing consumption while fertilizer production continued to expand—with the result that prices in 1975 declined one-half to one-third from their 1974 record high.

The longer-range world outlook is for sizable increases in fertilizer output in the late 1970s, especially in nitrogen and phosphate. Moreover, current projections show that a number of countries that are now large importers (People's Republic of China, Brazil, and India) may approach or achieve self-sufficiency in nitrogen and phosphate. Indonesia, Mexico, and Venezuela, and some Mideast countries may become fertilizer exporters. Thus, the outlook is for ample fertilizer supplies and moderate nitrogen and phosphate prices.

Climate and crop production.[22] Two kinds of climate changes may influence future world food production: (1) a possible long-term trend toward temperature change, either natural or caused by mankind's emissions of atmospheric pollutants, and (2) short-term climatic variations.

Historical data indicate the possibility of an eventual long-term cooling trend. Some researchers also argue that more carbon dioxide

[20] A. H. Boerma, "The World Could Be Fed," *Journal of Soil and Water Conservation*, vol. 30, no. 1 (January-February 1975), pp. 4-11.

[21] Richard B. Reidinger, *World Fertilizer Review and Prospects to 1980-81*, Foreign Agricultural Economic Report, no. 115, U.S. Department of Agriculture, Economic Research Service (Washington, D.C.: U.S. Government Printing Office, 1976).

[22] University of California Food Task Force, *A Hungry World*, pp. 79-81.

and particulates in the atmosphere may be lowering temperatures and decreasing rainfall. In addition, there is general agreement that atmospheric pollutants reduce the amount of solar radiation reaching the earth's surface. Trends in these factors, if they exist and prove significant, could affect crop production drastically. A drop in average temperatures of three degrees Centigrade would shift the United States wheat crop southward, squeezing out competing crops, and would markedly cut wheat production in Canada and the Soviet Union.

Studies in short-term climatic variability indicate relatively limited changes in weather in the last forty years. Recent evidence, however, suggests to some a possible return to more extreme variation. In addition, worldwide food production is becoming more sensitive to climatic change for various reasons: more intensive land use, which exposes more production to local extremes; expansion of cultivation to lands of marginal productivity; genetic tailoring of crops, especially grains, to narrow climatic ranges; and large areas of single-crop culture, increasing vulnerability to massive failures.

In a recent report of the Congress Budget Office on the subject of food and agricultural policy, the conclusion about weather trends was: "The evidence to answer these questions is incomplete and likely to remain so for many years. What is more certain, however, is that precipitation will continue to be highly variable from year to year and region to region." [23]

U.S. Agriculture: Changing Structure and Capacity

This section reviews some key characteristics of the U.S. agricultural economy and the changing nature of its structure and productive capacity—a continuing concern because of its dominant position in world agriculture.

Resource Use and Productivity. During the past four decades there have been dramatic changes in output, productivity, and the proportions in which farm inputs are used (Table 8). The U.S. land base (cropland used for crops) has remained practically unchanged, declining slightly from the 1950s to the early 1970s and increasing in the last few years with acres brought back in production. Labor has continually moved out of agriculture at a rapid rate, the outflow

[23] U.S. Congress, Congress Budget Office, *U.S. Agricultural Policy in the World Economy* (Washington, D.C.: U.S. Government Printing Office, 1976).

Table 8
ANNUAL AVERAGE RATES OF CHANGE IN OUTPUT, INPUT, AND PRODUCTIVITY IN U.S. AGRICULTURE, 1929–1975
(in percent)

	1929–40	1940–50	1950–60	1960–70	1970–75
Selected inputs					
Labor	−1.0	−2.6	−3.3	−3.8	−1.3
Cropland	−.2	.3	−.6	−.6	2.1[a]
Mechanical power and machinery	0.7	10.2	1.5	0.2	1.0
Agricultural chemicals	2.7	13.1	6.7	12.0	4.7
Total input	−0.2	0.5	−0.4	0.3	0.2
Total output	1.0	2.3	2.3	1.1	2.6
Productivity	1.3	1.8	2.7	0.9	2.0

[a] Only 1970-74.

Source: Calculated from data contained in: *Economic Report of the President* (Washington, D.C.: U.S. Government Printing Office, January 1976); and U.S. Department of Agriculture, Economic Research Service, *1975 Changes in Farm Production and Efficiency—A Summary Report*, Bulletin no. 548 (September 1975).

peaking in the 1960s with an annual decrease of 3.8 percent. The rapid move of labor out of agriculture has slowed in the 1970s to an average annual rate of 1.3 percent. Currently, farm population represents 4.2 percent of the total U.S. population, a marked decrease from the early 1930s when one out of four persons lived on farms.[24]

The use of capital in the form of mechanical power on farms increased rapidly in the 1940s and only gradually thereafter. Use of agricultural chemicals (fertilizers and pesticides) has shown marked increase over the last thirty-five years. Thus, large infusions of capital items produced in the nonfarm sector have increased the productivity of labor and land in agriculture and have effectively served as substitutes for these two resources. Steady decline in the number of farms and the farm population has accompanied these changes in factor proportions. The number of farms is now about one-half what it was in 1940.

Productivity (by whatever measure) has climbed in each of the last four decades.[25] However, total productivity gains (per unit of

[24] *Economic Report of the President*, p. 270.
[25] Willard W. Cochrane, "Food, Agriculture, and Rural Welfare: Domestic Policies in an Uncertain World," *American Journal of Agricultural Economics*, vol. 56, no. 5 (December 1974), p. 990.

total input) in the 1960s took place at only one-third the rate experienced in the 1950s. This dampening of productivity growth trends in the latter half of the 1960s caused some speculation that United States farm efficiency advances would become halting and irregular during the coming decade.[26] Output per unit of input shot upward in 1971 and has been relatively level thereafter. Yet for the 1971–1975 period the average annual increase has been 2 percent, second only to the high productivity growth gains of the 1950s (2.7 percent).

Supply of Prime Land. The diminishing supply of prime agricultural land in the United States has become a concern to many. Moreover, the extent of the agricultural reserve capacity attributed to land withheld from production by government programs in the 1960s is in question; the amount was generally assumed to be about 60 million acres or about one-sixth the nation's cropland. But this land has been referred to as an illusory land reserve or as "phantom acres" because all land did not return to production after the federal acreage set-aside program was relaxed in 1973. According to U.S. Department of Agriculture crop production data, in 1973 only 24 million additional acres came back into production.[27] In 1974 farmers reported intentions to plant 17 million acres more, but for various reasons including bad weather they expanded only by 10 million. Another 4 million acres came into production in 1975. Thus, three years after controls were removed, crop acreage rose by only 38 million acres, suggesting less excess capacity than had been generally believed.[28]

However, additional reserve capacity is available from land not previously cropped but still potentially arable. A U.S. Department of Agriculture report has provided estimates of the amount of U.S. land

[26] National Academy of Sciences, *Agricultural Production Efficiency* (Washington, D.C.: National Academy of Sciences, 1975), p. 38. The report notes several measurement difficulties, among them difficulties arising from the failure of current measures to reflect changes in the quality of inputs. The case of labor is one example: no account has been taken of the substantial increases in the level of education of the farm labor force that has occurred over the past decade, or the changes in age and sex distribution. In conclusion, the National Academy of Sciences' report states: "The available measures of inputs and outputs for U.S. agriculture are presently inadequate to provide evidence on the changes in the efficiency of agricultural production" (p. 38).

[27] U.S. Department of Agriculture, Statistical Reporting Service, *Crop Production, 1975 Annual Summary* (Washington, D.C.: U.S. Government Printing Office, January 1976), p. B-2.

[28] L. Tweeten and J. Plaxico, "U.S. Policies for Food and Agriculture in an Unstable World," *American Journal of Agricultural Economics*, vol. 56, no. 2 (May 1974), p. 365, conclude, after taking various factors into account, that reserve capacity probably averaged no more than 4 to 5 percent in the decade preceding 1972.

suitable for crop cultivation. Of the total amount of the top three soil classes (I, II, III), 365 million acres (58 percent) were being used as cropland and 265 million acres (42 percent) were in other uses (mainly forest and grass) but considered suitable for regular cultivation. The 265 million acres of potential cropland were stratified according to feasibility for reclamation. The U.S. Department of Agriculture estimated that about 152 million acres have high or medium potential for conversion to cropland.[29] Even if this reclaimed land would have yields considerably below those of existing land, this still provides a significant amount of reserve production capacity.

Recent Farm Income Gains. One result of the expanded export demand for U.S. products in the 1972–1975 period has been a narrowing of the income gap between the farm and nonfarm population. At the depth of the depression per capita personal income for the farm population was less than one-third per capita income for the nonfarm population (Table 9). During the 1950s it was still in the 50 to 60 percent range and just before the surge in export demand in 1972 slightly more than 70 percent—with part of the gain the result of government payments. However, record prices of 1973 lifted personal disposal farm income above nonfarm levels, with payments being a relatively minor portion of the total. Currently, the level is around 90 percent of nonfarm income levels.

How has this recent income gain been distributed among farmers of different sizes? Not surprisingly, increased prices have mostly benefitted the large and efficient farmers, just as government payments benefitted them in past years. Table 10 shows realized net income per farm by sales classes for the period 1960–1974. Farms with sales above $40,000 (which now account for about 17 percent of all farms) have realized the greatest net income change. Farms with sales in the $20,000 to $40,000 range (making up a fifth of the total farms) have realized only a slight gain. The farms with sales below $20,000 (accounting for about 60 percent of the total of all farms) experienced relatively small income gains considering the magnitude of the farm price changes in the past few years. Thus, as might be generally expected, sharply higher farm prices and higher farm incomes have not reduced the intrasectoral income gaps that have

---

[29] U.S. Department of Agriculture, Economic Research Service, *Farmland: Will There Be Enough?* no. 584 (Washington, D.C.: U.S. Government Printing Office, 1975). This acreage was further divided into short-run and long-run. Short-run acreage (about 63 percent of the total) could be converted to crop uses virtually from one year to the next and long-run acreage would require construction of works of improvement taking a longer time.

Table 9
DISPOSABLE PERSONAL INCOME PER CAPITA, FARM AND
NONFARM POPULATION, SELECTED YEARS, 1934–1974

| Year | Per Capita Income from All Sources | | | Farm as Percentage of Nonfarm (percent) |
	Farm population (dollars)	Nonfarm population (dollars)	Total population (dollars)	
1934	163	500	414	32.6
1940	245	671	573	36.5
1950	840	1,458	1,364	57.6
1960	1,073	2,019	1,937	53.1
1970	2,460	3,422	3,376	71.9
1971	2,643	3,651	3,605	72.4
1972	3,133	3,877	3,843	80.8
1973	4,572	4,282	4,295	106.8
1974	4,258	4,640	4,624	91.8

Source: U.S. Department of Agriculture, Economic Research Service, *Farm Income Statistics*, Statistical Bulletin no. 547 (July 1975).

characterized agriculture for many years. The arguments are still persuasive that farm commodity programs should deal with the adjustment problems of commercial farms; different programs should be used to improve the well-being of low-income people in rural areas or wherever they reside.

Policy Issues and Directions

This section indentifies feasible directions in policy available to the United States as the world's foremost agricultural producer, to deal with what are now perceived by most as the major food policy problems—instability of agricultural markets and insecurity of food supplies. These are not new problems; [30] but they were of less consequence before the "food crisis" of 1972–1973—when "burdensome" grain surpluses tended to moderate price changes—than they are now. Before we turn to policy directions, it will be useful to summarize

[30] Much has been written about instability in American agriculture. See, for example, a classic analysis by T. W. Schultz, *Agriculture in an Unstable Economy* (New York: McGraw-Hill, 1945). There is also substantial literature on the welfare aspects of stability.

Table 10

REALIZED NET INCOME PER FARM BY SALES CLASSES, 1960–1974

| | Farms With Sales: | | | | | | | | All Farms | |
| | $100,000 & over | | $40,000–99,000 | | $20,000–39,999 | | Under $20,000 | | | |
Year	Number (thousands)	Income (dollars)	Number (thousands)	Income (dollars)	Number (thousands)	Income (dollars)	Number (thousands)	Income (dollars)	Number (thousands)	Income (dollars)
1960	23	30,826	90	13,812	227	8,034	3,623	2,024	3,963	2,806
1961	26	31,653	97	14,578	239	8,431	3,463	2,126	3,825	3,036
1962	29	30,171	106	14,302	254	8,256	3,303	2,101	3,692	3,095
1963	31	29,322	113	13,983	267	8,026	3,161	2,052	3,572	3,112
1964	32	21,313	114	12,500	268	8,413	3,043	2,166	3,457	3,261
1965	36	32,750	125	15,064	280	8,543	2,915	2,180	3,356	3,519
1966	43	44,186	143	18,043	304	10,091	2,767	2,324	3,257	4,292
1967	43	29,327	142	14,992	299	8,753	2,678	2,077	3,162	3,659
1968	45	30,867	149	15,478	306	9,235	2,571	2,132	3,071	3,909
1969	51	40,371	168	16,220	330	10,400	2,450	2,256	2,999	4,639
1970	55	38,600	178	16,664	343	10,120	2,378	2,196	2,954	4,665
1971	58	33,242	188	15,164	356	9,334	2,307	2,035	2,909	4,399
1972	70	51,801	222	18,351	403	10,912	2,175	2,396	2,870	6,032
1973	106	93,264	328	22,864	550	12,678	1,860	2,749	2,844	10,363
1974	115	83,234	355	20,192	588	11,234	1,772	2,461	2,830	9,789

Source: U.S. Department of Agriculture, Economic Research Service, *Farm Income Statistics*, Statistical Bulletin no. 547 (July 1975), p. 39.

the previous sections on U.S. and world food trends and speculate on likely directions of change in the next ten years.

Some Perceptions on the Direction of Major Economic Variables. In previous sections on world and U.S. food trends and constraints, we noted that the evidence is mixed and that there is a fair amount of uncertainty in the minds of agricultural analysts and observers—both in their perceptions of the problem and in their recommendations as to what should be done. Some tentative generalizations for the next decade are given here:

(1) There is general but not complete consensus that the world's population/food balance is not undergoing a fundamental transformation toward chronic food shortages. Admittedly, in several regions, population gains will largely offset food production increases and intensify food supply problems for many more years as they have intensified them in the past. Meanwhile, market surpluses—that is, actual supplies in excess of effective demand (at politically acceptable prices)—will recur in the major producing countries of the world and particularly in North America.

(2) Rapidly expanding world fertilizer plant capacity has significantly lessened the fertilizer price and supply problems that peaked about two years ago.

(3) The agricultural productive capacity of the United States is basically strong and there is potential for expansion in the resource base and for continued productivity growth. One possible problem is that capacity may be developed at a rate faster than the ability of markets to absorb the increased output at acceptable producer prices. The situation for many other developed countries is similar.

(4) The real price of grain will remain roughly constant for a few years (depending on the form of the commodity program and reserve-stocks policy adopted) and then likely begin to decline again. This assumes a near constant real world price for oil and no sustained changes in weather patterns. Also, investment in agricultural research and development is assumed to accelerate. Accordingly, food price rises will be more moderate than in the last three years with most of the rise in prices coming largely from increases in processing and marketing costs.

The Institutional Environment for Policy. Government intervention in agriculture, both in the United States and abroad, has been substantial for many years. Thus, consideration of future policy direction requires a brief mention of the way we got where we are now.

U.S. policy evolution. In broad terms, farm and food policy was concerned first with efficiency of the farm, shifted in the 1930s to a concern for farm prices and incomes, and in the past twenty years has shown increasing concern for income distribution of domestic and foreign food aid programs, although that has not been the major focus.[31]

Beginning with the 1933 Agricultural Adjustment Act, policy instruments for intervention in agriculture included high price supports, marketing quotas, tariffs and quotas, subsidies, and acreage diversion. A transition in U.S. farm policy began in the 1960s. In an effort to reduce "burdensome" surpluses, price supports were lowered and farmers offered direct payments for acreage voluntarily withheld. Direct payments were continued (with payment limitations added) under the Agricultural Act of 1970 and general land diversion (set-aside) replaced crop-by-crop land withdrawal. Present legislation (the 1973 Agricultural and Consumer Protection Act) retains direct payments (and payment limitation) but the payments are tied to "target" price levels that can be raised as production costs increase. If market prices for feed grains, wheat, and cotton fall below the target levels, deficiency payments are made. Loan rates provide only a floor price.

Provisions remain for set-aside with payments, if needed. A program similar to that for feed grains, wheat, and cotton is now in effect for rice. Only peanuts, tobacco, and long-staple cotton are now covered by rigid control programs. Thus, there has been a gradual evolution away from rigid government intervention toward more market orientation. Compared to their previous levels, government payments are now minimal. Other general program provisions that currently are in effect include (1) price supports without production controls for dairy products at a specified minimal level of parity, (2) compensatory payments for wool production (without production provisions) to achieve a minimal specified national average unit return, (3) marketing orders and agreements for milk and selected fruit and vegetables, (4) food stamp program and other food distribution activities, (5) foreign aid with agricultural products available with concessions of credit, grants, and gifts, and (6) import and export embargo authority under specified trigger conditions and "national interest" authority.[32]

---

[31] R. G. F. Spitze, "Policy Issues and the Public Decision-Making Environment," and Leo V. Mayer, "Policy Issues and the Public Decision-Making Environment: Discussion." Both of these papers were prepared for the Policy Research Workshop on Public Agriculture and Food, Price and Income Policy Research, Washington, D.C., January 15-16, 1976.

[32] Spitze, "Policy Issues," p. 4.

The international policy environment. Johnson and Schnittker identify three main groups of nations with differing agricultural and food policies: [33]

(1) The largest group (by population) includes nations that depend upon their own farmers for most of their food requirements (within limits of climate). Their farmers are insulated from world markets with price guarantees, variable levies, import restrictions, and so on. Examples of nations in this group are those in the European Economic Community, the Soviet Union, People's Republic of China, and India. In total, nations following such highly protectionist policies account for well over half the world's population. Unfortunately, those countries that effectively insulate their markets from world prices exacerbate these problems for the remaining participants, particularly for a dominant residual supplier like the United States. The problem worsens when U.S. grain producers and exporters have limited trade information about markets dominated on the import side by a large government trader like the Soviet Union.

(2) A second group includes nations that import a large portion of their food needs and tailor price and income protection to their own farmers accordingly. Japan is the best example. The United Kingdom fell in this group before joining the European Economic Community in 1973. Only a small percentage of the world's population is now represented by this group.

(3) The third group includes the major exporting nations that compete with each other for world markets. They still retain protectionist policies for certain agricultural sectors. This group includes the United States, Canada, Australia, Argentina, New Zealand, and possibly Brazil as its main members.

Since it is generally conceded that domestic agricultural policies respond largely to domestic political forces and not to international interests, the obstacles to international cooperation and agreement on food and agricultural policy are formidable in the face of such diverse national policies. The World Food Conference and some of the follow-up structures and institutions may, in time, alter this situation and provide a reasonably cohesive international framework for individual countries to formulate their domestic and trade policies.[34]

---

[33] D. Gale Johnson and John A. Schnittker, *U.S. Agriculture in a World Context: Policies and Approaches for the Next Decade* (New York: Praeger Publishers, 1974).

[34] Nathan M. Koffsky, "What Has Happened since the World Food Conference," paper presented at the National Agricultural Outlook Conference, sponsored by U.S. Department of Agriculture, Washington, D.C., November 17-20, 1975.

Major Directions for Stabilization Policies. Acceptable political solutions for stabilizing markets are difficult to achieve in practice because the goals of price and commodity stability have different meanings to different groups within the U.S. economy and among our trading partners. Consumers everywhere are most concerned with the threat of rapidly rising food prices, yet they are more than willing to condone sharp food price drops—should they ever occur. Grain producers want price stability mainly on the down side to prevent disastrous dips in income in years of abundant supplies; conversely, they can accept rapid price increases. Livestock operators and processors would find themselves in concert with consumers for price "lids" for grain and concentrate, but not (of course) for the products they sell. To many importing countries, stability means reliable supplies— either as aid or commercial purchases. Nonetheless, while criteria for judging stability performance may not be uniform, there seems to be consensus that increased stability is a desirable goal.

The need for a flexible domestic policy. The 1973 Agricultural and Consumer Protection Act will expire at the end of 1977. One major advantage of a renewal of the legislation (with modifications) is that it would continue to provide the secretary of agriculture with considerable discretionary authority for coping with a variety of circumstances that could be encountered in changing agricultural markets. This is essential at least until world reserve stock can be accumulated to a reasonable level. Tweeten and Plaxico's reference to the 1973 act as a "policy for all seasons" underscores its flexibility: the secretary of agriculture "either can stabilize market prices through adjustments in stocks and set-aside requirements or can allow market prices to vary widely within a relatively uncontrolled farm economy." [35] The danger in excessive discretionary authority is the temptation to use it (or not to use it) in certain even-numbered years—especially those divisible by four. Yet the possible dangers loom even greater from being locked into a rigid program as the supply-demand situation changes rapidly.

Reserves. The 1973 act does not deal with the reserve stock question—an omission that needs correcting, especially in view of the fact that there appears little likelihood of moving toward freer world trade. Indeed, the act was designed to avoid the build-up of large government reserve stock by keeping loan rates for wheat, feed grains, and cotton almost at distress levels. If domestic reserves are desired, then an explicit policy for their accumulation is necessary. Our most

---

[35] Tweeten and Plaxico, "U.S. Policies for Food and Agriculture," p. 370.

recent experience with food reserves was actually an experience with large and chronic surpluses and many participants and observers retain unpleasant memories.

Studies of reserves, either domestic or international, point to two problems. First, there is a need for emergency stocks to meet disastrous declines in food production from adverse weather or disease, particularly in developing countries: the reserves needed for such contingencies probably would be a small proportion of annual world grain production. At the September 1975 preparatory meeting of the International Wheat Council, the United States proposed the establishment of a global reserve of 30 million tons of food grains (25 million tons of wheat and 5 million tons of rice): this reserve, it was claimed, would be sufficient to offset over 90 percent of world production shortfalls from trend.[36] If net accumulations were used to build such a reserve over a period of three or four years, international trade would not be adversely affected, although there might be some small temporary increases in international grain prices, depending on world supply conditions.

Second, a conscious reserve-stocks policy could be designed to mitigate wide variations in world grain market supplies and prices. Producers could be protected against inadequate markets and unduly low prices in years of high production or depressed demand. Such a policy could also protect consumers against rapid price increases during periods of depressed crop production or extraordinary demand. However, reserves may have detrimental effects as well. If they cause low prices that reduce farmer incentives, then output in the longer run may be reduced, especially in developing countries.

As with many policy instruments, it is easier to agree on the principles than on the program. For international reserves, the magnitude and incidence of the costs of maintaining world grain stocks are difficult to assess.[37] Ideally, the costs of acquiring and holding government stocks would be allocated among participating nations according to the benefits derived. However, among the potential beneficiaries are many developing countries with limited ability to carry their share of the costs. The developed nations would therefore carry a major share of the financial responsibility. European grain-importing countries would be expected to participate in the financing

[36] U.S. Congress, Congress Budget Office, *Agricultural Policy in the World Economy*, p. 65.
[37] Jimmye Hillman, D. Gale Johnson, and Roger Gray, *Food Reserve Policies for World Food Security: A Consultant Study on Alternative Approaches*, prepared for United Nations Food and Agriculture Organization, January 1975.

more than they have in the past when exporters have carried the burden of financing world grain stocks.

The guidelines or mechanics of operating the program—including the location of stocks (private or government) and procedures for releasing them from storage in short years are important but not unresolvable questions.[38]

---

[38] Numerous papers have been written on this subject. See Shlomo Reutlinger, "A Simulation Model for Evaluating Worldwide Buffer Stocks of Wheat," *American Journal of Agricultural Economics*, vol. 58, no. 1 (February 1976), pp. 1-12; Abraham Subotnik and James P. Houck, "Welfare Implications of Stabilizing Consumption and Production," *American Journal of Agricultural Economics*, vol. 58, no. 1 (February 1976), pp. 13-20; Willard W. Cochrane and Yigal Danin, *Reserve Stock Grain Models, The World and the United States, 1975-85*, Agricultural Experiment Station, Technical Bulletin no. 305 (Minneapolis: University of Minnesota, 1976); Jerry A. Sharples and Rudie W. Slaughter, Jr., "A Producer Price and Income Stabilization Program and Implications for Research," prepared for Policy Research Workshop on Public Agriculture and Food, Price and Income Policy Research, Washington, D.C., January 15-16, 1976; and Luther G. Tweeten, Dale Kalbfleisch, and Y. C. Lu, *An Economic Analysis of Carryover Policies for the United States Wheat Industry*, Oklahoma Agricultural Experiment Station Technical Bulletin, T-132 (Stillwater, Okla.: Oklahoma State University, 1971).

INTERNATIONAL RAW MATERIALS DEVELOPMENTS: OIL AND METALS

Richard Erb

Summary

This study provides separate examinations of recent international developments in the markets for crude oil and for metals and analyzes some of the policy implications of these developments. The major conclusions on international oil can be summarized as follows:

(1) The cartel capabilities of the Organization of Petroleum Exporting Countries (OPEC) have yet to be tested inasmuch as it has not been necessary for the members of OPEC to devise an explicit system for allocating production.

(2) As the world economy emerges from recession over the next two years, the demand for OPEC oil is likely to increase. Above 1975 levels of demand the prospects for a real price increase (or decline) will depend primarily on Saudi Arabia's actions since Saudi Arabia is able to adjust its own production levels to offset production increases or decreases by other OPEC members in order to achieve an oil price level that is in its long-run interests.

(3) The oil producers, including Saudi Arabia, are not as rich as is implied by their per capita oil revenue data. It is misleading to compare the oil revenues of the oil-producing countries, and, in particular, those as dependent on oil as Saudi Arabia, Libya, Kuwait, and the United Arab Emirates, with measures of income (GNP) for industrialized countries. Oil revenues represent a sale of depleting assets, and once these assets are depleted, income will drop unless alternative sources of income have been developed.

I would like to acknowledge the assistance of Stephen J. Maatsch and Lawrence R. Kahn in the preparation of this paper.

(4) *From an economic perspective, the underlying decision to produce oil is essentially an investment decision for a country like Saudi Arabia. That decision requires judgments about the expected return and risks of three investment alternatives: domestic development investments, foreign financial investments, and keeping oil in the ground. The higher the return and the lower the risks of investing in domestic development programs and foreign financial assets, the more it is in Saudi Arabia's long-run economic interest to increase production and lower oil prices.*

(5) *Given Saudi Arabia's economic trade-offs, both a more positive U.S. attitude toward Arab equity investments and continued involvement by the U.S. government and U.S. corporations in Saudi Arabia's domestic development program will be conducive to lower oil prices. Alternatively, should the U.S. Congress approve legislation restricting U.S. corporate activity in the Middle East and restricting Arab investments in the United States, the result is likely to be higher oil prices, inasmuch as Saudi Arabia would then have little economic justification for resisting the pressures of other OPEC members to raise the real price of oil.*

(6) *Saudi Arabia's price and production decisions are affected by a number of political considerations, the most significant of which is the Arab-Israeli conflict. If another Arab-Israeli war breaks out over the next few years, Saudi Arabia—along with the other Arab oil producers—possesses sufficient market power to pressure the industrialized world by imposing production cuts and an embargo. Settlement of the Arab-Israeli conflict would not only eliminate the major part of the risk of production cuts and embargo, but would also create economic and political conditions conducive to lower oil prices, since a settlement would reduce the risks attendant on the investing of large sums of Arab money in the United States and possibly accelerate Saudi domestic growth possibilities.*

(7) *While a settlement of the Arab-Israeli conflict and a positive U.S. response to Saudi economic requirements (specifically to their domestic development programs and foreign financial investments) would be conducive to lower real oil prices, a significant decline in the price of oil is not likely unless the world supply of alternative energy is increased and world demand for oil is reduced. Domestic price controls on U.S. crude oil and natural gas, however, not only encourage demand but discourage supply in the largest energy consumption market in the world.*

The major conclusions concerning international metals market developments are these:

(1) When metals prices for the last five years are adjusted to remove the effect of overall inflation, their behavior was not extraordinary in light of the slowdown in world economic activity during 1970–1971, the acceleration in world economic activity during 1972–1973, and the actual decline during 1974–1975. Increased price stability in the metals markets will be achieved only if a more stable rate of economic growth and lower rates of inflation are achieved.

(2) The primary structural changes in the metals industry have come from attempts by the governments of developing countries to increase their influence over their natural resources—these attempts including decisions involving prices, production, and investment. These governments are thus behaving like the governments of most of the major developed countries including the United States. Because of the complicated nature of the metals industry—with a relatively high degree of substitution possible among metals, long investment periods, multi-stage processing, and metal ore inputs that are not homogeneous—it will take the governments an extended period of time to learn how to price their raw materials and to manage their investments in new facilities. Foreign governments, the major metals companies, and the governments of the industrialized countries will be groping for many years for ways to bargain over prices and investments.

(3) As the world economy moves out of its current recession and demand for metals increases, moderate price increases are to be expected for most metals. The prospects for additional price increases as a result of unilateral or cartel-type actions on the part of metals-producing countries, however, are not very high—unless the world economy enters a two- or three-year period of above average economic growth. Under those circumstances, bauxite would be the most likely candidate for short-run monopoly price increases.

(4) From a long-run perspective, there exists a concern that recent structural changes in the metals industry will reduce investments in new mines, thus increasing the prospects for higher prices in five to ten years as a result of inadequate capacity. That concern is one motive behind the recent U.S. proposal for an International Resource Bank. Before such a bank is established, however, there must be a more certain justification than we now have for its existence—which means there must be a more detailed evaluation of current investment plans in relation to future capacity requirements for different metals.

(5) The United States has been under considerable pressure from the developing countries to enter into comprehensive commodity agreements with the objective of stabilizing commodity prices, includ-

ing metals prices. However, a related objective of the developing countries—to bring about increased transfer of resources—would make it extremely difficult for governments to operate a buffer-stock system since producer countries would attempt to use an increase in buffer stocks to raise prices over time. Thus, even if the U.S. government agreed to enter into commodity buffer-stock arrangements, the political conflicts between the developed and developing countries over commodity prices would not be likely to be reduced, and might even be exacerbated.

Introduction

During the past five years, in a world of rapid and unexpected economic changes, raw material markets have seemed to bear more than their share of stresses and strains. At times, commodities suffered from the backwash of overall economic forces—for example, most commodity prices rode the waves of inflation and expansion to new highs during 1973 and early 1974, and then collapsed with the worldwide recession in late 1974 and 1975. In other instances, commodity developments seemed to play an independent role and exacerbate overall political and economic instability—this was the case with the Arab oil embargoes, the U.S. embargo on soybean exports, the OPEC oil price increases, and the droughts that cut food production in several parts of the world.

In such an environment, it is not surprising that a bewildering array of commodity problems should bubble to the surface. Some were new, some old, some recycled. There were modern reincarnations of Malthus—armed with complex computer programs—who warned that the world would face severe raw material shortages within the next fifty years. Modern-day versions of Paul Revere warned that more OPECs were coming and that the industrialized world faced the threat of commodity wars from less developed countries. From the group of less developed countries there came proclamations of a New World Economic Order and demands for an array of consumer-producer commodity programs. In December 1975, multilateral discussions between representatives of developed and developing countries were begun under the Conference on International Economic Cooperation. As a consequence, the U.S. government has been facing strong foreign pressures to agree to a series of commodity buffer stock arrangements. Congressional committees have held hearings on raw materials shortages, a National Commission on

Supplies and Shortages has been established to develop legislation dealing with raw materials problems, and over fifty raw-materials-related bills were introduced in Congress in 1974 and 1975. Not since the early 1950s had so much attention been focused on the subject of raw materials. There were those who believed that greater government control was necessary over raw materials, and those who opposed government intervention, with the latter borrowing a phrase from the radical 1960s and asserting that governments were part of the problem, not part of the solution.

The list of issues is almost as long as the commodity lists themselves and the ranking of issues by order of importance almost as volatile as commodity prices. In 1973, in a world of "shortages," industrialized countries raised the issue of access to raw materials; by 1975, producer nations were seeking commodity stockpiles in order to reduce the price effects of the glut of raw materials. About the only thing remaining constant was the volume of rhetoric.

This study examines recent international developments in the markets for crude oil and metals and analyzes some of the policy implications of those developments. Although similarities exist between oil and metals, the differences between the two are more significant. The behavior of metals prices over the past five years has been determined primarily by world inflation and world economic instability, while the behavior of oil prices has been determined primarily by the supply actions initiated by the major oil-producing countries. Oil and metals also differ in their relative economic importance. Even before the 1973 oil price increases, total U.S. consumption of crude oil products (measured in dollars) was more than twice the U.S. consumption of pig iron and six times the U.S. consumption of aluminum, the two metals most widely used in the United States. Developments in the oil sector thus have had a more significant feedback effect on U.S. economic growth and inflation than developments in any of the metals markets. Perhaps the most important differences, however, reside in the relative market power and the underlying economic interests of the major oil producers. In contrast to most metals-producing countries, the dominant oil-producing countries have limited alternative expenditure and investment opportunities. As a result, these nations have less need for substantial current revenues than the metals-producing nations, and thus less need to produce. As a consequence, the oil price increases of 1973 were sustained without significant challenges to OPEC's ability to behave as a cartel. Because of these differences, metals and oil are treated separately in this study, with Part I devoted to oil and Part II to metals.

Part I—International Crude Oil Developments

During the past three decades, international petroleum prices and production have undergone dramatic shifts. Immediately following World War II, the price of crude oil declined until the late 1940s, rose until the mid-1950s, and then declined until the early 1970s. As measured by the price of Saudi Arabia light crude oil (which has become the oil standard for OPEC price quotations), the price of oil reached a level of almost $2.00 per barrel in the mid-1950s and then began a steady decline which ended at $1.30 per barrel in early 1970. During 1970 the major oil-producing countries began to gain control over the price, and, by early 1973, the price level of the Saudi light crude oil was back up to $2.00 per barrel. As a result of the late 1973 increases, the price of the Saudi crude was $9.50 at the beginning of 1974. As a result of price increases in December 1974 and again in September 1975, the price for the Saudi Arabia light crude was $11.51 during the first half of 1976.[1]

Adjusted for inflation (according to the U.N. export index for manufactured goods), the 1970 price of crude oil was about one-half the mid-1950s price level. Following the price increases of 1970–1973, the inflation-adjusted price level at the beginning of 1974 was almost three times the mid-1950s price. Although there were oil price increases between the end of 1973 and the end of 1975, the rate of inflation as measured by the U.N. export index for manufactured goods was such that the inflation-adjusted oil price remained about constant. Since the oil price increases of 1973 contributed to overall inflation in 1974, that outcome was partly, although inadvertently, self-induced. As discussed shortly, that outcome also moved the price of oil in a direction preferred by Saudi Arabia and not by some of the other members who preferred a higher real price.

At the beginning of 1950, production of crude oil outside of China and the Soviet bloc countries amounted to 8.8 million barrels a day. Growing at a compound annual rate of 7.5 percent, production reached 43.7 million barrels a day by 1972.[2] During 1950, the countries that eventually became members of OPEC accounted for only

---

[1] Because of the complex methods for pricing oil, it is extremely difficult to find a consistent historical series. For the purposes of this study, Saudi Arabia realized-price data are used as reported in International Bank for Reconstruction and Development, International Development Association, *Commodity Trade and Price Trends*, 1975 ed. (Washington, D.C.: World Bank, 1975), p. 84.

[2] U.S. Congress, House of Representatives, Committee on Banking and Currency, *Oil Imports and Energy Security: An Analysis of the Current Situation and Future Prospects*, 93rd Congress, 2nd session, September 1974, p. 40.

Table 1
OPEC-MEMBER PRODUCTION LEVELS

	Millions of Barrels a Day		1975 as Percent of 1973
	1973	1975	
Saudi Arabia	7.6	7.1	93
Kuwait	3.0	2.1	69
Libya	2.2	1.5	69
Venezuela	3.4	2.3	70
Iran	5.9	5.4	91
Nigeria	2.1	1.8	87
Algeria	1.1	1.0	100
United Arab Emirates	1.5	1.7	131
Iraq	2.0	2.3	115
Indonesia	1.3	1.3	98
Other	.8	.7	90
Total OPEC	30.9	27.2	88

Source: *Oil and Gas Journal*, February 25, 1974; February 16, 1976, p. 29.

20 percent of total production. In September 1973, just before the major 1973 price increases, production by all the OPEC members reached a peak at around 32 million barrels a day,[3] or over 70 percent of world production. The oil embargo and production cutbacks implemented by the Arab producers in October 1973 brought about an immediate decline in production, creating shortages in Europe and the United States. The embargo and production cutbacks were removed in 1974, but by that time the worldwide recession, and to some extent the higher price level per se, had begun to have an impact on the demand for OPEC oil. During 1974, the demand for (and thus production of) OPEC oil dropped to an average 29 million barrels a day. By early 1975, at the bottom of the world recession, the demand for OPEC oil was down to around 25 million barrels a day. Because of increased demand later in 1975, OPEC produced at an average rate of 27 million barrels a day for the year.[4]

Because of the reduction in the demand for OPEC oil since 1973, and because some OPEC members have increased their levels of production since 1973, it has been necessary for other OPEC members to cut production below 1973 levels. Table 1 compares 1975 with 1973

[3] *Petroleum Intelligence Weekly*, vol. 14, no. 43 (October 27, 1975), p. 7.
[4] *Oil and Gas Journal*, vol. 74, no. 7 (February 16, 1976), p. 29.

production levels for each OPEC member. Except for Iraq and the United Arab Emirates (which increased production) and Algeria and Indonesia (which maintained 1973 production levels), production cuts from 1973 levels were significant (more so for Libya, Kuwait, and Venezuela, and slightly less so for Iran, Nigeria, and Saudi Arabia). The distribution of demand among the members of OPEC was not part of an explicit agreement allocating production, but occurred because of differences in the prices charged.

As is suggested by the production increases for Iraq and the United Arab Emirates and the different degrees to which other members reduced production, each member has the means to increase or decrease its market share vis-à-vis the other members. Although it is the practice for the members of OPEC to agree on the price level for oil of a single quality (Saudi Arabia light crude oil), the individual members independently vary prices around that reference price depending on the quality of their oil and on transportation factors. Producers close to consumer markets or selling oil of higher quality are supposed to add a premium to the basic price while producers selling lower quality oils are allowed to give a discount. The discounts and premiums (or price differentials, as they are often called) that individual members are allowed to charge have not been determined by OPEC as a whole. Price differentials were the main issue addressed at the December 1975 OPEC petroleum ministers' meeting which was aborted when the ministers were kidnapped.[5] In effect, the kidnappers saved the ministers from having to admit that they could not resolve the extremely difficult problem of setting price differentials.

Not only are price differentials technically difficult to set, but the fixing of price differentials touches on the fundamental test of any cartel—how to allocate production among the members when demand is less than capacity. OPEC has not met that test, and, as a consequence, internal conflicts have arisen as individual members have used their freedom to set price differentials so as to increase their market share. During 1975 and 1976, criticism aimed at the fairness of the differentials set by the Iraqi government was especially strong,[6] and several Arabian Gulf producers, including Iran, adjusted their price differentials downward in early 1976 in the face of declining demand for their oil.[7] Those price changes, as well as a pickup in consumer demand, eased the pressures slightly, but in early May 1976, Iran's

---

[5] *Middle East Economic Survey*, vol. 19, no. 10 (December 26, 1975), pp. 1-3.

[6] Ibid., vol. 19, no. 27 (April 26, 1976), pp. 1-2.

[7] Ibid., vol. 19, no. 18 (February 20, 1976), pp. 1-3.

chief oil negotiator, Jamshid Amuzegar, commented that the issue of price differentials "could have grave consequences for the unity" of OPEC.[8]

Whether the issue of price differentials and the underlying "gut issue" of production allocation will have grave consequences for OPEC unity depends primarily on the future demand for OPEC oil. If the demand for OPEC oil rises above the 1975 level of 27 million barrels a day, the issue of price differentials will increasingly become a non-issue for OPEC's members. Above that level, the prospects for a significant price decline (or increase) will depend primarily on the way in which Saudi Arabia perceives its own interests, since Saudi Arabia has the capability of adjusting its own production levels to offset production increases or decreases on the part of other OPEC members in order to prevent the price level from moving very far in any direction. Even if OPEC broke apart, there would not necessarily be a significant price decline. If the demand for OPEC oil falls below 1975 levels, it would become increasingly necessary for the members to develop a system of allocating production or face a decline in the real price of oil. While at levels of OPEC demand below 1975, Saudi Arabia alone could reduce production to maintain the price (assuming the other members did not increase production), Saudi Arabia would be pursuing a high-risk economic strategy if it did so. The remainder of this part of the study will analyze the near-term prospect for the demand for OPEC oil, with this analysis followed by an examination of Saudi Arabia's interests and likely actions.

The Demand for OPEC Oil. Among the energy experts scattered around the world, there exists a wide range of views about the future demand for OPEC oil. Some forecasts have put the 1980 demand for OPEC oil as low as 23 million barrels a day, while others have put the demand as high as 36 million barrels a day.[9] The range between the two reflects the wide array of unknowns underlying the forecasts. Both demand and supply responses to the 1973 price increases remain uncertain. At least five to ten years will be necessary (1) for the consumer to make full adjustment to the higher real price, (2) for exploration and development to produce new sources of oil, and (3) for alternative sources of fuel and energy to be developed and utilized.

---

[8] *New York Times*, May 3, 1976, p. 1.

[9] U.S. Congress, Joint Committee on Atomic Energy, *Towards Project Independence: Energy in the Coming Decade*, 94th Congress, 1st session, December 1975, p. 59.

Recognizing the enormous uncertainties that underlie any oil demand forecast, we may more reasonably forecast the 1980 demand for OPEC oil at somewhere in the range of 27 to 32 million barrels a day, and more than likely at the upper end of that range. New sources of oil are not now being discovered or developed at the rate anticipated just two years ago, and the cost of new sources is turning out to be higher than expected, as in the case of Alaskan and North Sea oil.[10] Major alternative sources of energy—nuclear power, coal, shale oil, and solar power—are either priced above the current price of oil (as in the case of shale oil),[11] or pose serious environmental problems (as in the case of nuclear power), or are not yet technologically feasible on a mass scale (as in the case of solar power).

Another reason for believing that the 1980 demand for OPEC oil will rise from 1975 levels may be found in the actions taken by the U.S. Congress during the past year. The two most significant actions were the decision by Congress not to remove the price ceilings that apply to gas sold outside a state in which it is produced (interstate gas) and the decision to roll back the price of domestic oil, with the rollback to be followed by limited price increases. Because interstate gas was not deregulated, it is currently selling at a price 50 to 100 percent below that of unregulated intrastate gas.[12] As a result, not only is consumption of gas encouraged, but development of new gas supplies is discouraged.

The 1975 Energy Policy and Conservation Act rolled back the average price of oil sold in the United States by approximately $1.00 to $7.66 per barrel of oil, and removed the $2.00 per barrel import tariff. The bill permits an upward adjustment in the composite price to take inflation into account and also permits (if the President should find it necessary) an additional price increase of no more than 3 percent per year as a production incentive.[13] The sum of the two adjustments, however, must not exceed 10 percent in any one year without congressional approval. The oil price controls are supposed to be removed by 1979. However, even if the controlled U.S. price of oil were to rise at the maximum allowable annual rate of 10 percent, at the end of the price control period the U.S. domestic price level would be about 15 percent below the price level of imported oil if the price

---

[10] Ibid., pp. 22-27.

[11] Federal Energy Administration, *National Energy Outlook, February 1976* (Washington, D.C.: U.S. Government Printing Office, 1976), pp. 38-39, 154-56; *New York Times*, February 10, 1976, p. 53.

[12] Federal Energy Administration, *National Energy Outlook*, p. 9.

[13] *Wall Street Journal*, December 18, 1975, p. 5.

of imported oil were to remain constant.[14] If, as is more likely, the members of OPEC continue to increase their price to keep up with inflation, the gap will be wider. If Congress were faced with the prospect of a substantial jump in oil prices at that time, it is not at all likely that the price controls would be removed. In the meantime, and probably beyond, the controls will result in higher levels of consumption and lower levels of production than if U.S. prices were as high as world prices.

Saudi Arabia's Role and Interests. No other oil-producing country has the degree of oil market power possessed by Saudi Arabia—a power derived from three fundamental sources. The first, and most significant, is Saudi Arabia's excess production capacity. Saudi Arabia currently has sufficient excess production capacity almost to double its 1975 level of production from 7 million barrels a day to 12 million barrels a day.[15] By 1980, Saudi Arabia is likely to have a total capacity of around 16 to 17 million barrels a day.[16] That excess capacity is a source of intimidation not only to the other members of OPEC, but, even more important, to any business or government planning to make large investments in high-cost energy sources. By raising production to capacity, Saudi Arabia could conceivably drive the price back to early 1970 levels. Because of Saudi Arabia's ability to lower the price for oil, other OPEC members must weigh the effect of their actions on Saudi Arabia. If they try to take too great a market share, they face the risk of a large Saudi production increase as a form of retribution and a means of bringing them back in line. Potential producers of high-cost oil-energy alternatives outside of OPEC are faced with the risk of having the demand pulled out from under them as the result of a large decline in the price of oil induced by Saudi production increases. Without a guaranteed price, a private corporation would be taking a significant risk if it invested large amounts of capital in high-cost (equivalent to $8.00 per barrel of oil or above) energy alternatives.

Second, Saudi Arabia's market power derives from the large gap between its import requirements and its revenues. In 1975, Saudi revenues amounted to around $27 billion while the country's import requirements were only about $6 billion.[17] Thus Saudi Arabia could cut production by 5 million barrels a day and still have a financial

---

[14] *Monthly Energy Review*, March 1976, p. 72.

[15] *Petroleum Intelligence Weekly*, vol. 15, no. 14 (April 5, 1976), p. 11.

[16] Ibid., vol. 14, no. 48 (December 1, 1975), p. 8.

[17] U.S. Treasury, Office of Middle East Affairs, January 1976 report.

surplus. A third related source of oil market power lies in Saudi Arabia's vast financial holdings, which at the end of 1975 were sufficient to finance over five years of imports.

One way of illustrating Saudi Arabia's significance is to examine what would happen if some of the other major members of OPEC increased production from 1975 levels. The most likely candidates to make such an increase are Iraq, Iran and Nigeria. As production increases during 1974 and 1975 suggest, Iraq's government appears intent upon increasing its level of production from levels relatively low in comparison to those of the other major producers in the Middle East, Iran and Saudi Arabia. Given current capacity levels,[18] however, Iraq could increase production only .5 million barrels a day. Given current plans to expand capacity,[19] Iraq could increase production from 1975 levels by only 1.5 million barrels a day by 1980. Over the next two years, Iran and Nigeria will face balance-of-payment pressures to expand production to capacity levels in order to finance internal development programs. Given existing capacity,[20] that would mean at most an additional 2 million barrels a day from both countries. Indonesia, another country with major domestic revenue requirements, might be able to increase production by less than .5 million barrels a day for short periods of time, but not for any extended period. Algeria is in a similar position. Venezuela, another country with significant domestic development requirements, recently announced a new five-year development plan—accompanying it by a statement that production would not be increased above 1975 levels.[21]

Among the other producers, Libya and Kuwait each have the ability to increase production levels by 1 million barrels a day.[22] Both countries, however, have a conscious government policy of maintaining production below capacity levels. Limited domestic development requirements and a desire to conserve oil for the future have been the primary motives underlying these policies. The United Arab Emirates have been increasing production, but further increases to capacity at most would amount to .5 million barrels a day.[23]

Thus, if the OPEC members most likely to increase production in fact produced at capacity levels within the next few years, they would produce around 4 million barrels a day above 1975 levels.

[18] *Petroleum Intelligence Weekly*, vol. 14, no. 43 (October 27, 1975), p. 7.
[19] Ibid., vol. 14, no. 4 (January 27, 1975), p. 1.
[20] Ibid., vol. 14, no. 43 (October 27, 1975), p. 7.
[21] *The Financial Times* (London), April 9, 1976, p. 4.
[22] *Petroleum Intelligence Weekly*, vol. 14, no. 43 (October 27, 1975), p. 7.
[23] Ibid.

Even if the demand for OPEC oil remained around the 1975 level of 27 million barrels a day, the oil price implications of those production increases would depend on Saudi Arabia's decision whether to cut production from 7 million barrels a day to 3 million barrels a day, or somewhere in between. If the demand for OPEC oil were to rise to 31 million barrels a day, the price effect of production increases by other members would depend on Saudi Arabia's decision whether to maintain production at 7 million barrels a day. If the demand for OPEC oil were to exceed 31 million barrels a day, the price implications would depend on Saudi Arabia's decision whether to increase production from 1975 levels.

What considerations underlie Saudi Arabia's price and production choices? They are economic, social, religious, and political in nature. From an economic perspective, oil is currently Saudi Arabia's dominant form of economic wealth. As put by Sheikh Ahmed Zaki Yamani, Saudi Arabia's minister of petroleum:

> Oil is a non-renewable resource, and to the peoples of the OPEC countries it constitutes the greatest if not the entire source of livelihood. The revenues earned from its trade should meet not only the current requirements of the exporting nations, but also their future needs when this resource is entirely depleted.[24]

Three concepts flow together in Sheikh Yamani's statement, concepts that are fundamental to the economic decision making of an owner of oil no matter whether that owner is an individual, corporation, or government. First, oil is a form of wealth which provides an annual income, but only when it is pumped out of the ground and sold: that income provides a means for current consumption, as well as for investment in other forms of wealth that will generate income in the future. Second, the stock of oil possessed by an individual country will eventually be exhausted: in contrast to most goods and services, it is not reproducible. Third, a corollary of the first, unless some part of the income earned each year is invested in other forms of national wealth, future income (and thus future consumption) will drop when the stock of oil is exhausted. The major alternative forms of investment for Saudi Arabia are domestic development programs (including education, infrastructure, and physical plant and equipment) and financial investments outside Saudi Arabia.

Saudi Arabia, along with the other oil producers, is usually thought of as being extremely wealthy. That view of Saudi wealth is

---

[24] *Middle East Economic Survey*, vol. 17, no. 48 (September 20, 1974), p. Supp. 3.

reinforced when (as is often the case) oil revenues are translated into per capita GNP. Saudi per capita income is around $5,000, slightly below the per capita income of France, West Germany, Canada, and the United States.[25] It is inappropriate and misleading, moreover, to consider the oil revenue of the oil producers in the same light as GNP in the United States or any other industrialized country. Oil is a depletable resource, and when oil runs out, so will the revenues. The GNP accounting system does not take depletion into account—a weakness that is not so misleading for an industrialized country as it is for a resource-dependent country. Oil production depletes an asset, and unless some portion of the income from the sale of that asset is reinvested in assets capable of generating income in the future, Saudi Arabia or any other less developed oil producer will end up with a limited economic base with which to sustain its population. (At 1975 rates of production, Saudi Arabia has about seventy-five years of production given current known reserves.[26] At a 2 percent annual growth rate, Saudi Arabia's population would amount to around 20 million in seventy-five years.) That is a danger confronting all the oil producers, and especially those with populations initially larger than Saudi Arabia's. (Although it is not often recognized as such, that danger also confronts oil states such as Texas, Alaska, and Louisiana. Unless each of these states builds up a nonoil industrial base, the state governments will not only lose their tax base, but their citizens also will suffer a loss of income and employment when oil runs out. Reversing the migration of the last twenty years, there would be a large out-migration along with requests for federal support.)

Although no one really knows how the Saudis make their decisions, or what weights they give to different factors when making them, or what uncertainties they have about the future, it is possible to speculate on the direction of impact and the relative importance of different factors and to put reasonable boundaries on the choices likely to be made. Many of the social, religious, and political factors often completely override those that are economic. Although the primary focus of this study is economic, noneconomic factors will be discussed when they have an important bearing on oil price and production decisions.

As has already been mentioned, oil revenues can be used to support current consumption. Consumption, in this study, is defined

[25] World Bank Atlas: Population, Per Capita Product and Growth Rates (Washington, D.C.: World Bank, 1974), p. 7.
[26] Oil and Gas Journal, vol. 73, no. 52 (December 29, 1975), p. 86.

broadly to include private and social consumption goods, military expenditures, and foreign aid. Saudi Arabia currently has a relatively small population, estimated to be in the range of 5 to 6 million people, which is also a very poor population. Through a variety of public programs and private income transfers, the Saudi government is seeking to raise consumption standards. It is not very likely, however, to require more than 6 to 7 billion (1975) dollars in oil income to finance annual consumption imports by 1980. That would mean a threefold increase from 1975 per capita consumption levels and would put Saudi Arabia's consumption levels more or less on a par with consumption levels found in Kuwait. The other major current expenditure categories are defense and foreign aid. Although it is difficult to derive concrete estimates for either category, the import requirements for defense along with foreign aid could require between $5 and $6 billion a year of oil revenues by 1980. (The Saudis have been criticized for not giving more foreign aid than they do.[27] In light of the difference between GNP and oil revenues discussed previously, the ratio of aid to GNP for Saudi Arabia understates the relative economic contribution of Saudi Arabia vis-à-vis the contribution of the industrialized countries.) Thus, total import requirements to support current expenditure plans could range between $10 and $12 billion in 1975 dollars. In order to finance those current expenditures, Saudi Arabia would need to export less than 3 million barrels a day at 1975 price levels.

Since the Saudis are concerned about meeting the needs of future generations, decisions to produce above 3 million barrels a day should be viewed as investment decisions. In other words, in order for the Saudis to maximize income over time, their choice to produce more than required for current expenditures should depend on the difference between the expected rate of return to be earned on alternative forms of national wealth and the expected rate of return to be earned by holding oil in the ground and selling it in the future. Since the future cannot be projected with any certainty, their production decisions should also depend on their judgment of the risks underlying the alternative forms of investment and of the risk of holding the oil in the ground.

Saudi Arabia's relatively small and uneducated population also places a limit on the number of development projects that can earn a positive rate of return if undertaken within the near term. In fact, if too many projects are attempted, the rate of return will be negative

---

[27] Maurice J. Williams, "The Aid Programs of the OPEC Countries," *Foreign Affairs*, vol. 54, no. 2 (January 1976), pp. 308-24.

as a result of waste and induced inflation. Already in Saudi Arabia, as in other oil-producing countries, there exist major bottlenecks and manpower shortages impeding the flow of goods and the implementation of development projects.

Domestic development expenditures also are not without risks. In addition to the normal economic risks inherent in any venture, the Saudi government also faces the risk that too rapid an attempt to develop the economy will increase the danger of internal social and political instability. Imported labor and foreign corporations will enable the Saudis to carry out projects they would not otherwise be able to carry out, but too large an influx of foreigners will weaken cultural and religious traditions (something that has occurred already in Kuwait and the United Arab Emirates). Within Saudi Arabia there already exist conservative voices, from religious and political quarters, protesting the rapid changes that have already taken place. Thus, even if large amounts of domestic investment could be justified on economic grounds, there are compelling noneconomic reasons for slowing the rate of domestic growth.

Taking all of these factors into account, we can reasonably forecast that domestic development expenditures will result in annual import requirements no higher than $4 to $5 billion by 1980. (Our forecast is based on the assumption that foreign corporations will play a significant role in Saudi Arabia's development.) In order to finance these imports out of current revenues, Saudi Arabia would need to export an additional 1 million barrels a day at 1975 prices. Thus, a total of 4 million barrels a day would be more than enough to finance current expenditures and economically stable domestic projects. If anything, the forecast errs on the side of being too high, but it is consistent with the judgments of major Saudi officials.[28]

The other major investment alternative for Saudi Arabia is investment in foreign financial assets. Because of the size and depth of U.S. equity markets, the United States is the only market in the world that offers the Saudis the ability to invest large amounts of money without causing major price changes by their own buying and selling. European markets are relatively small, and large direct equity investments in European companies are not welcomed. Historically, after adjustment for inflation, long-run real rates of return on equity investments in the United States have been in the neighborhood of 7 percent. Thus, if the Saudis could invest all of their oil revenues in

---

[28] Hisham Nazer, Saudi minister of planning, in *Middle East Economic Survey*, vol. 19, nos. 14 and 15 (January 23 and 30, 1976), pp. 1-2. Ahmed Zaki Yamani, in *Middle East Economic Survey*, vol. 17, no. 27 (April 26, 1974), p. Supp. 20.

the U.S. market, they could expect to earn around 7 percent a year over the long run.

The alternatives to holding equity assets are holding short-term money instruments and holding long-term debt instruments. Once again the United States offers the largest money and debt markets with a wide array of government and corporate debt instruments to choose from, but in contrast to equities there are also significant opportunities for such investments in other countries, often in the form of direct government loans, as well as in Eurodollars and Euro-bonds. If we use long-run historical rates of return found in U.S. markets as a guide, we find that after adjusting for inflation the real rate of return that can be expected on long-term debt instruments is around 2 percent, while the real rates of return on short-term assets are even lower. Thus, unless the Saudis can invest a high proportion of their financial assets in equity investments, they will be limited to a rate of return of 1 to 2 percent.[29]

Moreover, there are the risks associated with investing in foreign financial assets. During the past two years, the oil-producing countries have found in Europe and the United States relatively suspicious (if not absolutely hostile) reactions towards the possibilities of their making large equity investments. Although the executive branch of the U.S. government has encouraged equity investments,[30] the Saudis remain uncertain what the U.S. Congress might do in the future. Given the economic and political risks associated with foreign financial assets, the question confronting the Saudis is whether the return on those investments is worth pumping oil out of the ground.

The answer to that question depends to a large extent on Saudi expectations about the future price level of oil. If the Saudis expect the real price of oil to decline from current levels, then (putting risk considerations aside for the moment) foreign financial assets earning 1 to 2 percent would provide a better return than holding oil in the ground. If the Saudis expect the real price to rise modestly, then foreign investments would be less attractive.

There are risks associated with holding oil, however—risks that would justify a build-up of foreign financial holdings from current levels even if the Saudis expected the real price of oil to rise significantly over time. While holdings of foreign financial assets are subject to economic and political risks, there is also a risk associated with

---

[29] The basis on which the historical real rates of return for debt and equity securities were estimated is more fully described in a forthcoming study of OPEC by the author.

[30] *Treasury Papers*, August 1975, p. 24.

being too dependent on one resource for future income. Expectations about future oil prices may turn out to be wrong and prices may drop sharply. Foreign financial assets provide (up to a point) a means of diversifying the overall economy in case of an unexpected price decline for oil. Of course, beyond some level (perhaps $150 billion), the political and economic risks of additional financial accumulations would begin to outweigh the benefits of additional diversification.

What are Saudi expectations about the future price of oil? On this the evidence is mixed. Ever since the price increases of 1973, Saudi Arabian officials have let it be known that they thought prices were too high.[31] Press stories covering the September 1975 OPEC meeting were filled with reports of heated debates between Saudi Arabia, which opposed a price increase, and the other OPEC members, which sought one.[32] The compromise was a 10 percent increase in the market price, which, in real terms, meant a slight decrease. On the basis of Saudi statements made in early 1976 that the price should not be increased at the May 1976 OPEC meeting, the Saudis appear to be willing to allow the real price to erode further.

During the past two years, however, Saudi Arabia appears to have been primarily concerned with the impact of the price increase on the world economy, and thus on the political stability of Western non-Communist governments. Sheikh Ahmed Zaki Yamani has stated publicly that it was a mistake to increase the price as rapidly as it was increased over a short period of time, but that from the perspective of long-run supply and demand conditions and the high costs of alternative sources of energy, the price was not inappropriate.[33]

How are the Saudis likely to behave over the next two or three years? Although their public statements imply that they are confident that the current price is appropriate from a long-run supply and demand perspective, the leadership of Saudi Arabia is too intelligent and sophisticated to ignore the uncertainties involved in making any forecast about future oil demand. Historically, oil price forecasts by industry specialists have generally been remarkably wrong. Thus, if the demand for OPEC oil remains around 27 million barrels a day as the world economy emerges out of its recession, the Saudis (and the other OPEC members) are likely to become more uncertain about

---

[31] Ahmed Zaki Yamani in *Middle East Economic Survey*, vol. 17, no. 48 (September 20, 1974), p. Supp. 4 and *Middle East Economic Survey*, vol. 18, no. 23 (March 28, 1975), p. 2.

[32] *Wall Street Journal*, September 25, 1975, p. 2, *Wall Street Journal*, September 26, 1975), p. 3, and *Wall Street Journal*, September 29, 1975, pp. 3 and 6.

[33] Ahmed Zaki Yamani in *Middle East Economic Survey*, vol. 19, no. 8 (December 12, 1975), pp. Supp. 6-8.

their judgment. If the demand for OPEC oil does not increase as the world economy returns to full growth, it will mean that the 1973 price increases have had a substantial short-run impact. Since the long-run adjustments to the price increase have yet to be completed, the prospects for further declines in demand would be relatively high. At a demand level below 27 million barrels a day, OPEC would have to behave more like a cartel than it has up to the present and allocate production among the members. If that happens, the 1975–1976 disputes over price differentials would seem like minor squabbles. In order to reduce the risk of a sharp future price decline it is likely that Saudi Arabia would become more assertive than in the past and bring about a near-term price reduction—if the demand remains around 27 million barrels a day. To do otherwise would be a high-risk strategy.

If the demand for OPEC oil rises to 30 million barrels a day over the next two years, Saudi Arabia will be faced with different pressures. Under such circumstances the other members will be in a stronger position to seek real price increases, especially if they maintain production below capacity levels. Saudi Arabia could prevent such increases with increases in production, but that would mean even greater accumulations of foreign financial assets. It would also increase the prospects of a future price decline if a higher real price intensified U.S. efforts to subsidize and protect energy investments with import barriers. This brings us back to Saudi Arabia's risk-return trade-offs. Although it may be presumptuous for us to guess what the Saudis would do if the demand were to rise to 30 million barrels a day over the next three years, we can reasonably conclude they are not likely to follow a high-risk strategy and allow the price to rise more than the rate of inflation. There are other considerations, however, that would affect that judgment—among them considerations related to U.S. policies.

U.S. Policy Implications. Saudi Arabia's economic trade-offs among domestic development, foreign investments, and holding oil in the ground are in fact significantly influenced by U.S. policies. A less hostile investment environment in the United States, especially a less hostile environment for equity investments, would improve the Saudi trade-off between keeping oil in the ground (with an attendant higher oil price) and larger foreign investments (with a lower oil price). If a reduction in oil prices is desired by the U.S. government, more efforts should be made, with the explicit approval of the Congress, to ensure that foreign government investments are welcome in the United States and to establish explicit ground rules that would apply to all foreign government investments. In addition, communication and cooperation between the Saudi central bank and the U.S. Federal Reserve Board and the U.S. Treasury should be expanded and strengthened. Saudi Arabia should be invited to become an active member of multilateral financial forums including the Bank for International Settlements and possibly even the Organization for Economic Cooperation and Development.

In addition to improving the overall political climate in which Saudi Arabia will be making its decisions, continued U.S. government assistance through the Saudi-U.S. joint commission on economic cooperation [34] as well as extensive participation on the part of the U.S. corporations in Saudi Arabia's development program would improve the Saudi economic trade-off between keeping oil in the ground and domestic development expenditures. Of course, the Saudis are also seeking assistance from European governments and corporations, but without U.S. corporate involvement, many of the development projects being considered will be dropped.

Although it is predominantly a political issue, the implications of the Arab-Israeli conflict on oil cannot be ignored, especially since the U.S. government plays a critical role in that conflict. The conflict not only creates the possibility of another embargo, but also influences Saudi economic trade-offs among oil production, domestic development, and foreign investments. The Saudis recognize that if war broke out, their financial assets held in the United States might be frozen or seized, especially if they imposed an oil embargo. The Arab-Israeli conflict thus raises the risk of holding foreign financial assets relative to the risk of holding oil in the ground. The Arab boycott of corporations having extensive relations with Israel is another factor that may indirectly affect Saudi economic decisions to produce oil. The boycott issue generates strong emotions among the supporters of Israel as well as among the Arabs who see the boycott as a legitimate economic weapon in a political war against Israel. If the Arab boycott issue degenerates into an open conflict—with the U.S. Congress restricting U.S. corporate involvement in the Middle East—or if Saudi Arabia were to expand the boycott, the Saudis would not be able to develop as rapidly as they could under a continuation of present circumstances. Since there would then be less need for Saudi Arabia to generate current revenues to finance current development expendi-

---

[34] The U.S.-Saudi Arabian Joint Commission on Economic Cooperation was established in June 1974 to help promote Saudi economic and social development. See *Treasury Papers*, April 1976, p. 11.

tures, there would be less incentive to increase oil production. While resolution of the Arab-Israeli conflict would not be likely to result in a significant decline in the price of oil, it would provide a greater incentive for the Saudis to seek higher levels of income (and thus production), because it would lower the risks inherent in foreign investment and improve Saudi Arabia's domestic development opportunities.

The Arab-Israeli conflict has implications for future oil developments in a different and perhaps more significant way. Should the conflict erupt into another war, the Arab oil producers are politically committed to imposing another embargo. There is currently greater excess capacity among the non-Arab members of OPEC, however, than there was in 1973 when almost all countries were producing at full capacity. Moreover, Arab countries such as Libya and Kuwait are producing at substantially lower levels than they were at the beginning of the 1973 embargo. The burden of an Arab boycott would fall primarily on Saudi Arabia, and, to a lesser extent, the United Arab Emirates. Since Iraq is producing at higher levels than in 1975, it would face greater Arab pressure to participate in the embargo than it apparently did in 1973, when Iraq in fact increased production during the months of the embargo.[35]

In 1973, Saudi Arabia reduced production by almost 30 percent. In 1976–1977, assuming that overall OPEC demand remained around 27 million barrels a day and that the non-Arab countries increased production to capacity levels during an embargo (the worst assumptions from the Arab perspective), Saudi Arabia would have to reduce production by over 50 percent to put pressure on the industrialized world. Such a reduction, however, would not be a difficult burden for the Saudis to bear. At higher levels of OPEC demand, Saudi Arabia's ability to put pressure on the West increases. Although Saudi Arabia is not likely to use the embargo weapon to "strangle" the industrialized world, it would be able to employ production cutbacks as a means for pressuring the industrialized world to resolve any Arab-Israeli war. A political settlement of the Arab-Israeli conflict, however, would eliminate the risk of future economic instability because of an embargo, and, furthermore, would have a beneficial impact on prices since it would improve the climate for Saudi investments in the United States as well as strengthen the prospects for economic development not only in Saudi Arabia, but also the entire Middle East.

---

[35] *The Petroleum Economist*, vol. 41, no. 12 (December 1974); see table, p. 480.

Part II—International Metals Market Developments

The analysis presented in this part of the study is divided into two major sections. In the first section below, metals price fluctuations during the past five years are examined in relation to overall world inflationary trends as well as instability in world economic activity. In the second section, three different but related changes in the structure of the metals industry are analyzed. The policy implications of these developments are examined within each section.

1970–1975: A Time of Inflation and Economic Instability. Beginning in the third quarter of 1972, and ending around the first quarter of 1974, metal price increases ranged from 28 percent for aluminum to 350 percent for zinc. By mid-1974, as illustrated by the movements of the price indexes for individual metals in Figure 1, most metal prices were declining as fast as they had risen. Underlying the price movements [36] were an accelerating rate of world inflation and the shifts in overall economic growth that began in the early 1970s.

One of the features that distinguished the early 1970s from the 1960s was the erratic state of the world economy. This economic instability is illustrated in the top half of Figure 2, where the industrial production index for the member countries of the Organization for Economic Cooperation and Development (OECD) is plotted (top solid line) for the period between 1955 and 1975. While the members of the OECD do not comprise the entire world economy, total GNP for the OECD accounts for about 70 percent of world GNP. Because of the linkages between the non-OECD and OECD countries, as well as the relatively small size of the non-OECD countries, economic activity in the rest of the world is pulled by business activity in the industrialized countries.

After the world recession of 1958, during which industrial production for the OECD countries declined by 3 percent, the OECD group of economies followed a path of rapid but relatively stable growth. The average annual growth rate between 1958 and 1969 was 6.2 percent. The lowest annual growth rate during that period, 2.8 percent, occurred in 1967. The highest growth rate, 7.8 percent, occurred in 1969. However, led by a decline of 3.7 percent in the U.S. economy during 1970, the rate of OECD growth for 1970 and

---

[36] Other recently published commodity price studies which the reader will find of value are Richard N. Cooper and Robert Z. Lawrence, "The 1972-1975 Commodity Boom," *Brookings Papers on Economic Activity*, 1975(3), pp. 671-723, and Edward M. Bernstein, Ltd., *The Rise and Fall of Basic Commodity Prices*, Report No. 76/2 (Washington, D.C.: Edward M. Bernstein, January 1976).

344

Figure 1

METAL PRICE MOVEMENTS

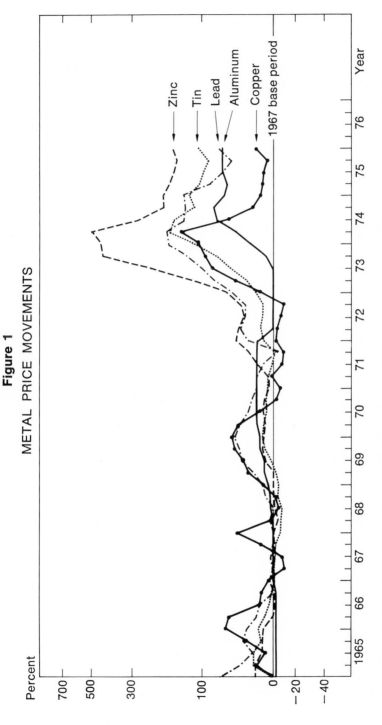

Sources: International Monetary Fund, *International Financial Statistics*, various issues; and the American Metals Market, *Metal Statistics*, various issues. Market price data through March 1976 were used to compute indexes on the basis of 1967 = 100.

345

1971 averaged only 1.5 percent. By 1972, however, the OECD growth rate was up to 6.9 percent, and the 1973 growth rate of 9.9 percent was the highest rate of growth for any one year during the postwar period. (In spite of the rapid growth in 1972 and 1973, however, the level of OECD industrial production did not exceed the overall level of industrial production that would have occurred if the 1960s growth trend had continued. The 1960–1970 trend level for OECD industrial production is represented by the dotted line in the top half of Figure 2.) During 1974, OECD industrial production declined by 6 percent, and during 1975 by another 5 percent. Thus, it may be seen that, within a period of five years, the world economy suffered significant fluctuations in economic growth.

A more dramatic economic development, and one that was a prelude to the economic instability of the early 1970s, began around 1965 with an acceleration in the rate of inflation. That development is illustrated on the lower portion of Figure 2, in which is plotted the U.N. price index for exported manufactured goods. This index is chosen as a measure of worldwide inflationary pressures in part because it can be viewed as a measure of the overall rate of increase in the costs of developing mines and metal refining facilities. The pattern of movement in this index, for example, coincides with that in U.S. price indices for heavy construction and mining equipment.

Between 1955 and 1965, the annual rate of increase in the U.N. export price index averaged about 1 percent. If that rate had continued beyond 1965, the U.N. export price index would have followed the path denoted by the dotted line in the bottom half of Figure 2. Between 1965 and 1970, however, the annual rate of increase in the export prices averaged 2.5 percent. In spite of the slowdown in world economic growth during 1970 and 1971, the rate of inflation accelerated, and rose 5.8 percent during 1970 and 6.4 percent during 1971. In other words, price increases were greater in years of slow economic growth than in the years of rapid economic growth. In 1973 and 1974, the rate of inflation rose to 16 percent and 19 percent respectively.

What were the underlying causes of the instability in economic activity and what were the causes of the sustained inflation? It will take a long time for economists to sort out all the forces at work, and opinions will differ depending on what economic theories are behind those opinions. However, there is considerable evidence that a primary cause was the acceleration in central bank monetary expansion that began in the early 1960s. Between 1955 and 1960 the average annual increase in the money stock of the six major developed countries

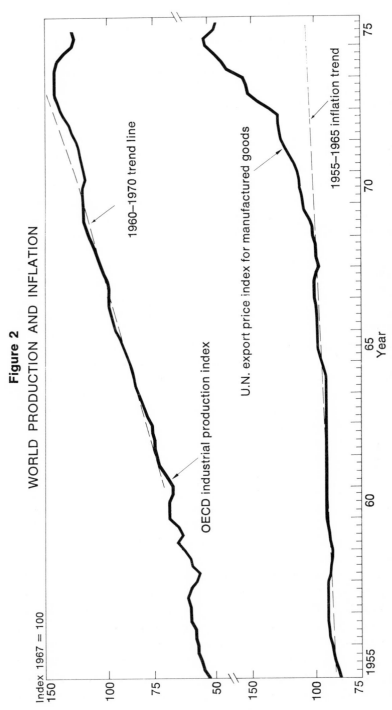

Figure 2

WORLD PRODUCTION AND INFLATION

Index 1967 = 100

1960–1970 trend line

OECD industrial production index

U.N. export price index for manufactured goods

1955–1965 inflation trend

Year

Sources: U.N. export price index calculated from United Nations, *Statistical Yearbook*. OECD industrial production from Organization for Economic Cooperation and Development, *Industrial Production*, 1955-1971. For both indexes, 1967 = 100.

347

was 3 percent.[37] Between 1960 and 1965, immediately before the rate of inflation began to accelerate, the average annual rate of growth in the money stock of the major developed countries more than doubled, reaching 7 percent. Between 1966 and 1970, the annual rate of increase was 8 percent, followed by rates of growth of 13 percent, 19 percent, and 16 percent for 1971, 1972, and 1973 respectively.[38]

In order to compare the price movements in metals to price movements for other goods, as well as to compare metals price movements for the 1970–1975 period to metals price movements in previous periods, we need to adjust the metals market prices for overall inflation. Failure to adjust for inflation can be misleading. For example, the December 1975 OECD *Economic Outlook* said it was "striking" that metals prices had not fallen further during 1975.[39] However, as illustrated below, when metals prices are adjusted for inflation, the decline in prices for most of the metals was very substantial. With 1967 as a base period, the market prices for each metal are divided by the U.N. export price index for manufactured goods. Figure 3 compares the market price index (solid line) with the price index adjusted for inflation (broken line) for each metal. The horizontal solid line represents the price level for each metal during the 1967 base period. The year 1967 is also the starting point for comparing the divergence between market prices and inflation-adjusted prices. For all the metals, the inflation-adjusted price and the market price did not diverge much until 1970, inasmuch as the rate of inflation did not begin to rise rapidly until that year. During 1970, 1971, and early 1972, the inflation-adjusted prices for all metals fell below 1967 base prices.

The decline in the inflation-adjusted prices during 1970–1971 is consistent with the slowdown in world economic activity that occurred during those years. As Figure 2 shows, in 1970 and 1971, the OECD industrial production index was substantially below what the index would have been if the trend established in the 1960s had continued forward. It seems reasonable to suppose that the mining and refining capacity that came on line worldwide during 1970 and 1971—capacity that had been planned during the middle and late 1960s—was geared

---

[37] Included are Italy, Japan, Canada, France, West Germany, and the United States. United Kingdom money supply data were not included. *Internaiional Financial Statistics* (Washington, D.C.: International Monetary Fund), various issues from 1955 to 1976.

[38] Ibid.

[39] Organization for Economic Cooperation and Development, *Economic Outlook* (Paris, France: OECD, 1975), p. 48.

toward the growth trend of the world economy during the 1960s and not toward the lower rates of growth in 1970 and 1971. Although worldwide measures of excess capacity for mining and refining are not available, available measures of overall U.S. excess capacity for durable goods confirm this view. For example, the Wharton index of excess capacity for durable goods increased from a low of 4.8 percent in 1969 to 18.3 percent in 1971.[40]

Inflation-adjusted prices began to rise for lead and zinc in late 1971, for tin and copper in late 1972, and for aluminum in mid-1973. Although world economic activity began to increase in early 1972, the increase did not immediately affect tin, copper, and aluminum prices because excess capacity and private-sector stocks had been built up during 1970 and 1971. Zinc prices may have begun their rise in 1971 because U.S. zinc refinery capacity was reduced by 17 percent during 1971, to a large extent because of pollution controls.

Increases in inflation-adjusted metals prices continued through 1973 and into early 1974. The rate of increase might have appeared dramatic, but that appearance came from the fact that prices were moving from a relatively low base as a result of the 1970–1971 economic slowdown. At their peak in 1974, copper, tin, and lead prices, after adjusting for inflation, were respectively only 40 percent, 55 percent and 75 percent above their 1967 base-period prices. Such movements are not especially abnormal in an industry characterized by delayed supply responses to demand shifts, and in late 1973 demand appears to have been pressing capacity. The Wharton index of average U.S. capacity utilization for durable goods production showed that by the third quarter of 1973 excess capacity was down to 4.0 percent.[41] Even as late in the boom as early 1974, there were those who seemed to expect demand to continue to grow from the already high levels. A Department of Commerce survey of plant and equipment showed that as late as March 1974, 51 percent of primary-metals manufacturers believed that more plant and equipment was necessary, 48 percent felt that existing capacity was adequate, and only 1 percent believed that capacity exceeded needs.[42]

As Figure 3 shows, the 1974 inflation-adjusted price level for copper and lead was not very different from the price peaks reached in 1969, the last time that overall U.S. capacity measures reported

[40] *Economic Report of the President, 1976* (Washington, D.C.: U.S. Government Printing Office, 1976), p. 211.
[41] Ibid.
[42] United States Department of Commerce, *Survey of Current Business*, vol. 55, no. 6 (1976), Table 4, p. 16.

Figure 3

MARKET PRICES VERSUS INFLATION-ADJUSTED PRICES

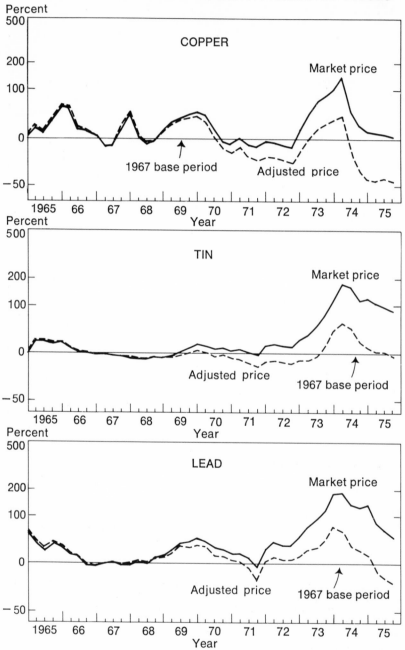

Figure 3
MARKET PRICES VERSUS INFLATION-ADJUSTED PRICES

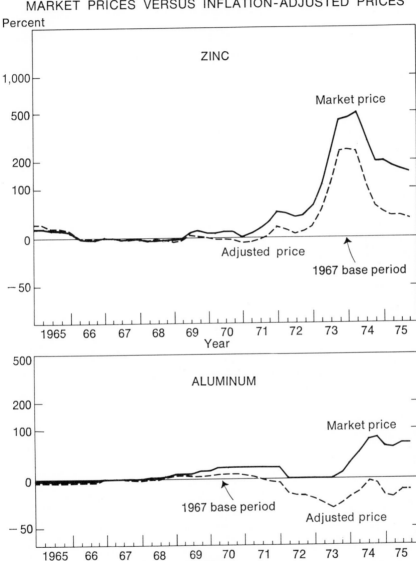

Source: Except for aluminum, all indexes are based on London Metal Exchange market prices as reported in the *International Financial Statistics*. The aluminum price index is the New York price for primary aluminum (99+ percent virgin ingots) according to the American Metals Market's *Metal Statistics* market price. For each chart, the time period includes the first quarter of 1965 through the fourth quarter of 1975.

such low levels of excess capacity. After adjusting for inflation, zinc prices increased to 244 percent above the 1967 reference base, but the U.S. zinc industry continued to be hit especially hard by pollution controls. In 1973, during a year of growing demand, U.S. zinc refining capacity declined an additional 31 percent. Although inflation-adjusted aluminum prices increased in late 1973 and early 1974, they never rose above their 1967 reference base.

Although the causes of the 1973–1974 real price increases for most of the major metals can be found primarily in the underlying state of the world economy, beginning with the slowdown of 1970–1971 and followed by the acceleration of 1972–1973, the inflation-adjusted prices were probably given some additional impetus by over-all inflationary expectations and the fears of shortages in 1973. In June 1973, the United States imposed an embargo on soybeans which hit one trading partner, Japan, especially hard. It is therefore not surprising that there were press trade stories about Japanese purchases of commodities, including metals, as a protection against future short-ages.[43] With official holdings of foreign currencies amounting to $18 billion at the start of 1973, the Japanese government was capable of supporting large transactions by domestic corporations.[44] Late 1973 was also, of course, the time of the Arab oil embargo. In addi-tion to creating actual fuel shortages and long gasoline lines in the United States, the embargo contributed to the fears of shortages in other areas, as well as reinforcing speculation about the possibility of trade wars between the developing world and the industrialized world, with the developing world using access to raw materials as a weapon.[45]

Instability in the foreign exchange markets may also have con-tributed to individual and governmental desires to hold metals as an alternative to holding currencies. The behavior of gold prices during the period confirms this view.[46] At a time when inflation rates were doubling and tripling, metals were also advertised as good hedges against inflation. The threefold OPEC oil price increase of late 1973 not only contributed to overall inflation fears, but also reinforced the perception that natural resources were a good hedge against inflation. The latter belief was given some credence by the debate over

---

[43] *New York Times*, October 14, 1974, p. 7.

[44] International Monetary Fund, *International Financial Statistics*, vol. 26, no. 12 (1973).

[45] C. Fred Bergsten, "The Threat Is Real," and Zuhay Mikdashi, "Collusion Could Work," *Foreign Policy*, no. 14 (Spring 1974), pp. 84-90 and 57-67.

[46] Cooper and Lawrence, "The 1972-1975 Commodity Boom."

the prospects of global scarcity, and in a world that appeared about to run out of raw materials, raw materials appeared to be good investments.[47]

By the second quarter of 1974, most metals market prices were beginning to decline. By early 1975, the market price for copper fell to its 1967 base level which (after adjustment for inflation) meant a decline of 44 percent below the base period price. The real price of lead was about 30 percent below the base period price while the price of tin was 10 percent below the 1967 base. The less volatile behavior of tin prices compared to those of the other metals may reflect the stockpile sales and purchases of the International Tin Council. The price of zinc, which increased more than any other metals price, declined the least and by 1975 was at a level about 36 percent above the 1967 reference base. The relatively greater zinc price increase may reflect the impact of pollution controls in the United States.

Although the overall behavior of metals prices can be explained largely by overall inflation and fluctuations in world demand, the explanations for the reasons the prices of individual metals differed in behavior from each other can only be suggestive. It would require a much more detailed study than this to develop more complete explanations. In addition, more time than has yet passed is needed to assess whether there have been any changes in relative prices among the major metals. The repercussions of the overall inflationary pressures on relative metals prices will take some time to sort out. Moreover, the large increases in energy prices have not worked their way through the economics of the metals industry because of the long supply and demand adjustment lags. And yet, higher energy prices should have a differential impact because each metal has different energy requirements.[48] Because of the relatively high importance of energy in aluminum costs, for example, it would not be surprising to find the real price of aluminum rising relative to other metals, resulting in a reduced rate of increase in aluminum consumption.

Given expected rates of economic growth, it will take the industrialized countries until some time in 1977 to achieve the level of business activity reached in 1973 and early 1974. Since 1973, there have been additions to capacity in both the mining and refining sectors of the metals industries, but at the same time a number of

[47] Donnella H. Meadows et al., The Limits to Growth (New York: Universe Books, 1972).
[48] National Commission on Materials Policy, Final Report of the National Commission on Materials Policy (Washington, D.C.: U.S. Government Printing Office, 1973), pp. 40-49.

mines and refineries have been closed down. Some of those that have been closed, however, can be reopened within relatively short periods of time. Thus, for the next two years, there should not be any fundamental capacity shortages in the production of any metals. However, that judgment must be qualified inasmuch as there are no adequate measures of productive capacity either for the current period or for future periods.

There also exist relatively large stocks for some metals. For example, 1975 year-end aluminum and bauxite stocks in the hands of U.S. producers and consumers were 28 percent higher than the previous peak stock levels of 1971. Refined copper stocks in the hands of U.S. producers were 46 percent above the previous peak levels of 1970, and almost five times greater than the average for the late 1960s. Stock holdings of the International Tin Council also are at their historical highs. The high stock levels will not prevent future price increases, but they will slow down rates of price increase. As world demand accelerates, copper is the most likely candidate for market price increases because its real price level is relatively low when compared to the 1967 base period price. In order to return to its 1967 level in real terms, the London Metals Exchange copper price would need to rise from the current (May 1976) level of almost 70 cents a pound to a range of 90 cents to $1.00 per pound. In order to return to its 1967 level in real terms, aluminum would need to rise from the current 41 cents to a range of 45 to 50 cents a pound. As of May 1976, the other major metals were at or above their 1967 base period prices in real terms, suggesting that price increases in those metals will not be as great as for the other metals.

For all metals, substantial price increases above their 1967 base period prices are not very likely as long as the governments of the industrialized world can manage their exit from the recent recession without producing excessively high rates of growth in 1977 and beyond. Using the 1960s average annual growth rate of 6.2 percent in the OECD industrial production index as a reference, we may conclude that, because of current excess capacity, a rate of growth above that level during 1976 is not likely to pose serious problems for the metals industry. If growth above that level continues during 1977 and beyond, however, capacity limits are likely to be approached and inflation-adjusted prices will rise substantially above their 1967 base period levels. A strong case can be made that during the period from 1977 to 1979, government policy makers would need to stabilize growth in a range of only 4 to 5 percent in order to avoid major increases in metals prices. The reason is that capacity additions in the second half of the 1970s will reflect investment decisions made during the early 1970s, a time of instability and lower overall investment levels. Growth rates in excess of 4 to 5 percent will press capacity (even though that rate is less than the average growth rate for the 1960s) and will thus cause metals price increases to exceed the rate of overall inflation. In addition, because of recent structural changes in the metals industry, higher growth rates (and concomitant capacity shortages) will increase the likelihood of price increases caused by producers attempting to take advantage of short-run monopoly positions. These structural changes and the risks they pose are analyzed in the next section.

Structural Changes in the Metals Industry. During the past ten years, the structure of the international metals industry has undergone an evolutionary change in three related ways. First and most significant, individual countries have sought greater control over production and investment decisions. Although a wide range of techniques has been employed, the basic intent of all the techniques is the same. Second, the metals-producing countries are attempting to develop mechanisms for coordinating their price and production policies. The success of OPEC provided a model for this movement, but the recession of 1974–1975 dashed the optimistic expectations of the OPEC imitators. In spite of that setback, however, efforts to build producer organizations have continued, albeit on a more realistic basis. Third, developing countries (including but not limited to those producing metals) are making broad efforts to improve their economic bargaining power by integrating their approach to different commodities (including other raw materials in addition to metals). The forces underlying these changes are political as well as economic and in the economic arena issues of resource transfer are of greater importance than the issues of economic efficiency. The developing countries seek a larger transfer of resources from the developed countries, and in the commodity arena this translates into a desire for higher prices, even if such prices result in a misallocation of resources.[49]

---

[49] Other recently published studies dealing with these and related developments and their policy implications include Roger D. Hansen, A "New International Economic Order"? An Outline for a Constructive U.S. Response, Development Paper No. 19 (Washington, D.C.: Overseas Development Council, 1975); James W. Howe, The U.S. and World Development Agenda for Action 1975 (New York: Praeger Publishers, 1975); Raymond F. Mikesell, Nonfuel Minerals: U.S. Investment Policies Abroad, The Washington Papers, vol. 3, no. 23 (Beverly Hills, Cal.: Sage, 1975); and Harald B. Malmgren, The Raw Material and Commodity Controversy (Washington, D.C.: International Economic Studies Institute, 1975).

There is little persuasive evidence that these developments have had much impact on metals prices in recent years. For what will happen in the future, there exists a range of views. At one extreme, there are those who believe that a fundamental change is taking place in the balance of economic power and that raw-materials-producing countries will be able to extract increasing amounts of real income for their resources.[50] Toward the other end of the range, there are those who do not believe that increased government controls and producer organizations will produce a major transfer of real income.[51] As discussed below, it also is conceivable that, because of the actions being taken by the developing countries to improve their bargaining power and their real income through more direct controls over prices, they are likely to end up being worse off in the future as a result of the countervailing economic forces set in motion by those actions. Economic power comes not from resources alone, but from the ability to develop those resources, or to develop substitutes. In that sense, the real economic power is in the hands of the industrialized countries and their major corporations, not in the hands of the developing countries.

National economic determinism. World War II and its aftermath saw a rapid decline in the control of Western European countries over their resource-rich colonies and protectorates in Africa and Asia. In our own hemisphere, individual countries sought to break or at least reduce the political power of the United States over the region. As Western domination declined, countries entered extended periods of political upheaval as factions sought political power and control. Even today, political stability is more of a wish than a reality in most developing countries, especially in some of the metals-producing countries.

For many countries, political independence did not result in immediate economic independence, and the most influential and visible vestiges of foreign domination were the foreign corporations. Although foreign corporations brought income and capital in, they also took natural resources out. Moreover, it was frequently claimed that the income and capital that remained behind went only into privileged enclaves. Rightly or wrongly, many governments began to believe

---

[50] Bergsten, "The Threat Is Real," and Mikdashi, "Collusion Could Work."

[51] Raymond F. Mikesell, "More Third World Cartels Ahead?" *Challenge,* November-December 1974, pp. 24-31, and Dr. James C. Burrows, Bension Varon, and Kenji Takenchi, Testimony before the Subcommittee on Economic Growth of the Joint Economic Committee, July 1974, pp. 71, 121-28, and Stephen D. Krasner, "Oil Is the Exception," *Foreign Policy,* no. 14 (Spring 1974), pp. 68-83.

that the contractual arrangements with foreign corporations were substantially biased in favor of the corporations. The role of foreign corporations became a controversial domestic political issue, and the political leaders faced (if they had not indeed encouraged) domestic pressures to "do something about it." Nor were such pressures limited to developing countries. In recent years, the role of foreign investments became a controversial political issue in such countries as Canada and Australia.

Many different techniques have been used to increase control over domestic resources, ranging from outright nationalization of foreign operations, to partial but controlling joint ownership arrangements, to restrictive investment guidelines for foreign corporations and aggressive use of taxes and royalties. Between 1960 and 1974, there were roughly 150 complete or partial nationalizations of foreign mining enterprises.[52] In the copper sector, for example, Chile nationalized or took majority control over six mining operations between 1967 and 1974. Peru, Zaire, and Zambia also purchased partial (and at times complete) control over foreign copper operations in their countries. In other countries, controls over foreign investments increased, with some governments (such as Australia's) requiring foreign corporations to provide for joint ownership with Australian nationals. Taxes on foreign corporations also were increased. In some countries, actions were taken not only at the national level but also by local governments. In Canada, for example, there is a conflict between the national government and the provincial governments over which should have the dominant control over natural resources.

In spite of the movement toward economic self-determination, and in spite of the rhetoric, the governments of most developing countries recognize (although grudgingly) that they need the active involvement of foreign corporations to bring in capital, skilled manpower, high technology, and management and marketing skills. They also need markets in which to sell their resources, and foreign corporations have access to and knowledge of a wide range of markets. In many of the developing countries, it will take decades to build up a cadre of trained personnel capable of managing all phases of investment, production, and marketing.

In recognition of what foreign corporations bring, some governments currently are relaxing controls and restrictions on foreign investments. Bolivia, for example, one of the first countries to nation-

---

[52] United Nations Report of the Economic and Social Council to the Secretary-General, *Permanent Sovereignty over Natural Resources* (New York: United Nations, September 1974).

alize foreign operations, has recently been seeking to encourage more foreign exploration and investment.[53] The new government of Australia recently announced a liberalization of the investment controls established by the previous government. Such steps, however, should be viewed as relaxing rather than as eliminating control.

The trend toward more active government control over prices and production means the dis-integration of what has traditionally been a vertically integrated industry. It is a fundamental belief of many of the governments of the metals-producing countries that there are profits they might earn from their raw materials that they believe have been captured in the later stages of processing by integrated companies from the industrialized world. Metals companies, however, argue that the prices they receive for their refined metals cover only production costs plus a profit return necessary to attract capital to a risky business.[54] It is further argued that the price of a refined metal (and thus the implicit value of the underlying metal ore) are determined partly by the prices of other refined metals offering substitution possibilities, and that there is a high degree of competition in the metals business.

Where does the truth lie? Free-market and Marxist ideologies aside, no one knows for sure what if any the magnitude of monopoly profits is for each metal. One thing that is relatively certain, however, is that since governments have only recently begun more active management of prices for their natural resources, there is an extensive learning process they must go through in order to understand the economic factors influencing the prices they can charge and thus the profits they can earn. For those countries hitherto involved only at the early stages of production, there will be problems in determining the optimum price inasmuch as they may not have sufficient knowledge of the demand and supply of refined metals. Because metal ores are not homogeneous commodities, prices will also vary according to a range of quality and location factors, thus posing further complications in the setting of prices. In addition, because metals markets are relatively volatile—a volatility stemming from changes in overall economic activity as well as from changes in the metals markets themselves—the prices charged for ore will vary over time. During the learning process, these governments will be dealing with corpora-

---

[53] *Copper Studies*, vol. 2, no. 49 (May 8, 1975).

[54] Rate-of-return data for several of the major aluminum companies over the last ten years more than support the latter view, at least for the aluminum industry, since their rates of return rank below most U.S. corporations. See *Report of the Federal Trade Commission on Rates of Return in Selected Manufacturing Industries, 1964-1973* (Washington, D.C.: U.S. Government Printing Office, 1975).

tions they do not trust in an economic world they believe is biased against them.

Because of these structural changes, there may be increased price instability in some of the metals markets over the near term. As already noted, that possibility is not very high unless world economic growth moves to a higher than average growth rate after emerging from the 1974–1975 recession. If demand grows too rapidly and begins to press capacity, some countries may try to take advantage of short-run monopoly opportunities to extract larger profits. Because Jamaica produces a significant portion of total output, bauxite is a possible candidate for such a development even without the support of other producers.

For the longer term, the question raised by these developments is whether future production capacity will be adequate, since many private corporations may now be reluctant to undertake major investments because of the risk that their investments may be seized or that their future profits squeezed by higher foreign government taxes and royalties. If corporations perceive such risks to be higher now than in the past, they will be more reluctant than in the past to undertake new investments, and the result will be higher prices in the future.

Alternatively, it can be argued that the uncertainties created by the structural changes discussed in this section have induced multinational corporations to diversify exploration and mine development among a wider range of countries. Although such countries also will want to exercise control over foreign corporations, their individual market power will be reduced because production will be spread over a wider range. At the same time, the greater the number of national entities involved, the lower the likelihood of cartel activities being successful.

Unfortunately, there exists relatively little in the way of hard data on the worldwide magnitude of investments now being considered or about to be implemented for individual metals. Metal trade journal reports on mine exploration and development support both of the possibilities described above.[55] During recent years, there have been reports of reduced exploration and development in countries where there is uncertainty about future government policies. At the same time, there have been reports that exploration activities have intensified in areas and countries that had not been thoroughly explored before or where limited development of known ore deposits

---

[55] "The Changing Exploration Picture," parts I, III, and IV; and *Copper Studies*, vol. 2, nos. 48, 50, and 51 (April 30, May 16, and May 23, 1975).

had taken place. In addition, new money is being invested in exploring and developing mining opportunities in the oceans. Not only are private corporations funding such explorations, but during the past three years the United Nations has been financing more intensive exploration in many parts of the world through the Energy and Mineral Development Branch of the U.N. Centre for Natural Resources, Energy, and Transport.[56]

Whether future production from the new areas being discovered and developed will effect a potential reduction in investment in more established (but also more risky) mining areas is a major source of uncertainty at the present moment. That is one reason why the U.S. government has proposed an International Resources Bank (IRB) to be associated with the World Bank. The primary objectives of that bank were described in Secretary Kissinger's Nairobi speech of May 6, 1976:

> This new institution would promote more rational, systematic and equitable development of resources in developing nations. It would facilitate technological development and management training in the developing countries. It would help ensure supplies of raw materials to sustain the expansion of the global economy, and help moderate commodity price fluctuations.[57]

At the time of this publication, not enough detailed information was publicly available to allow extensive analysis of the proposal. The secretary's general description, however, suggests that the potential role of the IRB in international raw materials development would be quite broad, with the possibility of financing buffer stocks included. Concerning the subject of investment financing per se, three questions arise. The first concerns whether such a facility is indeed necessary. More systematic information is necessary on world investment plans before this can be decided. The second question concerns the nature of the investment "subsidy" to be provided. The secretary's speech suggests that the bank would provide guarantees in order to reduce noncommercial risks. If in fact guarantees are to be provided, the third question is whether the bank would bring about an even greater concentration of mining developments among countries that are already producing metal ores. If such a bank eliminates noncom-

---

[56] "UNDP Role in Mining," *Mining Journal*, vol. 284, no. 7286 (April 11, 1975), pp. 270-71.

[57] Henry Kissinger, "Address by the Honorable Henry Kissinger before the Fourth Ministerial Meeting of the United Nations Conference on Trade and Development," Nairobi, Kenya, May 5, 1976, in Department of State Press Release, no. 224.

mercial risks, private corporations will have no risk incentives to diversify and develop resources in new areas. Because of the lower costs of developing established fields, they will have an economic incentive to concentrate metals mining further, and the result will be even greater market power in the hands of the current producers of metal ores. Thus, if such a bank is considered necessary to finance mine investments, it would be necessary to build in explicit requirements that mine investments be diversified so that more developing countries with undeveloped metal resources would benefit and so that existing metals-producing countries would not increase their market power.

Producer organizations. Among the several producer organizations formed in recent years is the International Bauxite Association, formed in 1974. Its members include the major producers—Australia, Jamaica, Surinam, and Guyana—that account for over 60 percent of world output. CIPEC, an acronym based on the French name of the International Council of Copper Exporting Countries, was formed in 1967 by the four major copper exporters—Chile, Peru, Zambia, and Zaire—which account for about 30 percent of world output. In 1975, an Association of Iron Ore Exporting Countries was formed with eleven original members that jointly produce more than 50 percent of world production. Other recent attempts at forming producer organizations include attempts to organize producers of the metals mercury and tungsten. In April 1975, in La Paz, Bolivia, representatives from Australia, Bolivia, Peru, Portugal, and Thailand agreed to form a producers organization for tungsten.[58]

A different kind of producer organization is the International Tin Council, which is indeed not strictly a producer organization since it includes both producer and consumer countries. The history of this organization goes back at least to 1931, when the first international tin agreement was adopted.[59] In late 1975, the U.S. government agreed to become a member of the organization, an agreement which currently is before the Congress for approval. The International Tin Council's objective is to reduce the magnitude of price fluctuations in the tin market. To achieve that goal, the principal tool used is a buffer stock of tin contributed by the producing members of the council. Floor and ceiling prices are set by the council, and the manager of the buffer stock must buy at the floor price if the market

---

[58] For a more detailed history of these organizations, see Kenneth W. Clarfield et al., *Eight Mineral Cartels: The New Challenge to Industrialized Nations* (New York: McGraw-Hill, 1975), p. 169.

[59] Ibid., pp. 22-25.

price drops below it and must sell from the buffer stock if the market price is above the ceiling. The council can impose export controls during periods of rapid price declines, or recommend to the producers to increase production during times of shortages.

To date, there is no evidence that these producer organizations have had a major (if any) impact on prices. Although the tin council appears to have been able to moderate price fluctuations, it has not (as is suggested by Figure 3) been able to prevent real price declines during periods of excess supply or real price increases during periods of excess demand. Although the CIPEC members gave the appearance of acting as a cartel by agreeing to reduce exports in December 1974 and again in April 1975,[60] they were in effect agreeing to do what they would have done in any case in the face of weak demand for copper. And, as shown in Figure 2, copper prices rose less and declined substantially more in the period between 1972 and 1975 than the prices of other major metals.

In 1973 and 1974, the bauxite producers raised the price of bauxite by increasing taxes and royalties, but that was more as a result of the independent initiatives taken by Jamaica, the dominant producer, than of an explicit agreement among the producers.[61] In spite of the price increases, and in contrast to the oil producers, the producers of bauxite were not able to prevent a decline in income as a result of the recession-induced decline in demand during 1975. Bauxite is the one metal, however, for which industry specialists are concerned about the likelihood of cartel-type activities being successful at least over the next five years. Production is highly concentrated, with Jamaica and Australia together accounting for 46 percent of the market. While it is conceivable that these two countries could collude and extract a large monopoly price by cutting back on production, participation by Australia in such an agreement would conflict with its overall trade commitments. More important, maximizing short-run revenues would be a costly long-run strategy since it would encourage exploration and development in other countries. Over the long run, there are limits on the price of bauxite because there are substitutes in abundant world supply, especially in the United States. Australia has a long-run economic interest in making sure bauxite prices do not rise above the costs of the alternatives to bauxite for any sustained period of time.

To a large extent, the producer organizations have served as a forum for developing better information about prices, production, and

---

[60] Ibid., p. 95.
[61] Ibid., pp. 123-25.

investments. For example, in 1974 a working group of tungsten producers sought a comprehensive survey of the actual prices at which tungsten is traded.[62] It was hoped that such a survey would enable the U.S. General Services Administration to sell its stockpile of tungsten without disrupting the market. The Association of Iron Ore Exporting Countries has primarily become a forum for consultation and the exchange of information.[63] At a March 1976 meeting of the copper producers in Geneva, there was general agreement that more information needed to be collected on prices, exploration, investment, and potential demand.[64]

As already mentioned, the International Tin Council includes both consumers and producers. Within the iron organization, some members are demanding that the interests of the consumers be represented, perhaps by consumer membership.[65] Consumer countries (including the United States) also participated in the March 1976 meeting of the copper producers. Thus, producer organizations in the metals industry appear to be moving in the direction of becoming councils wherein producers and consumer countries can carry on discussions. In that sense, they may serve as a useful umbrella under which individual countries and private corporations can carry out their specific negotiations over prices, production, and investment.

Rich against poor nations. During the past ten years, developing countries also have intensified their efforts to bargain as a cohesive unit with the industrialized countries. A variety of forums have been used, including the World Bank, the International Monetary Fund, and the United Nations. Within each of these institutions, the developing countries have taken steps not only to work more effectively as a group but also concomitantly to gain more power within each institution. In addition, flexible use is made of ad hoc forums, such as the recently established Conference on International Economic Cooperation. This conference is an outgrowth of efforts by France to bring oil-producing and oil-consuming countries together on energy-related issues. Under the pressure of the oil-producing countries, the scope of the conference was broadened to encompass other raw material commodities, including metals and agricultural products.

Although the developing countries are a diverse group, a number of common bonds work to pull them together. For most, there is

---

[62] Ibid., p. 169.
[63] Ibid., pp. 142-43.
[64] *Wall Street Journal*, March 10, 1976, p. 20.
[65] Clarfield et al., *Eight Mineral Cartels*, p. 142.

the shared heritage of having been politically dominated—if not colonized—by the United States and Western Europe. Among the more vocal leaders, for example, are the governments of countries like Algeria, which earned its independence only fourteen years ago. The psychological bond created by the common historical experience of having been subjected to Western imperialism is a force whose cohesive power is often underestimated by Westerners.

From an economic perspective, those countries share the characteristics of being poor and less developed. There is also a recognition that the relative degree of poverty is increasing, not decreasing, with time. For example, as reported by the World Bank, income disparities have continued to increase between the developed and developing countries.[66] The relative importance of the developing countries in international trade also has declined over the past thirty years, contributing further to their sense of increasing economic isolation. In the early 1960s, developing country exports accounted for 23 percent of total world exports. By the early 1970s, that proportion had declined to around 17 percent.[67] There is also a strong belief on their part that their terms of trade have declined because the rate of inflation on goods exported from industrialized countries has been higher than the rate of inflation on the exports of underdeveloped countries. As reported in the 1972 Proceedings of the United Nations Conference on Trade and Development: "Even before allowance is made for the recent changes in currency valuations, the terms of trade had deteriorated between 1959–1960 and 1969–1970 for forty-nine out of the eighty-seven countries for which the relevant indices are available, and of these the deterioration exceeded 1.0 percent per annum, on average, for twenty-two countries." [68]

There is also a sense of unity that stems from their believing that the international economic system is biased against them. From their perspective, the world is not made up of freely operating markets subject to the forces of competition but rather of large monopolistic corporations supported by their national governments. Japan, Europe, and the United States are seen as market fortresses protected by a variety of tariff and nontariff barriers that make it difficult for developing countries to sell goods. Even the oil producers at one time during the late 1950s and through the 1960s found import barriers

[66] World Bank Atlas, p. 4.

[67] United Nations, Yearbook of International Trade Statistics—1974 (New York: United Nations, 1975).

[68] United Nations Conference on Trade and Development, Third Session, Merchandise Trade—Volume 2 (New York: United Nations, 1973), p. 58.

restricting the amount of oil they could sell to the United States and Europe. Now they listen to the free-market gospel preached by the leaders of the consumer countries with more than a grain of skepticism.

To what extent the grievances against the international economic system derive from real abuses, to what extent from ideology, and to what extent from the feedback effect of their own rhetoric is a subject for separate study. The reason for describing their perceptions here, however, is not to determine the strength of their case, but to underline the kinds of forces that motivate and work to hold the developing countries together. Those forces provide a sense of unity, often in the face of very divergent interests. In part, this is why so many developing countries have continued to support OPEC, in spite of the fact that the oil price increases severely damaged their own economies.

During the past fifteen years, the developing countries have collectively pursued a wide range of objectives, some successfully and some unsuccessfully. Within the international monetary realm, unsuccessful attempts have been made to link development aid to the creation of Special Drawing Rights—the international currency that can be used to settle accounts among governments. Developing countries, however, have been successful in expanding their borrowing capacity at the IMF and World Bank. Developing countries have also been successful in reducing some of the trade barriers among the industrialized countries.

Because raw materials are a significant part of developing country exports, they have been the focus of special attention. The basic negotiating strategy of the developing countries has been to lump all commodities together and pursue integrated solutions for dealing with an array of commodities. (The commodities considered most important are cocoa, coffee, tea, sugar, bananas, wheat, rice, meat, cotton, rubber, jute, wool, hard fibers, copper, iron ore, tin, and bauxite.) [69] The primary objective underlying this lumping together of commodities is to reduce the opportunities for the industrialized countries to divide and conquer by enabling the developing countries to maintain overall political cohesion. The U.S. government, however, has taken the position that raw materials differ sufficiently among themselves that only a commodity-by-commodity approach is workable. The commodity-by-commodity technique is the one being used

[69] United Nations Conference on Trade and Development, Third Session, *An Integrated Program for Commodities* (New York: United Nations, October 28, 1975), p. 4.

currently under the Conference on International Economic Cooperation negotiations.

Objectives of the Developing Countries. For commodities in general
the developing countries have set out the following objectives for
themselves:

(1) To reduce excessive fluctuations in commodity prices and
supplies.

(2) To establish and maintain commodity prices at levels which,
in real terms, are equitable to consumers and remunerative
to producers.

(3) To assure access to supplies by raw material-importing countries.

(4) To assure access to markets by raw material-exporting countries.

(5) To expand processing activities in the developing countries.[70]

A related objective is the desire to achieve greater stability in export
earnings. While the latter is especially important to commodity-
producing countries which are subject to frequent shifts in demand,
it is also an objective of all the developing countries because of the
impact of price and demand fluctuations caused by developments in
the industrialized world.

A number of specific proposals have been put forward for
achieving these objectives, the two most important being a series of
international commodity stocks and the establishment of a common
fund for financing the commodity stocks. The developing countries
also seek a system under which commodity prices would be indexed
so that prices would rise with overall inflation rates.[71] Commodity
buffer stocks, similar to the tin buffer stock, would be established in
an attempt to maintain price stability with purchases during periods
of slack demand and commodity sales during periods of rapid growth
in demand. Supplementing the buffer stock agreements would be
arrangements to control exports of producing countries, as well as
long-term trade commitments, so that prices could be maintained
in real terms.

Another proposal involves a system of compensatory financing
that would be available to individual countries facing temporary balance-of-payments shortfalls. While in theory the buffer stocks would
be used to smooth out fluctuations in commodity prices for all pro-

---

[70] Ibid., pp. 2-3.

[71] Ibid., p. 5.

ducers of a commodity, they would not be useful for an individual country facing a greater than average balance-of-payments shortfall, and this is one rationale for additional financial support through compensatory financing. In January 1976 the International Monetary Fund compensatory financing arrangements were expanded,[72] but the magnitudes and conditions of the IMF arrangements do not fully meet the objectives of the developing countries.

A practical question is whether the proposals for establishing buffer stocks would achieve the primary objectives of the developing countries. In theory, short-term price fluctuations may be reduced by buffer stock arrangements in conjunction with export controls, but, unless they are open-ended in the size of the stocks that can be accumulated, buffer stock arrangements are not capable of maintaining real commodity prices in the face of shifting demand and supply trends over time. Indeed, the existence of the buffer stock arrangements may induce countries to make even larger investments in mining facilities, which would then work on the supply side to bring real prices down. A decline in real prices thus would bring about pressure from the producing members for increases in the buffer stock. Another well-known problem with buffer stock arrangements is the difficulty of distinguishing a cyclical movement from more fundamental trends in demand and supply. Metals producers will interpret price declines as being caused by cyclical movements and price increases as a reflection of long-run trends. Consumer countries will have the opposite bias. If consumer countries resist buffer stock increases to maintain the price, there will be conflicts. If consumer countries give in to short-run producer country pressures, it will eventually become obvious, as the buffer stock increases, that the price is out of line. When that occurs there will occur significant price instability. Thus, establishment of buffer stocks would not necessarily reduce tensions among governments since management of the stocks would result in continued disputes. In addition, the stocks themselves may be the cause of market instability.

The subject of investment is not usually given much attention in discussions about maintaining commodity price stability, and yet investment in new mining facilities not only plays a primary role in determining the long-run trend of real prices but also affects prices in the short run when there is excess or inadequate capacity as a result of fluctuations in investment. To the extent that investment is discussed, it is usually discussed in terms of the need to stimulate investment through subsidies in mining facilities among underde-

---

[72] International Monetary Fund, *IMF Survey*, January 5, 1976, p. 1.

veloped countries. The International Finance Corporation and the World Bank are actively considering ways of expanding their assistance for mining and metals investments—an area they have traditionally left to private corporations.[73] Subsidized investments or investment guarantees, however, may defeat the objective of developing countries to maintain (or increase) the real price over the long run because such investments will increase the available supply of raw materials and thus bring about lower prices. Investment subsidies may also cause short-run price fluctuations if the availability of subsidized credit becomes the primary determinant of investment rather than expectations of higher future demand.

U.S. policy issues. During the past three years, an extensive debate has taken place within and outside the U.S. government concerning the way the United States should respond to the commodity initiatives of the developing countries. The U.S. government has been criticized for not responding quickly enough to these initiatives and then for responding inadequately. Those who believe that there should be an accommodation to foreign pressures for comprehensive commodity arrangements—as a way of relieving these foreign pressures—often forget that the arrangements are going to generate economic problems that will produce different but equally strong political pressures. In effect, one political problem will be substituted for another. Those who support commodity arrangements for humanitarian reasons—to bring about a transfer of income from the rich to the poor—often do not seek to find out whether the means being proposed will accomplish the objective.

There are, however, more fundamental reasons for moving slowly on attempts to develop intergovernmental programs for managing prices and investment. The metals business is extremely complex. Prices of refined metals are difficult to manage because of the high degree of substitution among metals. At earlier stages of production, the problem of pricing is even more complex than the pricing of refined metals since the ores from which a metal is produced are not homogeneous but differ in quality, concentration, and location. Moreover, recycled materials can be utilized as a substitute for ore. The price that a producer can charge for his ore depends not only on the price that can be charged for the refined metal—which depends also on the prices for other metals—but also on the prices of other ores and of metal scrap. It is even more difficult to manage the investment process for metals than for other endeavors—not only because of the opera-

---

[73] *World Bank Annual Report 1975* (Washington, D.C.: World Bank, 1975), p. 7.

tional and technical problems of developing new mines and refining systems, but also because of the long lag between decisions to increase mining and refining capacity and the opening of a mine and refinery. Thus, by the time new capacity comes on line, demand conditions may differ substantially from the conditions that motivated the building of new capacity.

For these reasons, as well as the different and often conflicting objectives motivating different governments, I remain extremely skeptical whether the array of commodity proposals that have been put forward to date would achieve the objectives of the proponents. At the same time, it is necessary to face the fact that the metals industry is now dominated by governments. The full ramifications of this fact are difficult to predict, and there are dangers to underreacting as well as to overreacting: this is an area where different bilateral and multilateral policy approaches need to be explored and debated. Out of that debate a consistent and cohesive U.S. policy will (one hopes) emerge—one that is durable and in the interests (economic, political, and humanitarian) of the United States. In the meantime, the primary means of bringing about stability in the metals industry lies not with those government officials who deal with commodity issues, but those officials who manage fiscal and monetary policies for the major industrialized countries. No matter what commodity arrangements are agreed upon for prices and investments, unless more stable rates of growth at lower rates of inflation are achieved, there will not be stability in the international metals markets.

Cover and book design: Pat Taylor